Abstracts of the
DEBT BOOKS
of the
PROVINCIAL LAND OFFICE OF MARYLAND

Queen Anne's County

Volume I

Liber 36: 1734, 1747, 1754, 1756, 1757
Liber 37: 1745, 1756 (2nd version)

By
V. L. Skinner, Jr.

CLEARFIELD

Copyright © 2017
Vernon L. Skinner, Jr.
All Rights Reserved

Printed for Clearfield Company by
Genealogical Publishing Company
Baltimore, Maryland
2017

ISBN 978-0-8063-5851-2

Introduction

The Provincial Land Office of Maryland was responsible for the dispensing of land from 1634 to 1777. Land was initially acquired by a warrant and was then patented. Information concerning these documents are found in the Warrants and Patents series of the Provincial Land Office located at the Maryland State Archives and are indexed by Peter Wilson Coldham in his five-volume series *Settlers of Maryland*, published by Genealogical Publishing Company.

Land was patented according to the desires of the patentee, and the name given to a patent was not necessarily unique within any particular jurisdiction.

The Lord Proprietor's personal hold on land affairs was much weakened during the royal period from 1689 to 1715. However, it was immediately revived when his proprietary rights were restored in 1715 (Hartsook and Skordas, *Land Office and Prerogative Court Records*). Both the Rent Rolls and the Debt Books date from this restoration period.

The Rent Rolls and the Debt Books are the means by which the Lord Proprietor kept track of the rents due him. Each piece of land granted to a person was subject to a yearly rent according to the terms of the patent.

A Rent Roll consists of entries for each tract of land patented, plus the name of the person for whom it was originally surveyed, the present owner, the acreage, and the rent. Alienations, or subsequent sales and leases of the piece of land, are also included.

A Debt Book consists of a list of persons owning land with the names and rents of each tract that he or she owned, all listed in one place under his or her name.

The Debt Books

The Debt Books are arranged by county, by year, and then by the name of the person paying the rent. There are a total of 54 libers, covering all of the counties. The extant Debt Books for the Western Shore counties are essentially annual, dating from 1753 to 1774. (The Debt Books for 1750 for five Western Shore counties–Anne Arundel, Baltimore, Charles, Prince George's, Frederick–are found in the Calvert Papers, located at the Maryland State Archives.) The extant Debt Books for the Eastern Shore counties are also essentially annual, dating from 1733 to 1775.

Each liber contains information for only one county, but for multiple years. For purposes of identification, each section (i.e., year) of any particular liber is given the denotation of the specific year.

Tracking land ownership over various years is particularly important for intestate estates, land inherited by women, and land that is not specified in a will.

The information in this series is presented in a tabular form:

- liber and folio citation, with any pertinent date.
- name of the person paying the taxes.
- name of the tract of land.
- acreage.

Notes to Reader

The following conventions are used in this book:

1. "The" and "A" at the beginning of any tract name has been omitted.
2. The index contains both tract names and surnames, sorted together.

3. "Crossed out" entries in the original libers have been included, as such.
4. Names have been transcribed as they are written; no attempt has been made to standardize any spelling.
5. Introduction and index pages of the original libers have been omitted.

Abbreviations

AA	Anne Arundel County	o/c	overcharged
ACC	Accomac County	o/o	orphans of
a/s	alias	PA	Pennsylvania
BA	Baltimore County	PG	Prince George's County
CE	Cecil County	PW	Prince William County
CH	Charles County	pt	part of
cnp	name continued on next page	QA	Queen Anne's County
c/o	child/children of	RI	Rhode Island
CR	Caroline County	SM	St. Mary's County
CV	Calvert County	SO	Somerset County
DE	Delaware	s.p.	square poles
DO	Dorchester County	SU	Sussex County
d/o	daughter of	s/o	son of
FR	Frederick County	<t>	torn
h/o	heir(s) of	TA	Talbot County
KE	Kent County MD	tbc	to be charged to
KEDE	Kent County DE	unr	unreadable
KI	Kent Island	VA	Virginia
n/a	not available	w/o	widow of
NE	New England	WO	Worcester County
n/g	not given		

Contents of this volume

This book is the first of two volumes for Queen Anne's County. The debt books for Queen Anne's County cover the following years: 1734, 1745, 1747, 1754, 1756, 1756 (2nd version), 1757, 1757 (2nd version), 1758, 1763, 1765, 1766, 1767, 1769. There is an additional debt book for 1775 for that portion of Queen Anne's County that became Caroline County.

From the Debt Books entries, several interesting facts are evident: (1) Queen Anne's County had a Free School established by 1735; and, (2) Bridgetown, Kings Town, and Ogle Town were established communities, with several lots occupied by 1747. The leading landowners were: the Lloyd Family, the Tilghman Family, and the Wright Family. Some Queen Anne's County landowners were cited as inhabiting the following jurisdictions: Anne Arundel County, Baltimore County, Calvert County, Cecil County, Dorchester County, Kent County, Prince George's County, Somerset County, St. Mary's County, Talbot County, Annapolis, Chestertown, Kent Island, Delaware, Duck Creek, Kent County Delaware, New Castle County, Sussex County, Carolina, Jersey, Pennsylvania, Philadelphia, Virginia, London, Bristol, England, Ireland, Biddeford, Chester, Newfoundland, White Haven..

Queen Anne's County - 1734

36:1734:1 ...		Acres
James & William Kerby	"Bodys Neck" tbc Benjamin Clouds for h/o Benjamin Kerby	200
	"Allens Deceipt" tbc: • Robert Walters – 40 a. • Walter Kerby – 210 a.	250
	"Kerbys Addition" tbc Walter Kerby	50
John Guin	"Kerbys Prevention" – for h/o Josua Crocker tbc Robert Walters who married the daughter of (N) Cockar	50
Nathaniel Connor	pt. "Wood Yard Thickett" tbc Mathew Brown	205
John Stevens	"Stevens Adventure" tbc John Stevens, Jr. (heir)	255
	½ "Little Ease" tbc John Stevens, Jr. (heir)	150
	"Nineveth" – denied, supposed to lie in KE	600
Alexander Downey & John Cockey	"Pigg Quarter Neck" tbc Valentine Downey	100
	"Southerins Addition" tbc Valentine Downey & Joseph Sadler	80
	"Pigg Quarter Neck" – another tract; denied	100
Vallentine Downy	<n/g> – tract of land from Vallentine Downy; denied, as charged to Alexander Downy	100
Edward Brown	pt. "Sallen" tbc: • John Brown (KE) – 100 a. • Mathew Brown – 100 a.	200
	pt. "Batchellor" tbc John Brown (KE)	100
Phill. Connor	pt. "Connors Neck" tbc Phill. Connor	180
	"Woodyard Thickett" – denied; included in a tract of same name	300
	pt. "Woodyard Thickett" tbc Charles Connor (f. 8)	205
36:1734:2 ...		
Charles Connor	pt. "Woodyard Thickett"	205
Lewis DeRochburne	"Friendship" tbc Joseph DeRochburne	200
Lewis Merridith	"Stooply Gibson" tbc Francis Bright	150
Mr. John Wells	"Tarr Kill" tbc John Stevens	150
	pt. "Winchester" tbc George Jackson	125
	"Hills Cabbin" tbc Jos. Tucker	100
	"Broad Creek Resurveyed"	830
h/o Robert Small	"Ship Point" tbc Robert Small	100
h/o Robert Small	"Coopers Hills" tbc William Joyner	100

Queen Anne's County - 1734

w/o Christopher Granger	"Adventure" – heir knows no such land	50
	"Errecksons Island" tbc Christopher Granger	20
Ralph Distance	"Isaac Chance" tbc John Dayly	
	"Ralphs Frolick" tbc John Dayly; denied, says in elder survey	67
Isa Winchester	"Purlivant" tbc Jacob Winchester	180
	"Isaac Addition" tbc Jacob Winchester	80
Alexander Walters	"Dundee" tbc Robert Walters	100
	"Piney Neck" tbc Robert Walters	50
	"Maidens Choice" tbc Robert Walters	65
	"Walters Addition" tbc Robert Walters	50
36:1734:3 ...		
William Willson	pt. "Easterne Island" tbc John Willson	50
	"Williams Adventure" tbc John Willson	54
John Hocken now James Hutchins	"Wrights Fortune"	120
	"Condon" – for Edward Jones	326
Morrice Slinah	"Timber Ridge" tbc James Slyney	250
Christopher Goodhand	pt. "Sillin" tbc Marmaduke Goodhand	200
	pt. "Point Love" tbc Marmaduke Goodhand	200
	"Broad Oak" tbc Marmaduke Goodhand	500
	"Poplar Neck" tbc Marmaduke Goodhand	300
Benjamin Wicks	pt. "Point Love" tbc Joseph Wicks	400
John Coppidge	"Indian Spring" tbc Phill. Coppidge	100
Elizabeth & Martha Coppidge	"Beaver Neck Resurveyed" tbc John Rowles	320
Jacob Blangy	"Upper Deale" tbc: • Benjamin Clouds – 200 a. • John Evans – 300 a.	500
	pt. "Sillin" tbc: • Benjamin Clouds for h/o Jacob Blangy – 66⅔ a. • John Evans – 133⅓ a.	200
James Sudler	"Johns Hole etc. Resurveyed"	276
36:1734:4 ...		
h/o Thomas Marsh	"Warners Discovery" tbc William Vickers (TA)	200
	"Little Thickett" tbc Thomas Marsh	200
	"Marshes Forbearance" tbc Thomas Marsh	150
	"Cabbin Neck" tbc Thomas Marsh	350

Queen Anne's County - 1734

William Elliott	"Forlorne Hope" tbc Christopher Granger for h/o William Elliott	100
	"Elliotts Choice" tbc Christopher Granger for h/o William Elliott	100
	"Elliotts Choice" – denied	120
	"Addition" – denied	200
Mathew Erickson	"Stenton Erickson" tbc Mathew Errickson	200
	"Sarahs Portion" tbc John Errickson	
	"Marys Portion" tbc Mathew Errickson s/o Charles	150
	"Mathews Enlargement" tbc Mathew Errickson s/o Charles	135
	"Stoopley Gibson" tbc Fra. Bright	150
	"Conny Hall" tbc John Walters	100
Thomas Baxter	"Upper Blunt Point" tbc Capt. William Elliott for h/o Thomas Baxter	200
Robert Blunt	"Blunts Marsh" tbc: • Richard Blunt – 110 a. • Robert Blunt – 110 a. • Samuel Blunt – 110 a.	330
h/o Mathias Pooley for h/o William Osborne	"Tyburn Neck" a/s "Timber Neck" tbc William Osborne	100
	"Martins Neck Resurveyed" tbc William Osborne	234
36:1734:5 ...		
Thomas Godman	"Parsons Point" tbc: • Mary Wright (KI) for h/o Samuel Wright – 400 a. • Penelope Wright – 100 a.	500
	"Cocks Neck" a/s "Cox's Neck" tbc James Ringold – 2 barrels of wheat	1000
James Evans	"Wallnutt Neck Resurveyed"	109
	"Barren Ridge"	100
Francis Benton	"Pentrogay" tbc John Taylor for h/o Fra. Benton	50
	"Pentrogay" tbc John Taylor for h/o Fra. Benton	203
William White	"Workmans Hazard"	150
	"Sparks Point"	50
	"Coopers Quarter" tbc Fra. Bright	50
Thomas Tanner	"Chance"	50
	"Providence"	100
	"Tanners Advantage"	39

Queen Anne's County - 1734

h/o Alexander Forbes	pt. "Parsons Neck" tbc Ann Price	45
	pt. "Parsons Lott" a/s "Pascos's Lott" tbc Ann Price	100
	pt. "Eastern Island" tbc Ann Price	14
	pt. "Addition" tbc Ann Price	49
Mark Benton	"Georges Codd" tbc Elizabeth Maconakin	100
h/o John Dobbs	"Dobbs Adventure"	36
36:1734:6 ...		
John Sutton	"Sandy Hurst" tbc James Sutton	400
John Sutton for h/o Roger Baxter	pt. "Pascos's Lott" tbc Ann Price	100
	"Ashford" tbc Thomas Tanner	100
Thomas Cooper	"Parsons Neck" tbc h/o Thomas Cooper	80
Fra. Barns	pt. "Pitts Gift" tbc Thomas Barns	15
	pt. "Belcher" – included in "Barnes Satisfaction"	<n/g>
Mathew Griffith	"Little Neck" tbc James Sudler for h/o Samuel Griffith	55
	"Barnstable Hill" tbc John Walters in right of his wife the daughter of (N) Reddar	100
	pt. "Broad Creek" – in bounds of "Little Neck"	<n/g>
Thomas Rouse	pt. "Commins Freehold" tbc Sarah Rouse	50
Vallentine Carter	"Copartnership" tbc: • Richard Carter – 52 a. • William Price – 52 a.	104
	"Jones Plott" tbc: • Richard Carter – 45 a. • William Price – 45 a.	90
	"Dunns Hazard" tbc: • William Price – 75 a. • Richard Carter – 75 a.	150
	"Carters Addition" tbc: • Richard Carter – 25 a. • William Price – 25 a.	50
	"Chance" tbc: • Richard Carter – 25 a. • William Price – 25 a.	50
	"Barns Satisfaction" tbc: • William Price – 50 a. • Richard Carter – 50 a.	100
36:1734:7 ...		

Queen Anne's County - 1734

John Oldson	"Oldsons Pasture" tbc h/o John Oldson (minors)	20
	pt. "Hawkins Pharsalia" tbc: • Abraham Williams for h/o Henry Outson – 100 a. • Edwin Godwin – 100 a., being Andrew & Thomas Outson's part	200
Madam Alice Loyd	pt. "Loyds Meadows"	891
	"Loyds Meadows Addition"	334
Mr. Charles Blake	"Rufsindale" tbc John Sayer Blake	250
	"Coursey" tbc John Sayer Blake	250
	"Hoggs Hole" tbc John Sayer Blake	100
	"Jenkins Neck" tbc John Sayer Blake	250
	"Cold Harbour" tbc John Sayer Blake; included in "Sayers Forrest"	100
	"Sayers Forrest" tbc John Sayer Blake	2250
	"Gore"	175
	"Jacksons Choice" tbc John Sayer Blake	100
	"Sayers Range" tbc William Scott (TA)	300
	"Inkersell" tbc Ed. Chetham	134
	"Blakeford" tbc Phill. Charles Blake	555
Dr. Andrew Imbert now Capt. William Greenwood	"Jacksons Boggs" tbc Capt. William Greenwood	46
	"Wrexhams Plains" tbc: • Henry Wright – 90 a. • 70 a. denied	160
	"Smiths Forrest" tbc: • Henry Wright – 210 a. • 29 a. denied	239
	"Plain Dealing" tbc Capt. William Greenwood	727
	"Broad Neck" tbc Capt. William Greenwood	100
h/o Thomas Jackson	"Jacksons Choice" tbc ~~John Sayer~~ Christopher Blake	100
36:1734:8 ...		
Thomas Jackson	pt. "Winchester" tbc George Jackson	125
	"Barbarahs Choice" tbc George Jackson	80
	pt. "Jaspars Lott" tbc Francis Jackson who is runaway	200
John Downs	"Downs Chance"	150
	pt. "Nobles Range"	142
	"Shoreditch"	150

Queen Anne's County - 1734

John Nabb	"Jones Fortune"	100
	"Tilghmans Addition"	100
	pt. "Clouds Adventure"	200
Nathaniel Tucker	"Jones Addition" tbc John Tucker	200
	"Adventure" tbc John Tucker	100
	pt. "Batchellors Plains" tbc John Tucker	100
Henry Williams	pt. "Chestnutt Meadows" tbc Ann Williams	100
George Phillips	"Smiths Lott" tbc Christopher Phillips	200
Robert Kent	"Neglect" tbc William Kent	100
	pt. "Batchellors Plains" tbc John Caradine	200
Richard Hynson	pt. "Fair Play" tbc T. Hynson Wright; refused to pay, included in "New Hynson Town"	54
36:1734:9 ...		
Mathew Mason	pt. "Barbadoes Hall" – denied	100
	pt. "Bishops Outlett" – for o/o of Wat. Jones; denied	150
	pt. "Chesterfield"	100
Andrew King for h/o Robert Macklyn	"Reward" tbc: • John Coursey – 200 a. • William Elbert – 200 a.	400
	"Yarmouth" – twice charged; denied	100
	"Macklins Beginning" tbc William Elbert	400
	"Macklins Fancy" tbc: • William Elbert – 250 a.; denied • John Coursey – 250 a.	500
	"Ashbury Addition" tbc: • John Coursey – 17½ a. • William Elbert – 17½ a.	35
	"Yarmouth" – twice charged; denied	100
	"Macklyns Addition" tbc: • William Elbert – 18 a. • John Coursey – 18 a.	36
Thomas Lewis	pt. "Boagley"	175
Jeffry Mathewshaw	"Jamaica" tbc George Mathewshaw	100
h/o Mathew Read	"New Reading" – contains pt. "Reading" (357 a.) & "Adventure" (100 a.) tbc: • Nathaniel Reed – 100 a. • Elizabeth Reed for Mathew Reed – 120 a. • T. H. Wright – 80 a. • 157 a. – denied	300

John Tryall	pt. "Smithfield" tbc Joseph Tryall	100
36:1734:10 ...		
h/o Maj. William Turloe	pt. "Trustram" tbc William Dawson	233
	pt. "Smeath" tbc Phill. Emerson	106
	pt. "Stagwell" tbc Phill. Emerson	42
	"Hackers Meadows" tbc Phill. Emerson, who denied	460
Nathaniel Scott	pt. "Sayers Range Addition"	400
	"Scott Inclosure"	150
	pt. "Marshy Crook"	50
	"Partnership" – for self & William Young tbc: • self – 250 a. • William Young – 50 a.	300
Charles Seth	pt. "Mount Mill"	317
	"Addition"	40
	pt. "Sheppard Discovery & Henfield" – denied	76
William Clayton	"Prouse Park" a/s "Pauls Park" tbc Solomon Clayton	300
	"Collins Range" tbc William Clayton (TA)	300
William Campbell	pt. "Ditteridge"	166
	pt. "Anthorp"	197
	pt. "Hamiltons Hermitage"	250
	pt. "Bishopton"	68
Edward Harris	pt. "Ditteridge"	272
John Welch	pt. "Ditteridge"	83
	pt. "Partnership" – see TA Rent Roll	200
36:1734:11 ...		
Edmund Prior for h/o Arthur Emory	"Batchellors Chance" tbc John Emory	300
	"Arthurs Chance" – denied	300
	"Saint Pauls" tbc Col. Hawkins; denied	100
Mr. Arthur Emory, Sr.	pt. "Trustram" tbc Arthur Emory	170
	pt. "Coursey Upon Wye" tbc Arthur Emory	30
w/o Richard Stevenson now Thomas Hollingsworth	pt. "Forrest Lodge" a/s "Forrest Lodge Resurveyed"	80
	"Bennetts Adventure" – included in "Forrest Lodge Resurveyed"	150

Richard Wells	pt. "Bath" tbc: • Richard Wells – 100 a. • Humphrey Wells – 150 a.	250
	pt. "Bath Addition" tbc Richard Wells (100 a.)	150
	"Welsh Ridge Addition" – denied; taken in elder survey called "Darland"	300
William Hopper	"Vanderford" a/s "Partnership"	150
Robert Colt	pt. "Saint Paul" a/s "Pauls Fort" tbc William Tilghman	200
w/o William Hollingworth	"Spring Branch" tbc James Gould	100
	"Refuse" a/s "Refuge" tbc William Hollinsworth	100
	"Beginning" tbc William Hollinsworth; denied	100
36:1734:12 ...		
Col. Richard Tilghman (cnp)	"Tilghmans Hermitage" – included in resurvey of same name	400
	pt. "Tilghmans Addition" – included in "Forlorne Hope"	300
	pt. "Tilghmans Discovery" – included in "Forlorne Hope"	490
	pt. "Forlorne Hope" – included in tract of same name	200
	pt. "Hynsons Towne" – included in "Tilghmans Hermitage"	200
	"Goose Quarter" – included in "Tilghmans Hermitage"	50
	"Tilghmans Range" – included in "Tilghmans Hermitage"	98
	"Rosseth" – included in "Union"	350
	"Bockin" – included in "Union"	500
	"Tilghmans Lott" – let fall	500
	"Tilghmans Pasture" – included in "Tilghmans Hermitage"	300
	"Recovery" – denied	100
	"Tilghmans Freshes"	600
	"Adventure Addition" tbc James Earle	400
	"Tilghmans Forrest"	1400
	pt. "Bristoll Marsh" tbc William Tilghman	140
	pt. "Pauls Fort" tbc William Tilghman	200
	pt. "Bristoll Marsh"	50

Queen Anne's County - 1734

	pt. "Wilkinsons Addition" – included in "Tilghmans Hermitage"	50
	pt. "Waltham" – included in "Tilghmans Hermitage"	50
	"Nottleys Enjoyment"	500
	pt. "Spriglye" – included in "Tilghmans Hermitage"	235
	"Carpenters Meadow"	50
	"Salisbury"	500
	pt. "Adventure"	1635
	pt. "Molton"	239
	"Rings End"	100
	"Delmore End"	500
	"Forlorne Hope" – included in tract of same name	935
	pt. "Adventure" tbc: • Col. Richard Tilghman – 50 a. • William Burner – 50 a.	100
	"Andover"	500
	"Willmores Range" tbc Aug. Thompson	250
	"Jerusalem" tbc: • Col. Tilghman – 200 a. • Isaac Dixon (TA) – 200 a.	400
	"Tilghmans Meadows"	270
	"Forlorne Hope"	1830
	pt. "Forlorne Hope" tbc: • John Carradine – 50 a. • Richard Tilghman, Jr. – 1050 a.	1100
	"Snod Land" tbc Richard Tilghman, Jr.	284
	"Friendship" tbc: • James Massey – 120 a. • John Hadley – 80 a. • T. H. Wright – 150 a. • Col. Richard Tilghman, since sold to Jonathan Spry – 170 a.	520
	pt. "Adventure" – denied; taken away by "Loyds Towne"	630
36:1734:13 ...		

h/o Christopher Denny	½ "Waltham" tbc: • Ann Denny for h/o Christopher Denny – 25 a. • Terrence Gilaspy for h/o John Earle Denny – 25 a.	50
	pt. "Wilkinsons Addition" tbc: • Ann Denny – 25 a. • Terrence Gilaspy – 25 a.	50
h/o Michael Earle	"Smith Lott" tbc James Earle	100
	pt. "Sprigly" – denied	65
	pt. "Carpenters Outlett" – denied	68
	"Wood Land Neck" tbc James Earle	200
h/o Richard Jones	"Jones Hall" tbc Ner. Jones	200
	pt. "Jones Plackett Addition" tbc Ner. Jones	100
	"Labour in Vain" tbc Ner. Jones	20
	"Jones Addition" tbc Ner. Jones	50
	"Hynson Town Addition" tbc Ner. Jones	100
	"Jones Plackett" tbc Ner. Jones	50
John Jones	"Jones Tryangle" – not known; included in "Loyds Town"	50
h/o Mathew Smith	"Content" tbc Thomas Gall in right of his wife Jan	100
	"Jamaica" tbc Mat. Nevill	150
	"Smiths Begining" tbc William Smith	200
John Coursey	"Courseys Range"	600
Mr. Otho Coursey	"Lords Gift" tbc William Coursey	1050
36:1734:14 ...		
Richard Bennett, Esq. (cnp)	"Morgans Neck"	300
	"Bluff Point Resurveyed"	496
	pt. "Stagwell"	526
	"Wilton"	650
	"Shover"	200
	"Hoggs Hole"	50
	pt. "Addition"	600
	"Dungarnen"	300
	pt. "Wadeing Place"	800
	"Neglect"	400
	"James's Lott"	150
	pt. "Boagley"	175

	"Maxby"	100
	pt. "Smiths Addition"	250
	"Smiths Inlett"	200
	"Smiths Polygon"	400
	pt. "Windfield"	287
	"Smiths Chance"	50
	"Windsor Forrest"	250
	"Brocknock"	100
	"Drumfield"	400
	"Hemsleys Reserve Rectified"	185
	"Edmundsons Green Close"	400
	"Bennetts Out Lett Resurveyed"	695
	"Nuttwells Chance Resurveyed"	294
	"Burton Upon Walsey Resurveyed"	388
	"Bennetts Choice Resurveyed"	1392
	"Browley Lambeth Resurveyed"	1750
	"Hynsons Hill"	150
	"Stagwells Addition"	129
	pt. "Bishops Addition"	330
	pt. "Bishops Outlett"	
	pt. "Stevensfield"	600
	"Salsbury"	300
	"Oakenthorpe Resurveyed"	4000
	"Bennetts Regulation"	1306
	"Bennetts Toulson"	93
	"Neglect"	58
	"Morgans Neck"	40
36:1734:15 ...		
Col. Ernault Hawkins (cnp)	"Bowlingly" tbc Ernault Hawkins	250
	"Macklin" tbc Ernault Hawkins	100
	"Jaspars Lott" – denied	570
	"Barren Neck" tbc Da. McLean	227
	pt. "Hawkins Pharsalia" – denied	500
	"Beverdams"	160
	"Bramptons Addition" – denied	314
	"Hawkins Range" tbc John Hawkins	90

	"Green Spring"	650
	"Stratton" – denied; not to be found	1000
	"Carmans Neck" tbc: • Col. Hawkins – 100 a. • Charles Vanderford – 50 a.	150
	pt. "St. Pauls" tbc: • Col. Hawkins – 50 a. • Charles Vanderford – 50 a.	100
	pt. "Smith Ridge" tbc Christopher Cox	100
	pt. "Wadeing Place"	200
	pt. "Smiths Ridge" tbc Christopher Cox	200
	"Hawkins Farme" – denied	500
Thomas Crupper	"Good Increase"	200
John Hammond	"Forrests Plains"	150
John Beck	pt. "Smeath"	412
	"Anns Portion" tbc Richard Hyndson	150
	pt. "Smeath"	50
William Emory	pt. "Pharsalia" tbc: • John Emory – 100 a. • William Emory – 100 a.	200
	pt. "Partnership" tbc William Emory	100
Mr. William Coursey	"Cheston"	800
	pt. "Coursey Upon Wye"	290
36:1734:16 ...		
Edmund & Trustram Thomas	pt. "Trustram" tbc: • William Willson for h/o Edmund Thomas – 364 a. • Trustram Thomas, Jr. – 300	664
	"Hoggs Hole" tbc William Jarman	130
	pt. "Winfield" tbc Thomas Thomas	145
John Clayland	pt. "Trustram"	233
h/o William Merson	"Liberty" tbc Patrick Sexton	100
	"Peale Place" tbc William Ferrill & Precilla Burke	32
	"Addyhouse" tbc William Ferrill & Precilla Burke	68
	"Midle Plantation" tbc William Ferrill & Precilla Burke	200
John Green (cnp)	"Carpenters Square" – included in "Greens Adventure Upon Carpenter Square"; denied	200

	"Greens Adventure" – included in "Greens Adventure Upon Carpenter Square"; denied	300
	"Greens Adventure Upon Carpenter Square"	212
Charles Neale	"Lincolne" tbc Charles Price	200
	pt. "Winkfield Park"	100
James Hicks	pt. "Costtens Park" tbc John Hicks	21
36:1734:17 ...		
Anthony Ivey – lands supposed to belong to a minor in KE the h/o Robert Smith Ivey h/o Anthony Ivey	"Tell Tales Loss"	100
	pt. "Smithfield"	100
	"Adventure" tbc John Alley (100 a., f. 21)	200
	"Salisbury" tbc R. Bennett	200
	"Smiths Reserve"	84
	"Tryangle"	100
	pt. "Gloster"	350
	pt. "Winfield" tbc R. Bennett (287 a., f. 14)	313
	pt. "Bristoll Marsh"	50
	"Smiths Range Addition" tbc Mary Cole	290
	"Reason"	360
	"Enjoyment"	85
	"Chance"	100
	pt. "Double Kill"	60
	"Smiths Forrest Addition"	140
	pt. "Smiths Reserve"	100
	pt. "Confusion"	55
	"Wrexhams Plains"	200
	pt. "Smiths Range"	61
	"Tryangle Addition"	360
Henry Costin	pt. "Costins Park"	279
	"Newington" tbc Richard Costin	80
	pt. "Lambeth" tbc James Hicks	79
John Jones	"Deluge"	180
	pt. "Nobles Range"	52
Norton Knatchbull	pt. "Youngs Chance" tbc Norton Knatchbull (minor, ENG)	270
	pt. "Lambeth Fields" tbc Norton Knatchbull (minor, ENG)	132
John Walters	pt. "Smeath"	100

36:1734:18	...		
Mary Serjeant	"Robinsons Farme" tbc Katharine Hammond (TA)	200
William Wrench	"Vineyard" – included in "Wrenches Farme Resurveyed"	700
	pt. "Wrexhams Plains"	100
	pt. "Brigland & Briglands Addition" tbc Robert Grundy	86
	"Wrenches Lott"	300
	"Wrenches Farme" – included in "Wrenches Farme Resurveyed"	100
	"Wrenches Farme Resurveyed"	800
Robert Grundy for h/o John Pemberton	"Boston" tbc Grundy Pemberton	300
	"Bostons Addition" tbc Elizabeth Pemberton (TA)	150
	"King Sale Addition" tbc Elizabeth Pemberton (TA)	100
	"Change" tbc Elizabeth Pemberton (TA)	250
	pt. "Dawsons Neck" tbc Grundy Pemberton	142
Robert Grundy for self	pt. "Beiglin & Beignlin Addition" tbc Grundy Pemberton	114
	"Wrenches Discovery" tbc Grundy Pemberton	386
Charles Snowden	pt. "Grantham" – appears to belong to h/o William Elbert (TA)	100
h/o Dr. Edward Chattam	"Inkersell" tbc Edward Chattam	200
	"Collins's Lott" tbc: • William Edwards – 56 a. • William Pinder – 116 a. • denied – 28 a.	200
	"Timberland" tbc Ed. Chattam	400
	pt. "Partnership" tbc Richard Grafton (NC)	500
	"Pascalls Chance" tbc Edward Chattam	250
	"Timberland" – twice charged	400
36:1734:19	...		
h/o William Sweatnam	"Bridgwater" tbc William Hopper	300
	pt. "Chesterfield" tbc William Hopper	800
	pt. "Providence" tbc William Hopper	200
	"Paxtons Lott" – denied	100
Henry Green	"Coston's Hope"	200

James Countis	pt. "Wrenhams Plains" tbc Peter Countis & Mathew Williams	100
	"Dublin" tbc: • James Countis – 150 a. • William Countis – 150 a.	300
Renatus Smith	pt. "Brampton" tbc Mary Cole	100
	pt. "Larrington" tbc Mary Cole	125
	pt. "Conquest" tbc Mary Cole	273
	"Malden" – denied by Mary Cole	283
John Hamour	"Hamours Choice" – denied	200
	"Hamours Lott" tbc John Hamour, Jr.	200
	pt. "Mocklinborough Division" a/s "Incklingborough" tbs Solomon Clayton	100
	"High Gale" tbc Solomon Clayton	50
	½ "Royston" tbc Fra. Foreman	600
w/o William Austin	"Waterford" tbc William Austin	400
	"Smithfield" – denied	200
Henry Green	"Alder Branch" tbc Ann w/o Henry Green	100
36:1734:20 ...		
William Sparks	pt. "Adventure" tbc John Sparks	100
	½ "Royston" tbc: • Charles Wilkinson – 475 a. • Thomas Wilkinson – 100 a. • denied, lost by water – 24 a.	600
Richard Power	pt. "Macklingboroug" tbc Edward Brown & John Hawkins, Jr., who refuse to pay	340
John Loyd	"Crumpton" – supposed to belong to James Heath	50
Thomas Bayly	"Adventure" tbc: • John Merrydith – 50 a. • included in "Baileys Delight" – 100 a.	150
	"Bradbeans Delight" – included in "Baileys Delight"	100
	"Bradburns Purchase" – included in "Baileys Delight"	91
George Elliott	"Rawlins Chance" tbc: • George Elliott – 150 a. • William Elliott – 100 a.	250
	pt. "Mount Hope" tbc George Elliott	53
	"Elliotts Addition" tbc John Elliott	100

William Hamilton & James Cassey	pt. "Treshford" tbc: • Thomas Whittington (TA) – 60 a. • Henry Johnson – 130 a.	190
36:1734:21 ...		
Stephen Rich	"Willin" – denied	100
	"Hitt or Miss" – denied	150
Thomas Puney	½ "Jones Park" tbc Thomas Punney	100
	pt. "Norrests Addition" tbc Thomas Punney	20
	pt. "Providence" tbc Henry Covington	100
Patrick Obryan	"Pleasant Spring" tbc Thomas Obryan	300
	pt. "Batchelors Plains" tbc John Carradine	200
Thomas Obryan	pt. "Smiths Reserve"	150
John Alla	pt. "Daventport" – denied	16
	pt. "Adventure"	100
	pt. "Confusion" tbc: • John Alla – 41 a. • Richard Keiran – 100 a.	141
	pt. "Bradburns Delight" – for (N) Start; denied, charged to Thomas Bailey in "Baileys Delight Resurveyed"	100
h/o Richard Bishop	"Courseys Point" tbc William Bishop, included in "Resurvey of Smiths Mistake"	1350
	"Mill Range" tbc William Bishop, included in "Resurvey of Smiths Mistake"	163
	pt. "Bishops Outlett" tbc William Bishop, included in "Resurvey of Smiths Mistake"	350
	pt. "Bishops Addition" tbc William Bishop, included in "Resurvey of Smiths Mistake"	50
	"Mistake" – included in "Resurvey of Smiths Mistake"	400
	"Smiths Mistake Resurveyed" tbc William Bishop	1520
John Davis	pt. "Confusion"	220
36:1734:22 ...		
John Chaires	"Lentley" tbc Solomon Clayton	450
	"Chaires Addition" tbc James Chairs as "Reare Guard Addition"	100
	"Batchellors Adventure" tbc Thomas Chairs	150
	"Rear Guard" – denied	400

Queen Anne's County - 1734

Richard Moore	pt. "Norrests Addition" tbc Katherine Davis	100
	pt. "Smiths Forrest" tbc Charles Moor	61
	pt. "Confusion" tbc Charles Moor	159
Nathaniel Cleaves	"Astrick" tbc: • Thomas Davis – 120 a. • George Smith for h/o (N) Screvener – 105 a.	225
	"Exchange" tbc Nathaniel Cleave	100
	pt. "Todley" tbc Nathaniel Cleave	187
	"Mangey Pockey" tbc Nathaniel Cleave	100
Nathaniel Cleaves for Richard Scrivener	pt. "Shepards Fold" tbc Christopher Tillottson	100
John Hollinsworth	pt. "Partnership" tbc Edward Wright	250
	pt. "Anthorp" tbc John Hollingsworth	203
	pt. "Collins's Lott" – denied	50
36:1734:23 ...		
George Smith	pt. "Salisbury Plain" tbc James Williams	200
Edward Godwyn	pt. "Wrights Choice" tbc William Godwyn	100
Mr. Solomon Wright	pt. "Guilford" tbc John Pickering for h/o Nathaniel Wright	100
	"Warplesdone" tbc T. Hynson Wright	300
	pt. "Marlborough" tbc: • T. Hynson Wright & John Tillotson for h/o John Wright – 250 a. • Edward Roe – 250 a.	500
	pt. "Lowes Arcadia" tbc John Pickering for h/o N. Wright	300
	"Hog Harbour" tbc Mary Wright for h/o Solomon Wright	100
Thomas Goddin	pt. "Wrights Choice" tbc Thomas Godwyn	100
Thomas Head	pt. "Tullys Delight" tbc John Ricketts	100
William Boulton	pt. "Tullys Delight" tbc John Boulton	100
	"Boultons Delight" tbc Daniel Boulton	140
Robert Wharton	"Whartons Marsh"	27
	"High Gate Lane" tbc Robert Wharton, but land is called "New Hall" for John Lang	100
36:1734:24 ...		
Richard Keys	pt. "Collington" tbc Rev. Mr. Arthur Holt	150
John Lawrence	pt. "Partnership" tbc Grundy Pemberton	180

Henry Ayler	"Inclosure" tbc: • John Jackson – 73 a. • James Ayler – 50 a. • supposed to belong to h/o Henry Ayler – 177 a.	300
	"Dawsons Neck" – supposed to belong to h/o Henry Ayler	70
William Cooper	"Hills Out Lett"	100
John Worley	"Vaughans Discovery" tbc Thomas Burke	150
	pt. "Vaughans Discovery" tbc Thomas Burke	50
	pt. "Courseys Addition" tbc Thomas Burke	50
Thomas Fisher	"Long Range" – denied	147
	"Large Range" tbc: • Sarah Aussiter – 500 a. • James Barwick – 100 a. • Ed. Barwick – 100 a. • h/o Thomas Fisher – 300 a.	1000
	pt. "Coddshead Mannor" tbc Sarah Aussiter	884
	"Suffolk" tbc: • Thomas Fisher – 300 a. • John Fisher – 300 a. • Go. Fisher (DO) – 115 a.	600
William Jump	"Pockedy Ridge"	100
	pt. "Jumps Choice"	50
	"Jumps Addition"	49
	pt. "Jumps Chance" tbc: • William Jump – 250 a. • Thomas Swan – 50 a.	300
	"Jumps Lott" tbc William Jump, Jr.	50
36:1734:25 ...		
Thomas Swan	pt. "Jumps Choice" tbc Thomas Swann as "Jumps Chance"	100
Seth Gawell	"Grovely Hoe" tbc James Kenton	150
William Boone (cnp)	pt. "Oake Ridge" tbc Jacob Boon	175
	"Boons Park" tbc Jacob Boon	200
	"Jumps Lane" tbc William Purnell	100
	"Purnalls Forrest" tbc William Purnell	500
	pt. "Hadden" tbc Jacob Boon for legatees of William Boon as "Hadding"	200
	pt. "Partnership" tbc Jacob Boon	150

Queen Anne's County - 1734

	pt. "Partnership" – for his son John tbc Jacob Boon	150
	"Boons Pleasure" tbc Jacob Boon	250
	"Garden of Roses" tbc Jacob Boon	540
William Kenting	"Upland" tbc William Driskell	300
Thomas Roe	"Woodland" tbc John Roe	100
	"Dudleighs Desire" tbc: • Thomas Roe – 100 a. • William Roe – 100 a.	200
	pt. "Shephards Fortune" tbc Thomas Roe (Island Hundred)	100
	"Musketa Ridge" tbc Thomas Roe	50
	"Clouds Range" – from (N) Yewell tbc Thomas Roe (Island Hundred)	100
	pt. "Hackett Garden" tbc Thomas Roe	100
Benjamin Silvester	"Mischiefe" – heirs not known	100
John Thomas	pt. "Bramfield" – heirs not known	100
	"Carmathan" tbc James Silvester	100
James Kirkham	"Young Hall" tbc William Kirkham	175
	"Tuttlefields" tbc Samuel Dickinson (TA)	200
36:1734:26 ...		
Samuel Jommett	"Wooverton" tbc Jonathan Greenwood for h/o Samuel Jennett	250
John Lane	pt. "Lambeth" tbc Timothy Lane as "Lambert"	100
	pt. "Lanes Forrest" tbc John Lane, denied	60
	"Lanes Folly" tbc William Lane	100
	pt. "Killeroy" tbc Mary Lane	100
	"Lowes Bennington" tbc John Lane, denied	250
	"Lanes Folly Addition" tbc John Lane, rent refused	130
	"Scotts Chance" tbc John Lane, denied	100
George Golt	½ "Millford" tbc: • Hawkins Downs – 150 a. • William Gold – 50 a.	200
William Golt	pt. "Milford" tbc William Golt (minor)	50
John Leonard	½ "Millford"	200
	pt. "Hacton"	200
	pt. "Killkenny"	100
Thomas Banning	pt. "Lanes Forrest" tbc h/o Thomas Banning	80
Richard Webb	"Webbs Chance" tbc John Webb (TA)	150

36:1734:27	...	
Thomas Baynard	"Jones Plackett" tbc John Baynard	100
	pt. "Bear Garden" tbc William Willson & Rachel his wife (TA)	150
	pt. "Reliefe" tbc: • Esther Baynard for Nathan Bayanrd – 476 a. • Esther Baynard for George Baynard – 500 a.	976
John Baynard	"Pitts Vineyard" tbc: • John Baynard – 166⅔ a. • Esther Baynard for Nathan Baynard – 166⅔ a. • Esther Baynard for Susanna Baynard – 166⅔ a.	500
John Brown	pt. "Batchellors Hope"	60
Phill. Loyd, Esq.	"Loyds Insula" tbc Mr. Samuel Chew, Jr.	1793
	"Purchase" tbc Mr. Samuel Chew, Jr.	1000
	"Loyds Costin" tbc William Elbert (TA)	500
	pt. "Willenlew" tbc Samuel Chew, Jr.	682
Mr. William Hemsley	pt. "Fair Play" tbc. T. Hynson Wright, denied as included in "New Hynson Town"	40
	pt. "Loyds Meadows" tbc William Hemsley	66
	"Hardest Fend Off" tbc William Hemsley	150
	"Tewton Fields" tbc William Hemsley	460
	pt. "Loyds Meadows" tbc William Hemsley; denied	66
	"Hemsleys Park" tbc William Hemsley	800
	"Cloverfeilds" tbc William Hemsley	1622
	remaining part of "Trustram Wells" tbc William Hemsley	68
	"Hamesleys Discovery" tbc William Hemsley	91
	"Towton Fields Addition" tbc William Hemsley	140
	"Hemsleys Adventure" tbc William Hemsley	200
36:1734:28	...	
John Primrose	pt. "Hamiltons Hermitage" tbc: • John Primrose – 75 a. • William Primrose – 75 a. • William Campbell – 150 a.	300
	pt. "Shephards Fortune" tbc George Primrose	100
	"Adventure" tbc John Primrose	30

Queen Anne's County - 1734

John Hackett	pt. "Hamiltons Hermitage" tbc: • Daniel Newman – 33⅓ a. • John Hollinsworth – 33⅓ a. • Richard Wells – 33⅓ a.	100
	pt. "Prices Hill" tbc: • John Hackett – 200 a. • Thomas Hackett – 100 a.	300
John Offley	"Ponderfield" tbc h/o John Offley	200
William Wilkinson	"Shephards Redoubt" tbc: • Nath. Comegys – 60 a. • James Roberts – 100 a. • William Wilkinson – 140 a.	300
James Gould	pt. "Ripley"	400
	pt. "Spread Eagle"	75
	pt. "Comberwell"	100
	"Goulds Purchase"	195
Charles Vanderford	"Vanderfords Agreement" – denied	100
	"Fortune" tbc: • Charles Vanderford – 60 a. • Thomas Bellin – 40 a.	100
	<n/g> – from Major Hawkins tbc Charles Vanderford	100
John Parsons	"Mount Pleasant" tbc Aug. Thompson	50
	pt. "Enjoyment" tbc Aug. Thompson	50
	"Franckford" tbc h/o John Parsons (minors, KE)	200
	"Killmanams Plains Addition" tbc John Parsons who refused to pay	500
36:1734:29 ...		
Thomas Sayward	"Bishops Fields"	350
	"Dangerfield" – denied	200
	"Out Range"	174
Henry Johnson	pt. "Notlars Delight"	80
	"Alberts Delight"	200
Thomas Hinds	pt. "Spread Eagle" tbc: • Thomas Hinds – 50 a. • Mary Hinds – 150 a.	200
John Collins (cnp)	pt. "Spread Eagle"	425
	"Castle Miles" – included in resurvey of "Levells"	200
	"Offleys Fortune"	136

		pt. "Spread Eagle" – denied	200
	John Gibbs	pt. "Killmanams Plains"	200
	Charles Ryley	"Bradford" tbc John Ricketts	100
	William Merridith	pt. "Shrewsberry"	150
		"Plains" – denied	110
		pt. "Smeath" tbc John Beck	175
		"Shrewsberry Addition" tbc William Merrydith	100
	John Tillotson	½ "Lords Gift"	150
	Mathew Collier	pt. "Bishops Outlett" tbc Allice Collier	75
		pt. "Bishops Addition" tbc Allice Collier	75
36:1734:30	...		
	John Fowler	pt. "Shrewsberry" tbc h/o John Fowler	150
	Richard Collins	pt. "Tottenham"	300
	Samuel Taylor	"Lower Arcadia" tbc: • Thomas Shoebrook – 100 a. • David Phillips – 100 a. • T. H. Wright – 100 a. • lost in dividing – 26 a.	326
	Daniel Wild	pt. "Smiths Farme" – no such land & since taken up by Peter Wild as "Peters Lott"	150
	Charles Wright	"Clarksons Hills" tbc Ka. Davis	150
		pt. "Shephards Fortune" tbc: • Thomas Roe from (N) Shephard – 100 a. • William Ratcliffe from William Shephard – 150 a. • William Shephard – 150 a.	400
		"Cork House" tbc Robert Nor. Wright	200
		"White Marsh" tbc Robert Nor. Wright	400
		"White Marsh Addition" tbc Robert Nor. Wright	300
		"Collington" tbc Robert Nor. Wright	120
36:1734:31	...		
	William Harris	"Crumps Chance" tbc: • Joseph Harris – 50 a. • John Harris – 50 a. • William Harris – 50 a.	150
		pt. "Contention" tbc John Harris	200
	w/o Robert Norris	"Clarksons Hills Addition" tbc Katharine Davis	80
		pt. "Joanes Park" tbc Katharine Davis	100

Queen Anne's County - 1734

Henry Wilcocks	pt. "Mount Hope" tbc Henry Willcocks	250
	"Mount Hope Addition" tbc Henry Willcocks	100
Daniel Walker	pt. "Salisbury Plains"	100
Edward Cash	pt. "Carmans & Burton" & pt. "Covington" tbc Nicholas Broadway who married h/o said Cash	175
James Salisbury	"Sintra" tbc James Salisbury, resurveyed for John Salisbury in tract of same name for 187 a.	350
Capt. William Hackett	pt. "Ripley" tbc James Brown	250
	"Contest" tbc James Brown	50
	"Hacketts Lott" tbc James Brown; denied	150
John Johnson	pt. "Ripley"	300
	"Bee Tree Ridge"	50
36:1734:32 ...		
Thomas Ford	"Barton" tbc: • Solomon Seney – 110 a. • Walter Nevill – 40 a.	150
	"Fords Folly" tbc Stephen Deer	20
	"Fords Park" tbc Stephen Deer	30
	"Hopewell" tbc David Harrington	100
Isaac Abrams	pt. "Devenish's Chance" tbc Isaac Abrams (minor)	150
James Cassey	pt. "Connoway" tbc: • James Cassey – 189 a. • Christopher Williams – 111 a.	300
William Pinder	pt. "Bishopton"	250
	"Knave Stand Off"	50
	pt. "Ashton"	75
	"Collins Lott"	116
William Lee	pt. "Camberwell" tbc John Lee	100
Charles Lowther	"James Choice" tbc: • David Newnam, Jr. – 200 a. • Charles Louther – 100 a.	300
	pt. "Connoway" tbc Charles Louther	70
	"Chance" tbc John Swift	66
	"Fork" – for you & (N) Elliott tbc Caleb Esgate & his wife	200
Thomas Wyatt	"Constantinople" tbc John Swift	100

Nicholas Massey	"Masseys Hazard" – denied, included in "Johnsons Adventure"	90
	"Johnsons Adventure" tbc w/o Nicholas Massey	100
36:1734:33 ...		
Nicholas Clouds	pt. "Bishopton" tbc: • William Campbell – 68 a. • Richard Clouds (heir, minor) – 32 a. • William Pinder – 50 a., denied	150
	pt. "Fox Harbour" tbc Richard Clouds	50
	"Notlars Desire" tbc Richard Clouds	160
	"Notlars Delight" tbc: • Sarah Wright now John Hays, Jr. – 33 a. • Thomas Vanderford – 37 a.	70
	"Kilkenny" tbc John Harris	200
	"Willsons Beginning" tbc Richard Clouds, denied as being in elder surveys	250
	"Clouds Range" tbc Thomas Roe	100
	"Clouds Hermitage" tbc George Elliott	200
George Powell	pt. "Tilghmans Discovery" tbc Thomas Powell	80
	pt. "Partnership" tbc: • James Powell – 214 a., denied as being in elder surveys • William Carmichall – 36 a.	250
James Wyatt	"Manton" tbc John Hawkins Hamilton	300
	pt. "Ryhall" tbc Edward Crew (KE) for h/o James Wyatt	40
	"Clockerton" tbc John Hawkins Hamilton	200
	"Harmans Lott" tbc James Wyatt (KE) now possessed by William Carmichall	304
John Nevell	"Farrington" tbc John Nevill	250
	"Willsons Beginning" tbc John Roylen	100
	"Longs Desire" tbc John Nevill	50
	"Powells Fancy" tbc John Nevill	94
John Whittington	pt. "Whittingtons Lott" tbc John Dempster	350
	pt. "Hemsleys Brittland" tbc John Dempster	300
	pt. "Whittingtons Luck" – denied, not to be found	100
36:1734:34 ...		
Thomas Stanton	"Forrest of Sherwood"	200

Mr. Augustine Thompson	"Courseys Towne" tbc A. Thompson	600
	pt. "Prices Hills" tbc A. Thompson	80
	pt. "Hemsleys Britland" tbc A. Thompson	200
	pt. "Shephard Discovery" tbc A. Thompson	200
	"Addition" tbc A. Thompson, let fall	250
	"Parsons Marsh Addition" tbc A. Thompson	10
	"Good Luck" tbc A. Thompson	100
	pt. "Providence" tbc A. Thompson	200
	pt. "Henfield" & pt. "Shephards Discovery" tbc John Gibbs	161
	pt. "Sparks Choice" tbc Augustine Thompson	250
	pt. "Prices Hill" tbc Augustine Thompson	100
	"Ashford" tbc Augustine Thompson	200
	pt. "Willmores Range" tbc Augustine Thompson	700
	"Bears Harbour" tbc Solomon Parsons (KE)	50
	pt. "Rambles" tbc Augustine Thompson	200
	"Parsons Marsh" – from (N) Parsons tbc Augustine Thompson	22
	<n/g> – another parcel from (N) Parsons tbc Augustine Thompson	12
	"Sparks Choice" tbc Thomas Henry	50
William Ringold for h/o Herbert Morgan	"Hogg Pen Neck" tbc: • Andrew Toulson – 50 a. • Benjamin Clouds – 50 a.	100
	"Morgans Enlargement" tbc: • Andrew Toulson – 130 a. • Benjamin Clouds – 130 a.	260
Mr. Foster Turbut	pt. "Thompsons Manor" tbc h/o Foster Turbut (TA)	430
Michael Miller	"Coopers Freehold" tbc John Knowles & included in "Widdows Lott Resurveyed"	80
	"Crawford Resurveyed" tbc Michael Miller (KE)	264
36:1734:35 ... [Pages 35 through 44 are out of order]		
Robert Betts	"Westberry" tbc h/o Robert Betts	100
	"Addition" tbc Oliver Millington (TA)	100
	"Westbury" tbc h/o Robert Betts	100
Edgarr Webb	pt. "Lyford" tbc James Webb	780

Queen Anne's County - 1734

Col. Mathew Ward	"Adventure" tbc Col. Mathew Tilghman Ward (TA)	100
	"Winton" tbc Col. Mathew Tilghman Ward (TA)	500
	"Nineveth" tbc Col. Mathew Tilghman Ward (TA)	600
	"Winton Addition" tbc Col. Ward	50
	"Wards Hermitage"– denied, included in "Bridge North Resurveyed" for John Leatherberry	400
	"Wintons Addition" tbc Col. Ward	25
	"Nineveth Addition" tbc Col. Ward	200
Mr. Richard Carter	pt. "Lambeth Fields" – denied by (N) Cockayne & said to belong to h/o Norton Knatchbull	68
	pt. "Vaughans Dives" tbc Richard Phillips	20
	"Betts Range" tbc Thomas Cockayne (TA)	400
	pt. "Stevensfield" – denied, said to belong to h/o (N) Carter	200
h/o John Norwood in ENG	"Norwood"	1000
Thomas Brown, Sr.	pt. "Devenish Chance" – for h/o Anthony Cox	200
36:1734:36 ... [Pages 35 through 44 are out of order]		
Thomas Marshall	"Purchase" tbc Solomon Yewell	100
w/o Robert Harding	pt. "Dawsons Neck" tbc h/o Robert Harding	58
h/o Daniel Glover	"Grays Inn" tbc T. H. Wright	75
h/o Mr. John Lillingston	"Cheshire" tbc Thomas Hammond	200
	pt. "Carpenters Outlett" tbc Henry Jacobs, denied	68
	"Parke" tbc William Tillinpher	500
	"Lillingstons Castle" tbc Mordicai Hammond & his wife (AA)	500
	"Lillingstons Addition" tbc Mordicai Hammond	350
	pt. "Spriglye" tbc Henry Jacobs	300
	"Berks" tbc John Lillingston, let fall	200
John Gwyn	"Gunners Harbour" tbc John Gwinn	100
Peter Walls	"Bear Point" tbc Richard Chance	200
h/o Jacob Hyndman	pt. "Lexon" tbc Jacob Hyndman (DO)	184
John Woodall	pt. "Lexon"	51
	"Crumpton"	220
	"Hope" tbc John Woodall, Jr.	100
36:1734:37 ... [Pages 35 through 44 are out of order]		
William Bell	"Purnalls Addition"	150

Queen Anne's County - 1734

Phill. Feddeman	pt. "Hacketts Garden" tbc Elizabeth Feddeman	500
Samuel Groom (London)	"Partnership" tbc John Ratcliffe & George Gale (SO)	1000
	"Ratcliffe" tbc John Ratcliffe & George Gale (SO)	1000
Oliver Millington	"Epsom" tbc Oliver Millington (TA)	100
	"Addition" tbc Oliver Millington (TA)	100
Richard Purnall	"Dudleighs Chance" tbc Thomas Purnall (TA)	200
	pt. "Partnership" tbc Thomas Purnall (TA)	200
Henry Price	"Margaretts Hills" – denied	200
	pt. "Copartnership" – denied	186
Richard Chance	pt. "Boons Hope"	50
	"Littleworth"	100
Edward Starkey	pt. "Boons Hope" tbc h/o Edward Starkey, who will disclaim	50
h/o William Darvill	"Hills Addition"	50
h/o Col. Edward Loyd	"Darland" tbc Rebecca Loyd	400
	"Loyds Towne" tbc Rebecca Loyd	1000
	"Loyds Freshes" tbc Ed. Loyd (TA)	1000
36:1734:38	... [Pages 35 through 44 are out of order]	
Thomas Gadd	"Addition" tbc h/o Thomas Gadd	50
w/o Richard Jones, Jr.	pt. "Joans Plackett Addition" tbc Neriah Jones	50
h/o Henry Gills	pt. "Providence" – included in "Rowlands Hazard"	100
h/o Stephen Tully	pt. "Providence" – escheated	100
	"Tullington" tbc h/o Stephen Tully; not known	300
	"Sandwich" tbc h/o Stephen Tully, not known	150
Benjamin Clarke	"Sayers Addition" tbc Ed. Willaby	100
	pt. "Brandfield" tbc h/o (N) Clark, unknown	50
Richard Mitchell (ENG)	"Colne" – heirs unknown	500
John Lewis	"Lewis Chance" tbc Thomas Lewis	50
Daniel Wheatly	"Daniels Fields" tbc John Wheatly	80
William Ringold & Row White	"Youngs Adventure" tbc William Ringold & h/o Row White	175
	pt. "Grantham" tbc h/o William Elbert (TA)	100
36:1734:39	... [Pages 35 through 44 are out of order]	
h/o Simon West	"Stepney" tbc h/o Francis West	200
Richard Jones (smith, Pockety)	"Youngs Chance" tbc h/o Richard Jones (smith, Pockety)	100

Queen Anne's County - 1734

Richard Mason	pt. "Winchester Folly"	130
Dennis Hopkins	"Limrich" tbc John Legg	100
h/o Charles Ferris	"Maxfield"	100
	pt. "Dancy"	100
Nicholas Bancks	"Banks Fork"	200
	pt. "Hadden" tbc: • James Boon – 160 a., as "Hadding" • Moses Boon – 40 a., as "Hadding"	200
	"Banks Addition" tbc h/o Nicholas Banks	160
Thomas Alcock	pt. "Brandfield" tbc Samuel Chew	228
Nicholas Lowe (TA)	pt. "Controversey" tbc Robert Gouldsborough (TA)	250
James Ross (Bristoll)	"Bangor" tbc h/o James Ross	300
	pt. "Coddshead Mannor" tbc: • Sarah Anssiter for h/o Thomas Fisher – 96 a. • h/o James Ross – 904 a.	1000
Robert Brodaway	"Muskata Range" tbc h/o Robert Broadaway (runaway)	51
36:1734:40 ... [Pages 35 through 44 are out of order]		
Andrew Skinner	"Skinners Expectation" tbc Samuel Chew, Jr. & Henrietta Maria his wife	480
William Clayland	"Claylands Purchase" tbc John Clayland, who refuses	200
	"Glocester" tbc William Clayland (TA)	300
Dun Monrowe	"Bridgnorth" tbc: • James Berry – 50 a. • Elizabeth Mathews – 50 a. • Solomon Clayton – 50 a. from John Monroe	150
Capt. Richard Cheshire (Bristoll)	"Cheshires Delight" tbc h/o Richard Cheshire (Bristoll)	600
Christopher Sprye	"Doddington" tbc h/o Christopher Sprye (TA)	200
	pt. "Devenish Chance" tbc Christopher Sprye (TA)	100
	"Doddington" tbc h/o Christopher Sprye (TA)	200
Richard Dudleigh	"Dudleighs Demeans" tbc h/o Richard Dudleigh (TA)	200
w/o Dennis Connelly	"Connollys Park" tbc h/o Dennis Connolly	200
William Dickenson	"Dickensons Plains" tbc James Dickenson (TA)	860
	"Swanbrook" tbc John Bartlett (Mill Hundred, TA)	770

Queen Anne's County - 1734

36:1734:41	... [Pages 35 through 44 are out of order]	
John Harrington	"Purnalls Chance" tbc h/o John Harrington	100
John Freeman	"Plains" tbc Thomas Hammond	105
Fran. Neale	"Shadwell" tbc Francis Neale (Bullingbrook Hundred, TA)	100
Samuel Broadway	pt. "Townton Fields" tbc h/o Samuel Broadway (TA)	460
h/o John Walker	"Walkers Square" tbc William Campbell	300
James Hurlock	"Yarnton" a/s "Yarton" tbc h/o James Hurlock	200
Thomas Yewell	"Purchase" tbc Solomon Yewell	86
Dr. John Carr	pt. "Lanes Forrest" tbc: • h/o John Carr – 212 a. • supposed to be included in "Turners Lane" & "Turners Plains" for Rebecca & Ester Turner – 88 a.	300
James Dawson who married h/o (N) Impey	"Padan Haran" tbc John Dawson (TA)	500
	"Kniver Heath" tbc John Dawson (TA)	500
36:1734:42	... [Pages 35 through 44 are out of order]	
Solomon Clayton & Thomas Butler	pt. "Bradburns Delight" tbc Thomas Bayly, included in "Bailys Delight"	100
	pt. "Smiths Ridge" tbc William Clayton (TA)	300
	"Chesterfield" tbc: • Thomas Butler – 200 a. • Solomon Clayton – 200 a.	400
	pt. "Shephards Forrest" tbc: • Solomon Clayton – 100 a. • Thomas Butler – 100 a.	200
	"Tryangle" tbc: • Thomas Butler – 25 a. • Solomon Clayton – 25 a.	50
Mr. James Heath (cnp)	pt. "Tottenham" tbc James Paul Heath (CE)	300
	"Heaths Discovery" tbc Peter Froon & his wife a/s Elizabeth Earle	23
	pt. "Upper Heath Worth" a/s "Upper Heath" tbc James Paul Heath	429
	pt. "Crumps Forrest" tbc Thomas Shoebrook	125
	"Collins Refusall" tbc James Paul Heath	129
	"Heaths Forrest" tbc: • James Paul Heath – 100 a. • Thomas Ruth – 50 a.	150

Queen Anne's County - 1734

	"Heaths Parcell" tbc James Paul Heath, lies in CE	195
	"Chethams Landing" tbc Edward Chetham	90
	pt. "Park" tbc Edward Chetham	500
	pt. "Larrington" tbc John Ruth	125
	"Crumpton" tbc James Paul Heath	50
Flower Walker	pt. "Prices Hill" for h/o Flower Walker (NC)	400
John Price	"Goodhap" tbc Henry Price	126
36:1734:43	... [Pages 35 through 44 are out of order]	
Quakers – for a meeting house	"Land of Prophecy" tbc Body of Quakers	2
Ralph Fishburne	pt. "Providence" tbc William Fishburne (Philadelphia)	200
Daniel Whale	pt. "Collington" – escheated by Rev. Mr. Arthur Holt	50
w/o Michael Hackett	pt. "Adventure" tbc h/o Michael Hackett	100
	"Hacketts Chance" tbc h/o Michael Hackett	250
William Burton	pt. "Spread Eagle"	100
	pt. "Carman & Burton"	75
Thomas Hopkins	"Elliott" tbc h/o Thomas Hopkins (TA)	100
John Hamilton	pt. "Wrights Choice" tbc: • John Hamilton – 70 a., denied • John Hamilton – 30 a., as "Wrights Choice"	100
	pt. "Neglect"	50
	"Hamiltons Range"	100
	"Mary Ann Lott"	100
William Turbutt	"Long Neck"	400
	"Coursey on Wye"	600
Darby Ryan	"Tullys Lott"	300
h/o Mr. Christopher Rousby (ENG)	"Rousbye"	500
36:1734:44	... [Pages 35 through 44 are out of order]	
Robert Crump	"Crumps Fancy"	50
h/o John Whittall	"Whittall" tbc Nicholas Broadaway	38
William Sheppard	pt. "Sheppard Forrests" – denied	27
	pt. "Sheppard Folds" – denied, taken away by elder survey	160
	"Sheppards Forrest" – denied	200
Sarah Collins	"Freshfords Addition" tbc Sarah Collins (TA)	100

John Hughes	pt. "Lords Gift" tbc John Tillottson, included in resurvey of same name (f. 94)	150
h/o Col. Vincent Lowe	"Addition"	500
	"Expectation"	300
William Sigbye	pt. "Mount Pleasant" tbc h/o William Sigbye	100
	pt. "Double Kill" tbc h/o William Sigbye	100
Robert Hill	"Woolverhampton" tbc Augustine Thompson	200
	"Gwyders Lott" tbc h/o Robert Hill	250
Timothy Manah	pt. "Chance" – included in resurvey of same name	100
36:1734:45 ...		
Jeremiah Milles	"Hitt or Miss" tbc James Millis	50
Charles Baker	pt. "Adventure" – included in "Adventure" tbc Col. Tilghman	60
h/o Lawrence Knowles	"Partnership"	400
	"Discovery"	220
	"Knowls Range"	500
Thomas Jackson (Plymouth)	"Boothbys Fortune" tbc h/o Thomas Jackson (Plymouth)	500
Joseph Cassey	pt. "Connaway" tbc James Cassey	100
h/o James Ridley	"Ridleys Chance"	200
Andrew Abington	"Abingtons Square" tbc James Bowles (SM)	300
	"Abington" tbc John Abington (Piscataway Hundred, PG)	500
Dorrothy Offly	"Castle Miles" tbc John Collins, included in tract "Lewells"	200
h/o John Lundy	"Batchellors Plains"	216
	"John Forrest"	200
	"Lundy"	200
	pt. "Woodhouse"	200
	"Waterford"	200
36:1734:46 ...		
Denis Seney	pt. "Clouds Adventure" tbc James Ponder	150
John Reynolds	"Chesterton" tbc h/o John Reynolds (Duck Creek)	150
Henry Martin	"Chance" tbc h/o Henry Martin	100
James Ponder	pt. "Clouds Adventure"	100
Charles Lane	"Gwyders Range" tbc h/o Charles Lane	500

Henry Bastin (Plymouth)	"Harmonton" – escheated by James Wyatt & included in tract of same name	250
Daniel Glover	"Hope" – denied by h/o (N) Glover	200
Teague Malloony	pt. "Killmanams Plains" – died & left no heirs	100
Walter Ridley	"Lampton" tbc h/o Walter Ridley (TA)	135
Phill. Davis	"Mount Moluck" tbc Phill. Davis (KE)	150
36:1734:47 ...		
h/o William Nutthead	"Nutheads Coyce"	300
Robert Greene	pt. "Outrange" tbc Robert Green (KE)	200
legatees of George Robotham	"Robotham Park" tbc George Robatham	500
Edward Wilkinson	"Rattle Snake Ridge" tbc John Baker	150
h/o John Starkey	"Randon" tbc John Starkey, denied	100
h/o Col. Thomas Smithson	"Reviving Spring" tbc Mary Wrightson (TA)	500
Walter Nevill	"Southampton" tbc: • Walter Nevill, Jr. – 75 a. • Walter Nevill – 82 a.	157
	pt. "Barton"	40
	"Smiths Addition"	106
James Smith	"Tautnell" tbc h/o James Smith	100
	"Painters Point" tbc h/o James Smith	50
	"Fresh Run" – from (N) Sigley tbc James Smith (KE)	160
~~John Price~~	~~"Good Hope"~~	~~126~~
36:1734:48 ...		
Edward Holt	pt. "Whittingtons Luck" – land & owner not to be found	100
William Ailward (IRE)	"Ailwards Town" tbc h/o William Ailward (IRE)	500
James Hutchins (KI)	"James Camp" tbc James Hutchins, who disowns	1000
	"Castle Town" tbc James Hutchins, who disowns	100
	"Lanes Ridge" tbc James Hutchins, who disowns	200
James Murphy	"Churnells Neck" tbc Stephen Bordley	200
Simon Stevens	pt. "Providence" tbc: • John Miller for h/o Charles Stevens – 150 a. • Elizabeth Stevens (TA) – 150 a.	300
w/o (N) Mountsier	"Hacketts Delight" tbc Thomas Mountseer	150
	½ "Outrange" tbc Henry Short	200

Queen Anne's County - 1734

Daniel Perry	"Stafford" tbc John Perry	100
	"Sherin" tbc Daniel Newnam	100
36:1734:49 ...		
John Carter	"Coppedge Range" tbc: • John Carter – 200 a. • Alexander Toulson – 81 a. • Thomas Norman – 30 a. • Susanna Toulson – 100 a. • denied – 9 a.	440
	"Oar Mine"	200
	pt. "Mattapax Neck"	98
	"On Long Creek"	187
	"Crany Neck Resurveyed"	160
Edward Roe	"Neds Beginning"	30
	pt. "Hyndsleys Plains"	140
	½ "Tullys Addition"	150
Mr. Thomas Hynson Wright	"Toms Fancy" – denied	100
	pt. "Providence"	802
	pt. "Reading" –included in resurvey called "New Hynson Town"	93
	pt. "Hynson Towne" – included in resurvey called "New Hynson Town"	200
	"Addition" – included in resurvey called "New Hynson Town"	100
	"Foul Play" – let fall	500
	pt. "Grays Inn"	50
	"Hemsleys Britland" – included in resurvey called "Hemsley Britland Rectified"	740
	"Conclusion" tbc William Parker	150
	"Neglect" tbc: • John Hamilton – 50 a. • Solomon Clayton – 200 a.	250
	"Reliefe" tbc George Baynard	169
	"Smiths Neglect" tbc Ann Marshall	150
	"Warplesdon Addition"	280
36:1734:50 ...		
Daniel Newman (cnp)	"Addition" tbc Daniel Newnam	24
	"Williams Lott" tbc Daniel Newnam	50
	"Newnams Hermitage" tbc Daniel Newnam	50

Queen Anne's County - 1734

	pt. "Devenish Chance" tbc Daniel Newnam	50
	"Scottings Addition" tbc Daniel Newnam	60
	"Shervin" tbc Daniel Newnam	100
Humphrey Wells	"Landing"	30
	"Sheife Keep Out" tbc Christopher Sprye & wife	100
	pt. "Bath"	250
	pt. "Bath Addition"	150
	"Calebs Lott"	80
	"Prices Land"	200
	"Low Land"	45
Benjamin Faulkner	"Faulkners Lott"	50
	"Marshy Creek"	60
John Roe	"Roes Addition"	70
	"Downs Forrest"	300
	½ "Tullys Addition" – from (N) Pooley	150
George Cummerford	"Neglect" tbc Jos. Elliott for h/o (N) Cummerford	200
Edward Turner	"Abners Park" tbc Edward Turner (TA)	130
Gabriel Johnson	"Chichester" tbc Gabriel Johnson (KE)	50
36:1734:51 ...		
John Swift	"Timber Ridge"	70
	"Johns Meadows" tbc Da. Newman	100
	pt. "Isaac's Chance"	10
	pt. "Lowes Desire"	100
	"Swifts Out Lett"	140
	"Philadelphia"	50
John Long	"Longs Chance" tbc John Long (KEDE)	50
	"Sandy Hurst" tbc John Long	50
John Emory, Sr.	pt. "Partnership" tbc: • William Emory – 100 a. • John Emory – 90 a. • William Hopper – 100 a.	290
	pt. "Pharsalia" tbc John Emory	100
Benjamin Ball	"Cloverfields Resurveyed" tbc: • Augustine Thompson – 335 a. • Daniel Richardson – 335 a. • Nathaniel Richardson (AA) – 100 a.	770
James Earle, Jr.	"Cove Point Resurveyed" tbc James Earle	200

Queen Anne's County - 1734

Thomas Butler	"Butlers Owne"	50
Gilbert Falconar	"Edenburgh" tbc Mr. Gilbert Falconar (KE)	1074
36:1734:52 ...		
Edward Wright	"Collonells Quarter"	100
	"Hazard"	100
	½ "Content"	100
	"Content Addition"	200
	"Tullys Reserve"	300
	"Guilford" tbc Mary Wright	300
	"Out Lett"	50
	"Brotherhood" tbc Nathaniel Wright	50
	"Canaan"	50
	"Millford Addition" tbc Thomas Allaband	100
Ralph Swift	"Content"	50
John Timm	"Society Hill"	50
	"Timms Arcadia"	50
William Swift	"Williams Hazard" – denies, lost in Old Town	50
	"Swifts Meadows" tbc John Swift	100
	"Swifts Forrest"	50
	"Swifts Forrest Addition"	50
	"Williams Pasture"	54
John Merridith	"Merridith Adventure" tbc h/o John Merridith	100
	pt. "Plean Dealing" tbc John Merrydith	75
	pt. "Adventure" tbc John Merrydith	100
	"Trustram Ridge" – from (N) Thomas tbc John Merrydith	150
36:1734:53 ...		
William Burroughs	"Buck Road"	100
	pt. "Adventure"	50
Samuel Hunter	"Hunters Forrest" tbc: • James Hunter – 100 a. • Lawrence Everett (KI) – 100 a.	200
Benjamin Clouds	"Clouds Choice"	200
William Morrice	"Watry Plains" tbc Samuel Morris	150
	"Salisbury Plains" tbc Richard Scotten	150
Anne Morrice	"Morris's Chance" tbc Ann Morris (runaway)	100

Benjamin Ellis	"Benjamins Parke" tbc: • Benjamin Blackstone, Jr. (KE) – 80 a. • denied – 20 a.	100
Phill. Wooters	"Wooters Choice" tbc John Atkinson	100
George Edwards	"Edwards Chance"	50
Neriah Wright	"Beaverdam Addition"	150
Morris Cloake	"Tilbury"	50
	"Andeavour"	50
36:1734:54 ...		
Thomas King	"Fosters Folly" tbc Jo. Hobbs for h/o Thomas King	50
William Wheeler	"Kill Maiden"	100
Jer Jadwin & William Mountecue	"Cows Range" tbc Jeremiah Jadwin	100
William Parsons	"Friendship" tbc: • Thomas Mooth – 25 a. • Charles Tillottson – 50 a. • Trustram Thomas, Jr. for h/o Benoni Wattson – 25 a.	100
Samuel Parsons	"Marys Chance" tbc George Ayres	30
Richard Costin	"Newington Addition"	50
Fran. Sprye	"Sprys Adventure" tbc Francis Sprye	150
	"Friendship" tbc Francis Sprye	200
William Wyatt	"Wyatts Lott" tbc Stephens Andrews for h/o (N) Wyatt	150
	pt. "Tilghmans Discovery" tbc Stephen Andrews for h/o (N) Wyatt	100
	pt.. "Tilghmans Discovery" tbc Stephen Andrews for h/o (N) Wyatt	100
36:1734:55 ...		
Thomas Parsons	"Neglect" tbc: • Thomas Parsons – 51 a. • John Brown – 49 a.	100
	pt. "Batchellors Hope"	90
Thomas Elsbury	"Dogwood Ridge" tbc Charles Lemarr	100
George Hollyday	"Wood Ridge"	200
	"Wood Ridge Addition"	100
Lewis Blangey	"France" tbc h/o Lewis Blangey, said to be let fall	100

Queen Anne's County - 1734

John Rousby, Esq.	pt. "Mattapax Neck" – resurveyed & now tbc John Carter & Edward Cockey	25½
	"Ridge" – resurveyed & now tbc John Carter & Edward Cockey	300
	"Sledmore" tbc Walter Smith (CV)	800
Mr. Charles Carroll	"Thompsons Mannor" tbc h/o Charles Carroll	1000
Maj. Nicholas Sewell	a tract nameless	1000
	"Sewells Mannor" tbc: • h/o Nicholas Sewell – 2000 a. • Benjamin Tasker & Charles and Daniel Carroll – 2000 a. (KE)	4000
36:1734:56 ...		
h/o Thomas Phillips	"Cabbin Branch" – escheated	200
William Sudborough	"Sudboroughill" – owner unknown	200
Richard Johns (CV)	"Cold Spring" tbc: • Aaron Parrott (TA) – 162 a. • Richard Johns (CV) – 438 a.	600
	"Silvesters Addition" tbc John Webb (TA)	40
John Webb	½ "Redford" tbc John Webb (Trade Heaven Hundred, TA)	150
James Knowles	"Ulthorpe" tbc Ernault Hawkins	100
	"Wrights Chance" tbc Ernault Hawkins	124
John Baker (SM)	"Bakers Plains" tbc h/o John Baker (SM)	600
Edward Diggs	"Brandford" tbc: • Richard Richards – 318 a. • lost by "St. Martins" – 41 a.	359
Charles Stevens	pt. "Providence" tbc: • John Miller (TA) – 150 a. • Elizabeth Stevens – 150 a.	300
	pt. "Willenlew" tbc John Miller (TA)	218
36:1734:57 ...		
John Robinson	"Robinsons Adventure" tbc h/o John Robinson	200
John Emerson	pt. "Addition"	100
Timothy Lane	pt. "Lambeth"	100
Robert Gouldsborough	pt. "Controversey" tbc Robert Gouldsborough (TA)	250
Richard Hopewell (SM)	"Bloomsberry" tbc h/o Richard Hopewell	400
	"Irish Discovery" tbc h/o Richard Hopewell	350
William Finney	pt. "Dancey" tbc Rachell Finney (TA)	300
h/o John Bourks	"Old Indian Cabbin" tbc h/o John Bourk	50

Queen Anne's County - 1734

William Pratt	"Grantham" tbc William Elbert (TA)	100
Christopher Wise	"Naseby" tbc h/o Christopher Wise (TA)	100
h/o Samuel Randall	"Freshford" tbc h/o Samuel Randall	250
36:1734:58 ...		
James Edmundson (TA)	pt. "Willmores Range" tbc Augustine Thompson	50
Samuel Hollyday	"Parkers Lott" tbc Francis Gould, included in a tract called "Goulds Purchase" for 195 a.	200
Richard Smith (CV)	"Smiths Forrest" tbc Samuel Hyde (merchant, London)	2000
John Gresham (AA)	"Pockhiccory Ridge" tbc h/o John Gresham & lies in KE	1000
	"Brothers Annexion" tbc John Gresham (AA)	1000
	"Salisbury Meadows" tbc John Gresham (AA)	34
John Davis (TA)	"Davis Pharsalia" tbc John Davis (heir, TA)	350
	"Davis Range" a/s "Wrixham" tbc: • William Elbert (TA) – 400 a. • Rev. Mr. Beckeld (SU) – 200 a.	600
John Allen (TA)	"Allens Neck" tbc: • William Carmichall – 117 a. • William Thomas – 83 a., taken away by elder surveys	200
h/o Thomas Smith	"Bonnams Addition" tbc John Ross, included in a resurvey called "Westminster"	100
	"Barbars Delight" tbc John Ross, included in a resurvey called "Westminster"	170
36:1734:59 ...		
Richard Bruff (TA)	"Ramseys Folly" tbc h/o Richard Bruffe (TA)	200
Edward Day (SO)	"Providence"	1100
h/o Katharine Smith	"Broad Creek" – supposed to be lost	200
h/o Thomas Butler	"Butlers Marsh" – no owner	50
h/o John Butler	"Butlers Neck" – no owner found	200
h/o Thomas Allen	"Allens Neck" – no owner	66
h/o Thomas Petts	"Petts Neck" – no owner	100
h/o Thomas Adams	"Priors Mannor" – either let fall or taken up	1000
h/o Giles Bashaw	"Pears Plantation" – no owner & supposed to lie in "Kent Fort Manor"	75
36:1734:60 ...		
h/o Thomas Wetherell	"Wetherell" – thought to be same land as "Martins Neck"	100

h/o Edward Burton	"Burtons Lott" – no owner found	200
h/o John Wright	"Wrights Chance" – no owner found	200
	"Marborough Addition" tbc: • T. H. Wright for h/o John Wright – 50 a. • John Tillottson for h/o John Wright – 50 a.	100
	"Littleworth" tbc T. H. Wright & John Tillottson for h/o John Wright	50
h/o John Coursey	"Caedar Branch" tbc Col. Tilghman & included in "Tilghmans Hermitage"	400
h/o Deliverance Lovely	"Lovely" – lies in bounds of lands of Col. Coursey	200
John Singleton & h/o Richard Jones	"Addition" tbc h/o John Singleton, disclaimed & taken away by elder surveys, now land of Michael Earle	50
h/o Jonathan Syberry	"Wickersby" – supposed to lie in His Lordships Mannor	500
36:1734:61 ...		
John Willson (Tuckahoe)	pt. "Brandfield & Sayers Addition" tbc Mary Willson	570
	"Good Luck Range" tbc Mary Willson	50
James Dalton	"New London" tbc Isaac Payne	150
Thomas Williams	"Doctors Folly" tbc Thomas Wilkinson	60
Thomas Shoebrook	"Stoke Addition"	50
	pt. "Lows Arcadia" a/s "Lowes Arcadia"	100
	pt. "Crumps Forrests"	50
	pt. "Upper Heath"	100
	pt. "Crumps Forrest"	100
	"Stoke"	100
John Wiggins	"New Nottingham" tbc William Dulany	100
John Wooters	"New Buckley" tbc Jacob Wooters	100
Barnaby Sinnold	"Addition"	50
Thomas Hynesby	"Hynsley Choice" tbc Peter Hynesly	100
	"Addition" – denied	50
	pt. "Oakenthorp" tbc Peter Hynesly	40
	pt. "Daventport" tbc Thomas Davis, included in "Content Resurveyed"	164
	"Hynsleys Reserve" tbc Thomas Davis, included in "Content Resurveyed"	100
36:1734:62 ...		

Edward Cossens	"Cossens Neck" tbc h/o Edward Cossens, called by name of "Cossens Lott" & supposed to be in KE	100
George Bowes	pt. "Kendall" tbc h/o George Bowes (TA)	100
Timothy Toole	pt. "Kendall" tbc h/o Timothy Toole	88
Mr. Solomon Clayton	"Forrest"	100
	"Solomons Fancy"	50
	"Winterhouse"	50
	"Chestnutt Meadows"	100
	"Neglect"	50
	"Sheppards Hook"	200
	"Sleeford"	200
	"Lott" tbc William Scandell	50
	pt. "Brampton" – denied	150
	"Chesterfield Addition"	70
	"Hogg Pen Neck"	55
	"Hogg Hole"	50
	pt. "Conquest"	127
Daniel Mullican	"Mullicans Delight" tbc h/o Daniel Mullican (KE)	150
Benjamin Shurman	"Spicie Grove" tbc Benjamin Shurman (KEDE)	250
	"Tappahanah" tbc Benjamin Shurman (KEDE)	1375
John Knott	"Littleworth" tbc John Loyd for h/o John Knott	50
36:1734:63 ...		
George Whitehead	"Tappanah" tbc George Whitehead & Co. (Easton)	1000
	"Addition to Fruth" tbc George Whitehead & Co. (Easton)	725
h/o Nathaniel Wright	"Beginning" tbc John Pickering for h/o Nathaniel Wright	85
	"Beaver Dams" tbc John Pickering for h/o Nathaniel Wright	50
	"Wrights Chance" tbc Nathaniel Wright	300
John Granger	pt. "Connors Neck" tbc John Grainger (KE)	100
Isaac Harris	"Gouldhawks Enlargement" tbc Benjamin Elliott for h/o Workman Harris	70
	pt. "Cummins Freehold" tbc Benjamin Elliott for h/o Workman Harris	50
	"Mersons Freehold" tbc Benjamin Elliott for h/o Workman Harris	50
	"Claxton"	100

Queen Anne's County - 1734

Vestry of Christ Church Parish	"Little Ease" tbc Rev. Mr. Thomas Phillips, as glebe land	150
Daniel Richardson	"Pascos Adventure"	150
	"Wadeing Place"	300
Joseph Sudler	"Clay Pitt Neck" tbc James Sudler	100
	"Hills Cabbin" tbc Jos. Sudler	100
	"Beverton" tbc Jos. Sudler	100
	"Saw Pitt Neck" tbc James Sudler	78
36:1734:64 ...		
John Wright (KI)	pt. "Parsons Point" tbc Penelope Wright	100
Ann Price (widow)	"Primus" tbc h/o Ann Price	96
	pt. "Parsons Neck" tbc h/o Ann Price	75
	"Bonadventure" tbc h/o Ann Price	75
	"Addition" tbc h/o Ann Price	131
	"Easterne Part of Easterne Island" tbc h/o Ann Price	36
	"Rotterdam" tbc h/o Ann Price	50
	pt. "Parke" tbc: • Mathew Griffith – 220 a. • Benjamin Griffith – 220 a.	440
William Legg	"Limbrick" – from (N) Cooper tbc John Legg, Jr.	100
John Legg	"Woodland Neck"	50
Edmund Sheild	"Petts Gift" tbc Leonard Mason	85
Isaac Hudson	"Ashford" tbc Thomas Tanner	100
Andrew Toulson	pt. "Coppidge Range" tbc Susanna Toulson	100
Absolem Johnson	pt. "Sayers Range" tbc Albert Johnson, as "Sayers Range Addition"	100
William Murphy	"Oldsons Reliefe" tbc William Murphey	100
Christopher Birch	"Jamaica Addition" tbc Thomas Wilkinson	50
36:1734:65 ...		
Darby Dulany	"Powells Fancy" tbc Thomas Marsh	300
Edward Macdaniell	"Emorys Paxton" tbc Hugh Paxton, let fall	372
	"Range" tbc Hugh Paxton, denied	200
William Dulany	"Standford"	200
	pt. "Mount Mill" tbc: • William Dulany – 33 a. • Charles Seth – 27 a., denied	60
	"Vaughans Kindness"	200

Page 41

James Barkhurst	pt. "Henfield" & pt. "Sheppards Discovery" tbc Roger Hix & his wife (KE)	162
John Emory, Jr.	"Hemsley"	300
	"Emorys Neglect"	125
	"Emorys Addition"	50
	"Batterfield" tbc John Emory	200
	pt. "Forrest Lodge" tbc John Emory	20
Arthur Emory, Jr.	"Welsh Ridge"	500
	"Hap Hazard" – from Thomas Wilkinson	116
Visitors of Queen Anns Free School	pt. "Forlorne Hope"	100
Thomas Davis	pt. "Daventport" – denied	20
	pt. "Astrick" – denied	200
	pt. "Confusion"	200
36:1734:66 ...		
John Miller	pt. "Oakenthorpe" tbc John Miller (TA)	380
John Knowles	½ "Bedford"	150
	pt. "Hacton"	200
	"Wilsons Addition"	70
	"Jones Forrest"	500
Jos. DeRochburne	pt. "Vaughans Kindness"	200
William Pryor	pt. "Contention"	250
Thomas Murphy	"Hawkins Pharsalia" tbc Edwin Godwin	200
Michael Hussey	pt. "Hawkins Pharsalia" & pt. "Reliefe"	130
	pt. "Hynsleys Plains"	91
	pt. "Reliefe"	55
Henry Councill	pt. "Hawkins Pharsalia"	162
John Evans	pt. "Winfield"	55
John Carriday	pt. "Smiths Addition" – no such survey, denied	50
James Williams	pt. "Salisbury"	100
	pt. "Courseys Addition"	100
	pt. "Kendall"	100
36:1734:67 ...		
Thomas Robins	"Wallnutt Ridge" tbc George Robins (TA)	600
Thomas Wilkinson (cnp)	"Barbadoes Hall"	350
	pt. "Providence"	200

	pt. "Royston"	100
	"Hap Hazard" tbc Arthur Emory, Jr.	116
	"Hitt or Miss"	100
	"Discovery" tbc Rev. James Cox	100
	"Adventure"	84
William Satterfield	pt. "Winfield"	100
William Scandrett	pt. "Bristoll Marsh"	160
	pt. "Lexon"	235
	"Lott"	50
	pt. "Hynsley Plain"	76
John Greenwood	pt. "Gloster" tbc William Wilkinson	50
Fran. Rochester	"Winchester"	200
	"John & Rachell Choyce" – from (N) Layton	100
John Sparks	pt. "Sparks Choyce" tbc: • John Sparks – 100 a. • h/o John Sparks – 100 a.	200
	"Sparks Owne"	100
Fra. Pickering	"Pleasant Park" tbc Fra. Pickering (TA)	100
Michael Fling	"Milland" tbc Michael Fling (runaway, left no heir)	60
36:1734:68 ...		
Christopher Wilkinson	pt. "Royston"	475
Mr. James Earle	pt. "Land of Prophecy" tbc Peter Froen & his wife a/s Elizabeth Earle	497
	pt. "Freshford" a/s "Fresford" tbc Thomas Whittington (TA)	60
	"Upper Heathworth" tbc James Earle	161
	"Heathworth" tbc: • John Earle – 533 a. • denied – 20 a.	553
	"Boroughs Ridge" tbc Thomas Whittington (TA)	100
	pt. "Plain Dealing" tbc Christopher Cox	125
	"Ovall" a/s "Oval" – from (N) Thomas tbc James Earle	355
Richard Ponder	pt. "Smiths Delight" tbc: • Richard Ponder – 181½ a. • John Andrews – 118½ a.	200
	pt. "Smiths Delight" [above]	100
David Berry	pt. "Crumps Forrest"	150

Henry Covington	pt. "Providence"	100
Robert Certaine	"Jones Delight" tbc Robert Certain	200
Edward Jones	"Beaverdam Fork"	100
Mathew Williams	pt. "Salisbury Plains" tbc: • Mathew Williams – 100 a. • James Williams – 100 a. • James Williams – 100 a., denied	300
36:1734:69 ...		
James Harris	pt. "Guilford" tbc Terr. Gillespy	200
James Massy	pt. "Solomon Friendship" tbc James Massey, as "Friendship", denied	100
Morrice Macarthy	"Smiths Range" tbc Susanna Harris (KE)	239
	pt. "Malton" tbc Susanna Harris	150
Thomas Horney	"Sparks Outlett"	114
	pt. "Sparks Choice"	50
Richard Turner	"Hackers Adventure" tbc Thomas Roe	250
Charles Bradley	"Aylers Hope"	100
Henry Jones	pt. "Wooleys Outrange"	50
Thomas Jump	"Horse Pasture"	200
	"Jumps Chance"	100
Mathew Chilton	"New Cunningham"	100
Gallan Lane	pt. "Lambeth" tbc Timothy Lane	100
36:1734:70 ...		
James London	"Kirkhams Lott" tbc Robert Hardcastle for h/o James London	200
William Eagle	"Lambeth Addition"	170
Thomas Richardson	"Limrick" tbc Anthony Richardson (TA)	50
	"Richardson Adventure" tbc Anthony Richardson (TA)	80
Charles Downes	pt. "Fair Play"	116
George Vanderford	pt. "Fox Hill"	56¾
	"Dispute" a/s "Brotherhood" – from (N) Wright	47
Thomas Vanderford	pt. "Fox Hill"	56¾
	pt. "Notleys Delight"	37
William Vanderford	pt. "Fox Hill"	56¾
	"Dispute" a/s "Brotherhood" – from (N) Wright	47
James Horseley	pt. "Bishopsfields"	50

William Ratcliff	pt. "Spread Eagle"	100
	pt. "Collins Owne"	92
	pt. "Sheppards Fortune"	150
36:1734:71 ...		
Mary Willson & Hanah Phillips	pt. "Bishops Outlett" tbc Alice Collier	75
	pt. "Bishops Addition" tbc Alice Collier	75
Ann Tomelin	pt. "Lowes Arcadia" tbc John Deford & his wife a/s Ann Tomlin	70
Mary Wright	"Long Run" tbc Ed. Goodwin	100
	"Guildford Addition"	150
Timothy Mathews	pt. "Isaac Chance" tbc h/o Timothy Mathews	40
William Edwards	pt. "Fox Harbour"	100
	pt. "Collins Lott"	56
Thomas Coleman	pt. "Tilghmans Discovery"	80
George Aires	pt. "Ryhall"	184
Thomas Routh	"Leicester Fields" tbc William Jones & his wife	200
Jos. Clarke	pt. "Lyford" tbc: • Robert Jadwin – 70 a. • Joshua Clarke (TA) – 150 a.	220
Richard Phillips	pt. "Vaughans Discovery"	230
36:1734:72 ...		
Thomas Burke	pt. "Dawsons Neck"	136
	pt. "Dawsons Neck"	36
	"Welsh Poole"	250
John Fieldin	pt. "Saint Martins" tbc William Meeds from Robert Jarman	100
Thomas Hamond	pt. "Grays Inn"	75
Mr. William Till	pt. "Pack" tbc William Till, Esq. (Philadelphia)	500
John Carpenter	"Porters Lodge"	300
John Baggs	pt. "Old Towne"	266
John Banning	pt. "Golden Lyon" tbc William Banning	100
Thomas Moscropp	pt. "Old Towne" tbc Nicholas Goldsborough (TA)	500
John Bell	pt. "Golden Lyon" tbc James Bell	100
Margaret Purnell	"Purnells Addition" tbc William Bell	150
Fard Callaghan	pt. "Lambeth" tbc Fard Callaghan (TA)	38
36:1734:73 ...		
Henry Wright	"Smiths Ridge" tbc John Clements	100

Fra. Bullock	"Chance" – from (N) Taylor tbc John Cooper, presumed let fall or belongs to h/o H. Marks	200
John Cooper	"Chance" – from (N) Taylor	200
Edmund Cahall	"Daniels Field"	120
James Harvey	pt. "Winchester Folly" tbc James Harvey (TA)	100
William Vickars	pt. "Alcocks Pharsalia" tbc William Vickars (TA)	100
	"Warners Fairest Discovery" – from (N) Dudleigh to William Vickars (TA)	200
Thomas Pamphillion	"Spryley" tbc Thomas Pamphillion (Oxford, TA)	200
Thomas Turner & Charles Clymer	pt. "Shadwells Addition" tbc: • John Russum – 100 a. • Park Webb (TA) for h/o Jonathan Neale (TA) – 50 a. • h/o T. Turner & C. Clymer – 50 a.	200
John Dwiggin	pt. "Shadwells Addition" tbc Robert Floyd	50
36:1734:74 ...		
<t>	"Shadwells Addition" tbc Fra. Neale	100
	"Jones Forrest" tbc Neriah Jones	100
Edward Jones	pt. "Sandy Hurst" tbc: • Ed. Jones – 100 a. • h/o Edward Jones – 30 a.	130
John Wheadle	pt. "Sandy Hurst" tbc John Woodall	216
Henry Ward	pt. "Sandy Hurst"	25
William Tarboton	pt. "Crumps Forrest" tbc Thomas Shoebrook	50
Thomas Ruth	pt. "Heaths Forrest"	50
Samuel Shefeild	pt. "Spread Eagle" tbc William Burton, resurveyed by the name of "Littleworth"	100
Morgan Ponder	pt. "Poplar Hill" tbc John Blake	100
John Bath	pt. "Poplar Hill"	100
Mary Ann Turbut	"Sandish Woods" tbc: • Hercules Cook – 335 a. • John Robins & his wife (TA) – 665 a.	1000
36:1734:75 ...		
Ephraim Winn	pt. "Toadley"	193
Jos. & Benjamin Elliott	pt. "Slaughterton"	200
John Elliott	pt. "Slaughterton"	200
Phill. Coppidge	pt. "Slaughterton"	200
George Haddaway	pt. "Lowes Desire" tbc Thomas Sands	200
James Roberts	pt. "Lowes Desire"	100

Nathaniel Comegies	pt. "Sheppards Forrest"	173
Robert Finley & William Sweatnam	pt. "Camberwell"	300
	"Stepney"	300
John Evans	"Timber Fork" tbc w/o John Evans (KE)	500
	"Negligence" tbc w/o John Evans (KE)	45
Thomas Haddaway	pt. "Lowes Desire" tbc Thomas Haddaway (TA)	100
36:1734:76 ...		
Edward Scott (KE)	"Poplar Plains"	500
Rebecca Ashbury	pt. "Clouds Adventure" tbc James Ashbury	50
Thomas Peacock Betts	pt. "Providence"	100
Lewis Cloather	"Plain Dealing"	100
George & Henry Clift	pt. "Stevens Fields" tbc Henry Clift	200
William Starkey	"Oak Ridge" tbc: • Jacob Boon – 175 a. • William Starkey – 175 a.	350
	pt. "Coddshead Mannor"	116
Thomas Campe	"Willenlew" tbc h/o Thomas Campe	106
Thomas Bostick	"Hynesleys Fancy"	50
	"Bosticks Chance"	50
	"Northumberland" tbc John Swift	100
Albert Johnson	"Sayers Range Addition"	100
Nathaniel Smith	"Taylerton"	800
36:1734:77 ...		
John & Fr. Johnson	"Clouden"	200
Joseph Earle	pt. "Emorys Fortune"	314
	pt. "Golden Groves"	
	pt. "Vanderford"	
	pt. "Addition"	
	"Hazard"	175
	"Emorys Fortune Addition"	72
Jos. Wicks & John Rowles	"Widdows Lott" tbc John Rowls	287
Alexander Toulson	"Phillpotts Neck"	690
Caleb Clarke	"Clarks Adventure"	12
	"Clarks Lott"	112
	"Clarks Delight"	76

Queen Anne's County - 1734

William Massey	"Hazard" tbc William Hazard, denied being taken away by land called "Dixons Gift"	100
	"Pocolett" tbc William Hazard, denied being taken away by land called "Dixons Gift"	18
Patrick Robinson	"Tally Gardin"	50
William Ridgers	"Ridgers Lott"	100
Nathaniel Wright	"Wrights Plains" tbc John Downs, Jr.	100
	"Brotherhood"	50
	"Wrights Chance"	300
	"Malborough" tbc: • Na. Wright – 250 a. • Mary Wright for Sarah Wright – 250 a.	500
36:1734:78 ...		
William Cole (TA)	"Coles Endeavour" tbc William Cole	150
James Millis	"Chance Hills" tbc James Hill	50
Archibald Jackson	"Sandy Hill"	50
	"Hazard" – from (N) Boggs	54½
	"Hazard"	50
Edward Cockey	"Hog Pen Neck, Goose Hill, Mattapax Neck, & Ridge" tbc: • Edward Cockey – 285 a. • John Carter – 187 a.	472
Richard Fisher	"Large Range Addition" tbc James & Edward Barwick	150
James Slaughter	"Ferne Ridge"	50
George Lambden	"Lambden Adventure"	100
Thomas Powell	"Toms Adventure" tbc Thomas Powell & Mary his wife (KEDE)	56
David Mills, Jr.	"David Prospect"	75
Fra. Wattson	"Wattsons Lott" tbc Thomas Lee	50
36:1734:79 ...		
Elizabeth Wattson	"Swine Range" tbc Teus. Thomas, Jr.	30
	"Widdows Folly" tbc Teus Thomas, Jr.	70
William Wattson	"Wattson Chance"	50
	"Grubby Neck"	50
	"Long Marsh Ridge"	50
William Whittby	"Whittbys Forrest"	50
Thomas Rowland	"Rowlands Hazard"	257

Queen Anne's County - 1734

John Lang	"Newhall" tbc John Lang (AA)	90
James Hobbs	"Hobbs Venture"	50
John Pitts	pt. "Coleraine" tbc h/o John Pitts (TA)	308
Robert Jadwin	"Lyford" – from (N) Clark	70
Abner Dudley	pt. "Sarahs Portion" tbc h/o Abner Dudley (TA)	140
Marsh Dudley	"Sarahs Portion" tbc h/o Marsh Dudley (TA)	160
36:1734:80 ...		
Thomas Barnes	"Barns Satisfaction" tbc: • Thomas Barns – 223 a. • Richard Carter – 50 a. • William Price – 50 a.	323
Rev. Mr. James Cox	"Denby" – included in "Denby" for John Smith (f. 87)	250
	"Denbys Addition" – included in "Denby" for John Smith (f. 87)	27
Robert Jarman	pt. "Hogg Hole" tbc William Jarman	180
	"St. Martins"	400
	"Brandford" tbc: • John Meads – 100 a. • Stephen Yeo – 68 a. • Thomas Price – 103 a.	591
William Ford	pt. "Ashton"	158
	pt. "Ashton" tbc William Pinder	150
John Wicks	pt. "Mount Pleasant" tbc: • John Wicks – 186 a. • denied as taken away in elder survey – 64 a.	250
	pt. "Enjoyment" tbc: • John Wicks – 79 a. • denied as taken away in elder survey – 86 a.	165
Mathew Dockwra	pt. "Royston" tbc Fra. Foreman	567½
	pt. "Fishingham" tbc: • Mathew Docraw – 100 a. • Fr. Foreman – 65 a.	165
William Elliott	"Rawlins Chance"	80
Jacob Bayley	pt. "Bishops Outlett"	200
36:1734:81 ...		
Thomas Sodden	pt. "Worleys Outrange"	50

Queen Anne's County - 1734

Edward Barrick	pt. "Large Range" & pt. "Large Range Addition"	100
	pt. "Jumps Choice"	50
James Barrick	pt. "Large Range" & pt. "Large Range Addition"	100
Samuel Dickenson	"Tutlefields"	200
	"Poplar Ridge"	150
	"Poplar Ridge Addition"	200
	"Gorsuch Triangle"	63
Christopher Williams	"Lowerfords"	200
Fran. Foreman	pt. "Royston"	567½
	pt. "Fishingham" tbc: • Mathew Docwra – 50 a. • Mathew Docwra – 50 a. [!]	100
John Macconakin	pt. "Barton" tbc: • Solomon Seney – 100 a. • Walter Nevill – 40 a.	150
John Andrews	pt. "Smiths Delight" & pt. "Hammers Addition"	118½
	"Mount Gilboa"	50
36:1734:82 ...		
Andrew Findley	pt. "Ramble"	150
John Jarman	pt. "Brandford" & pt. "St. Martins"	100
William Mead	pt. "Brandford" & pt. "St. Martins"	200
Anthony Richardson	pt. "Hacketts Garden" tbc Anthony Richardson (TA)	300
William Carey	pt. "Silvesters Forrest" tbc Charles Lowd (TA)	105
	"Silvesters Addition" tbc: • John Webb (TA) – 40 a. • William Carey (TA) – 174 a. • denied – 86 a., as tract is only 214 a.	300
James Silvester	"Bear Garden Point"	53
Thomas Silvester	pt. "Bear Garden" tbc William Willson (TA)	150
John Meads	pt. "Brandford"	100
James Hollyday, Esq.	"Bermmington" – denied, being in "Redburne"	<n/g>
	"Redburne Rectified"	1440
36:1734:83 ...		
John Blake	pt. "Poplar Hills"	100
Nicholas Broadway	pt. "Whitthall"	62
	pt. "Nottleys Desire"	38

Casparus Smith	"Jones Fancy" tbc: • Da. Smith – 50 a. • Benjamin Smith – 50 a. • Casparus Smith – 50 a.	150
John Biscoe	"Pleasant Spring" tbc John Biscoe (SM)	500
James Downs	pt. "Smiths Neglect" tbc Stephen Ritch for h/o James Downs	150
Richard Harrington	"Solomons Lott"	100
David Harrington	"Hopewell"	100
William Stavely & James Bennett	"Kent Fort Mannor" tbc Benjamin Tasker, Esq.	1000
Mary Carroll	"Sewells Fort" tbc: • John Nevill – 500 a. • Frances Gould – 500 a.	1000
Susanna Douglass	"Poplar Ridge" tbc Susanna Douglass (CE)	500
Richard Smith (CV)	"Sebergham" tbc h/o Richard Smith (minor)	800
36:1734:84 ...		
Edward Fotterell	"Halls Harbour" tbc Henry Rippon (KE)	500
William Fray	"Nodd" tbc Archibald Jackson	113
William Dehorty	pt. "Heneslys Plains" tbc William Dehorty (TA)	52
Edward Ricketts	pt. "Hynesly Plains"	59
Nathaniel Hynesly	"Oakenthorpe"	60
Charles Hynesly	pt. "Hyneslys Plains" tbc: • Michael Hussy – 91 a. • denied – 10 a.	101
Archibald Douglass	pt. "Kendall" tbc Archibald Douglass (TA)	85
Nicholas Shirlock	pt. "Pharsalia" tbc Nicholas Shurlock	150
William Carman	"Bradfords Addition" tbc William & John Carman	100
James Cook	"Campersons Choice"	100
John Croney	pt. "Coleraine" tbc: • Mary Crony – 150 a. • John Burke – 100 a. • denied, being twice conveyed – 150 a.	400
	"Godfreys Folly" tbc Mary Croney for h/o John Crony	50
36:1734:85 ...		
James Jordan	pt. "Coleraine" tbc Andrew Jordan for h/o James Jordan	567
John Burke	pt. "Coleraine"	100

Queen Anne's County - 1734

Richard Ross	pt. "Coleraine" – which is the new name (John Ross is struck out)	125
James Knotts	pt. "Emorys Rich Land" – from (N) Emory	95
Baldwin Kemp	"Emorys Rich Land" – from (N) Emory	150
Dorothy Esgate	"Fork" – from (N) Elliott tbc Caleb Esgate	200
Hance Hamilton	"Barron Neck" – from (N) Hawkins tbc Da. Maclean	227
	"James Lott" tbc Da. Maclean	50
William Driskell	"Newington" – from (N) Lewis, denied	250
John Gregory	"Benjamin Infancy" – from (N) Pemberton tbc h/o (N) Gregory	50
Thomas Meads	"Beginning" – from (N) Royston	200
William Roberts	"Skinners Pleasure" – from (N) Skinner	50
36:1734:86 ...		
Jos. George	"Chesterfield" tbc Jos. George (CE)	500
Daniel Pearce	pt. "Poplar Hill" tbc John Dempster	300
John Blackwell	"Alcocks Pharsalia" tbc John Blackwell (TA)	100
Daniel Cornelius	"Daniels Fancy" tbc Daniel Cornelius (KE)	100
Jonathan Raymond	"Raymond Folly" tbc Jonathan Raymond (KEDE), by name of "Raymonds Travells" 100 a.	50
Godfrey Viney	"Godfreys Folly" tbc Mary Crony for h/o (N) Crony	50
James Willson	"Willsons Chance"	100
Robert Rich	"Bridge Town" tbc Peter Rich	31
John Nicholson	"Hopewell" tbc Thomas Jackson	50
	"Nicholsons Addition"	50
Richard Lawrence	"Lawrence Delight" tbc Henry Johnson	100
Nathaniel Knotts	"Knotts Addition"	50
Thomas Grace	"Alcocks Pharsalia" tbc Thomas Grace (TA)	100
36:1734:87 ...		
James Hunter	"Hunters Chance"	100
	"Hunters Hope"	50
Isaac Merrick	"Merricks Delight"	50
James Rawlins	"Josephs Lott" tbc William Harrington	150
Jeremiah Neale	"Chance" tbc Jeremiah Neale (TA)	50
William Dobson	"Dobsons Westmoreland" tbc William Dobson (TA)	150

Queen Anne's County - 1734

Burton Fra Faulkonar	"Chestnutt Ridge" tbc Burton Fr. Faulkonar & John Faulkner	200
James Blades	"Goodwill"	50
Fra. Bright	"Stooply Bright"	200
William Bell	"Bells Adventure"	50
John Smith	"Denby Resurveyed" tbc Rev. Mr. James Cox	275
Jacob Ford	pt. "Ashton"	75
Patrick Sexton	"Liberty"	100
36:1734:88 ...		
Capt. Henry Rippon	"Halls Harbour" tbc Henry Rippon (KE)	500
Hawkins Downs	½ "Milford" tbc: • Hawkins Downs – 150 a. • William Gold – 50 a. (f. 27)	200
Thomas Chairs	"Storeys Park"	100
Thomas Price	pt. "Brandford" a/s "Brentford"	103
Stephen Yeo	pt. "Brandford"	68
Mary Cole	"Smiths Range Addition"	290
Ri Cole	"Brampton" tbc: • Solomon Clayton – 100 a. • Mary Cole – 150 a.	250
William Parker	"Branford" a/s "Brandford"	31
Isaac Paine	"New London"	150
John & George Gale	"Partnership" tbc John & George Gale (SO)	1000
	"Ratclife" tbc John & George Gale (SO)	1000
36:1734:89 ...		
Edward Wright	"Brotherhood Resurveyed" tbc: • George Vanderford – 47 a. • William Vandeford – 47 a. • Richard Clouds – 45 a. • Dr. William Edwards – 42½ a. • Sarah Wright for h/o Edward Wright – 618½ a.	800
Robert Nor. Wright	"Wrights Park" tbc T. H. Wright	100
Mrs. Rebecca Loyd	"Dareland Resurveyed"	1750
MM Benjamin Tasker, Charles & Daniell Carroll	pt. "Sewells Mannor" tbc Benjamin Tasker & Co., land lies in KE	2000
John Doile	"Waxford" tbc h/o John Doile	100
Charles Marshall	"Marshall Outlett" – surrendered by Act of Assembly to creditors of (N) Marshall	600

John Scott	"Scotts Chance" tbc h/o John Scott	100
John Lancaster	"Lancaster" tbc h/o John Lancaster	119
Jane Wyatt	"Jennys Beginning" tbc h/o Jane Wyatt	100
36:1734:90 ...		
Jeffry Horney	"Dixons Gift" tbc Jeffry Horney (TA)	100
John Jackson	"Barbarys Inlett" tbc Joseph Jackson	263
William Britton	"Bragholt" tbc Augustine Thompson, by name of "Barefield"	200
Christopher Tillottson	pt. "Sheppards Fold"	140
John Williams	pt. "Salisbury"	100
John Clemens	pt. "Edmundsons Green Close" tbc John Clemonds	200
Edward Carslake	pt. "Drumfield"	100
Phill. Charles Blake	"Blakeford"	555

36:1734:91	Additional Debt Book for QA – 9 October 1734	
Peter Wild	"Peters Lott"	150
Rachell Bartlett	"Turners Plain Addition"	298
Robert Wharton & William Pinder	"Wharton & Pinders Outrange" tbc: • Robert Wharton – 58 a. • Mary Pinder for h/o William Pinder – 67 a. • John Rayley – 75 a.	300
	"Wharton Addition" – for (N) Wharton tbc: • Robert Wharton – 31 a. • Alexander Lee & his wife – 19 a.	50
Joseph Fisher	"Fishers Chance" tbc Jos. Millis	100
John Errickson	"Johnson Lott" – escheated	46
Richard Tilghman, Esq.	"Pearl" tbc Col. Tilghman	1000
	"Tilghmans Hermitage" tbc Col. Tilghman	1843
Rebecca Turner	"Turner Plains" tbc h/o Edward Turner	128
Archibald Turner	"Speedy Contract"	10
Christopher Birch	"Doctors Folly" – escheated, tbc Thomas Wilkinson	60
36:1734:92 ...		
William Murphy	"Murphys Chance" tbc Edward Godwin	50
William Swift	"Indian Tract"	50
William Robison	"Anns Lott" tbc William Robison, Jr.	100
John Emory	"Emorys Rich Land" tbc: • Balwin Kemp – 150 a. (f. 85) • James Knotts – 90 a. (f. 85)	240
Walter Lane	"Lanes Folly on Resurvey"	160
Easter Turner wife of Joseph Turner	"Turners Lane"	100
Thomas Nicholson	"Nicholsons Chance"	50
John Timm	"Golden Rod Ridge"	50
Humphry Wells	"Wells's Park"	110
	"Crumps Advice"	50
Josias Clapham	"Soot Hill" tbc Thomas Bayley & William Nevill	200
Patrick Linsey	"Jadwins Hazard"	61
36:1734:93 ...		
Henry Johnson	"Johnsons Addition"	100

Edward Wright	"Reserve Addition"	50
	"Beverdams"	50
	"Millford" tbc Abraham Williams	123
Thomas Hynson Wright	"New Hynson Town Resurveyed"	360
	"Toms Fancy Resurveyed" tbc: • Thomas Hynson Wright – 1850 a. • Fairclough Wright – 150 a. • George Smith – 100 a.	2100
	"Hemsleys Britland Rectified" tbc T. H. Wright tbc: • T. H. Wright – 273 a. • Jane Smith for h/o John Smith – 57 a.	330
	"Timber Swamp" tbc T. H. Wright	200
Mathew & Nathaniel Reed	"New Reading on Resurvey" tbc: • Elizabeth Reed – 120 a. • Noll. Reed – 100 a. • T. H. Wright – 80 a.	300
John Bermingham	"Berminghams Fortune"	100
William Driskell	"Uplands Addition"	50
John Powell	"Tryangle"	50
Thomas King	"Fosters Folly" – see f. 54	50
John Cobrieth	"Holly Neck"	200
John Hollingsworth	"Exchange" tbc T. H. Wright	60
36:1734:94 ...		
Thomas Bayley	"Bayleys Delight on Resurvey"	356
Edward Roe	"Roes Lane"	22
Jeremiah Jadwin	"Timms Neglect"	50
Richard Turbutt	"Controversey" – taken away by "Ratcliffe Resurveyed"	200
Nathaniel Cleaves	"Cleaves Rambles"	230
Stephen Rich	"Miss Hitt"	250
John Tillottson	"Lords Gift Resurveyed"	350
Richard Bennett, Esq.	"Bennetts Toulson"	930
William Burton	"Littleworth" – eacheated	100
Robert Buckley	"Buckleys Delight"	50

Queen Anne's County - 1734

36:1734:95	Additional Debt Book for QA – 11 February 1735	
John Welch	"King Hammer on Resurvey"	182
Col. Richard Tilghman	"Union on Resurvey" tbc Col. Tilghman	770
Fra. Wattson	"Wattsons Desire" tbc Fra. Wattson (DO)	50
	"Wattsons Delight" tbc Thomas Mooth	50
Andrew & Prudence Price	"Andrew & Prudence Satisfied on Resurvey"	696
Thomas Hynson Wright	"Exchange" tbc T. H. Wright	470
	"Moore Hope" tbc John Moore	100
Thomas Curtis	"Curtis's Lott"	50
Richard Chance	"Littleworth Addition"	50
John Emory	"Jacks Purchase"	750
	"Emorys Chance"	100
36:1734:96 ...		
Richard Bennett, Esq.	"Neglect Resurveyed"	580
	"Bennetts Regulation on Resurvey"	1306
Robert Scrivenor	"Neglect Resurveyed" tbc George Smith for h/o (N) Scrivenor	190
John Ross (Annapolis)	"Westminster" – on escheat	297
Thomas Hollingworth	"Forrest Lodge on Resurvey" tbc Col. Ernault Hawkins	152
James Hutchins	"Little Thickett" tbc James Hutchins (KI), on escheat	435
John Emory, Sr.	"Partnership" – composed of several tracts tbc John Emory	350
	"Bee Tree" tbc John Emory	500
John Scotten	"Scottens Folly"	50
William Keary	"Kearys Discovery" tbc: • John Cooper – 60 a. • Thomas Stuard – 50 a. • Charles Lowder – 90 a.	200
John Baynard	"Baynards Chance"	54
	"Vineyard Addition"	28½
Henry Burt	"Burts Fancy"	50
36:1734:97 ...		
Solomon Clayton	"Hogg Harbour"	125
Thomas Crupper	"Good Encrease" – see f. 15	200
Joshua Clarke	"Clarks Venture" tbc Joshua Clarke (TA)	35
James Bell	"Mary Branch"	85

John Collins	"Levells" – composed of several tracts	250
Edward Clark	"Clarks Strugle"	65
Josiah Crouch	"John & Rachells Choice" tbc Fra. Rochester	100
Richard Bennett, Esq.	"Morgans Neck" tbc Richard Bennett, Esq. & his wife	400
Thomas Davis	"Content" – composed of several tracts	470
John Burk	"Lock Point"	50

36:1734:98	Following Tracts are Transcribed in KE Rent Rolls	
Daniel Perry	"Shearing" tbc Daniel Newman (f. 48)	100
Nicholas Clouds	"Clouds Range" tbc Thomas Roe (f. 33)	100
	"Clouds Hermitage" tbc George Elliott (f. 20)	200
John Doile	"Wexford" tbc h/o John Doile (f. 89)	100
Charles Marshall	"Marshalls Outlett" – given up to creditors of Charles Marshall by Act of Assembly (f. 89)	600
Nathaniel Wright	"Wrights Chance" – see f. 77	300
Robert Smith	"Reareguard" tbc Mary Cole, denied	100
John Hammer	"Hammers Lott" – see f. 19	200
George Whitehead & Co.	"Addition to Freith" – see f. 63	725
John Lancaster	"Lancaster" – see f. 89	119
John Scott	"Scotts Chance" – see f. 26	100
36:1734:99 ...		
William Bolton	"Boltons Delight" tbc Daniel Bolton (f. 23)	140
John Parsons	"Parsons Chance" tbc George Aires	115
Charles Lowther	"Chance" tbc John Swift	66
Edward Elliott & Charles Lowder	"Fork" tbc Caleb Esgate (f. 32)	200
Robert Smith	"Stroke" tbc Thomas Shoebrook (f. 61)	100
Jane Wyatt	"Jennys Beginning" tbc h/o Jane Weyatt (f. 89)	100
Nathaniel Cleave	"Mangy" a/s "Mangy Pockey" (f. 22)	100
William Hollingsworth	"Beginning" tbc w/o William Hollingsworth (f. 11)	100
Jeffry Horney	"Dixons Gift" tbc Jeffry Horney (TA) (f. 90)	100
Nathaniel Scott & William Young	"Partnership" tbc: • Nathaniel Scott – 250 a. (f. 10) • Joham Young – 50 a.	300
Timothy Meanah	"Meanahs Chance"	150
Thomas Bostick	"Northumberland" tbc John Swift (f. 76)	100

36:1734:100	Lands in DO belonging to Persons living in QA	
h/o Jacob Seth	pt. "Hunting Field" tbc Charles Seth, denied	100
Mr. James Earle	"Fork" – denied	300
Phill. Feddeman	"Fedeman Purchase" – dead & widow knows nothing of the land	205
	"Prevention" – dead & widow knows nothing of the land	85
	"Fedemon Hill" – dead & widow knows nothing of the land	30
Elizabeth Feddeman wife of Phill. Feddeman	pt. "Danby" – knows nothing of the land	100
Lands Lying in TA to Persons Living in QA		
h/o John Emerson	"Vincents Lot"	43
Jeremiah Jadwin	pt. "Hampton" & pt. "Parkers Range"	44
Timothy Tool	"Kendal"	275
h/o Benjamin Pemberton	pt. "Partnership"	1050
Samuel Bussey	pt. "Mount Hope"	150
36:1734:101 ...		
h/o William Sweetnam	"Browns Lott"	200
Charles Blake	"Sayers Forrest"	2250
	"Upper Range"	200
	"Adventure"	446
Richard Wooters	"Richard & Mary's Forrest"	80
Col. Arnal Hawkins	"Sandy Bite"	50
	"Good Luck" & pt. "Grafton Mannor" – from (N) Low	28
John Chais	"Hole Haven"	100
John Climer	"Ann's Chance"	50
William Cross	"Branfield"	800
Henry Price	"Copartnership"	373
Bartholomew Greenwood	pt. "Hampton" – from Bartholomew Greenwood	<n/g>
Mathew Docwray	"Storys Park"	100
John Downes	pt. "Hemsleys Arcadia"	75
36:1734:<unnumbered> ...		
Thomas Curtis	pt. "Mount Hope"	181
John Lawrence	pt. "Partnership"	180
Andrew Price	½ "Todcaster"	500

Samuel Wright	"Harris's Range"	400
William Haddin	pt. "Ramseys Forest"	107
	"Inclosure"	150
Henry Downes	pt. "Carters Chance"	109
h/o William Kenting	"Edmonsons Freshes"	100
	"Bloomsberry"	200
Mr. Thomas Wright	pt. "Dover"	40
John Hawkins, Jr.	"Hoopers Ensel"	200
Mr. Charles Blake	"Upper Range"	200
36:1734:<unnumbered>	**Recapitulation**	
36:1734:<unnumbered>	**Lands Lying in TA to Persons Living in QA**	
William Clayton	"Coles Bank" – land lies in QA	300
John Hawkins, Jr.	"Freemans Forest"	50
Andrew Price & Thomas Bullin	"Todcaster"	1000
Samuel Dickenson	"Mount Hope"	150
Edward Godwin	"Parkers Freshes"	300
Thomas Purnal	"Dudleys Choice"	100
Mr. Charles Blake	"Adventure"	446
Grundy Pemberton	"Long Point"	42
Timothy Tool	"Kendall"	273
h/o William Kenting	"Bloomsberry"	200
Henry Downes	pt. "Coston"	109
h/o John Emerson	"Vincents Lott"	43
<n/g>	"Newington" – from Ch. Lewis	240
Edward Roe	pt. "Tullys Addition"	150
36:1734:<unnumbered>	**...**	
Joseph Longfellow	"Josephs Hope"	50
William Shepherd	"Shepherds Fold"	160
William Ridger	"Hope"	50
William Ridger	"Small Hope"	50
Richard Tilghman, Esq.	"Tilghmans Gift"	650
Daniel Smith	"Manton Addition"	5
William Bishop	"Out Range"	174
William Bishop	"Dangerfield"	200
William Bishop	"Fox Hill"	170

Rev. Arthur Holt	"Holts Castle Hill"	245
36:1734:<unnumbered> ...		
Henry Price	"Copartnership"	379
Mathew Griffen	"Griffens Adventure"	220
Mr. Charles Blake	"Sayers Forrest"	2250
Richard Wooters	"Richard & Marys Forrest"	80
Benjamin Pemberton	pt. "Partnership"	1050
Thomas Chairs	"Storys Park"	100
Additional Rent Roll – 14 May 1738		
William Montecue	"Montecues Luck"	40
William Jackson, Jr.	"Triangle"	50
William Ubank	"Out Range"	50
James Silvester	"Grubby Neck"	150
John Roe	"Roes Addition"	70
Edward Williams	"Williams Adventure"	50
William Whitby	"Buck Range"	100

Queen Anne's County - 1745

37:1758:1		No. 1: Lands in QA – included in Resurveys & Escheated		
Land	Acres	Taker Up	For Whom Resurveyed	Acres
"Abbot's Ash"	40	John Abbot	Martha & Elizabeth Coppidge as "Beaver's Neck"	320
pt. "Adventure"	100	Richard Jones	Thomas Baily as "Baily's Delight"	356
pt. "Astrick"	105	Robert Smith	Robert Scriviner as "Neglect"	190
pt. "Astrick"	120	Robert Smith	Thomas Davis as "Content"	470
pt. "Belcher"	200	Thomas Belcher	Francis Barnes as "Barnes's Satisfaction"	323
"Batts Neck"	50	Matthew Reed	James Sudler as "John's Hole"	276
"Broad Creek"	400	Thomas Broadnox	John Wells	830
"Burton Upon Wallsey"	200	Edmund Burton	Otho Coursey	388
"Bluff Point"	200	Henry Morgan	Madam Frances Sayer	496
"Beedles Outlett"	400	Henry Beedle	Richard Bennett, Esq. as "Bennett's Outlett"	695
"Broomley"	200	Henry Parker	Richard Bennett, Esq. as "Broomley Lambeth"	1750
"Bocking"	500	William Smith	Col. Richard Tilghman	500
"Bashaw"	100	Andrew Bashaw & James Cloughton	Martha & Elizabeth Coppidge as "Beaver's Neck"	320
"Bradbourne's Delight"	200	unknown	Thomas Baily as "Baily's Delight"	356
"Bocking"	500	Richard Tilghman	Richard Tilghman as "Union"	770
pt. "Boagley"	175	John Boage	Richard Bennett as "Bennetts Regulation"	1306
"Bennetts Addition"	150	Deborah Bennett	Thomas Hollingsworth as "Forrest Lodge"	152
"Carpenter's Square"	200	William Young	John Green as "Green's Adventure Upon Carpenter's Square"	212
"Coursey's Point"	1350	Henry Coursey	William Bishop as "Smith's Mistake"	1520
"Cooper's Freehold"	80	Robert Cooper	Jane Coppidge as "Widow's Lott"	287
"Craney Neck"	400	Robert Huet & Henry Belamy	John Carter	160
"Crawford"	100	Henry Coursey	Michael Miller	264
"Coursey's Neck"	140	Henry Coursey	Charles Blake as "Blakeford"	555

"Coursey's Choice"	1000	Henry Coursey, Jr.	Richard Bennett, Esq. as "Bennett's Choice"	1392
"Cove Point"	200	Nathaniel Evett	James Earle on escheat	200
"Connors Neck"	100	Philip Connor	Philip Connor	280
"Cedar Branch"	400	John Coursey	Richard Tilghman as "Tilghman's Hermitage"	400
"Carpenters Meadows"	50	Simon Carpenter	Simon Carpenter	1843
"Castle Miles"	200	Thomas Collins	John Collins as "Levell"	250
pt. "Confusion"	200	Anthony Ivy	Thomas Davis as "Content"	470
pt. "Collington"	200	Thomas Collings	Rev. Mr. Arthur Holt as "Holts Castle Hill"	245
"Clay Neck" or "Stint Land"	100	Isaac Ilive	James Sudler as "Stint on Sudler"	173
"Darland"	400	Philemon Lloyd	Rebecca Lloyd	1750
"Denbigh"	250	Richard Jones	John Smith	275
"Denbigh Addition"	27	John Johnson		
"Doctors Folley"	60	Thomas Williams	Christopher Birch	60
pt. "Ditterage"	83	Richard Bridges	John Welch as "King Hammer"	182
"Elliott"	200	William Elliott	Benjamin Ball as "Cloverfields"	770
"Forlorne Hope"	935	Robert Smith	Richard Tilghman	1830
"Forrest Lodge"	100	Patrick Forrest	Thomas Hollingsworth	152
"Green's Adventure"	300	John Green	John Green as "Green's Adventure Upon Carpenter's Square"	212
"Goose Quarter"	50	John Singleton & Richard Jones	Richard Tilghman as "Tilghman's Hermitage"	1843
"Harmonton"	250	Henry Bastin	James Wyatt as "Harmon's Lott" on escheat	304
"Hogg Pen Neck & Goose Hill"	220	William Medcalfe & Thomas Yewell	John Rousby as "Hogg Pen Neck"	570
"Hemsly's Choice"	300	William Hemsley	Charles Blake as "Blakeford"	555
"Hackney Marsh"	300	James Sedgwick	Richard Bennett, Esq. as "Bennett's Outlett"	695
"Horse Pasture"	200	William Jump	Thomas Jump	200
"High Gate Lane"	100	Michael Hacket	John Lang as "New Hall"	90

"Hemsley's Reserve"	231	Philemon Hemsley	Richard Bennett, Esq. as "Hemsley's Reserve Rectified"	155
"Hopewell"	200	William Young	William Hemsley as "Cloverfields"	1622
"Hale's Neck"	50	Thomas Hale	John Erickson as "Johnson's Lott"	46
pt. "Hynson Town"	200	Thomas Hynson	Thomas Hynson Wright as "New Hynson Town"	360
"Hemsley's Britland"	40	William Hemsley	Thomas Hynson Wright as "Hemsley's Britland Rectified"	330
pt. "Hynson Town"	100	Thomas Hynson	Richard Tilghman as "Tilghman's Hermitage"	1843
37:1758:2	...			
"Jackson's Choice"	200	Richard Jackson	Andrew Imbert as "Plain Dealing"	727
"Joane's Hole"	150	Thomas Miles	James Sudler as "John's Hole"	276
"Jones's Armour"	180	John Johnes	Richard Bennett, Esq. as "Broomly Lambeth"	1750
"Inkersel"	200	Jonathan Silbery	Charles Blake	134
"James's Lott"	150	James Scott	Richard Bennett, Esq. as "Bennett's Regulation"	1306
"Long Neglect"	60	Henry Coursey	Charles Blake as "Blakeford"	555
"Lloyd's Meadows"	600	Philemon Lloyd	Madam Alice Lloyd	957
pt. "Lambeth"	240	Henry Costin	Richard Bennett, Esq. as "Broomley Lambeth"	1750
pt. "Lane's Forrest"	128	John Lane	Edward Turner as "Turners Plains"	298
"Lane's Folly"	100	John Lane	Walter Lane	160
pt. "Lane's Forrest"	100	John Lane	Esther Turner as "Turner's Lane"	100
"Lord's Gift"	300	Stephen Tully	John Tillotson	350
"Mistake"	400	Richard Bishop	William Bishop as "Smiths Mistake"	1520
"Mattapax"	350	William Medcalf & Thomas Yewell	John Rousby as "Hogg Pen Neck"	570
"Martin's Neck"	100	Robert Martin	William Osborne	234
pt. "Mount Mill"	50	Robert Morris	William Hemsley as "Cloverfields"	1622
"Maxby"	100	Alexander Maxwell	Richard Bennett, Esq. as "Bennett's Regulation"	1306
"Morgan's Neck"	300	Henry Morgan	Richard Bennett, Esq.	400

Queen Anne's County - 1745

"No Name"	600	Robert Philpott	Alexander Toulson as "Philpott's Neck"	690
"Nuthall's Chance"	300	Elias Nuthall	Richard Bennett, Esq.	294
"Neglect"	400	Henry Coursey	Richard Bennett, Esq. as "Neglect"	580
"Oakenthorpe"	1000	Col. Vincent Lowe	Richard Bennett, Esq.	1000
"Pett's Gift"	15	Thomas Pett	Francis Barnes as "Barnes's Satisfaction"	323
pt. "Providence"	200	Steven Tully & John Robinson	Thomas Rowland as "Rowland's Hazard" on escheat	257
"Parker's Lott"	200	Henry Parker	James Gould as "Gould's Purchase"	195
"Plain Dealing"	470	Andrew Imbert	Andrew Imbert	727
"Phillpott's Neck"	350	Robert Phillpott	Alexander Toulson	690
"Price's Hills"	300	William Price	Philemon Lloyd, Esq. as "Lloyd's Insula"	1795
"Partnership"	1000	Samuel Groom	John & George Gale	575
"Ridge"	300	John Rousby	John Rousby as "Hogg Pen Neck"	570
"Readbourne"	1000	George Read	James Hollyday, Esq. as "Readbourne Rectified"	1440
"Reading"	450	Matthew Read	Mat. & Nat. Read as "New Reading"	300
"Rosseth"	350	Philemon Lloyd	Richard Tilghman as "Union"	770
"Roe's Addition"	70	John Roe	John Roe	70
"Sintra"	350	Andrew Elina	John Salisbury	187
"Stoopley Gibson"	150	Henry Stoop & John Gibson	Francis Bright	200
pt. "Smeath"	175	Robert Smith	John Beck	412
"Stagwell"	300	Thomas Stagwell	Richard Bennett, Esq.	526
pt. "Sillin"	200	Thomas Broadnox	Nathaniel Hynson	200
pt. "Sprigley"	235	Thomas Sprigg	Richard Tilghman as "Tilghman's Hermitage"	1843
pt. "Spread Eagle"	100	Daniel Jenifer	John Feney as "Littleworth"	100
"Smith's Addition"	300	Robert Smith		

"Smith's Inlett"	200	Robert Smith	Richard Bennett, Esq. as "Bennett's Regulation"	1306
"Smith's Chance"	50	Robert Smith		
"Smith's Polygon"	400	Robert Smith		
"Shepherds Field"	400	Francis Shepherd	William Shepherd	160
"Sawpitt Neck" a/s "Sawpitt"	78	Francis Bright	James Sudler as "Stint on Sudler"	173
37:1758:3	...			
"Fork"	100	Evan Morgan	Peter Sayer as "Sayre's Forrest"	2250
pt. "Forlorne Hope"	300	John Singleton & Robert Jones	Richard Tilghman as "Forlorne Hope"	1200
pt. "Tilghmans Addition"	300	Richard Tilghman		
"Trustram Wells"	382	John Wells	William Hemsly as "Cloverfields"	1622
"Triangle"	125	Andrew Skinner		
"North East Thickett"	200	John Russell	Benjamin Ball as "Cloverfield"	770
"Addition"	100	Thomas Hynson	Thomas Hynson Wright as "New Hynson Town"	360
"Tom's Fancy"	100	Thomas Hynson Wright	Thomas Hynson Wright as "Tom's Fancy Enlarged"	2100
"Adventure"	100	Thomas Hallings	Mat. & Nat. Reed as "New Reading"	300
"Vineyard"	700	George Rowbotham & Andrew Abington	William Wrench as "Wrenche's Farme"	800
"Vanderfort"	350	Michael Paul Vanderfort	John Beck as "Partnership"	340
"Woodyard Thickett"	300	Philip Connor	Philip Connor	410
"Wrenches Farme"	100	George Rowbotham	William Wrench	800
"Ward's Hermitage"	400	Matthew Ward	John & Mary Lillingston as "Bridge North"	150
"Winton"	300	John Winchester	Nathaniel Evett	500
"Walnutt Ridge"	100	John Wright & Thomas Collins	James Evans as "Walnutt Neck"	109

Queen Anne's County - 1745

"Walcutt's Addition"	40	John Walcutt	Martha & Elizabeth Coppidge as "Beaver Neck"	320
"Wilkinson's Addition"	50	John Wilkinson	Richard Tilghman as "Tilghman's Hermitage"	1843
pt. "Waltham"	50	Thomas Hynson	Richard Tilghman as "Tilghman's Hermitage"	1843
pt. "Young's Chance"	94	John Grey & William Young	William Hemsley as "Cloverfields"	1622
pt. "Young's Chance"	86	John Grey & William Young	Thomas Marshall as "Purchase"	86
"Young's Fortune"	200	William Young	William Hemsley as "Cloverfields"	1622
"Barber's Delight"	170	William Bonham	John Ross, Esq. as "Westminster Escheated"	297
"Bonham's Addition"	100	William Bonham		
"Little Thickett"	200	Giles Gasha	James Hutchins, escheated	435
pt. "Lane's Forrest"	85	John Lane	James Bell as "Mirely Branch"	85
pt. "Lloyd's Freshes"	190	Philemon Lloyd, Esq.	William Ratcliffe as "Ratcliff's Part of Lloyd's Freshes"	190
"Toulson"	1000	Thomas Toulson	Richard Bennett, Esq. as "Bennett's Toulson"	930
"Tilghman's Hermitage"	400	Richard Tilghman	Richard Tilghman as "Tilghman's Hermitage"	1843
"Tilghman's Range"	98	Richard Tilghman		
"Tilghman's Pasture"	300	William Tilghman		
"Tilghman's Pasture"	500	Richard Tilghman		
"Good Increase"	200	Andrew Price	Thomas Crupper	200
"Hynson's Hill"	150	Thomas Hynson	Richard Bennett, Esq. as "Bennett's Regulation"	1306
"Hinesly's Reserve"	100	Thomas Hinesly	Thomas Davis as "Content"	470
Accepted on 31 May 1745 by Edward Tilghman.				

Queen Anne's County - 1745

37:1758:4	No. 2: Lands in QA – Twice Entered on Rent Roll	
Land	**Acres**	**Charged to:**
"Addition"	1000	Robert Bitts
"Ashford"	100	Walter Kirby
"Batchelors Plains"	300	Robert Smith
"Broad Creek"	250	Katherine Smith & Thomas Bradnox
"Cabbin Branch"	200	Thomas Philips
"Cork"	100	John Lane
"Charleville"	150	John Lane
"Dangerfield"	200	William Bishop
"Doddington"	200	Peter Dodd
"Foster's Folly"	50	Thomas King
"Great Neck" a/s "Blunts Marsh"	330	Richard Blunt
"Fox Hill"	170	William Bishop
"Hamer's Lott"	200	John Hamer
"No Name" or "Connor's Neck"	100	Philip Connor
"Outrange"	174	William Bishop
"Pigg Quarter Neck"	100	Alexander Downy, John Cockey, & Val. Downy
"Paxton's Lott"	100	Hugh Paxton
"Providence"	600	Stephen Tully & John Robinson
"Parson's Neck" or "Pasco's Lott"	200	Pasco Dunn
"Robinsons Adventure"	200	John Robinson
"Sandwich"	150	Stephen Tully
"Saint Pauls"	300	Michael Paul Vanderford & Katherine Pryor
"Timberland"	400	James Scott
"Thief Keep Out" a/s "Liberty"	100	Andrew Price
"Turner's Lane"	100	Esther Turner
"Westbury"	100	Robert Betts
"Woodridge Addition"	100	George Hollyday
"Wright's Chance"	124	Samuel Wright
"Yarmouth"	100	Robert Macklyne
Accepted on 31 May 1745 by Edward Tilghman.		

37:1758:5	No. 3: Lands in QA – Owners being Foreigners	
Land	Acres	Owners
"Addition to Frieth"	725	George Whitehead & Co.
"Ailward Town"	500	William Ailward (IRE)
"Bangor" – since escheated	300	h/o James Ross (Bristol)
"Cheshires Delight"	600	Richard Cheshire (Bristol)
pt. "Codshead Mannor"	904	h/o James Ross (Bristol)
"Coln"	500	h/o Richard Mitchell
pt. "Collins's Refusal"	112	Samuel McCosh (PA)
pt. "Davis's Range"	200	(N) Beckett (SU)
"Kent Fort Manour"	1000	h/o William Brent (VA)
"Long's Chance"	50	John Long (KEDE)
"Rousby"	500	Christopher Rousby
"Raymond's Travels"	100	Jonathan Raymond (KEDE)
"Smith's Forrest"	2000	Samuel Hyde (London)
"Spicie Grove"	250	h/o Benjamin Shermer (KEDE)
pt. "Sandy Hurst"	50	John Long (KEDE)
"Tappahannah"	1000	George Whitehead & Co. (Bristol)
"Tappahannah"	1375	h/o Benjamin Shurmer (KEDE)
"Williams's Fancy"	40	James Williams (VA)
"Young's Chance"	100	h/o Richard Jones (KEDE)

37:1758:6	No. 4: Lands in QA – Owners on Western Shore	
Land	Acres	Owners
"Abbington Square"	300	h/o James Bowles (SM)
"Bloomsbury"	400	Richard Hopewell (SM)
"Baker's Plains"	600	John Baker (SM) – since sold William & Thomas Hughlett
pt. "Cold Spring"	438	h/o Richard Johns (CV)
"Gwider's Range"	500	h/o Charles Lane (SM)
"Guider's Lott"	250	Thomas Gwider or his heirs (SM)
"Irish Discovery"	350	Richard Hopewell (SM)
"New Hall"	90	John Land (AA)
pt. "Sewall's Manour"	3000	Benjamin Tasker, Esq. (AA)
"Sebergham"	800	John & Charles Egerton (SM)
"Westminster"	297	John Ross, Esq. (AA)
Accepted on 31 May 1745 by Edward Tilghman.		

37:1758:7 No. 5: Lands in QA – Owners in KE		
Land	Acres	Owners
pt. "Adventure"	100	h/o Michael Hackett
pt. "Adventure"	100	h/o Robert Smith Ivy (minor)
"Brother's Annextion"	1000	John Gresham
pt. "Bristol Marsh"	50	h/o Robert Smith Ivy (minor)
"Chichester"	50	h/o Gabriel Johnson
"Crawford"	264	h/o Michael Miller – since sold to P. Frisby
"Cousins Lott" a/s "Neck"	100	Edward Cousins
"Chance"	200	h/o Robert Smith Ivy (minor)
pt. "Confusion"	55	h/o Robert Smith Ivy (minor)
"Churnalls Neck"	200	Stephen Bordley – since sold to R. Porter
"Double Kill"	60	h/o Robert Smith Ivy (minor)
"Edinborough"	1074	Abraham Falconar
"Frankford"	200	h/o John Parson (minor)
"Glocester"	350	h/o Robert Smith Ivy (minor) – since sold
"Mount Malick"	150	Philip Davis – since paid by William Coursey for h/o (N) Clayton
"Ninevah"	600	John Stevens
"Pockhickory Ridge"	1000	John Gresham
"Reason"	360	h/o Robert Smith Ivy (minor) – since sold 129 a.
"Salisbury Meadows"	34½	John Gresham
"Shield" – in KE	41	Simon Wilmer
pt. "Smithfield"	100	h/o Robert Smith Ivy (minor) – since sold to D. Jackson
pt. "Smith's Reserve"	100	h/o Robert Smith Ivy (minor) – since sold 34 a. to N. Wright
"Smith's Forrest Addition"	140	h/o Robert Smith Ivy (minor)
pt. "Smith's Forrest"	29	h/o Robert Smith Ivy (minor)
pt. "Smith's Range"	61	h/o Robert Smith Ivy (minor)
37:1758:8 ...		
"Smith's Reserve"	84	h/o Robert Ivy (minor)
"Triangle"	100	h/o Robert Ivy (minor) – since sold to J. Wallace
pt. "Enjoyment"	85	h/o Robert Ivy (minor)
"Triangle Addition"	360	h/o Robert Ivy (minor) – since sold to J. Wallace
"Adventure"	160	h/o Robert Ivy (minor)

pt. "Wrexham Plains"	130	h/o Robert Ivy (minor)
pt. "Winfield"	313	h/o Robert Ivy (minor)
Accepted on 31 May 1745 by Edward Tilghman.		

37:1758:9	No. 6:	Lands in QA – Owners in TA
Land	Acres	Owners
"Allcocks Pharsalia"	200	John Blackwell & Thomas Grace
"Abner's Park"	130	h/o Edward Turner
"Addition"	100	Oliver Millington
pt. "Carter's Forrest"	168	h/o Richard Carter
pt. "Colerain"	500	Daniel Powell
"Chance"	50	Jeremiah Neale
"Connally's Park"	200	h/o Dennis Connally
"Charleville"	150	William Brown
"Cork"	100	
"Clarke's Struggle"	65	Edward Clark
"Cold Spring"	162	Aaron Parrott
"Dickinson's Plains"	860	James Dickinson
"Dudley's Demesne"	200	h/o Richard Dudley
"Doddington"	200	Christopher Spry
"Davis's Pharsalia"	350	h/o John Davis
"Drumfield"	400	William Lampson
"Dobson's Westmoreland"	150	William Dobson
pt. "Devonishs's Chance"	85	Christopher Spry
"Epsom"	100	Oliver Millington
"Gorsuch's Triangle"	63	Samuel Dickinson
"Glocester"	300	William Clayland
"Grantham"	200	widow Elbert
pt. "Hacketts Garden"	300	Anthony Richardson
pt. "Hemsleys Arcadia"	579	William Hemsley – to persons in TA
"Kniver Heath"	500	James Dawson
pt. "Kendall"	100	h/o George Bowes
pt. "Lambeth Fields"	68	h/o Richard Carter
pt. "Lane's Forrest"	127	h/o John Carr
pt. "Lowe's Desire"	100	Thomas Haddaway
"Lampton"	135	William Thomas
"Loyd Costin"	500	widow Elbert
37:1758:10 ...		
"Naseby"	100	Christopher Wise
"Negligence"	45	Dr. Richard Porter

"Poplar Ridge"	150	Samuel Dickenson
"Poplar Ridge Addition"	200	
"Padan Aaron"	500	James Dawson
pt. "Partnership"	200	Thomas Purnal
"Ramsey's Folley"	200	Richard Bruff
pt. "Stevens Fields"	200	h/o Richard Carter – said to lay in Tuckahoe Creek
pt. "Silvester's Addition"	174	William Carey
"Shadwell's Addition"	50	Thomas Turner & Charles Climer
"Sarah's Portion"	300	Abner & Marsh Dudley
"Turners Lane"	100	Esther Turner
"Tuttle Fields"	200	Samuel Dickinson
"Turner's Plains"	128	h/o Edward Turner
pt. "Thompsons Manour"	430	h/o Foster Turbutt
"Touton Fields"	460	Samuel Broadway
pt. "Turner's Plains Addition"	178	h/o Edward Turner
"Timber Fork"	500	Dr. Richard Porter
pt. "Willenlew"	212	h/o Charles Stevens
"Yarnton"	200	James Hurlock
Accepted on 31 May 1745 by Edward Tilghman.		
37:1758:11 <blank>		

37:1758:12		No. 7: Lands in QA – Rent Refused with Reasons	
Land	Acres	To Whom:	Reason
"Adventure"	50	Christopher Granger	knows not any such land
"Arthur's Chance"	300	Edmund Pryor	knows not any such land
pt. "Briglin" & pt. "Briglins Addition"	86	h/o William Wrench	says sold to (N) Grundy, whose heir supposes the land involved
"Carpenter's Outlett"	136	h/o John Lillingston & h/o Michael Earle	cannot find the land; since 9 a. to Col. Richard Tilghman
"Clayland's Purchase"	200	John Clayland	cannot find the land
pt. "Collins's Lott"	28	Edward Chetham	supposed to be left in dividing
pt. "Colerain"	183	h/o John Pitts	supposed wanting in the survey
"Hineslys Addition"	50	Thomas Hinesly	cannot find the land
"Hamer's Choice"	299	h/o John Hamer	cannot find the land
pt. "Hacker's Meadows"	246	John Hacker	denied, being left in a resurvey of the same name made by Maj. Turlo for 214 a.
"Hamer's Lott"	200	John Hamer	cannot find the land
"James's Camp"	1000	James Hutchings	cannot find the land
"Killmainam Plains Addition"	500	h/o John Parsons	cannot find the land
pt. "Long Range"	147	Thomas Fisher	heirs will disclaim
"Large Range"	300	Thomas Fisher	
"Lowe's Bennington"	250	John Lane	cannot find the land
"Lane's Folly Addition"	130		
pt. "Lambeth"	100	h/o John Lane	cannot find the land & will disclaim
"Large Range Addition"	26	h/o Richard Fisher	knows of no such land
pt. "Lowe's Arcadia"	50	Samuel Taylor	supposed to be left in dividing
"Macklyn's Fancy"	500	John Coursey & William Elbert who married heiresses of (N) Macklyn	cannot find the land
"Margarett's Hill"	200	Henry Price	cannot find the land
pt. "Macklinborough"	26	John Power	supposed to be left in dividing
pt. "Noble Range"	6	Robert Noble	supposed to be left in dividing
37:1758:13 ...			
pt. "Park"	10	Philemon Lloyd & Henry Costin	refused by heirs as wanting in the survey

Queen Anne's County - 1745

"Randon"	100	John Starkey	cannot find the land
"Rearguard"	100	h/o Robert Smith	refused till they inquire if not foul
pt. "Sprigley"	65	h/o Michael Eagle	wanting in the survey
pt. "Neglect"	155	Robert Kent	refused by the heirs as wanting in the survey
"Whittington's Luck"	200	h/o John Whittington	cannot find the land
"Westbury"	400	h/o Robert Betts	knows no such land
"Winchester"	250	John Winchester	knows no such land
"Wyatt's Lott"	150	h/o William Wyatt	knows no such land
Accepted on 31 May 1745 by Edward Tilghman.			

Queen Anne's County - 1745

37:1758:14		No. 8: Lands in QA – Owners Unknown or Out of Province	
Land	Acres	Former Possessor	
"Allen's Neck"	66	Thomas Allen	neither land nor owner known
"Burlers Marsh"	50	Thomas Butler	neither land nor owner known
"Butler's Neck"	200	Thomas Butler	neither land nor owner known
"Burton's Lott"	200	Edward Burton	neither land nor owner known
"Batchelors Plains"	216	John Lundy	to h/o John Lundy (unknown)
pt. "Conaway"	70	Gabriel Thomas	to h/o Gabriel Thomas
"Chestorton"	150	John Reynolds	to h/o John Reynolds
"Cabin Branch"	200	Thomas Phillips	land & owner unknown
pt. "Dancy"	100	Charles Ferris	to his heirs; supposed to be escheated
pt. "Dawson's Neck"	86	h/o Henry Ailer	supposed to live in Carolina
"Expectation"	300	Col. Vincent Lowe	to h/o Col. Vincent Lowe
"Freshford"	250	Samuel Randal	to his heirs; supposed escheated
"Hill's Addition"	50	William Darvill	to his heirs
"Jennys Beginning"	100	Jane Wyatt – since purchased by Humphry Wells	to her heirs
"John's Forrest"	200	John Lundy	to his heirs (unknown)
pt. "Killmainam Plains"	100	Teague Mallory	to his heirs, supposed escheated
"Lowe's Desire"	1000	Col. Vincent Lowe	to his heirs
"Lundy"	200	John Lundy	to his heirs (unknown)
"Land of Prophecy"	3	Daniel Jenifer	to the Quakers for a Meeting House
"Morris's Chance"	100	Ann Morris	to her heirs
"Maxfield"	100	Charles Ferris	to his heirs, supposed escheated
"Mill Land"	60	Michael Fling	to his heirs, supposed escheated
"Marshall's Outlett"	600	Charles Marshall	to his heirs, supposed escheated
37:1758:15 ...			
"Nuthead's Choice"	300	William Nuthead	to his heirs, supposed escheated
"Notlar's Desire"	80	Nicholas Clouds	to his heirs
"Oldsons Pasture"	20	John Oldson	to his heirs
"Petts Neck"	100	Thomas Pitt	land & owner unknown
"Pear Plantation"	75	Giles Bashaw	land & owner unknown
"Rowbotham's Park"	500	George Rowbotham	to his heirs, supposed escheated

Queen Anne's County - 1745

"Robinson's Adventure"	200	John Robinson	to his heirs, supposed escheated by Edward Roe & called "Roe's Chance"
pt. "Royton"	25	Richard Royston	said to be left in the survey
"Stepney"	200	Simon West	to his heirs
"Beginning"	500	Col. Vincent Lowe	to his heirs
"Addition"	500		
"Tatnell"	100	James Smith	to his heirs, supposed in KEDE
pt. "Inclosure"	169	h/o Henry Ailer	supposed to live in Carolina
"Tullington"	300	Stephen Tully	to his heirs
"Weatherall"	100	Thomas Weatheral	land & owner unknown
"Wrights Choice"	200	John Wright	land & owner unknown
pt. "Woodhouse"	200	John Lundy	to his heir (unknown)
"Waterford"	200	John Lundy	to his heir (unknown)
Accepted on 31 May 1745 by Edward Tilghman.			

37:1758:16		No. 9: Lands in QA – Rent is Unsettled	
Land	Acres	Former Possessor	
"Addition"	200	William Elliott – this is the same land William Coburn is charged	William Elliott (KI) – who can't find the land
"Beginning"	100	William Hollingsworth	h/o William Hollingsworth
"Banks's Fork"	200	Nicholas Banks	h/o Nicholas Banks
"Banks's Addition"	200		
pt. "Boones Hope"	50	Edward Starkey	& his heirs – 7¾ a. since purchased by Richard Chance
pt. "Brandfield"	102	Peter Sayer	h/o John Thomas
pt. "Bridge Town"	17	Peter Rich	Peter Rich (Town Land)
pt. "Bishop's Outlet"	150	Matthew Mason	John Davis Inch who married the heir
"Bishop's Fields"	350	William Bishop – purchased by William Clayton	William Bishop (the heir)
"Barren Ridge Addition"	60	Anthony Workman	h/o Anthony Workman
"Copartnership"	186½	Henry Price & (N) Dehiniosa	Henry Price (Tuckahoe) – purchase since by Robert Blunt
"Chance"	100	Henry Martin	h/o David Rogers
"Camberwell"	300	Robert Finley & William Sweatnam	h/o William Sweatnam
"Contention"	50	Henry Martin	h/o (N) Martin
"Controversy"	200	Samuel Turbutt	John Baggs
pt. "Cloverfields"	100	Benjamin Ball	Thomas Price s/o William – from Nathaniel Richardson
"Dangerfield"	200	William Bishop – since sold to Mat. Dockery	tbc William Bishop
"Dobbs Adventure"	36	Mark Benton	h/o John Dobbs (KI)
pt. "Devonishe's Chance"	150	Isaac Abrahams – since sold to Jo. Newnam	h/o (N) Abrahams
pt. "Devonishe's Chance"	200	Thomas Brown	h/o Anthony Cox
pt. "Double Kill"	100	William Sigley	his heirs
"Dunnington"	100	Maurice Woollahand	h/o Maurice Woollahand (KI)

Queen Anne's County - 1745

pt. "Elliotts Choice"	20	William Elliott	William Elliott (KI)
"Freshford Addition"	100	Sarah Collins	John Collins, Jr.
"Fosters Folley"	50	Thomas King	h/o Thomas King
"Friendship"	89	William Hemsley	Mr. Robert Lloyd for h/o (N) Hemsley
pt. "Freshford"	50	John Broadrib	William Calvin
pt. "Fox Harbour"	25	John Hollingsworth	h/o John Hollingsworth
pt. "Golden Grove"	96	Robert Smith	h/o Christopher Santee
pt. "Guilford"	100	Solomon Wright	John Pickeron for h/o Nat. Wright
pt. "Glocester"	50	William Wilkinson	John Scotton – purchased from (N) Wilkinson
pt. "Hawkins's Pharsalia"	8	Ernault Hawkins	Elizabeth Hawkins
"Hacker's Forrest"	200	John Hacker – since resurveyed	George Baynard
pt. "Hunter's Forrest"	100	Samuel Hunter	Lawrence Everard
"Hawkins's Farm"	500	John Hawkins – resurveyed	Mrs. Hawkins
"Hackett's Delight"	45	William Hackett – since paid by Thomas Mountsier & at this time by John Andrews	h/o William Hackett
37:1758:17 ...			
pt. "Jasper's Lott"	200	Thomas Jackson	h/o Francis Jackson
"Isaac's Chance"	50	Timothy Matthews	William Matthews
pt. "Jasper's Lott"	570	John Hawkins	Mrs. Hawkins & Robert Goldsborough, Jr.
pt. "Killeray"	100	John Lane – since paid for by Giles Hix	Giles Hicks
pt. "Kendall"	88	George Bowes	h/o Timothy Tool
"Knave Stand Off"	50	William Pindar	Elizabeth Lee
"Lancaster"	119	John Lancaster – since paid by Thomas Sands	his heirs
"Merediths Adventure"	100	John Meredith	William Meredith (Tully's Neck)
pt. "Millford"	50	William Golt	h/o Golt Minn
pt. "Mount Pleasant"	100	William Sigley	his heirs
"Mill Range"	163	Richard Bishop	William Bishop (the heir)

pt. "Narborough"	250	Nathaniel & Solomon Wright	Richard Bennett, Esq.
"Paxton's Lott"	100	William Sweatnam	William Hopper who married Sweatnam's heir
"Plain Dealing"	600	William Hemsley	Mr. Robert Lloyd for h/o (N) Hemsley
"Purnall's Chance"	100	John Harrington	h/o (N) Harrington
pt. "Parson's Neck"	80	Thomas Cooper	h/o Thomas Cooper
pt. "Ponderfield"	91	John Offley	h/o John Ponder
"Plain Dealing"	175	Elizabeth Hemsley	Mr. Robert Lloyd for h/o (N) Hemsley
pt. "Poplar Hill"	100	Morgan Ponder	John Williamson for h/o (N) Rippon
"Panther Point"	50	James Smith	Richard Smith for h/o James Smith
pt. "Pascoe's Lott"	100	John Sutton	h/o John Sutton
"Ralph's Frolick"	67	Ralph Distance	his heirs (KI) – John Gilbert & John Daily
pt. "Sayer's Range Addition"	58	Nathaniel Scott	h/o Nathaniel Scott
"Spark's Choice"	100	John Sparks	h/o John Sparks
pt. "Sandy Hurst"	34	Edward Jones	h/o Edward Jones
"Stepney"	300	Robert Finley & William Sweatnam	h/o William Sweatnam
"Sudborough Hill"	200	William Sudborough	h/o (N) Sudborough
"Stratton"	1000	Col. Vincent Lowe – since paid by <unr>	Mrs. Hawkins
pt. "Silvester's Forrest"	45	James Silvester	James Silvester, Jr. (the heir)
37:1758:18 ...			
"Addition"	50	Thomas Gadd	to his heirs
"Tryangle"	50	William Jackson – since charged to (N) Bailey	James Baily
"Vineyard Addition"	28½	John Baynard – since charged to (N) Baynard	John Baynard
"Willew"	100	Stephen Rich – since paid by (N) Shoebrook	Thomas Shoebrook

pt. "Winchester"	125	John Winchester tbc (N) Jacobs	Henry Jacobs for h/o Mr. John Wells
pt. "Willenlew"	106	Charles Stevens	h/o Thomas King
"Wexford"	100	John Doyle	h/o John Doyle
"Wharton's Addition"	19	Robert Wharton	Elizabeth Lee
"Young's Adventure"	175	William Young	h/o Rowland White
Accepted on 31 May 1745 by Edward Tilghman.			
37:1758:<unnumbered> **Payments Made**			

Queen Anne's County - 1745

37:1758:19		No. 10: Lands in QA – Let Fall or Involved	
Land	Acres	Takers Up	
"Addition"	250	John Salter	let fall by (N) Salter
pt. "Adventure"	620	Col. Tilghman	lost in "Lloyds Town"; recovered on ejectment
pt. "Allen's Neck" – see f. 9	83	William Allen	said to be involved in "Park"
pt. "Bishop's Addition"	50	William Bishop	said to be involved in "Smith's Mistake"
pt. "Benjamin's Parks"	20	Benjamin Ellis	taken away by "Forlorne Hope"
pt. "Brandford"	172	William Diggs	taken away by "Saint Martins"
"Berks"	200	John Lillingston	taken away by "Farrington"
"Brampton Addition"	314	John Hawkins	involved
"Bear Garden"	3	James Silvester	taken away by elder surveyes
"Brimmington"	300	Robert Smith	taken away by elder surveys by "Readbourne"
"Contention"	100	Robert Smith	taken away by "Stoke"
"Chance"	200	John Marks	let fall
"Camberwell"	500	James Sedgwick	let fall
pt. "Coppidge's Range"	13	John Coppidge	taken away by elder surveys
"Davenport"	400	Humphry Davenport	involved & so let fall
"Emory Paxton"	372	Edmund McDaniel	let fall
"Emory's Fortune"	190	William Turlo	supposed by (N) Emory to be taken by some other survey
"Elk Point"	1000	Richard Husbands	supposed to be the same as "Tully's Delight"
pt. "Enjoyment & Mount Pleasant"	321	John Lillingston	involved
"France"	100	Lewis Blangey	let fall
"Fool Play"	500	Thomas Collins	let fall being taken away by "Lloyds Freshes"
pt. "Fair Play"	40	Richard Hynson	involved
pt. "Fortune"	10	John Jackson	lost in elder surveys
"Hynson New Haven"	100	John Hynson	said to be let fall
"Hazard"	100	Nicholas Massy	taken away by "Dixon's Gift"
"Hill's Lott"	200	William Hill	same as "Adventure" surveyed for John Mitchell
"Hackett's Chance"	250	Michael Hackett	let fall

Queen Anne's County - 1745

pt. "Henfield" & pt. "Shepherds Discovery"	182	h/o Jacob Seth	involved
"Hackett's Lott"	150	William Hackett	let fall
37:1758:20 ...			
"Jones's Tryangle"	50	John Jones	in "Loyd Town"
pt. "Johnson's Adventure"	10	Henry Johnson – since paid by Capt. Seegar	involved
pt. "Lexon"	81	John Woodhall	taken away by "Barbados Hall"
"Lovely"	200	Deliverance Lovely	involved
"Little Thickett"	435	James Hutchins	involved
pt. "Lambeth"	39	Henry Costin	taken away by elder surveys
"Maclinborough Division"	700	John Power	involved in "Maclinburgh"
pt. "Massy's Hazard"	50	Nicholas Massey	involved in "Johnson's Adventure"
"Malden"	283	Renatus Smith	involved in "Conquest"
"Musketo Range"	51	Robert Broadaway	taken away by "Sayer's Forrest"
"Morgan's Hope"	400	Martin Morgan	supposed to be the same as "Collington" – surveyed for Thomas Collins
"Mischief"	100	James Silvester	not to be patented
"Mountague's Luck"	40	William Mountague	involved in "Ratcliffe"
"Norris Derry"	350	Thomas Norris	supposed to be the same as "Prophecy" & so neglected
"Norwood"	1000	John Norwood	involved in "Todcaster"
"No Name"	400	Joseph Wickes	taken into "Point Love"
"Old Indian Cabbin"	50	John Burke	taken away by "Sayer's Forrest"
"Outrange"	50	William Eubanks	involved in "Ratcliffe"
pt. "Partnership"	214	George Powell	involved in "Park"
"Pryor's Manour"	1000	Thomas Adams	surrendered per Liber R Folio 52
pt. "Poplar Plain"	118	Cornelius Comegys	involved in elder surveys
"Range"	200	Edmund McDaniel	let fall
"Rereguard"	400	John Chaires	taken away by "Walnutt Ridge" & let fall
pt. "Smith's Addition"	50	John Carradine	taken away by "Forlorne Hope" – the whole of this tract is in List No. 1
pt. "Smithfield"	150	w/o William Austin	lost in "Macklyn's Beginning"

"Sandwich"	150	Stephen Tully	taken away by "Oakenthorpe"
"Sadlers Rest"	400	Giles Sadler	let fall per Liber R Folio 175
pt. "Shepperd's Forrest"	27	William Sheppard	involved
pt. "St. Martins"	136	Thomas Goddard	involved in elder surveys
37:1758:21 ...			
"Addition"	50	John Singleton & Richard Jones	let fall, being taken by elder surveys
"Tell Tale's Loss"	100	Robert Smith	involved
"Barren Ridge"	100	John Hynson	said to be let fall
"Tilghman's Lott"	500	Richard Tilghman – h/o Thomas Carman	said to be let fall
"Plains"	110	Robert Broadaway	taken away by "Sayer's Forrest"
"Hope"	200	Daniel Glover	taken away by "Darland"
"Vanderforts Agreement"	100	Charles Vanderfort	taken away by elder surveys
"Welch Ridge Addition"	300	Richard Wells	taken away by "Darland"
"Willson's Beginning"	250	Nicholas Clouds	taken by elder surveys
"William's Hazard"	50	William Swift	taken away by "Old Town"
"Wrights Point"	50	John Wright	let fall & taken up by Robert Smith by the name of "Neglect"
"Week"	400	John Older	supposed to be the same as "Chesterfield" – surveyed for William Hemsley
"Wickersly"	500	Jonathan Sibery	supposed to be in His Lordships Manour
"Yarmouth"	100	Richard Macklyn	taken away by elder surveys
Accepted on 31 May 1745 by Edward Tilghman.			

37:1758:22 No. 11: Lands in QA – Owners Living in SO, DO, CE		
Land	Acres	Owners
pt. "Codshead Manour"	110	Joseph Fisher (DO)
pt. "Collins's Refusal"	17	James Paul Heath (CE)
"Crompton"	50	James Paul Heath (CE)
"Chesterfield" – in KE	500	Joshua George (CE)
"Denton Holm" – in DO	600	Richard Cooper (DO)
pt. "Heath's Forrest"	100	James Paul Heath (CE)
"Heath's Parcells"	195	James Paul Heath (CE)
pt. "Joseph's Lott"	50	Joseph Rawlins (DO)
"Partnership" – since sold to John Bartlet	575	John & George Gale (SO)
"Providence"	1100	Edward Day (SO)
pt. "Park"	50	James Paul Heath (CE)
"Poplar Ridge"	500	John Baldwin (CE)
"Ratcliffe"	670	John & George Gale (SO)
"Ridley's Chance"	200	Joseph Wilson (DO)
pt. "Sewalls Manour"	1000	Mrs. Elizabeth Frisby (CE)
"Taylerton"	800	h/o Nathaniel Smith (DO)
"Kindness"	400	h/o Nicholas Painter
pt. "Tottenham"	300	James Paul Heath (CE)
pt. "Upper Heath Worth"	423	James Paul Heath (CE)
"Wattson's Desire"	50	Francis Wattson (DO)
Accepted on 31 May 1745 by Edward Tilghman.		

37:1758:23		No. 12: Lands in QA – Rent is Overcharged
Land	Acres	Owner
"Addition"	200	William Osborne
"Blunts Marsh"	330	Richard Blunt
"Connor's Neck"	280	Philip Connor
"Condon"	326	Robert Smith
"Cloverfields"	770	Benjamin Ball
"Heathworth"	533	James Paul Heath
"Jump's Addition"	49	William Jump
"Millrange"	163	William Bishop
"Purlivant"	180	Jacob Winchester
"Smiths Mistake"	1520	William Bishop
"Southampton"	150	William Hackett
"Trustram"	1300	Trustram Thomas
"Gore"	175	John Sayre Blake
"Tilghman's Hermitage"	1843	Richard Tilghman
Accepted on 31 May 1745 by Edward Tilghman.		

37:1758:24		No. 13: Lands in QA – Rent Undercharged
Land	Acres	Owner
"Gould Hawk's Enlargement"	70	George Gould Hawk
"Golden Grove"	116	Robert Smith
"Young's Adventure"	175	William Young
Accepted on 31 May 1745 by Edward Tilghman.		

Queen Anne's County - 1745

37:1758:25	No. 14: Answers to the Additional Debt Book for Lands Transcribed from TA			
Land		Acres	Charged to	Reasons why Rent not Paid
pt. "Costin's Chance"		109	h/o Samuel Cockayne	lives in TA
pt. "Costin's Chance"		32	William Cole	lives in TA
"Coles Bank"		300	Thomas Lane	accounted for by the late Receiver for 6½ years for the year 1715
pt. "Griffin's Adventure"		120	Matthew Griffin	I have not had time to inquire who is the possessor
pt. "Griffin's Adventure"		100	Matthew Griffin	received by the late Receiver for 6½ years for the year 1715
"Hickory Ridge"		150	Jos. Jones & John Wild	received by the late Receiver for 6½ years for the year 1715 from William Starkey
"Lambeth"		200	John Kinnimont & Ferdinando Callaghane	John Kinnimont paid me for 11 years & I did not receive for want of direction
"Lambeth"		200	John Kinnimont & Ferdinando Callaghane	overcharged
"Mount Hope"		150	Samuel Dickinson	lives in KEDE
"Newington"		240	William Driskell	accounts for by the late Receiver for 6½ years for the year 1715
pt. "Parker's Freshes"		33	James Silvester	I have not had opportunity to demand
pt. "Parker's Freshes"		87	Hawkins Downs	accounted for by the late Receiver for 6½ years for the year 1715
pt. "Parker's Freshes"		180	Edward Godwin	denies, alleging it is taken away by "Edmundson's Green Close"
"Scarborough"		1400	William Harrison	lives in TA
"Storey's Park"		100	Thomas Chairs	accounted for by the late Receiver for 6½ years for the year 1715
"Todcaster"		1000	Andrew Price	500 a. included in a resurvey called "Andrew & Prudences Satisfaction"; 500 a. the possessor unknown
Accepted on 31 May 1745 by Edward Tilghman.				

37:1758:26	No. 15: Lands Discovered & Charged in Debt Book which are not on Rent Roll	
Land	Acres	Charged to:
"Adventure Addition"	40	James Tilghman – since patented
"Benjamin's Infancy"	250	sundrys – since patented
"Cole's Bank Addition"	165	Thomas Lane for his wife – since resurveyed
"Carter's Addition" – 2 parcels	191	Thomas Cockayne
"Fresh Run"	160	James Smith
"Green Hill"	100	John Hill
"Hogg Harbour"	300	Lawrence Hall – since patented
"Heath's Gift"	53	Thomas Ruth
"Hamer's Addition"	37	Richard Ponder – since denied
"Long Point" – in TA	42	Grundy Pemberton
"Newnam's Chance"	56	William Newname
pt. "Partnership"	200	John Welch
pt. "Partnership"	180	Grundy Pemberton
pt. "Poplar Neck"	200	John Colbreath
"Parson's Marsh"	34	Dowdall Thompson
pt. "Poplar Neck"	150	Joseph Willson (DO)
"Richard & Mary's Forrest" (TA)	80	Richard Wootters – lies in TA
"Beginning"	300	Thomas Meeds
"Trustram Ridge"	150	John Meredith
"Ovall" – resurveyed	355	James Earle
"Wyatt's Folley"	50	Henry Wilkinson
"Fentry" – in TA	100	Grundy Pemberton
Accepted on 31 May 1745 by Edward Tilghman.		

Queen Anne's County - 1745

No. 16: Lands Charged for a Greater Quantity than on Rent Roll			
Land	Acres		Charged to:
pt. "Bishop's Fields"	50	William Bishop	James Kersley
pt. "Ditteridge"	21	Richard Bridges	Thomas Harris
pt. "Emory's Chance"	10	John Emory	John Emory
pt. "Emory's Rich Land"	5	John Emory	John Emory
pt. "Hinesly's Plains"	61	Thomas Hindsly	sundrys
pt. "Hackton"	150	Nicholas Hackett	sundrys
pt. "Price's Hill"	80	John Price	Dowdell Thompson
pt. "Smeath"	156	Robert Smith	sundrys
pt. "Vaughan's Discovery"	30	Thomas Vaughan	John Philips
pt. "Providence"	13	Andrew Skinner	Dr. John Jackson
Accepted on 31 May 1745 by Edward Tilghman.			

Queen Anne's County - 1745

37:1758:27		Difference in Rent Charged by old Rent Roll & Additional Rent Roll for Years 1741, 1742, 1743, & 1744	
Land	Acres	For Whom Resurveyed	For Whom Surveyed Originally
"Friendship"	335	Joseph & Lewis Derochbrune	• "Friendship" – 200 a. by Thomas Waddy • "Lewis Addition" – not on Rent Roll
Additional Rent Roll 1742			
"Sudler's Purchase"	50	Joseph Sudler	• "Beverton" – 100 a. by Edward Coppin
Difference in Arrears in Additional Rent Roll for Year 1742			
"Skinner's Pleasure"	50	John Hadley	paid to Mr. Thomas Hynson Wright late Receiver
Additional Rent Roll 1743			
"Pemberton's Resurvey"	969	Grundy Pemberton	• "Brigling" – 100 a. by Margaret Ocklyn • pt. "Bridling's Addition" – 14 a. by William Wrench • "Wrenche's Discovery" – 386 a. by William Wrench • "Boston" – 300 a. by John Pemberton
"Wharton's Adventure"	570	Robert Wharton	• pt. "Sayer's Range Addition" – 342 a. by Peter Sayer • pt. "Wharton's & Pindar's Outrange" – 158 a. by Robert Wharton & William Pindar • pt. "Wharton's Addition" – 32 a. by Robert Wharton
"Holt"	506	Rev. Mr. Arthur Holt	pt. "Price's Hill" – 400 a. by John Price
"Holly Neck Resurveyed"	415	John Colbreath	"Holly Neck" – 200 a. by John Colbreath
"Sudler's Fortune"	186	Joseph Sudler	• "Hill's Cabbin" – 100 a. by Peter Johnson • "Southern's Addition" – 80 a. by Valentine Southerne

"Holt's Castle Hill Resurveyed"	304½	Rev. Mr. Arthur Holt	"Holts Castle Hill" – 245 a. by Rev. Mr. Arthur Holt
Additional Rent Roll 1744			
"Hawkins's Farme"	638	Mrs. Elizabeth Hawkins	"Hawkins's Farme" – 500 a. by John Hawkins
"Baynards Large Range Addition"	505	John Baynard	pt. "Large Range" – 283½ a. by Daniel Jenifer
"Adventure"	158	Rev. Mr. James Cox	pt. "Doctor's Folly" – 29 a. by Christopher Birch
"Sewell's Range"	1120	Richard Bennett, Esq.	"Sewell's Range" – 1000 a. by Maj. Nicholas Sewall
37:1758:28	**Difference in Rent Charged by old Rent Roll & Additional Rent Roll being the Second for Year 1744**		
"Parson's Neck"	64	William Bishop	pt. "Parson's Neck" – 64 a. by William Porter
"Hitt or Miss"	223	Dr. John Jackson	"Hitt or Miss" – 100 a. by Thomas Wilkinson
"Morgan's Inclosure"	437	Andrew Toulson & Rebecca his wife & Alexander Toulson & Mary his wife	• "Morgan's Enlargement" – 260 a. by Henry Morgan • "Hogg Pen Neck" – 100 a. by Thomas Keen
(N) Bishop says the above part of "Parsons Neck" is the same as paid for by William Joiner, Jr. or Andrew Price			
Accepted on 31 May 1745 by Edward Tilghman.			

37:1758:29 List of Arrears, arising due for Quit Rents from Michaelmas 1740 to Michaelmas 1744	
John Alley	William Bishop
Thomas Alleyband	Thomas Peacock Betts
James Ayler	Nicholas Broadway
Sarah Ausiter	Richard Buckley
Mark Anthony	John Buck, Esq.
William Austin	John Bermingham
John Austin	Margaret Bussells
John Andrews	William Burroughs
Stephen Andrews	Rev. Mr. Bradford
Jacob Alquare	Francis Bright
Joseph Ashbury	Samuel Blunt
John Abbington	Thomas Benton
Philemon Charles Blake	Let. Brown
John Sayre Blake	Edward Brown (KI)
John Burk s/o Thomas	Vincent Benton
Sarah Burk	George Burroughs
John Baker	William Barkhust
John Baynard	Thomas Baily s/o Thomas
Esther Baynard	William Barwick
John Burk, Sr.	h/o James Barkhust
William Banning	James Bailey
John Banning	William Baxtor
Thomas Bostock	John Brown
Charles Bradley	Anthony Bacon
James Blades	John Bartlett
John Baggs	William & Isaac Broadway
Henry Burt	Rizdon Bozman
Thomas Baggs	James Bartlett
James Boon	John Biscoe
Jacob Boon	Thomas Bartlett, Jr.
Isaac Boon	Sweatnam Bourn
Joseph Boon	Nathaniel Connor
Abraham Boon	John Carradine
Moses Boon	William Campbell

Benjamin Boon	Thomas Chaires
James Barwick	Rev. James Cox
Judith Burton	William Coursey
John Bolton	William Coursey for Edward Clayton
Daniel Bolton	John Coursey
Thomas Butler	John Clements
Thomas Baily s/o James	Peter Countiss
Thomas Baily	Christopher Cox
George Baynard	John Cooper, Jr.
Edward Brown (Chester)	Matthew Chilton
37:1758:30 ...	
Richard Coffin	Caleb Clark
Mary Croney	John Camper
James Chaires	James Claypole
Henry Clift	William Dawson
William Cooper	Daniel Dulany, Esq.
Edmund Cahall	Thomas Dockery
John Cooper	John Davis
John Croney	Thomas Davis
Thomas Curtice	Nathaniel Downes
James Countice	Mathew Dockery
William Countice	William Driskell
John Colbreath	Henry Downes
James Cook	John Downes
Ann Cruper	Hawkins Downes
Henry Covington	Stephen Deer
Henry Councill	Katherine Davis
Alice Collier	Dr. Duhamil
John Collins, Jr.	John Deford
John Carman	John Dempster
Thomas & John Carman	T. Valentine Downey
William Cannon	Jo. & Lewis Derochbrune
Thomas Colement	Jo. Derochbrune
John Comegys	William Dockery
Lewis Clothier	Robert Devonish
William Carmichall	William Durding

Queen Anne's County - 1745

Cornelius Comegys	Isaac Dixon
James Cassey	Samuel Dickinson
Maurice Cloak	Arthur Emory
James Clough	John Emory, Jr.
Mrs. Clouds	John Emory
Charles Connor	William Emory
Richard Carter	William Eagle
John Carter	George Edwards
Edward Cockey	Benjamin Endsworth
Philip Coppidge	William Ewbanks
Henry Culley	George Elliott
Jacob Carter	John Evans
William Carman	John Earle
John Cole	James Earle
Nathaniel Cleave	Caleb Esgate
Katherine Cleave	James Evans
Joseph Chaires	John Elliott, Jr.
John Clothier	Joseph Elliott
Nicholas Clouds	John Errickson
William Clayton	Benjamin Elliott
Hannah Cleave	John Elliott
Nat. Cleave s/o Benjamin	Lawrence Everett
Daniel Cheston	Roger Ellstone
Edward Crew	Henry Ellers
Daniel Cornelius	John Earle (sadler)
Thomas Cockayne	Philip Emerson
William Cary	Frances Elbert
37:1758:31 ...	
B. F. & John Falconar	John Higgens
h/o Benjamin Falconar	William Hopper
Peter Froom	Lawrence Hall
Robert Fowler	Robert Hardcastle
Francis Foreman	John Hill
William Firth	James Hix
William Ford	Joseph Hunter
Andrew Finley	David Harrington

Queen Anne's County - 1745

Flower Fisher	James Hobbs
Samuel Field	William Harrington
Henry Feddeman	Richard Harrington
John Fouracres	Rev. Mr. Arthur Holt
Capt. William Greenwood	William Hamer
John Gwinn	John Hawkins, Sr.
William Gregory	Ernault Hawkins
Matthew Griffith	Richard Hynson
Benjamin Griffin	Thomas Honey
Jonathan Greenwood	Peter Hinesly
Edward Garrett	Nathaniel Hinesly
Edward Godwin	Joseph Harris
Nicholas Glinn	William Harris
William Godwin	James Hambleton
Michael Green	James Hines s/o James
Archibald Greenfield	John Hackett
Thomas Godwin	Thomas Hackett
Richard Gould	John Hawkins Hambleton
Frances Gould	John Hamer
Charles Gafford	John Harris
John Gibb	John Hollingsworth
Marmaduke Goodhand	James Horsley
Christopher Granger	John Hays, Jr.
Jeremiah Grimes	John Haldey
Mat. Graves	John Hartshorne
Robert Gwinn	John Hamer (Carolina)
Philemon Greene	h/o James Hutchins
John Granger	Isaac Harris
Nicholas Goldsborough	John Hart
Robert Goldsborough	Ann Hines
Robert Goldsborough, Jr.	Charles Hines
Jeremiah Gressingham	William Holding
Col. George Gale	George Harrington
Richard Grafton	Susanna Harris
Mrs. Elizabeth Hawkins	Edward Harding
Thomas Hammond	Katherine Hammond

Thomas Harris	Jacob Hindman
37:1758:32 ...	
Henry Jacobs	John Legg
Mary Jackson	Thomas Litton
George Jackson	Edward Loyd
Nerish Jones	Thomas Lane
John Jerman	George Mattershaw
Joseph Jerman	Thomas Mooth
Henry Jones	William Merson
William Jones	William Mansfield
devisees of James Jordan	John Meeds
Robert Jadwin	Charles Moor
Thomas Jump	William Meeds
William Jump	Thomas Meredith
Jeremiah Jadwin	Abigail McClallyn
Archibald Jackson	Thomas Meeds
John Johnson (Ripley)	John Moffit
Edward Jones	John Mayne
Albert Johnson	Thomas Martindale
Thomas Jackson	Isaac Merrick
William Joiner	James Millis
Jonathan Jolly	Richard Mason
Dr. John Jackson	William Mountague
Edward Jump	Dr. McKittrick
Robert Kent	John Meredith
Richard Keys	Thomas Mounsieur
John Knowles	Susanna Manah
James Kenton	James Massey
Solomon Kenton	William Massey
James Kersey	William Mounsieur
Baldwin Kemp	John McConnikin
James Knotts	Elizabeth McConnikin
William Kent	John Meredith (KI)
John Keys, Jr.	Thomas Marsh
Walter Kirby	Joseph Merchant
John Kinnimont	Thomas McClannahan

Queen Anne's County - 1745

Thomas Kersey	James McCoy
Edmond Kelly	David Mills
Thomas Lewis	Samuel McCosh
Mrs. Alice Loyd	John Nabb
Robert Loyd	John Nevill
Ann Loyd	Elizabeth Nevill
James London	Daniel Newnam, Jr.
Timothy Lane	devisees of Daniel Newnam
Rebecca Leonard	Charles Nabb
James Lane	William Newnam
Patrick Linsey	Thomas Nickolson
Charles Lemare	William Nevill
Joseph Longfellow	Joseph Newnam
Thomas Lee	John Newnam (Choptank)
John Lambden	Francis Neal
Charles Lowther	Edward Neal
John Legg, Jr.	
37:1758:33 ...	
Charles Oneal	Anthony Roe
John Oldson	Patrick Robertson
Thomas OBryon	Peter Rich
Robert Offley	Thomas Roe (Choptank)
John Oldson	Thomas Roe (Chester)
Abraham Oldson	Edward Roe
John Oldson s/o Henry	Thomas Ruth
Samuel Osborne	John Ricketts
Edward Oldham	Edward Ricketts
Thomas Parsons	James Roberts
Christopher Phillips	Francis Rochester
William Prior	Francis Rochester, Jr.
Charles Price	John Railey
Thomas Price	William Ridger
William Pratt	Benjamin Richardson
Henry Pratt	John Ruth
Juliana Purnall	James Reed
Thomas Purnall	Thomas Roe, Jr. (Choptank)

Queen Anne's County - 1745

Grundy Pemberton	William Roberts
Elizabeth Pemberton	Mrs. Henrietta Maria Robins
Thomas Porter	Thomas Rowland
Henry Price	John Roe (DO)
Andrew Price	William Scandret
John Powell	James Saunders
David Phillips	John Sullivant
John Pickeron	Thomas Smith
Richard Ponder	Andrew Saunders
Margaret Pinder	Thomas Soder
James Ponder	Thomas Stuart
Richard Ponder, Jr.	Ralph Swift
Rachel Primrose	James Slaughter
William Primrose	James Sylvester
Thomas Powell (DO)	William Starkey
Violet Primrose	Richard Swift
John Parsons	John Swift, Jr.
John Perry	Emanuel Swift
Thomas Powell (For.)	Ralph Swift, Jr.
Andrew Price, Jr.	Nathaniel Scott, Jr.
George Primrose	William Shepherd
Morgan Ponder	Ann Sherlock
Daniel Paxton (Bridges)	Thomas Shoebrook
Richard Porter, Jr.	William Saterfield
Oneal Price	devisees of John Sparkes
Thomas Pamphilion	George Smith
Nathaniel Reed	James Salisbury
Richard Ross	John Sparkes for Caleb
John Ressum	Millington Sparkes
John Roe	William Scandrett, Jr.
William Roe	
37:1758:34 ...	
Richard Scrivener	Benjamin Toalson
Daniel Smith (planter)	Elizabeth Thompson
devisees of Francis Spry	Dowdal Thompson
Solomon Seney	Thomas Trickey

Queen Anne's County - 1745

Thomas Seward	William Trulock
Thomas Sands	William Thorn
Henry Short	William Till, Esq.
John Swift	William Thomas
Christopher Spry	Visitors of Queen Ann County School
Daniel Smith (joiner)	Vestry of St. Paul's Parish
William Swift	William Vanderford
William Shepherd (DE)	William Vickers
Thomas Stanton	John Walters
John Scotton	William Wilson
Richard Scotton	Thomas Hynson Wright
Sarah Sliney	Thomas Wilkinson
Dr. John Smith	John Walker
John Stevens, Jr.	William Wrench
John Stevens	Ambrose Wright
Robert Small	Daniel Wheatly
Joseph Sudler	Tabitha Williams
William Scott	James Walker
John Starkey	Richard Wootters
Richard Smith	James Webb
h/o Nathaniel Scott	Jacob Wootters
Thomas Scotton	Edward Willoby
James Scotton	John Wheatly
William Smith	John Wootters
Richard Sparkes	William Wheeler
James Smith	William Whitby
Elizabeth Stevens	Fairclough Wright
John Stant	Nathaniel Wright
Samuel Swift	Alice Wright
Richard & William Tilghman	Daniel Wilcox
William Tilghman	Robert Nor. Wright
Trustram Thomas	Abraham Williams
Nathaniel Tucker	Ephraim Winn
Trustram Thomas, Jr. (Wye)	John Woodall
John Tillotson	William Wilkinson (Island Hundred)
James Tilghman	Martha Woodall

Matthew Tilghman	Humphry Wells
John Timm	Christopher Wilkinson
Martha Tillotson	Thomas Wyatt
Trustram Thomas (Island Hundred)	Richard Wells
Thomas Thomas	Jos. & Benjamin Whittington
Rubin Taylor	Edward Williams
Trustram Thomas (Long Neck)	Christopher Williams
Thomas Tanner	Penelope Wright
Andrew Toalson	Ruth Wells
Anna Toalson	Robert Walters
Alexander Toalson	John Wilson
Richard Tickel	Jacob Winchester
Christopher Thomas	Hynson Wright
37:1758:35 ...	
Thomas Walker	Park Webb
James Wilcox	William Willson & wife
Richard Wells, Jr.	Joseph Willson
Zorobabel Wells	William Wattson
Timothy Webb	William Worthington (BA)
Henry Wilkinson	T. H. Wright for h/o John Wright
Lambert Wilmore	James Willson
John Williamson	William Wallis
John Webb	Solomon Yewell
Mrs. Margaret Ward	Stephen Yoe
Thomas Whittington	John Young s/o William
Accepted on 31 May 1745 by Edward Tilghman.	

37:1758:36-7 Recapitulation		
37:1758:38 Additional Notes		
Land	Acres	
pt. "Sillen"	200	undercharged
"St. Pauls"	100	undercharged to Mrs. Hawkins & Arthur Emory
"Forlorne Hope"	1830	
pt. "Coursey"	20	
"Baynard's Discovery"	50	charged instead of "Baynard's Chance" 54 a.
pt. "Barnes's Satisfaction"	50	charged to John Collins
"Morgan's Neck"	400	charged to Richard Bennett, Esq.
"Original of Friendship"	200	received from Jo. & Lewis Derochbrune
"Original Stagwell"	42	Mr. Phil. Emerson
"Highgate Lane"	100	paid by Robert Wharton; resurveyed by John Lang by name of "New Hall"
"Forrest Lodge"	20	paid by John Emory, Jr.; resurveyed by Thomas Hollingsworth
"Pennsylvania Border"	50	received from William Barkhust
Accepted on 31 May 1745 by Edward Tilghman.		

Queen Anne's County - 1747

36:1747:1	<missing>		Acres
<missing>		"Winfield" tbc: • William Emory, Jr. – pt. "Winfield" 287 a.	<n/g>
		"Stradtton" tbc: • John Young s/o William – pt. "Stradon" 50 a. • John Young – pt. "Stradon" 54½ a. • William Young – pt. "Stradon" 52 a.	<n/g>
36:1747:2	...		
Madam Anna Maria Tilghman		"Union"	770
Major William Tilghman		"Pauls Fort"	200
		pt. "Bristol Marsh"	140
		pt. "Tilghmans Discovery"	490
		"Salisbury"	500
		"Delmore End"	500
		"Andeaver"	500
		1 lot in Ogle Town	1
		pt. "Poplar Plains"	191
Madam Elizabeth Hawkins		pt. "Hawkins Farme Resurveyed" tbc William Dockery (8 a.) f. 101	20
		"Bowlingly"	250
		"Macklin"	100
		"Beaver Dam"	160
		"Green Spring"	600
		pt. "St. Pauls"	50
		pt. "Carmans Neck"	100
		"Forrest Lodge"	152
		"Partnership"	400
		"Discovery"	220
		pt. "Tulleys Delight"	200
Mr. Henry Jacobs		pt. "Sprigley"	300
		pt. "Winchester" – for his daughter	125
36:1747:3	...		
MM Richard & William Tilghman		"Covepoint on Resurvey" – for h/o Mr. James Earle	200
		"Smiths Lott" – for h/o Mr. James Earle	100
		"Woodland Neck" – for h/o Mr. James Earle	200
		"Adventure Addition" – for h/o Mr. James Earle	400

Mr. John Downes, Jr.	"Wrights Plains"	100
	pt. "Wrights Reserve"	160
	"Wrights Reserve Addition"	50
	pt. "Wrights Reserve" – from Thomas H. Wright for h/o John Beck	40
	pt. "Smeathen Resurvey"	412
	pt. "Smeathen Resurvey" – from (N) Barber	50
	pt. "Smeathen Resurvey" – from (N) Hynson	175
John Walters	pt. "Smeath"	250
	"Barnstable Hill"	100
	"Coney Hall"	100
	"Barnstable Hill Resurveyed" comprised of: • "Barnstable Hill" – 100 a. • "Coney Hall" – 100 a.	210
	"Westminster"	297
John Brown	pt. "Batchelors Hope"	60
	pt. "Neglect"	49
	"Claxton"	100
	1 lot in Ogle Town – No. 37	1
	"Marshy Brook"	100
	pt. "Goldhawks Enlargement" – for h/o his former wife Mary Harris	17½
	pt. "Commins's Freehold" – for h/o his former wife Mary Harris	12½
	pt. "Mersons Freehold" – for h/o his former wife Mary Harris	12½
36:1747:4 ...		
William Dawson	pt. "Trustam" – for Ralph Dawson	233
Nathaniel Conner	pt. "Mount Mill" – for h/o Charles Seth	317
	"Addition" – for h/o Charles Seth	40
William Dulany	"Standford"	200
	pt. "Mount Mill"	33
	pt. "Vaughans Kindness"	200
	"New Nothingham"	100
Daniel Dullany, Esq. (cnp)	"Loyds Insula"	1795
	"Purchase"	1000
	pt. "Willinlee"	682

	pt. "Brandfield"	228
	"Skinners Expectation"	480
Patrick Sexton	"Liberty"	100
36:1747:5 ...		
Mr. Philemon Charles Blake	"Blakeford"	555
	pt. "Loyds Meadows & Loyds Meadows Addition"	570
Thomas Lewis	pt. "Boagley"	175
	"Lewis's Chance"	50
Mr. John Sayre Blake	"Russendale"	250
	"Coursey"	250
	"Hogg Hole"	100
	"Jenkins Neck"	250
	"Sayres Forrest"	2250
	"Gore"	175
	"Jasson Choice"	100
	"Cold Harbour"	100
Margaret Berry	pt. "Bridge North"	150
Ann Caridine	pt. "Forlorne Hope" – for h/o John Caradine	50
36:1747:6 ...		
John Clayland	pt. "Trustram"	233
William Scandrett	pt. "Bristol Marsh"	160
	pt. "Lexton"	235
	"Lott"	50
	pt. "Hineslys Plains"	76
William Campbell	pt. "Ditteridge"	166
	pt. "Anthorpe"	197
	pt. "Hambletons Hermitage"	250
	pt. "Bishopton"	68
	"Walkers Square"	300
	pt. "Davis's Range"	185
Robert Kent	pt. "Batchelors Plains"	200
Thomas Parsons	pt. "Neglect"	51
	pt. "Batchelors Hope"	90
36:1747:7 ...		
John Nabb (cnp)	pt. "Tilghmans Addition"	100
	"Jones Fortune"	100

Mr. Charles Downes	pt. "Adventure"	7
	pt. "Fairplay"	116
	pt. "Macklinbourough" – for John Chairs	199
	"Highgate" – for John Chairs	50
	pt. "Lantley" – for John Chairs	325
Mr. Arther Emory	pt. "Trustram"	170
	pt. "Coursey Upon Wye"	30
	pt. "Fortune"	50
	pt. "Carmans Neck"	50
	pt. "Saint Pauls"	50
	pt. "Fortune" – from (N) Betton	40
John Emory, Jr.	"Hemsley"	300
	"Emorys Neglect"	125
	"Emory's Addition"	50
	"Butterfield"	200
	pt. "Forrest Lodge"	20
Trustram Thomas (Wye)	pt. "Trustram"	300
	"Hazard" – for Joseph Earle	175
36:1747:8 ...		
Mr. Thomas Hammond	pt. "Grays Inn"	75
	"Cheshire"	200
	"Plains"	105
John Welch	pt. "Partnership"	200
	"King Hammer"	182
George Mattershaw	"Jamaica"	100
Thomas Mooth	pt. "Friendship"	25
	"Wattsons Delight"	50
	"Wattsons Delight Addition"	30
William Wilson	pt. "Trustram" – for his wife	214
36:1747:9 ...		
Thomas Chairs	"Batchelors Adventure"	150
	"Storeys Park"	100
Christopher Philips	"Smiths Lott"	200
Rev. Mr. James Cox	"Denby Resurveyed"	275
	"Discovery"	100
	"Adventure Resurveyed"	158

Mr. William Coursey	"Cheston"	800
	pt. "Coursey Upon Wye"	290
	"Lords Gift"	1050
	pt. "Shepherds Forrest" – for his wife	100
	"Sleeford" – for his wife	200
	"Shepherds Hook" – for his wife	
	pt. "Conquest" – for Solomon Clayton	127
	pt. "Solomon's Fancy" for Solomon Clayton	50
	"Mount Moluck" – for Charles & Solomon Claton	150
	pt. "Chester Fields" – as guardian to Edward Clayton	200
	pt. "Neglect" as guardian to Edward Clayton	200
	"Chesterfields Addition" – as guardian to Edward Clayton	70
John Gwinn	"Gunners Harbour"	100
36:1747:10 ...		
William Merson	pt. "Peale Place" tbc John Davis, Jr.	22
	pt. "Addy House" tbc John Davis, Jr.	45½
	pt. "Middle Plantation"	133
Mr. Thomas Harris	pt. "Ditteridge"	272
	pt. "Long Neck"	20½
	pt. "Coursey Upon Wye"	258½
Mr. John Emory	pt. "Partnership"	90
	"Batchelors Chance"	300
	"Emorys Chance"	110
	"Bee Tree"	500
	pt. "Partnership"	175
	pt. "Powells Fancy"	90
	"Batchelors Chance Resurveyed" – 11 March 1744	253
Capt. William Greenwood	"Broad Neck"	100
	"Plain Dealing"	727
	"Jacksons Boggs"	46
William Elbert	½ "Reward"	200
	½ "Macklins Addition"	18
36:1747:11 ...		

Queen Anne's County - 1747

John Coursey	"Courseys Range"	600
	½ "Reward"	200
	½ "Macklins Addition"	18
	pt. "Hemsleys Brittland Rectified"	223
Francis Jackson	"Barbara Inlett"	263
William Mansfield	pt. "Waltham" – for h/o John Earle Denney	50
	pt. "Wilkinsons Addition" – for h/o John Earle Denney	50
	pt. "Goldhawks Enlargement" – for his wife	17½
	pt. "Commins Freehold" – for his wife	12½
	pt. "Mersons Freehold" – for his wife	12½
William Emory	pt. "Partnership"	100
	pt. "Hawkins's Pharsalia"	100
John Clement	pt. "Edmondsons Green Close"	200
	pt. "Smiths Ridge"	100
36:1747:12 ...		
George Jackson	pt. "Winchester"	125
	"Barbarahs Choice"	80
Nathaniel Reed	pt. "New Reading on Resurvey" – wrong charge	100
	pt. "Tom's Fancy Enlarged"	400
William Prior	pt. "Contention" – included in "Pryor's Chance"	250
	"Pryor's Chance"	271
Visitors of Queen Annes County School	pt. "Forelorne Hope"	100
James Saunders	pt. "Peale Place" – for wife	10
	pt. "Addy House" – for wife	22¾
	pt. "Middle Plantation"	66 1/6
Nathaniel Tucker	"Adventure Point"	61
	"Jones's Addition"	200
	pt. "Batchelors Plains"	100
36:1747:13 ...		
Dr. Charles Carroll	pt. "Loyds Meadows & Loyds Meadows Addition" – for his daughter Mary	655
John Sullivant	pt. "Fossetts Plains" – for h/o John Hammond	150
	pt. "Ponderfield"	109
	pt. "Dungarnow" – for h/o John Hammond	150

Trustram Thomas 3rd	pt. "Hemsleys Britland Rectified" – for h/o Jonathan Smith	57
Mr. Thomas Hynson Wright	pt. "Providence" – from (N) Wilkinson	100
	"New Hynson Town"	360
	pt. "New Reading"	200
	pt. "Grays Inn"	125
	pt. "Neglect"	45
	pt. "Hemsleys Britland Rectified"	50
	"Warplesdon"	300
	"Warplesdon Addition"	280
	"Solomons Friendship"	100
	pt. "Lowes Arcadia"	280
	pt. "Lowes Arcadia" – from (N) Deford	70
	pt. "Tom's Fancy Enlarged"	222
	"Wrights Park"	100
	pt. "Courseys Part" or "Smiths Mistake"	300
	pt. "Bishops Outlett"	300
	pt. "Providence"	352
	pt. "Wrights Reserve"	250
	pt. "Larrington"	100
	pt. "New Reading" – from Nathaniel Reed	100
36:1747:14 ...		
Edward Tilghman	"Forlorne Hope"	1830
	pt. "Malton"	239
	1 lot in Ogle Town	1
	"Porter's Lodge"	300
	pt. "Coursey Upon Wye"	20
	pt. "Long Neck"	377
	"Tilghman's Landings"	68
	"Tilghman's Resurvey of Long Neck" composed of: • pt. "Coursey Upon Wye" – 20 a. • pt. "Long Neck" – 377 a.	539
Mr. Thomas Wilkinson	"Barbadoes Hall"	350
	pt. "Providence"	100
	pt. "Doctors Folly"	30½
Thomas Smith	"Jacsons Choice" – for h/o Thomas Jackson	100

Queen Anne's County - 1747

Vestry of St. Pauls Parish	pt. "Doctors Folly"	½
John Higgens	pt. "Dungamon"	150
36:1747:15 ...		
Mrs. Neriah Jones	"Jones Hall"	200
	"Jones Plackett"	50
	"Jones Plackett Addition"	150
	"Labour in Vain"	20
	"Jones Addition"	50
	"Hyson Town Addition"	100
	"Jones Forrest"	100
Richard Keys	"Jaimaca Addition"	50
Mr. John Tillottson	"Inkersal" – for h/o (N) Chetham	134
	"Timberland" – for h/o (N) Chetham	400
	"Pascall's Chance" – for h/o (N) Chetham	250
	pt. "Park" – for h/o (N) Chetham	500
	"Chethams Landing" – for h/o (N) Chetham	90
	"Shepherds Folds on Resurvey"	140
Mr. James Tilghman	pt. "Adventure"	1030
	"Adventure Addition"	40
	"Tilghmans Freshes"	600
	pt. "Jurusalem"	200
Mathew Williams	pt. "Salisbury Plains"	100
36:1747:16 ...		
Mr. Mathew Tilghman	"Tilghmans Forrest"	1400
	"Rings End"	100
	"Nollars Enjoyment"	300
	1 lot in Ogle Town	1
	pt. "Poplar Plain"	191
Richard Kieron	pt. "Confusion"	100
Mr. William Hopper (cnp)	pt. "Chesterfield"	800
	pt. "Providence"	200
	"Bridge Walter"	300
	"Vanderford" a/s "Partnership"	150
	pt. "Guilfords"	200
	"Darkin"	210
	pt. "Courseys Point" or "Smiths Mistake"	200

	pt. "Providence" – from (N) Wilkinson, escheated	100
William Gregory	pt. "Benjamans Infancy"	50
John Green	"Greens Adventure Upon Carpenters Square Resurveyed"	212
36:1747:17 ...		
John Walker	pt. "Salisbury Plains"	100
Rebecca Countiss	pt. "Hawkins's Farm Resurveyed"	120
William Wrench	"Wrenches Lott"	300
	"Wrenches Farme Resurveyed"	600
	pt. "Hawkins's Farme Resurveyed"	326
Ambrose Wright	pt. "Smiths Forrest"	210
	pt. "Hawkins's Farme Resurveyed"	46
John Alley	pt. "Adventure"	100
	pt. "Confusion"	41
MM T. H. Wright & William Hopper	pt. "Smiths Mistake" – from William Bishop (f. 64)	520
36:1747:18 ...		
Charles Oneal	pt. "Winfield"	100
Charles Price	"Lincoln"	200
	pt. "Broomly Lambeth"	247
James Costin	pt. "Costins Park"	279
Lawrence Hall	"Hoggs Harbour"	300
Solomon Yewell	"Purchase"	86
Thomas Dockery	pt. "Fishingham"	100
36:1747:19 ...		
John Burk s/o Thomas	pt. "Dowsons Neck"	172
Edward Hall	pt. "Vaughans Discovery" – for his wife Elinor	200
Aaron Yoe	"Courseys Addition" – for his wife	50
John Hall	pt. "Welch Poole"	100
	pt. "Dancy"	300
Daniel Wheatly	pt. "Welch Poole"	150
Tabitha Williams	pt. "Salisbury" – for h/o John Williams	100
36:1747:20 ...		
Christopher Cox (cnp)	pt. "Smiths Ridge"	300
	pt. "Plain Dealing" – for his son Christopher	123
	pt. "Prophesy"	217

Queen Anne's County - 1747

	pt. "Heaths Discovery"	23
	pt. "Adventure"	39
Thomas Price	pt. "Brandford"	100
	"Conclusion"	150
	pt. "Chestnut Meadows"	100
	pt. "Brandford" – more	31
	pt. "Brandford" – from (N) Diggs	123
	pt. "Brandford" – from (N) Diggs, more	6
John Davis	pt. "Confusion"	220
John Gutteridge	"Rattle Snake Ridge" – for h/o John Baker	150
John Philips	pt. "Vaughans Discovery"	230
James Williams	pt. "Courseys Addition"	100
	pt. "Kendall"	100

36:1747:21 ...

h/o Henry Price Williams	pt. "Chestnutt Meadows"	100
Stephen Yoe	pt. "Brandford"	68
William Jerman	pt. "Hogg Hole" – for wife	130
John Meeds	pt. "Brandford"	100
Robert Jerman	pt. "Hogg Hole"	130
	pt. "Brandford" – from (N) Diggs	211
Thomas Davis	"Content"	470
	"Berverdams"	50
	"Hallow Hatt"	50

36:1747:22 ...

Charles Moore	pt. "Smiths Forrest"	61
	pt. "Confusion"	159
Mr. Robert Loyd (cnp)	pt. "Loyds Meadows" – for Philemon Hemsley	66
	"Hardestfindoff" – for Philemon Hemsley	150
	pt. "Townton Fields" – for Philemon Hemsley	460
	"Hemsleys Park" – for Philemon Hemsley	800
	"Clover Kelds" – for Philemon Hemsley	1622
	pt. "Trustram Wells" – for Philemon Hemsley	68
	"Hemsleys Discovery" – for Philemon Hemsley	91
	"Towntons Fields Addition" – for Philemon Hemsley	140
	"Hemsleys Adventure" – for Philemon Hemsley	200

	"Tilghman's Gift" – for William Hemsley	650
	"Tilghmans Meadows" – for his wife	270
	"Snodland" – for his wife	284
Thomas Allyband	"Millford Addition"	100
	"Allabands Hazard"	20
John Jerman	pt. "St. Martins"	82
	pt. "Brandford"	18
	pt. "Inclosure"	81
36:1747:23 ...		
James Ayler	pt. "Inclosure"	50
Arther Emory, Jr.	"Welch Ridge"	500
	"Haphazard"	116
	"Haphazard Addition"	50
Mr. William Anderson (London)	"Darland Resurveyed"	1750
	"Loyds Town"	1000
William Meeds	pt. "Brandford"	100
	pt. "Saint Martains"	100
William Greenhood	"Miss Hitt" – for h/o Stephen Rich	250
Nathaniel Downes	pt. "Smiths Neglect"	150
36:1747:24 ...		
Joseph Jerman	pt. "Brandford"	140
Matthew Dockrey	pt. "Fishingham"	100
	"Fishingham Addition"	13
	"Moores Hope"	100
	pt. "Moores Hope Addition"	208
William Pratt	"Liecester Fields"	200
	pt. "Chaires Addition"	54
Henry Pratt	"Pleasant Park"	100
Andrew Saunders	"Good Luck Range"	50
Anne Loyd	pt. "Wrexam Plains" – for h/o Edward Loyd	140
36:1747:25 ...		
Thomas Meredeth	"Alder Branch" – for Michael Green	100
John Davis, Jr.	pt. "Chesterfield" – for his wife	100
	"Peters Lott"	150
Matthew Griffith	pt. "Park"	200
Benjamin Griffith	pt. "Park"	200

John Knowles	pt. "Kendall" – for h/o Thomas Owen	85
William Driskell	pt. "Newington"	120
36:1747:26 ...		
John Cooper, Jr.	pt. "Hearys Discovery"	60
	"Grimes's Folly"	40
Matthew Chilton	"New Cunningham"	100
Mr. John Baynard	pt. "Large Range"	183⅓
	pt. "Large Range" – from (N) Barwick	100
	pt. "Hamton" & pt. "Rich Range" – in TA	130
	pt. "Range" – in DO	192
	"Baynards Large Range Addition"	505
	pt. "Pitts Vineyard"	166⅔
	"Jones Plackett"	100
Mr. John Baynard	pt. "Lyford" – for h/o Joshua Clarke	287
	pt. "Stephens Fields" – for h/o Joshua Clarke	412
Robert Hardcastle	pt. "Kirkhams Lott"	60
	pt. "Newington"	120
36:1747:27 ...		
James London	pt. "Kirkhams Lott"	140
Thomas Baynard s/o Robert	pt. "Pitts Vineyard"	166⅔
Nathan Baynard	pt. "Relief"	476
Henry Downes	pt. "Carters Forrest"	114
	pt. "Costins Chance" – in TA	109
John Downes	"Downes's Chance"	150
	pt. "Nobles Range"	142
	"Shore Ditch"	150
	pt. "Hemsleys Arcadia"	75
	pt. "Carters Forrest"	22
	pt. "Hemsleys Arcadia Moore"	75
Richard Costin	"Newington"	80
	"Newington Addition"	50
	pt. "Carters Forrest"	22
36:1747:28 ...		
Hawkins Downes	pt. "Millford"	150
	pt. "Parkers Freshes"	87
Mary Croney	pt. "Coldrain"	75

John Burk	pt. "Coldrain"	148
	"Locks Point"	50
James Chairs	pt. "Wrenches Farme" – for his wife	200
John Emerson	pt. "Addition"	100
	"Vincents Lott" – in TA	43
Henry Jones	pt. "Nobles Range"	32
	pt. "Deluge"	50
36:1747:29 ...		
Handcock Jones	pt. "Deluge"	80
William Jones	pt. "Deluge"	50
Thomas Soden	pt. "Worly's Outrange"	50
Richard Ross	pt. "Coldrain"	125
devisees of James Jordan	pt. "Coldrain"	241
Thomas Fisher	pt. "Suffolk"	300
36:1747:30 ...		
Abigail McClallyon	pt. "Suffolk"	300
Burton Francis Falconer & John	"Chestnut Ridge"	200
Henry Clift	pt. "Stephens Fields"	278
Juliana Purnal	"Purnals Forrest" – for h/o Mc. Purnal	500
	"Jumps Lane" – for h/o Mc. Purnal	100
Walter Laine	"Lanes Folly"	161
	pt. "Stephens Fields"	100
Thomas Swann	pt. "Jumps Chance"	150
	pt. "Jumps Choice"	2½
36:1747:31 ...		
William Eagle	"Lambeths Addition"	170
William Banning	pt. "Golden Lyon"	100
	"Clerks Venture"	35
h/o Samuel Jemmett	"Woolverton"	250
Richard Wootters	"Richard & Marys Forrest"	80
Robert Jadwin	pt. "Lyford"	70
William Cooper	"Hills Outlett"	100
36:1747:32 ...		
Thomas Stuart	pt. "Kearys Discovery"	50
Thomas Meeds	"Beginning"	300

John Banning	"Bells Venture" – for h/o William Bell	50
	"Purnalls Addition" – for h/o William Bell	300
Thomas Purnal	"Dudleys Chance"	200
	pt. "Rich Range" – in TA	50
	"Dudleys Choice" – in TA	100
Hannah Bell	pt. "Golden Lyon" – for h/o James Bell	100
	"Mire Branch" – for h/o James Bell	85
	pt. "Turners Plains Addition" – for h/o James Bell	120
Francis Climer	pt. "Shadwells Addition"	100
36:1747:33 ...		
Nathaniel Knotts	"Knotts Addition"	50
James Webb	pt. "Lyford"	648
David Mills	"Davids Prospect"	75
	1 lot in Kings Town	1
Mr. Grundy Pemberton	pt. "Dawsons Neck"	142
	pt. "Partnership"	180
	pt. "Hawkins Pharsalia"	600
	"Pembertons Resurvey"	969
	"Fentry" – in TA	100
	"Long Point" – in TA	42
John Hill	"Green Hill"	100
36:1747:34 ...		
James Willson	"Willsons Chance"	100
Mrs. Elizabeth Pemberton	pt. "Partnership" – for h/o Benjamin Pemberton, in TA	670
	"Bostons Addition" – for h/o Benjamin Pemberton	150
	"Kings Sale" – for h/o Benjamin Pemberton	250
	"Kings Sale Addition" – for h/o Benjamin Pemberton	100
	"Change" – for h/o Benjamin Pemberton	200
Jacob Wootters	"New Buckley"	100
	pt. "Smiths Clifts" – in TA	95
Edward Willoughby	pt. "Sayre's Addition"	100
Mary Cahal	pt. "Wheatlys" a/s "Daniels Fields" – for h/o Edm. Cahall	60
36:1747:35 ...		
John Wheatly	pt. "Wheatlys" a/s "Daniels Fields"	140

John Wheatly, Jr.	"Wheatlys Park"	100
John Cooper	"Taylors Chance"	200
Vincent Price	pt. "Lambert" – for h/o Timothy Lane	400
John Baynard s/o William	pt. "Pitts's Vineyard"	166⅔
Sarah Ausiter	pt. "Large Range" – for h/o Thomas Fisher	416⅔
36:1747:36 ...		
John Roe	"Woodland"	100
William Roe	pt. "Dudleys Desire"	100
Thomas Jump	"Horse Pasture"	200
	pt. "Jump's Chance"	100
Mr. William Jump	"Pokety Ridge"	100
	"Jumps Addition"	49
	"Jumps Chance"	200
Mr. John Mayne	"New London"	150
	pt. "Hacketts Garden"	500
Thomas Porter	pt. "Benjamins Infancy"	100
36:1747:37 ...		
h/o Henry Price	"Goodhope"	126
Capt. Andrew Price	"Andrew & Prudence's Satisfaction"	696
George Edwards	"Edwards Chance" – paid by Richard Wootters	50
James Kenton	"Grovely Hoe"	150
	pt. "Upland"	100
Mark Anthony	pt. "Hackton"	100
John Croney	pt. "Coldrain"	75
36:1747:38 ...		
Solomon Kenton	pt. "Upland"	200
	"Upland Addition"	50
Rebecca Leonard	pt. "Hackton"	100
Rebecca Curtice	"Curtice's Lott" – for h/o Thomas Curtice	50
	pt. "Mount Hope" – for h/o Thomas Curtice, in TA	181
Thomas Martaindale	pt. "Sylvesters Forrest"	100
James Lane	pt. "Worleys Outrange"	50
Anthony Roe	pt. "Sayres Range"	100
36:1747:39 ...		
James Hix	pt. "Edmondsons Green Close"	200

John Wootters	pt. "Jumps Choice"	50
	pt. "Smiths Clifts" – in TA	20
Joseph Hunter	"Hunters Chance"	100
	"Hunters Hope"	50
	"Jumps Lott"	50
	"Boones Ridge"	50
	"Hunters Hazard"	50
Isaac Ford	"Fords Folleys"	20
	"Fords Park"	30
	"Hopewell"	100
Ralph Swift	"Content"	50
36:1747:40 ...		
James Countiss	pt. "Dublin"	150
William Countiss	pt. "Dublin"	150
John Colbreath	"Poplar Neck"	200
	pt. "Solomons Lott Addition"	35
	"Holly Neck Resurveyed"	415
David Harrington	"Hopewell"	100
	"Beaverdambs Addition"	150
	"Harringtons Desire"	50
John Slaughter	"Fern Ridge"	50
	pt. "Partnership" a/s "Ratcliffe"	50
Thomas Bostock	"Hinesleys Fancy"	50
	"Bostocks Chance"	50
36:1747:41 ...		
Patrick Robertson	"Tully Barden"	50
	"Tully Bardens Addition"	62
	"Hunting Town"	100
John Adkinson	pt. "Friendship"	50
	pt. "Tom's Fancy Enlarged"	200
Charles Bradley	"Aylor's Hope"	100
James Blades	"Goodwill"	50
	pt. "Long Range" – in DO	50
Isaac Merrick	"Merricks Delight"	50
James Hobbs	"Hobbs's Venture"	50
	"Bear Harbour"	50

Queen Anne's County - 1747

36:1747:42	...		
Jeremiah Jadwin		"Cow Range"	100
		"Timm's Neglect"	50
		"Jadwin's Project"	40
		pt. "Hamton" & pt. "Parkers Range" – in TA	44
		pt. "Scarbrough" – in TA	200
John Timm		"Society Hill"	50
		"Timm's Arcadia"	50
		"Golden Rod Ridge"	50
John Baggs		"Hazard"	50
		pt. "Controversye"	22
Richard Harrington		"Solomons Lott"	100
		pt. "Solomons Lott Addition"	15
		pt. "Fishers Chance"	50
William Harrington		pt. "Josephs Lott"	100
36:1747:43	...		
Richard Chance		pt. "Boones Hope"	50
		"Little Worth"	100
		"Bear Point"	200
		"Little Worth Addition"	50
James Sylvester		pt. "Bear Garden"	200
		"Carmarthen"	100
		"Grubby Neck"	150
James Millis		"Chance Hill"	50
		"Hitt or Miss"	50
		"Fishers Chance"	100
		pt. "Cods Head Mannor"	20
Archebald Jackson		"Nodd"	113
		"Speedy Contract"	10
		pt. "Ratcliffe"	300
James Cook		"Campersons Choice"	100
William Whealor		"Kill Maiden"	100
		"Kill Maiden Addition"	15
36:1747:44	...		
John Powell (cnp)		"Tryangle"	50
		"Longs Desire"	50

Queen Anne's County - 1747

	"Powells Fancy"	94
h/o Benjamin Falconer	"Falconer's Lott"	50
William Starkey	pt. "Oak Ridge"	175
	"Hiccory Ridge"	150
	pt. "Codshead Mannor"	116
Henry Burt	"Burts Fancy"	50
	"Burts Delight"	100
Richard Swift	"Williams Pasture"	54
John Swift, Jr.	"Swifts Forrest"	50
36:1747:45 ...		
Emanuel Swift	"Swifts Forrest Addition"	52
John Newman (Choptank)	pt. "Swifts Meadows"	50
Peter Ritch	"Bridge Town"	11
	3 lots in Bridge Town – No. 4, No. 5, No. 6	3
	"Ritches Folly" – in DO	50
	"William, John, & Joseph's Lott" – in DO	294
	"Ritches Chance" – in DO	60
	pt. "Halls Fortune" – in DO	130
Partrick Lynsey	"Jadwins Hazard"	61
Charles Lemarre	"Doggwood Ridge"	100
Thomas Baggs	pt. "Old Town"	60
36:1747:46 ...		
Benjamin Endsworth	pt. "Brandfield & Sayres Addition" – for h/o John Willson	250
James Andrew	pt. "Brandfield & Sayres Addition" – for his wife	120
John Willson (Choptank)	pt. "Brandfield & Sayres Addition"	200
James Boone	pt. "Hadden"	160
	pt. "Partnership"	100
	pt. "Garden of Roses"	48
Jacob Boone	"Boone's Park"	200
	"Boone's Hazzard"	120
Isaac Boone	pt. "Hadden"	200
	pt. "Garden of Roses"	92
	"Boones Venture"	130
36:1747:47 <blank>		
36:1747:48 ...		

Queen Anne's County - 1747

Joseph Longfellow	"Josephs Hope"	50
Edward Garrett	"Sandy Hill"	50
w/o Fairclough Wright	"Soote Hill" – for his heirs	200
Ralph Swift, Jr.	"Indian Tract"	50
Thomas Roe (Choptank)	"Hackers Adventure"	250
William Ewbanks	pt. "Ratcliffe"	140
William Montague	pt. "Ratcliffe"	140

36:1747:49 ...

Nathaniel Scott	pt. "Toms Fancy Enlarged"	100
Rev. Mr. James Sterling	"Whartons Marsh" – for h/o Rev. Mr. Arther Holt	27
	"Highgate Lane" – for h/o Rev. Mr. Arther Holt	100
	"Holt" – for h/o Rev. Mr. Arther Holt	506
	"Holts Castle Hill Resurveyed" – for h/o Rev. Mr. Arther Holt	304½
John Oldson	pt. "Hawkins Pharsalia"	50
William Hamer	pt. "Wrights Choice"	70
James Barwick	pt. "Oakenthorpe"	185
Edward Goodwin	pt. "Hawkins Pharsalia"	200
	"Long Run"	100
	"Marphys Chance"	50

36:1747:50 ...

Nathaniel Wright	"Brother Hood"	50
	"Wrights Chance"	300
William Sheppard	pt. "Hindsleys Plains"	109
Mr. John Hawkins	pt. "Tulleys Delight"	600
	pt. "Macklinbourough"	175
Mr. John Collins	pt. "Spread Eagle"	425
	pt. "Levells"	170
	pt. "Barnes's Satisfaction"	50
	"Smiths Range Addition"	290
Benjamin Hines	"Good Increase"	200
Martha Tillotson	"Lords Gift on Resurvey"	350
	pt. "Tooley"	320
	"Tillottson's Chance"	100
	"Shepherds Folds on Resurvey"	140

36:1747:51 ...

Queen Anne's County - 1747

Alice Wright	"Tullys Reserve"	300
	"Hazard"	100
	½ "Content"	100
	"Colonels Quarter"	100
	"Content Addition"	200
	"Contents Outlett"	50
	"Canaan"	50
	"Reserve Addition"	50
	pt. "Partnership"	250
Judith Burton	pt. "Spread Eagle" – for h/o William Burton	100
	pt. "Carman & Burton" – for h/o William Burton	75
	"Little Worth" – for h/o William Burton	100
Ernault Hawkins	pt. "Brampton"	150
	pt. "Conquest" tbc David Register (130 a., f. 119)	267
	pt. "Tullys Delight"	200
	pt. "Bramton" – recovered from devisees of (N) Clayton	100
John Sinott	pt. "Hawkins Pharsalia"	150
36:1747:52 ...		
Thomas Roe (Chester)	"Clouds's Range"	100
	"Roes Addition"	70
	"Downes's Forrest"	300
Edward Roe	pt. "Tulleys Addition"	150
	"Nedds Begginning"	30
	pt. "Hindsleys Plains"	140
	"Roes Lane"	22
	pt. "Narborough"	250
	pt. "Oaken Thorpe"	226
	pt. "Tulleys Addition" – more	150
Daniel Willcox	pt. "Mount Hope"	55
	"Mount Hopes Addition"	100
James Kersey	pt. "Scotland"	100
Richard Lambert	pt. "Lowes Arcadia" – for Thomas Philips s/o David	100
36:1747:53 ...		

Mrs. Kathrine Davis	"Clarkson Hill Addition"	80
	"Clarkson Hill"	150
	pt. "Norrestts Addition"	100
	pt. "Jones's Park"	100
John Covington	pt. "Providence"	<n/g>
James Covington	pt. "Providence"	<n/g>
Mr. Robert Norrest Wright	pt. "White Marsh" & pt "White Marsh" [!] for Nathan Wright	400
	"White Marsh Addition"	300
	"Corke Horse"	200
	"Callington"	120
	pt. "Jones Park"	100
	pt. "Norrest Addition"	20
William Austin	pt. "Waterford"	382
36:1747:54 ...		
Henry Counell	pt. "Hawkins Pharsalia"	162
Baldwin Kemp	pt. "Emorys Rich Land"	150
	pt. "Hindsleys Plains"	91
Richard Hynson	"Anne's Portion"	150
Thomas Shoebrook	"Stoke"	100
	"Stroke Addition"	50
	pt. "Lowes Arcadia"	100
	pt. "Crumps Forrest"	150
	pt. "Upperheathworth"	100
	"Addition"	50
	"Wellies"	100
Mr. Nicholas Glinn	"Guilford Addition" – for his wife	150
	"Guilford" – for his wife	300
	pt. "Narborough" – for his wife	250
	"Hogg Harbour" – for his wife	100
36:1747:55 ...		
Abraham Williams	"Milford"	123
John Bolton	pt. "Tulleys Delight"	100
Daniel Bolton	pt. "Boltons Delight" & pt. "Parkers Lott"	140
Thomas Honey	"Sparks's Outlett"	114

Queen Anne's County - 1747

John Rogers	pt. "Chester Field" – for h/o Thomas Butler	200
	pt. "Sheperds Forrest" – for h/o Thomas Butler	100
	pt. "Tryangle" – for h/o Thomas Butler	25
	"Butlers Own" – for h/o Thomas Butler	50
	pt. "Fox Hill" – for h/o Thomas Butler	55
	pt. "Notlars Delight" – for h/o Thomas Butler	37
Ephraim Winn	pt. "Todley"	913
36:1747:56 ...		
Peter Hinesly	"Hineslys Choice"	100
	pt. "Oaken Thorpe"	40
Nathaniel Hinesley	pt. "Hineslys Plains"	56
Stephen Thomas	pt. "Hawkins Pharsalia"	80
Benjamin Thomas	pt. "Hawkins Pharsalia"	60
Philimon Thomas	pt. "Hawkins Pharsalia"	60
John Young s/o William	pt. "Partnership"	50
Dr. Andrew McKittrick	pt. "Crumps Forrest"	150
36:1747:57 ...		
Thomas OBryon	"Pleasant Spring"	300
	pt. "Smiths Reserve"	150
James Knotts	pt. "Relief"	55
	pt. "Emory's Rich Land"	95
	"Littleworth"	50
William Satterfield	pt. "Winfield"	100
Joseph Harris	pt. "Crumps Chance"	50
Volentine Honey	pt. "Adventure" – for h/o George Sparkes	25
	pt. 'Sparkes's Own" – for h/o George Sparkes	25
	pt. "Sparkes's Choice" – for h/o George Sparkes	25
	pt. "Tottingham" – for h/o George Sparkes	100
	pt. "Mitchells Adventure"	100
Absolom Sparkes	pt. "Sparkes Own"	25
	pt. "Sparkes Choice"	25
	pt. "Adventure"	25
36:1747:58 ...		
James Harriss	pt. "Crumps Chance"	50
William Godwin	pt. "Wrights Chance" a/s "Choice"	100

Queen Anne's County - 1747

George Smith	pt. "Tom's Fancy Enlarged"	100
	"Neglect"	190
James Hollyday, Esq.	"Readbourn Rectified"	1440
	pt. "Macklin Borough" – given to James Hollyday, Jr. (f. 119)	210
	pt. "Warterford"	18
Thomas Baily s/o Jacob	pt. "Bishops Outlet"	100
	pt. "Larington"	31
	"Exchange" – for his wife	100
James Salisbury	"Sintra Resurveyed"	187
36:1747:59 ...		
Alice Collier	pt. "Bishops Outlett"	75
	pt. "Bishops Addition"	75
	pt. both as charged Margaret Wattson & Hannah Philips	150
Caleb Sparkes	pt. "Adventure"	25
	pt. "Sparkes Own"	25
	pt. "Sparkes Choice"	25
Millington Sparkes	pt. "Adventure"	25
	pt. "Sparkes Own"	25
	pt. "Sparkes Choice"	25
Thomas Ruth	pt. "Heaths Forrest"	50
	pt. "Heaths Gift"	53
John Collins, Jr.	pt. "Follingham"	200
William Elliott	pt. "Rawlings Chance"	100
36:1747:60 ...		
John Meridith	pt. "Plain Dealing"	75
	pt. "Adventure"	100
	"Trustram Bridge"	150
w/o William Meridith	pt. "Shrewsberry" – for his heirs	150
	"Shrewsberry Addition" – for his heirs	100
George Elliott	pt. "Rawlings Chance"	230
	pt. "Mount Hope"	50
	"Clouds's Hermitage"	200
	pt. "Elliotts Addition"	50

James Hambleton	"Bacon Neck" a/s "Barren Neck"	227
	"Janes Lott"	50
John Woodall	"Hope"	100
Thomas Baily	pt. "Bailys Delight on Resurvey"	256
	pt. "Toms Fancy Enlarged"	150
36:1747:61 ...		
Thomas Thomas	pt. "Winfield"	134
John Evans	pt. "Winfield"	55
George Baynard	pt. "Relief"	500
	pt. "Relief" & pt. "Hawkins Pharsalia" – from (N) Hussy	187
	"Hackers Forrest"	200
John Hammilton	pt. "Wrights Chance" a/s "Choice"	30
	pt. "Neglect"	50
	"Hamiltons Range"	100
	"Mary Ann's Lott"	100
Michael Green	"Coston's Hope"	100
William Robinson	"Anns Lott"	100
	pt. "Elliotts Addition"	50
36:1747:62 ...		
Mr. John Earle	pt. "Upperheathworth"	167
	"Heathworth"	533
James Earle	"Ovall"	355
	pt. "Toms Fancy Enlarged"	162
Archebald Greenfield	4 lots in Ogle Town – No. 22, No. 38, No. 39, No. 39 [!]	4
William Scandrett, Jr.	1 lot in Ogle Town – No. 21	1
	pt. "Lexton"	\<n/g\>
Peter Foome (VA)	pt. "Land of Prophesy"	280
Thomas Godwin	pt. "Wrights Chance" a/s "Choice"	100
36:1747:63 ...		
John Ricketts	pt. "Tullys Delight"	100
	"Bradford" tbc William Green (f. 120)	100
Benjamin Hines	pt. "Spread Eagle"	150
	"Good Increase" – for h/o Thomas Crupper	200
Edward Brown (Chester)	pt. "Macklinborough"	200

John Pickeron	pt. "Lowes Arcadia" – for h/o Nathaniel Wright	300
	"Beginning" – for h/o Nathaniel Wright	85
	"Beaver Dams" – for h/o Nathaniel Wright	50
Ruebin Taylor	pt. "Lowes Arcadia"	100
John Carman	pt. "Hawkins Range"	90
36:1747:64 ...		
Thomas & James Carman	"Bradfords Addition"	100
Dr. Peter Duhamil	"Timber Swamp"	200
Richard Scrivner	pt. "Hackers Meadows"	214
John Austin	pt. "Bishops Outlett" – for Jacob Baily	100
John Deford	pt. "Toms Fancy Enlarged"	91
William Wilkinson (J.H.)	pt. "Glocester"	50
William Bishop	pt. "Courseys Point" or "Smiths Mistake" tbc MM T. H. Wright & William Hopper (f. 17)	520
	"Mill Range"	163
	"Parsons Neck"	64
36:1747:65 ...		
Edward Ricketts	pt. "Hinesleys Plain"	59
William Calvin	pt. "Freshford"	140
William Kent	pt. "Toms Fancy Enlarged"	150
Thomas Lee	"Wattsons Lott"	50
	pt. "Hawkins Pharsalia"	100
William Carman	pt. "Content"	100
John Miller	pt. "Oakenthorpe"	229
	pt. "Providence"	150
Robert Fowler	pt. "Shrewsberry"	150
36:1747:66 ...		
John Hackett	pt. "Prices Hill"	200
Thomas Hackett	pt. "Prices Hill"	100
	pt. "Shepherds Fortune" – for his wife	150
Thomas Mountsieur	pt. "Hacketts Delight"	105
John Nevill (cnp)	"Farrington"	250
	pt. "Wharton & Pinders Out Range"	75
	pt. "Sewalls Fork"	500
	"Nevills Outrange"	46½
	"Nevills Discovery"	3½

	pt. "Tilghmans Discovery"	200
	"Solomons Outlet"	50
	"Nevills Addition"	144
John Andrews	"Mount Gilboa"	50
	pt. "Hacketts Delight"	45
36:1747:67 ...		
Richard Ponder	pt. "Smiths Delight"	181½
	"Hamers Addition"	37
Martha Woodall	pt. "Crumpton"	210
	pt. "Sandy Hurst"	216
Thomas Peacock Betts	pt. "Providence"	200
John Johnson Ripley	pt. "Ripley"	300
	"Bee Tree Ridge"	50
Francis Foreman	pt. "Royston"	600
John Keys, Jr.	pt. "Rye Hall" – for h/o George Ayres	184
36:1747:68 ...		
John Coleman	pt. "Royston" – for his wife	50
Margaret Pinder	pt. "Bishoptan"	250
	pt. "Ashton"	75
	pt. "Collins's Lott"	116
	pt. "Wharton & Pinders Outrange"	67
Susannah Manah	"Manahs Chance Resurveyed" – for h/o Timothy Manah	150
James Ponder	pt. "Clouds's Adventure"	175
Richard Ponder, Jr.	pt. "Clouds's Adventure"	75
Elizabeth Nevill	pt. "Southampton" – for h/o Walter Nevill	75
36:1747:69 ...		
David Nevill	"Jamaica"	150
William Primrose	pt. "Hambletons Hermitage"	75
	pt. "Southamton" – for h/o Walter Nevil	75
	pt. "Barton" – for h/o Walter Nevil	40
	"Smiths Addition" – for h/o Walter Nevil	106
	pt. "Hambletons Hermitage" – for h/o Walter Nevil, more	75
Danniel Smith (planter)	pt. "Jones's Fancy"	75
Benjaman Smith	pt. "Jones's Fancy"	75

John Hawkins Hambleton	pt. "Manton" – for h/o James Wyatt	150
	pt. "Clockerton" – for h/o James Wyatt	100
36:1747:70 ...		
Mr. James Brown	pt. "Ripley"	250
	"Contest"	50
	pt. "Hambletons Hermitage"	33½
Mr. Humphry Wells	pt. "Bath"	400
	pt. "Bath Addition"	150
	"Landing"	30
	"Calebs Lott"	80
	"Pierce Land"	200
	"Lowe Lands"	45
	"Welles Park"	119
	"Crumps Advice"	100
	"Crumps Fancy"	50
	"Security"	100
	"Pierce Land Addition"	50
	"Red Lyon Point"	50
Edward Jones	pt. "Sandy Hurst"	100
	"Beaverdam Fork"	100
William Massy	"Pacolett"	18
John Spry	pt. "Friendship" – surveyed for (N) Tilghman	70
36:1747:71 ...		
Thomas Spry	pt. "Friendship" – surveyed for (N) Tilghman	55
	pt. "Friendship" – another	15
Christopher Spry	"Thief Keep Out"	100
	pt. "Friendship" – surveyed for (N) Tilghman	52
	pt. "Friendship" – another	18
	"Sprys Chance"	21
Francis Spry	pt. "Spry's Adventure"	75
Robert Wharton	"Whartons Adventure"	570
	pt. "Sprys Adventure" – for Jo. Spry	75
William Spry	pt. "Friendship" – surveyed for (N) Spry	160
William Vandeford	pt. "Fox Hill"	85
	pt. "Dispute" a/s "Brotherhood"	47
36:1747:72 ...		

James Massy	pt. "Friendship" – surveyed for (N) Tilghman	185
	pt. "Johnsons Adventure" tbc Peter Massey, Jr. (f. 141)	90
	pt. "Massys Hazard" tbc Peter Massey, Jr. (f. 141)	40
	pt. "Friendship" (above) – from (N) Certain	85
Rachel Primrose w/o John	"Adventure"	30
Mr. Stephen Bordley	"Churnalls Neck"	200
John Hamer	pt. "Spread Eagle" – for h/o William Ratcliffe	100
	"Collins's Own" – for h/o William Ratcliffe	92
	pt. "White Hall" – for h/o William Ratcliffe	18
	"Ratcliffs Part of Loyds Freshes" – for h/o William Ratcliffe	190
Solomon Seney	pt. "Barton"	100
John Harriss	pt. "Contention"	150
	"Killkenny"	200
36:1747:73 ...		
Thomas Powell (Double Creek)	pt. "Tilghmans Discovery"	1¼
Thomas Coleman	pt. "Tilghmans Discovery"	80
John Comegys	pt. "Sheperds Forrest"	173
	pt. "Sheperds Redoubt"	60
	pt. "Sheperds Redoubt" – from (N) Wilkinson	200
Thomas Seward	"Outrange"	174
Richard Gould	pt. "Ripley"	266⅔
	pt. "Goulds Purchase"	150
	pt. "Camberwell" – for Benjamin	66⅔
	pt. "Spread Eagle"	50
	pt. "Camberwel" – more	33⅓
	pt. "Spread Eagle" – more	25
William Firth	"Chesnutt Neck"	150
	"Smiths Beginning"	200
36:1747:74 ...		
Francis Gould (cnp)	"Spring Branch"	100
	pt. "Ripley"	133⅓
	pt. "Goulds Purchase"	65
	pt. "Camberwell"	33⅓
	pt. "Spread Eagle"	25

Queen Anne's County - 1747

	pt. "Sewalls Fork"	500
Trustram Thomas	"Swine Range" – for h/o Benony Wattson	30
	"Widows Folly" – for h/o Benony Wattson	70
	pt. "Friendship" – for h/o Benony Wattson	25
	"Grubby Neck"	50
	"Trustrams Ridge"	50
James Roberts	pt. "Lowes Desire"	100
	pt. "Shepherds Redoubt"	100
	"Dixsons Gift"	100
	"Roberts Meadow"	100
Thomas Sands	pt. "Lows Desire"	200
	"Sands Outlett"	100
	"Dubb Hen Ridge"	40
	"Timber Ridge"	70
	pt. "Swifts Outlett"	22
36:1747:75 ...		
Daniel Newnam, Jr.	pt. "Hambletons Hermitage"	33⅓
	pt. "James's Choice"	100
Winnefred Ford	pt. "Ashton" – for h/o William	225
Henry Short	pt. "Out Range"	200
devisees of Daniel Newnam	"Williams Lott"	50
	"Newnams Hermitage"	50
	pt. "Devonishes's Chance"	50
	pt. "Scottons Addition"	50
Albert Johnson	"Sayres Range Addition"	100
	"Alberts Delight"	100
	"Lawrence's Delight"	100
	"Johnsons Addition"	100
John Lambden	"Lambdens Adventure" – for h/o George Lambden, John Swift is guardian to heirs	100
36:1747:76 ...		
John Hollingsworth	pt. "Hambletons Hermitage"	33⅓
John Swift	"Chance"	66
	pt. "Swifts Outlett"	118
	"Northumberland"	100
	"Constantinople"	100

Lewis Clothier	"Plain Dealing"	100
Sarah Hollingsworth	"Refuse"	100
James Horsley	pt. "Bishops Fields"	50
Caleb Isgate	"Fork"	200
36:1747:77 ...		
Matthew Wickes	pt. "Injoyment"	79
John Wicks	pt. "Mount Pleasure"	32
Mr. John Dempster	pt. "Poplar Hill"	288
	pt. "Shepherds Fortune"	150
Stephen Wicks	pt. "Mount Pleasure"	134
Nicholas Broadway	pt. "White Hall"	82
	pt. "Callington"	100
	pt. "Notlars Desire"	38
	pt. "Carman & Burton"	75
	pt. "Anthorpe"	60
Francis Rochester	"Winchester"	200
	"John & Rachaels Choice"	100
	"Louder's Hazard"	77
	pt. "Fox Harbour"	100
36:1747:78 ...		
John Hays, Jr.	pt. "Dispute" a/s "Brotherhood"	47
	pt. "Brotherhood" – for h/o Edward Wright, Jr.	618
	pt. "Notlers Delight" – for h/o Edward Wright, Jr.	33
Mr. William Carmichall	pt. "Park"	500
	pt. "Allins Neck"	117
	pt. "Partnership"	36
	"Hermonton"	304
	"Allins Neck Outlett"	18¾
Francis Rochester, Jr.	"Watry Plains"	150
	pt. "Tulley's Lott"	200
Joseph Newnam	pt. "Sandish Wood" – for h/o Her. Cook	335
Richard Buckley	"Buckley's Delight"	50
James Sutton	pt. "Sandy Hurst"	100
36:1747:79 ...		
Stephen Andrews	pt. "Tilghman's Discovery" – for his wife	66⅔

John Hadley	pt. "Friendship"	80
	"Skinners Pleasure"	50
Christopher Wilkinson	pt. "Golden Grove"	20
	"Emorys Fortune Addition"	270
	pt. "Partnership"	175
John Buck, Esq.	pt. "Poplar Hill"	100
	2 lots in Ogle Town	2
John Bermingham	"Bermingham's Fortune"	100
John Lee	pt. "Camberwell"	100
36:1747:80 ...		
Thomas Wyatt	pt. "Lowes Desire"	100
	"Wyatts Range"	50
Richard Wells	pt. "Bath"	50
	pt. "Baths Addition"	100
Charles Lowther	pt. "James's Choice"	50
Andrew Finley	pt. "Ramble"	150
Daniel Smith (joiner)	pt. "Manton"	75
	pt. "Clockerton"	50
	"Mantons Addition"	5
Charles Nabb	pt. "Clouds's Adventure"	200
	pt. "Manton"	75
	pt. "Clockerton"	50
36:1747:81 ...		
Charles Gafford	"Macklins Beginning"	400
	pt. "Smithfield"	50
William Swift	pt. "Swifts Meadows"	50
Margarett Bussells	"Philadelphia" – for h/o John Bussells, Charles Lowther is guardian	50
Robert Offley	pt. "Levills"	80
Violett Primrose	pt. "Poplar Hill"	100
Cornelius Comegys	pt. "James's Choice"	150
	pt. "Crumps Choice"	50
John Johnson, Jr.	"Cloudent"	200
	pt. "Notlars Delight"	80
36:1747:82 ...		
Jacob Aliquare	pt. "Outrange" – for Robert Green	200

Queen Anne's County - 1747

William Sheppard	pt. "Shepherds Folds"	20
John Parsons	"Marys Chance"	30
	"Parsons Chance"	115
James Cassey	pt. "Cannoway"	289
William Newnam	"Newnams Chance"	56
	pt. "Johns Meadows"	60
	"Shaver"	200
William Mounsieur	"Alberts Delight"	200
Thomas Stanton	"Forrest of Sherwood"	200
36:1747:83 ...		
John Perry	"Stafford"	100
Joseph & Ben Whittington	"Whittingtons Lott"	400
	pt. "Hemsleys Britland"	300
	"Recovery"	100
Mr. John Gibb	pt. "Killmanam Plains"	200
	pt. "Knowles's Range"	244
William Burroughs	"Buck Road"	100
	pt. "Adventure"	50
Robert Certain	"Jones's Delight"	200
John Scotton	"Scottons Inclosure"	55
	"Scottons Folly"	50
36:1747:84 ...		
John Hartshorne	pt. "Woodhouse" tbc Thomas Nicholson (f. 85)	100
	"Woodhouse Addition" tbc Thomas Nicholson (f. 85)	25
Thomas Jackson	"Hopewell"	50
Maurice Cloak	"Tillbury"	50
	"Tillburys Addition"	50
Edward Williams	"Williams's Adventure"	50
John McConnikin	"Wood Ridge"	200
	"Wood Ridge Addition"	100
	"McConnikins Fortune"	399
John Hamer	"Hamer's Lott"	200
36:1747:85 ...		
Richard Scotton (cnp)	"Salisbury Plains"	150
	"Scottons Outlett"	50

		"Scottons Addition"	100
Thomas Powel		"Toms Adventure" tbc Thomas Walker (f. 56)	56
		"Powells Venture"	95½
Thomas Nickolson		"Nickolson's Chance"	50
		"Nickolson's Fancy"	50
		pt. "Woodhouse"	100
		"Woodhouse Addition"	25
William Ridger		"Hope"	50
		"Small Hopes"	50
		"Ridgers Lott"	100
		"Ridgways Chance"	50
Christopher Williams		pt. "Connoway"	111
James Clough		"Clough's Fancy"	50
36:1747:86 ...			
James Williams		"Williams's Fancy"	40
John Legg, Jr.		"Limrick"	100
		"Leggs Beginning"	100
		pt. <n/g> – from Thomas Benton by the name of "Pentreby"	14
Penelope Wright		pt. "Parsons Point"	100
Mrs. Ruth Wells who married Nicholas Clouds		"Broad Creek Resurveyed"	830
John Legg		"Woodland Neck"	50
		"Oldsons Relief"	100
Mr. Marmaduke Godhand		pt. "Sillin"	200
		pt. "Point Love"	200
		"Broad Oak"	500
		"Poplar Neck"	300
36:1747:87 ...			
Mrs. Elizabeth Bradford (CE)		pt. "Point Love" for h/o Mr. Jo. Wickes	400
		"Beaver Neck Resurveyed" – for h/o John Rowlens	320
		"Widows Lott" – for h/o John Rowlens	289
Warter Kirby		pt. "Allens Deceit"	210
		"Kirbys Addition"	50
Francis Bright (cnp)		"Stooply Gibson"	200
		"Coopers Quarter"	50

	"Brights Island"	28
Mrs. Elizabeth Clouds	"Clouds's Choice" – for h/o Nicholas Clouds	200
	"Clouds's Chance" – for h/o Nicholas Clouds	6
	pt. "Sillen" – for h/o (N) Blangy	66⅔
	pt. "Upper Deal" – for h/o (N) Blangy	200
	"Bodys Neck" – for h/o (N) Kirby	200
Rev. Mr. Samuel Hunter	pt. "Little Ease"	150
36:1747:88 ...		
Robert Walters	"Dundee"	100
	"Piney Neck"	50
	"Maidens Choice"	65
	"Kirbys Prevention" tbc his son Jacob Walters (f. 118)	50
	pt. "Allens Deceit" tbc his son Jacob Walters (f. 118)	40
	"Walters's Addition"	50
Thomas Tanner	"Chance"	50
	"Tanners Advantage"	39
	"Providence"	100
	"Ashford" – for h/o Isaac Hudson	100
William White	"Work Mans Hazard"	150
	"Sparkes's Point"	50
John Willson	pt. "Eastern Island"	50
	"Willsons Adventure"	54
	"Errickson's Island"	20
William Joiner	"Coopers Hill"	100
36:1747:89 ...		
Richard Blunt	pt. "Blunts Marsh" a/s Great Neck" – sold to Robert Blunt (below)	110
Robert Blunt	pt. "Blunts Marsh" a/s "Great Neck"	110
	pt. "Parsons Point" – for h/o Samuel Wright	400
	"Copartnership"	373
	pt. "Blunts Marsh" a/s "Great Neck" – more	110
Thomas Benton	"Pentrogay" tbc John Legg, Jr. (14 a.) (f. 86)	200
	"Pentrovay"	50
James Evans	"Walnutt Neck Resurveyed"	109
	"Barren Ridge"	100

Samuel Blunt	pt. "Blunts Marsh" a/s "Great Neck"	110
h/o John Evans	pt. "Upper Deal"	300
	pt. "Sillen"	133⅓
36:1747:90 ...		
Charles Conner	pt. "Woodyard Thickett"	205
Sarah Sliney	"Timber Ridge" – for h/o James Sliney	250
Richard Carter	pt. "Copartnership"	52
	pt. "Jones Plott"	45
	pt. "Dunn's Hazard"	75
	pt. "Carters Addition"	25
	"Chance"	25
	"Barnes's Satisfaction"	50
Volentine Downey	"Pigg Quarter Neck"	100
Mr. James Sudler	"Little Neck"	55
	"Griffiths Adventure"	100
	"Cox Neck" – for h/o James Ringold	1000
36:1747:91 ...		
Letitia Brown	pt. "Woodyard Thickett" – for h/o Mathew Brown	205
	pt. "Sillen" – for h/o Mathew Brown	200
Dr. John Smith	pt. "Pitts Gift" – for h/o Leonard Mayton	85
	"Timber Neck"	100
	"Addition"	200
	pt. "Martins Neck" – from William Osborne by lease for 20 years	117
John Elliott, Jr.	pt. "Copartnership" – for h/o William Price	52
	pt. "Jones's Plott" – for h/o William Price	45
	pt. "Duns Hazard" – for h/o William Price	75
	pt. "Carters Addition" – for h/o William Price	25
	pt. "Chance" – for h/o William Price	25
	pt. "Cloverfields" – for Thomas Price	100
Thomas Barnes	pt. "Barnes Satisfaction"	220
Elizabeth McConnikin	"Georges Codd"	100
36:1747:92 ...		
Mr. William Elliott	"Upper Blunt Point" – wrong charge	200
	"Forlorne Hope"	100
	"Elliotts Choice"	100

John Stephens, Jr.	"Stephens Adventure"	255
	pt. "Little Ease"	150
Benjamin Richardson	"Pasco's Adventure"	150
	"Wading Place"	300
	"Ashburys Addition"	35
	pt. "Cloverfields"	335
Andrew Toulson	½ "Morgans Inclosure" – for his wife	210½
h/o James Hutchins	"Wrights Fortune"	120
	pt. "Condone"	316
	"Lanes Ridge"	200
	"Castle Town"	100
36:1747:93 ...		
Mrs. Rebecca Sudler	"Jones Hole Resurveyed" – for h/o James Sudler	276
	"Stint on Sudlar" – for h/o James Sudler	137
Joseph Elliot	pt. "Slaughterton"	100
Mr. John Carter	pt. "Coppidges Range"	190
	"Craney Neck"	160
John Meridith	pt. "Connor's Neck" – for h/o Phill. Connor	180
Jos. & Lewis Derochbrume	"Friendship Resurveyed"	396
Alexander Toulson, Jr. s/o Andrew	pt. "Copidges Range"	100
36:1747:94 ...		
w/o Mr. Jacob Winchester	"Purlivant" – for his heirs	180
	"Isaac's Addition" – for his heirs	80
Joseph Derouchbrume	pt. "Vaughan's Kindness"	200
	"Joseph's Addition"	60
Edward Cockey	"Hoggpen Neck", "Goose Neck", & pt. "Ridge"	285
John Errickson	"Sarahs Portion"	150
	"Johnson's Lott" – escheat	46
Charles Errickson	"Stint on Errickson"	200
Mr. Christopher Granger	"Erricksons Island" – sold to John Willson (f. 88)	20
36:1747:95 ...		
Andrew Price, Jr. (cnp)	pt. "Parsons Neck"	60
	pt. "Pascoes Lott"	50
	pt. "Eastern Island"	25
	pt. "Addition"	90

	pt. "Primus"	40
	pt. "Bonadventure"	37½
	pt. "Rotterdam"	25
Mr. Thomas Marsh	"Little Thickett"	200
	"Marshes Forbearance"	150
	"Cabbin Neck"	350
	"Marshs Portion"	150
	"Neglect"	200
	2 lots in Kings Town – No. 4, No. 5	2
Philip Coppidge	"Indian Spring"	100
	pt. "Slaughterton"	200
John Stephens (KE)	"<unr> Kill"	150
Anna Toalson	"Phillpotts Neck" – for h/o Alexander Toalson	690
36:1747:96 ...		
James Harvy	pt. "Slaughterton"	100
	pt. "Gold Hawks Enlargement"	35
	pt. "Cummins's Freehold"	25
	pt. "Mersons Freehold"	25
Edward Brown	pt. "Pascoe's Lott" – for h/o John Griffith	50
	pt. "Eastern Island" – for h/o John Griffith	25
	pt. "Addition" – for h/o John Griffith	90
	pt. "Primus" – for h/o John Griffith	48
	pt. "Bonadventure" – for h/o John Griffith	37½
	pt. "Rotterdam" – for h/o John Griffith	25
	pt. "Parsons Neck" – for h/o John Griffith, sold to William Joiner, Jr. (below)	60
William Joiner, Jr.	pt. "Parsons Neck" – for his wife	60
Robert Small	"Ship Point"	100
Jeremiah Grimes	pt. "Cummins's Freehold"	50
36:1747:97 ...		
Sufia Elliott	pt. "Slaughterton" – for h/o John Elliott	100
	"Matthews Enlargement" – for h/o John Elliott	155
Volentine Carter	pt. "Ridge"	187
Alexander Toalson	½ "Morgans Inclosure" – for his wife Mary daughter of Herbert Morgan	218½

Queen Anne's County - 1747

Mr. Joseph Sudlar	"Sledmore"	800
	pt. "Devonishes Chance"	15
	"Sudlar's Purchase"	80
	"Sudlars Fortune"	186
	"Sudlar's Island"	64
Vincent Benton	pt. "Contention"	50
George Burroughs	"Georges Hazard"	50
36:1747:98 ...		
Mr. Henry Casson	pt. "Large Range Addition"	124
	"Mistake"	20
	"Jump's Claims"	80
	pt. "Dudleys Desire"	100
Joseph Merchant	"Jacks Purchase"	75
	"Musketo Ridge"	50
	"Fairplay" – in TA	50
Benjamin Denny	"Wootters's Choice"	100
Jonathan Jolley	"Andever" – from Maurice Cloak	50
	"Nicholson's Adventure"	50
	"Burton"	50
	"Lester"	50
William Barkhust	"Pensylvania Border"	50
36:1747:99 ...		
Hynson Wright	pt. "Tom's Fancy Enlarged"	100
Thomas Baily s/o Thomas	pt. "Outrange" – for your wife (N) daughter of Robert Green	40
William Scott	pt. "Sayre's Range"	200
Lawrence Everett	"Hunter's Forest"	200
John Ruth	pt. "Larrington"	119
	pt. "Smiths Neglect"	150
John Starkey	"Starkeys Folly"	50
36:1747:100 ...		
Richard Smith	"Smiths Desire"	50
	"Smiths Outlett"	100
John Kinnimont	pt. "Lambeth"	200
Timothy Tooll	pt. "Kendall"	88
Ralph Pearson	pt. "Bishopprick" – in TA	50

John Needles	"Griffiths Purchase" – in DO	155
	"Rings End" – in DO	200
h/o Dr. Thomas Bullin	"Todcaster" – in TA	500
36:1747:101 ...		
Phineas Willson	"Willsons Chance" – in DO	100
	"Johns Fortune" – in DO	100
	pt. "Willsons Chance" – in DO	200
	"Lanes Chance" – in DO	100
Richard Goodman	"Goodmans Purchase" – in DO	100
Mr. James Tuit	pt. "Youngs Chance"	270
	pt. "Lambeth Fields"	132
William Dockery	pt. "Moores Hope Addition"	192
	pt. "Hawkins's Farme Resurveyed"	8
Mr. Henry Culley	pt. "Poplar Hill"	12
	5 lots in Kings Town – No. 1, No. 12, No. 13, No. 24, No. 25	5
	pt. "Poplar Hill" – from Samuel Massy (f. 140)	27
William Carman	pt. "Scottland"	50
36:1747:102 ...		
Thomas Macclannahan	pt. "Fox Harbour"	100
	pt. "Collins's Lott"	56¼
	pt. "Brotherhood"	42½
Jacob Carter	"Oar Mine"	200
	pt. "Coppidges Range"	30
	"Mattapax Neck" – for Henry Carter	98
Thomas Kersey	pt. "Scotland"	50
Richard Tickett	1 lot in Kings Town – No. 22	1
Roger Ellstone	1 lot in Kings Town – No. 7	1
John Cole	"Coles Endeaver"	150
36:1747:103 ...		
Nathaniel Cleave	"Mangy Pocky"	100
Kath Cleave	pt. "Tooley"	187
Joseph Chairs	pt. "Lantley"	125
George Primrose	pt. "Shepherds Fortune"	200
James Reed	pt. "Providence"	50

h/o Nathaniel Scott	pt. "Partnership"	250
	"Scotts Inclosure"	150
	pt. "Toms Fancy Enlarged"	243
36:1747:104 ...		
John Hart	1 lot in Kings Town – No. 11	1
Morgan Ponder	"Wattsons Desire"	50
Daniel Bridges Paxton	pt. "Powells Fancy"	160
Marian Nevill	"Nevills Delight" – for h/o William Nevill	50
Thomas Roe, Jr. (Choptank)	"Roes Desire"	50
William Robberts	"Roberts's Range"	150
	"Roberts's Range Addition"	37
36:1747:105 ...		
Thomas Scotton	"Scottons Forrest"	50
Matthew Graves	"Graves's Beginning"	50
Thomas Walker	"Toms Adventure Addition"	50
	"Toms Adventure"	56
Abraham Oldson	pt. "Hawkins Pharsalia"	50
	pt. "Hawkins Farme Resurveyed"	126
James Scotton	pt. "Toms Fancy Enlarged"	50
Giles Hix	pt. "Hilleray"	100
William Smith	pt. "Salisbury Plains"	200
36:1747:106 ...		
William Barwick	pt. "Jumps Choice"	50
James Willcox	pt. "Mounthope"	100
Joseph Newnam	"Addition"	24
	pt. "Scotton's Addition"	10
	pt. "Johns Meadows"	40
	"Shearing"	100
	pt. "Devonish's Chance"	150
Ann Hines	pt. "Spread Eagle"	16 2/5
Charles Hines s/o Thomas	pt. "Spread Eagle"	33⅓
John Oldson s/o Henry	pt. "Hawkins Pharsalia"	100
36:1747:107 ...		
Richard Wells, Jr.	pt. "Bath"	50
	"Crumpton"	220
	"Williams's Adventure"	50

Zerobabel Wells	pt. "Bath's Addition"	50
Dr. Richard Porter, Jr.	pt. "Anthorp"	145
James McCoy	pt. "Smiths Delight"	118½
Timothy Webb	"Wattsons Lott"	50
Christopher Thomas	"Forrest Plains"	150
William Holding	pt. "Trustram" – for Edmund Thomas	150
36:1747:108 ...		
John Earle (sadler)	"Troy"	100
Joseph Ashbury	pt. "Clouds's Adventure"	50
Henry Willkinson	"Wattsons Chance"	50
	"Wyatts Folly"	50
William Durding	pt. "Powells Fancy"	50
Samuel McCosh	pt. "Upper Heath Worth"	88
	pt. "Collins's Refusall"	112
Oneal Price	pt. "Winfield"	11
Richard Sparkes – grandson of Richard Collins	1 lot in Ogle Town	1
36:1747:109 ...		
John Clothier	"Clothiers Pharsalia"	155
	"Addition" – for Tilden Thomas	227
Robert Gwinn	"Gwinns Hazard"	100
h/o James Barkhust	pt. "Shepherds Discovery" & pt. "Henfield"	162
Henry Ellors	pt. "Smiths Range" – for his wife (N) daughter of Maurice McCarty	239
Benjamin Toalson	pt. "Coppidge's Range"	111
Nicholas Clouds s/o Richard	pt. "Bishopton"	32
	pt. "Fox Harbour"	25
	pt. "Notlars Delight"	80
	pt. "Brotherhood"	45
36:1747:110 ...		
Mrs. Elizabeth Thompson	"Wilmores Range" – for her son Samuel	1000
	pt. "Cloverfields"	335
Dr. James Anderson (Chester Town)	pt. "Providence" – in right of his wife	200
	"Ashford" – in right of his wife	200
	pt. "Rambles" – in right of his wife	200
	"Shepherds Fields" a/s "Forrest"	200

Queen Anne's County - 1747

Mr. Dowdal Thompson	"Courseys Town"	600
	pt. "Prices Hill"	180
	pt. "Shepherds Discovery"	200
	"Parsons Marsh Addition"	10
	"Good Luck"	100
	pt. "Sparkes Choice"	200
	"Woolverhamton"	200
	pt. "Mount Pleasant"	50
	pt. "Enjoyment"	50
	"Barefield" a/s "Braghott"	200
	"Parson's Marsh"	34
	pt. "Shepherds Discovery" & pt. "Henfield"	218
	pt. "Sparkes Choice" – more	50
	pt. "Hemsleys Britland"	200
	"Coursey's Town Resurveyed" – includes: • "Hemsleys Britland" – 200 a. • "Courseys Town" – 600 a.	394
James Baily	pt. "Cleaves Ramble" – for his wife (N) daughter of Nathaniel Cleve	120
	"Tryangle"	50
36:1747:111 ...		
Mr. William Clayton, Jr.	"Prous's Park"	300
	pt. "Tryangle"	25
	"Forrest"	100
	"Winter House"	50
	"Hogg Penn Neck"	55
	"Hogg Hole"	50
	"Bishops Fields"	400
Benjamin Cleve (KE)	pt. "Cleves's Rambles" – for his son Nathaniel	110
Mr. Nathan Wright	pt. "Long Neck"	2½
	pt. "Coursey Upon Wye"	321½
Flower Fisher	pt. "Cods Head Manner"	850
Samuel Osborne	½ "Martains Neck Resurveyed"	117
William Baxter	"Upper Blunt Point"	200
36:1747:112 ...		
Thomas H. Wright (cnp)	pt. "Narborough" – for h/o John Wright	250
	"Narborough Addition" – for h/o John Wright	100

	"Littleworth"	50
Dr. John Jackson	"Hitt or Miss Resurveyed"	223
	pt. "Smithfield"	100
	pt. "Providence"	213
	"Smithfield Addition" – includes: • "Hitt or Miss Resurveyed" – 223 a. • pt. "Smithfield" – 100 a.	327¼
John Fouracres	pt. "Tulleys Lott"	100
Edmund Kelly	pt. "Isaac's Chance"	50
Samuel Swift	"Fosters Folly"	50
Sweatnam Burn	pt. "Royston"	475
36:1747:113 ...		
George Harrington	"Harringtons Venture"	100
w/o Thomas Trickey	"Woodberry"	100
James Cohee	"Cohee's Desire"	100
Philemon Green	"Greens Fortune"	80
	"Greens Fortune Addition"	75
John Stent	pt. "Coldrain"	103
Henry Fiddeman	pt. "Hacketts Garden"	100
36:1747:114 ...		
Anthony Harrington	pt. "Warners Discovery" – for his wife (N) d/o William Vickers	200
Edward Jump	"Godferys Folly"	50
William Wallis	"Boothby's Fortune"	500
John Railey	"Willsons Beginning"	100
Jane Ratcliff	½ "Ratcliffs Part of Lloyds Freshes"	95
36:1747:115 ...		
Ann Jackman (widow)	pt. "Sayre's Addition"	100
John Lord	pt. "Toms Fancy Enlarged"	132
Thomas Teat	"Mary's Chance" – from John Parsons (f. 82)	30
	"Teats Desire"	35
Mr. Michael Earle	pt. "Emorys Fortune Addition"	100
James Willcox	pt. "Mount Hope" – from Daniel Willcox	95
Richard Vandeford	pt. "Outrange" – in right of his wife Hannah d/o Robert Green	40
36:1747:116 ...		
Jacob Bell	"Wyatts Range" – from Thomas Wyatt (f. 30)	50

Mr. Charles Brown	pt. "Brad Burns Delight" a/s "Bailys Delight Attached" – from Thomas Baily	100
Mrs. Elizabeth Bradford (widow)	pt. "Point Love" – for h/o John Rowles	400
	"Beaver Neck Resurveyed" – for h/o Mr. Joseph Wicks	320
	"Widows Lott" – for h/o Mr. Joseph Wicks	287
Samuel Austin	pt. "Courseys Point" or "Smiths Mistake"	100
John Pratt	pt. "Vaughan's Discovery" – for his wife	100
36:1747:117 ...		
Nathaniel Clough	"Cloughs Hope"	50
Richard Cook	pt. "Partnership"	20
Absolom Sparkes (f. 57)	pt. "Sparkes Choice" – from Caleb Sparkes	\<n/g\>
	pt. "Sparkes Choice" – from Millington Sparkes	\<n/r\>
William Andrew	pt. "Ingrains Desire"	\<n/g\>
	pt. "Bridge Town"	\<n/g\>
Isabel Bath	1 lot in Ogle Town – No. 35	1
Margaret Carter	pt. "Bishops Addition"	\<n/g\>
	pt. "Bishops Outlett"	\<n/g\>
36:1747:118 ...		
Isaac Thorpe	pt. "Coleraine"	\<n/g\>
John Tittle	1 lot in Kings Town – No. 1	1
Jacob Walters	"Kirby's Prevention"	50
	"Allen's Deceit"	40
William Scandrett, Jr.	pt. "Lexton"	\<n/g\>
36:1747:119 ...		
James Gould	pt. "Goulds Purchase"	65
	pt. "Goulds Purchase" – more	130
John Hawkins, Jr.	"Hoopers Ensul" – in TA, for his wife (N) d/o John Power	200
	"Freeman's Rest" – in TA, for his wife (N) d/o John Power	50
Samuel Cocklin	"Wyatts Lott" – for h/o William Wyatt	150
Jonathan Wootters	"Oak Ridge"	20
David Register	pt. "Conquest" – from Ern. Hawkins (f. 51)	130
Mr. James Hollyday, Jr.	pt. "Macclinborough" – from James Hollyday, Esq. (F. 58)	\<n/g\>
36:1747:120 ...		

Robert Sumpter	"Patsy Plains" – from Nathan Wright, Jr.	50
William Green	"Bradford" – from William Ricketts s/o & h/o John Ricketts (f. 63)	100
William Emory, Jr.	pt. "Winfield" – from Richard Bennett, Esq. (f. 1)	287
Mr. John Granger	pt. "Connor's Neck"	100
36:1747:121 ...		
Mr. William Bancks	pt. "Pitts Vineyard" – from John Baynard s/o William (f. 35)	166⅔
Mr. Edward Neale	pt. "Hawkins Farm Resurveyed"	12
	"Bowtingly"	250
	"Macklin"	100
	"Beaverdamb"	160
	"Green Spring"	650
	pt. "St. Pauls"	50
	pt. "Carmans Neck"	100
	"Forrest Lodge"	152
	pt. "Knowles Range"	256
	"Partnership"	400
	"Discovery"	220
	pt. "Tully's Delight"	200
John Young	pt. "Stratton" – from Esquire Bennett (f. 1)	54½
William Young	pt. "Stratton" – from Esquire Bennett (f. 1)	52
36:1747:122 ...		
Joseph Boone	pt. "Boones Pleasure"	160
	pt. "Partnership"	100
Abraham Boone	pt. "Boones Pleasure"	90
	pt. "Partnership"	100
Benjamin Boone	pt. "Oak Ridge"	175
	pt. "Garden of Roses"	200
Moses Boone	pt. "Garden of Roses"	200
	pt. "Hodden"	40
Rebecca Mason	pt. "Winchesters Folly" – for h/o Richard Mason	230
	"Ephraims Hope" – for h/o Richard Mason	100
	"Winchesters Folly Resurveyed" – for h/o Richard Mason	539
William Whitby (cnp)	"Whitbys Forrest"	50
	"Buck Range"	100

Queen Anne's County - 1747

		pt. "Buck Range" – in TA	100
36:1747:123	<blank>		
36:1747:124-9	missing		
36:1747:130	Lands Lying in QA – the Owners in TA		
Edward Harding		pt. "Arcadia"	301
Mr. Philip Emerson		pt. "Smeath"	106
		pt. "Stagwell"	42
Francis Neal		"Shadwell" – for his son Francis	100
		pt. "Shadwell's Addition" – for h/o Robert Jones	100
John Webb		pt. "Redford"	150
		"Webbs Chance"	150
		pt. "Sylvester's Addition"	40
Mrs. Frances Elbert		pt. "Davis's Range"	400
Elizabeth Stevens		pt. "Providence"	150
36:1747:131	...		
William Vickers		pt. "Allcocks Pharsalia"	100
Mrs. Margaret Ward		"Ninevah"	600
		"Ninevah's Addition"	200
		"Mill Range"	163
Mrs. Henrietta Maria Robins		"Walnutt Ridge" – for h/o George Robins	600
		pt. "Sylvester's Forrest" – for h/o George Robins	105
		pt. "Keary's Discovery" – for h/o George Robins	90
		"Pearle"	1000
Mr. Nicholas Goldsborough		pt. "Old Town"	740
Mr. Anthony Bacon		"Limrick" – for h/o Anthony Richardson	50
		"Richardsons Adventure" – for h/o Anthony Richardson	80
Mr. Thomas Cockayne		"Betts Range"	400
		"Carters Addition"	191
36:1747:132	...		
Mrs. Katherine Hommond		"Robinsons Farme"	200
Thomas Whittington		pt. "Freshford"	60
		"Burroughs Ridge"	100
Isaac Dixon		pt. "Jerusalem" – part sold to John Dixon (below)	200
John Bartlett		"Swan Brook"	770

William Carey	pt. "Sylvester's Addition"	147
	"Baynards Discovery"	50
	pt. "Sylvesters Addition"	30
Edward Lloyd, Esq.	pt. "Loyds Freshes"	810
John Dixon	pt. "Jerusalem" – from Isaac Dixon (above)	<n/g>
36:1747:133 ...		
Mr. Robert Goldsborough	pt. "Controversey"	500
Samuel Fields	pt. "Benjamins Infancy"	100
Park Webb	pt. "Shadwells Addition" – for h/o Samuel Neal	50
William Wilson & his wife	pt. "Bear Garden"	150
William Thorpe	pt. "Coldraine"	50
Mr. Robert Goldsborough, Jr.	pt. "Sandishwood" – for his wife	665
36:1747:134 ...		
Thomas Pamphilion	"Spryley"	200
h/o Mr. James Dickinson	pt. "Dickinsons Plains"	860
h/o Caleb Clark	"Clarks Adventure"	12
	"Clerks Lott"	112
	"Clerks Delight"	76
Aron Parrott	pt. "Cold Spring"	162
William Lambden	pt. "Reviving Spring" – for his son William	166⅔
Samuel Brayley	pt. "Reviving Spring" – for his son John	166⅔
36:1747:135 ...		
John Camper	pt. "Reviving Spring" – for his son	166⅔
Thomas Rowland	"Rowland's Hazard"	257
William & Isaac Broadaway	pt. "Tenton Fields"	250
James Ratcliffe	pt. "Jerusalem"	100
Mr. Rizdon Bozman	pt. "Killeray"	100
	pt. "Millford"	200
	"Point Landing"	5¼
	"Killerays Addition"	34¾
Mr. Jonathan Nicols	"Jones's Forrest"	500
	pt. "Hackton"	200
	pt. "Redford"	150
	"Willsons Addition"	70
36:1747:136 ...		

Mr. Edward Oldham	"Exchange"	470
	pt. "Providence"	300
	"Exchange"	60
James Bartlett	"Partnership"	575
Mr. Jer. Gressingham	pt. "Davis's Range"	15
Mr. Thomas Lane	pt. "Smith's Ridge"	300
	"Collins's Ridge"	300
	"Coles Bank"	300
	"Coles Bank Addition"	165
	"Hogg Harbour"	125
Thomas Bartlett, Jr.	pt. "Turners Plains Addition"	420
William Thomas	"Lampton"	135
	pt. "Smiths Range"	100
36:1747:137 ...		
Edward Neal	pt. "Shadwells Addition"	50
	pt. "Shadwells Addition" – recovered from (N) Floyd	50
Mr. Jacob Hindman	pt. "Lexton"	184
Dr. Edward Knott	½ "Ratcliffes Part of Loyds Freshes" – in right of his wife Frances	90
Aron Higgs	"Skeggs Springs" – in TA	50
	"Skinners Swineyard" – in TA	200
36:1747:138 **Lands Lying in QA – the Owners in KE**		
Mr. Daniel Cheston	pt. "Condon"	10
	pt. "Crumpton"	10
Thomas Lihon	1 lot in Kings Town – No. 3	1
Mr. Lambert Wilmer	1 lot in Kings Town – No. 15	1
Mr. James Porter	"Halls Harbour" – in right of his wife (N) d/o Capt. Henry Rippon	500
	pt. "Poplar Hill"	50
(N)	pt. "Malton" – in right of his wife (N) d/o Major McCarty	150
Edward Crew	pt. "Rye Hall" – for Jo. Wyatt	40
36:1747:139 ...		
John Granger	pt. "Conners Neck"	100
Daniel Cornelius	"Daniels Fancy"	100

Mr. John Brown	pt. "Sillin"	100
	pt. "Belcher"	100
Benjamin Blackiston	pt. "Benjamin's Park"	80
Mr. James Smith	"Fresh Run"	160
William Trulock	"Lower Fords" – removed back to QA (f. 120)	200
36:1747:140 ...		
Samuel Massey	pt. "Poplar Hill" tbc Henry Culley (29 a. (f. 101)	50
	pt. "Royston"	50
	"Chestnutt Neck"	150
James Claypole	pt. "Lambeth"	187½
Edward Cousins	pt. "Outrange" – for his wife Elizabeth d/o Robert Green; from Jacob Alquare (f. 82)	40
Daniel Coaley	pt. "Outrange" – for his wife Mary d/o Robert Green; from Jacob Alquare (f. 82)	40
Rebecca Green d/o Robert Green	pt. "Outrange" – from Jacob Alquare (f. 82)	40
Robert Devonish	pt. "Lambeth"	62½
36:1747:141 ...		
Peter Massey, Jr.	pt. "Johnsons Adventure" with "Masseys Hazard"	140
36:1747:142	**Lands Lying in QA – the Owners in CE**	
Mr. Peregrine Frisby	"Crawford" – from Michael Miller	264
	"Coopers Freehold" – from Michael Miller	80
	Lands Lying in QA – the Owners in DO	
Joseph Willson	pt. "Poplar Neck"	150
John Roe	"Blair Crook, Athol, & Dunkelld"	60
36:1747:143	**Lands Lying in QA – the Owners in SO**	
George & John Gale	pt. "Ratcliffe"	420
	Lands Lying in QA – the Owners in SM	
John Biscoe	"Pleasant Spring"	500
	Lands Lying in QA – the Owners in AA	
John Ross, Esq.	"Westminster" tbc John Walters (f. 3)	297
Mr. Charles Carroll	pt. "Thompsons Manor" a/s "Poplar Island"	1000
	Lands Lying in QA – the Owners in BA	
William Worthington	"Lillingstons Castle"	500
	"Lillingstons Addition"	310
John Hallaway	"Little Ease"	400

36:1747:144	Lands Lying in QA – the Owners in PG	
Dr. Scott	"Abbington" – for h/o Mr. John Abbington	500
Lands Lying in QA – the Owners in Philadelphia		
William Till, Esq.	pt. "Park"	500
	"Winton"	500
	"Winton's Addition"	50
	"Wintons Addition"	25
Lands Lying in QA – the Owners on DE		
Mr. Samuel Dickinson (KEDE)	"Tuttle Fields"	200
	"Youghal"	175
h/o Mr. Richard Grafton	pt. "Partnership"	500
William Wattson (KEDE)	"Long Marsh Ridge"	50
	"Chance" – in DO	64
	"Goodridge Choice" – in DO	150
36:1747:145	Lands Lying in QA – the Owners are Foreigners	
Mr. Samuel Hyde (London)	"Smiths Forrest"	2000
Phillip Wootters (Carolina)	pt. "Holme Hill" – in TA	50
John, Thomas, & Richard Awbry (VA)	pt. "Prophecy"	217
	pt. "Heaths Discovery"	23
Robert Gilpin, Esq. (Whitehaven)	"Berrys Point" – in DO	50
Rev. Mr. Richard Molineaux	"Batchelors Plains"	216
	"John's Forrest"	200
	"Landy"	200
	"Woodhouse"	300
	"Waterford"	200
Wrightman Sipple (KEDE)	"Tappahannah"	1370
	"Spicey Grove"	250
	"Land of Benjamin"	275
36:1747:146 ...		
Charles & Ignatius Joy	pt. "Sebergham"	160
36:1747:<unnumbered> <blank>		

36:1754:<unnumbered>	Certification	
36:1754:1 ...		Acres
Alice Allyband	"Millford Addition" – take off	100
	"Allyband Hazard Enlarged"	114
James Ayler	pt. "Inclosure"	50
Mr. William Anderson (London)	"Darland Resurveyed"	1750
	"Loyds Town"	1000
Elinor Anthony (widow)	pt. "Hacton"	100
William Austin	pt. "Waterford"	382
John Atkinson	pt. "Toms Fancy Enlarged"	200
	pt. "Rawlings Chance" – for wife	230
	pt. "Mounthope"	50
	pt. "Elliotts Addition"	50
Dr. James Anderson	pt. "Providence"	200
	"Ashford"	200
	pt. "Rambles"	200
	"Shepards Fields" a/s "Forrest"	200
Samuell Austin	pt. "Courseys Point" a/s "Smiths Mistake"	22
	pt. "Bishops Outlett"	100
	pt. "Bishops Addition"	100
William All	pt. "Oakenthorpe" – for his son James	100
36:1754:2 ...		
Rebecca Ashbury	pt. "Fox Hill"	28⅓
	pt. "Dispute" a/s "Brotherhood"	15⅔
John Atkinson, Jr.	pt. "Toms Fancy Enlarged"	132
36:1754:3 ...		
Mr. Philemon Charles Blake	"Blakeford"	555
	pt. "Loyds Meadows & Loyds Meadows Addition"	570
	"Bennetts Regulation"	1306
Mrs. Sarah Blake (cnp)	"Russendale" – for h/o John Blake	250
	"Coursey" – for h/o John Blake	250
	"Hoggs Hole" – for h/o John Blake	100
	"Jenkins's Neck" – for h/o John Blake	250
	"Cold Harbour" – for h/o John Blake	100
	"Sayers Forrest" – for h/o John Blake	2250
	"Gore" – for h/o John Blake	175

	"Jacksons Choice" – for h/o John Blake	100
	"Wading Place" – for h/o John Blake	1000
	"Burton Upon Walsey" – for h/o John Blake	388
	pt. "Neglect" – for h/o John Blake	440
	"Ulthorpe" – for h/o John Blake	100
	"Wrights Chance" – for h/o John Blake	124
	pt. "Broomley Lambeth" – for h/o John Blake	1503
John Burk s/o Thomas	pt. "Dawsons Neck"	172
	"Falconars Lott"	50
Hannah Baynard (widow)	"Baynards Large Range Addition"	505
	pt. "Pitts Vineyard"	166⅔
	"Joans Placket"	100
	"Vineyard Addition"	28½
	"Baynards Chance"	54
William Banning	pt. "Golden Lyon"	100
	"Clarks Venture"	35
	"Bannings Discovery"	48
Mr. George Baynard	pt. "Relief"	500
	pt. "Hawkins Pharsalia" & pt. "Relief"	185
	"Baynards Pasture"	202
	"Roes Chance"	247
	"Hogg Harbour"	125
36:1754:4 ...		
Margarett Banning	"Bells Venture" – for h/o John Banning	50
	"Purnalls Addition" – for h/o John Banning	300
	"Widows Choice" – for h/o John Banning	83
Thomas Bostick	"Hinsleys Fancy"	50
	"Bosticks Chance"	50
	"Addition"	100
Charles Bradley	"Aylers Hope"	100
James Blades	"Goodwill"	50
John Baggs	"Hazard"	50
	pt. "Controversey"	22
Thomas Baggs	pt. "Old Town"	60
	"Chance Hitt"	50
	"Hunters Hope"	50

Henry Burt	"Burts Fancy"	50
	"Burts Delight"	100
	"Dogwood Ridge"	100
	"Elisbury"	33
Jacob Boone	"Boones Park"	240
	"Boones Hazard"	120
	"Boones Struggle"	30
	"Boones Hazard Addition"	46
	pt. "Brandfield" & pt. "Sayers Addition" – for his wife (N) w/o James Andrew	120
36:1754:5 ...		
Isaac Boone	pt. "Haddin"	200
	"Boones Venture"	130
Joseph Boone	pt. "Boones Pleasure"	160
	"Boones Addition"	39
Abraham Boone	pt. "Boones Pleasure"	90
	"Boones Covitt"	75
Moses Boone	pt. "Garden of Roses"	200
	pt. "Haddin"	40
Benjamin Boone	pt. "Oakridge"	175
	pt. "Garden of Roses"	177¾
James Barwick	pt. "Oakenthorpe"	185
William Bolton	pt. "Spread Eagle" – for his wife	100
	pt. "Carman & Burton" – for his wife	75
	"Littleworth" – for his wife	100
John Bolton	pt. "Tully's Delight"	100
Thomas Baily s/o Jacob	pt. "Todley"	187
36:1754:6 ...		
Thomas Baily	pt. "Baily's Delight on Resurvey"	156
Thomas Peacock Betts	pt. "Providence"	200
	"Come by Chance"	50
Mr. James Brown	pt. "Hambletons Hermitage"	33⅓
	"Ripley Resurveyed"	265
Robert Basnett	pt. "Mannahs Chance" – for h/o Timothy Mannah	100
Nicholas Broadaway (cnp)	pt. "White Hall"	82
	pt. "Collington"	100

Queen Anne's County - 1754

	pt. "Notlars Desire"	38
	pt. "Carman & Burton"	75
Katherine Buckley (widow)	pt. "Buckleys Delight"	16⅔
John Buck, Esq.	2 lots in Ogle Town	2
	pt. "Poplar Hill"	100
Charles Bermingham	"Berminghams Fortune"	100
Francis Bright	"Stoopley Gibson"	200
	"Brights Island"	28
Samuel Blunt	pt. "Blunts Marsh" a/s "Great Neck"	110
36:1754:7 ...		
Robert Blunt	pt. "Blunts Marsh" a/s "Great Neck"	220
	"Copartnership"	373
	pt. "Parsons Point"	400
Thomas Benton	pt. "Pentrogay"	186
	"Pentrovay"	50
Thomas Barnes	pt. "Barnes Satisfaction"	223
Edward Brown	pt. "Pascos Lott" – for h/o John Griffith	50
	pt. "Eastern Island" – for h/o John Griffith	25
	pt. "Addition" – for h/o John Griffith	90
	pt. "Primus" – for h/o John Griffith	48
	pt. "Bonadventure" – for h/o John Griffith	37½
	pt. "Rotterdam" – for h/o John Griffith	25
	pt. "Tullys Delight"	107
	<n/g> lots in Ogle Town – from John Hawkins	<n/g>
	"Sadlers Chance" – for h/o James Sadler	87½
Vincent Benton	pt. "Contention"	50
	"Bentons Hazard"	87
George Burroughs	"Georges Hazard"	50
William Barkhust	"Pensylvania Border"	50
	pt. "Golden Ridge"	80
James Baily	pt. "Cleaves's Ramble"	120
	"Bailys Addition"	70
	"Tryangle"	50
36:1754:8 ...		
William Baxter (cnp)	pt. "Parsons Neck" – as guardian for Thomas Price	60
	pt. "Pascos Lott" – as guardian for Thomas Price	50

	pt. "Eastern Island" – as guardian for Thomas Price	25
	pt. "Addition" – as guardian for Thomas Price	90
	pt. "Primus" – as guardian for Thomas Price	48
	pt. "Bonadventure" – as guardian for Thomas Price	37½
	pt. "Rotterdam" – as guardian for Thomas Price	25
	"Upper Blunt Point Resurveyed"	324
Sweatnam Burn	pt. "Royston"	525
Nathan Baynard	pt. "Reliefe"	476
h/o James Boone	pt. "Hadden"	160
	pt. "Garden of Roses"	48
Mr. Charles Brown	"Meaguholm"	608
	pt. "Bennetts Choice"	1180
	pt. "Neglect"	100
	"Halls Discovery"	150
	"Burks Expectation"	150
	"Butlers Own Resurveyed"	164
	"Piney Swamp Tract"	50
	"Canaan"	50
	"Alder Branch"	100
	"Watry Plains"	50
	pt. "Long Marsh Ridge Enlarged"	33½
	"Hobbs Venture"	281
	"Hope Resurveyed"	312
George Burroughs, Thomas, & John	"Buck Road"	100
36:1754:9 ...		
William Banckes	pt. "Pitts's Vineyard"	166⅔
	"Godfreys Folly"	50
	pt. "Pockety Ridge" & pt. "Jumps Chance"	126
	"Hunters Chance"	100
	"Backs's Addition"	665
	"Aylers Outlett"	97
	"James's Park"	50
	"Bancks's Delight"	773½
	pt. "Jumps Chance"	50

Queen Anne's County - 1754

Edward Brown, Jr. (KI)	pt. "Sillen"	100
	pt. "Belcher"	100
Thomas Butler	pt. "Chesterfield"	200
	pt. "Tryangle"	25
Mr. John Brown	pt. "Hambletons Hermitage"	33⅓
	"Sedge Harbour"	167
	"Huntley"	251
Thomas Burroughs	"Scottons Inclosure"	55
Mr. John Bracco	"Braco"	393
	"Bracco Addition"	98¾
	"Rattle Snake Ridge"	151
	pt. "Long Marsh Ridge Enlarged"	724
John Bostick	"Haysil Point"	75
36:1754:10 ...		
Samuell Blunt, Jr.	pt. "Fox Harbour"	50
	pt. "Bishopton" – for Nicholas Clouds s/o Richard	32
	pt. "Notlars Desire" – for Nicholas Clouds s/o Richard	80
	pt. "Brotherhood" – for Nicholas Clouds s/o Richard	45
Hannah Burroughs	pt. "Adventure"	50
William Bennett	"Bennetts Chance"	281
	"Lambdens Adventure"	100
Nathaniel Brown	pt. "Sillen"	66⅔
Turbutt Betten	pt. "Waltham"	21
	pt. "Wilkinsons Addition"	45
Robert Broady	pt. "Henrys Lott"	50
	"Roberts Outlett"	150
James Butler	pt. "Fox Hill"	85
	pt. "Notlars Delight"	37
Edward Brown (Chester)	pt. "Brampton"	124
Charles Baker	pt. "Salisbury Plains"	100
36:1754:11 ...		
John Barwick	"Jumps Choice"	97½
h/o William Bishop	"Parson's Neck"	64
36:1754:12 ...		

Anne Carradine	pt. "Forlorne Hope"	50
	pt. "Batchelors Plains"	200
Mr. William Campbell	pt. "Ditteridge"	166
	pt. "Anthorpe"	197
	pt. "Hambletons Hermitage"	250
	pt. "Bishopton"	68
	"Walkers Square"	300
	pt. "Davis's Range"	185
	pt. "Reason"	74
	pt. "Loyds Meadows"	66
	pt. "Anthorpe"	203
	"Churnells Neck"	200
	"Adventure" – from (N) Primrose	30
	pt. "Hambletons Hermitage" – from (N) Primrose	150
h/o or devisees of Rev. Mr. James Cox	"Denby Resurveyed"	275
	"Discovery"	100
	pt. "Adventure Resurveyed"	124
	pt. "Bridge North"	100
John Clemments	pt. "Edmondsons Green Close"	200
	pt. "Smiths Ridge"	100
Mr. Christopher Cox	pt. "Smiths Ridge"	300
	pt. "Prophecy"	217
	pt. "Heaths Discovery"	23
	pt. "Adventure"	39
	"Cox's Necessity"	½
	pt. "Partnership"	500
	"Plain Dealing Resurveyed"	350
	pt. "Lowes Arcadia"	233⅓
36:1754:13 ...		
Mr. John Coursey	½ "Reward"	200
	½ "Macklys Addition"	18
Mr. William Coursey (cnp)	"Cheston"	800
	pt. "Coursey Upon Wye"	290
	"Lords Gift"	1050
	pt. "Smeath"	25
	"Sleeford"	200

		"Shepherds Hook"	200
		pt. "Solomons Fancy"	50
James Clayland		pt. "Costins Park" – for h/o James Costin	279
John Cooper, Jr.		pt. "Kearys Discovery"	60
		"Grimes's Folly"	40
Matthew Chilton		"New Cunningham"	100
Richard Costin		"Newington"	80
		"Newington Addition"	50
		pt. "Carters Forrest"	22
		pt. "Toms Fancy Enlarged"	100
h/o John Croney		pt. "Coldraine"	75
John Cahal		pt. "Wheatleys" a/s "Daniels Fields" – for h/o Edward Cahal	60
36:1754:14 ...			
John Cooper		"Taylors Chance"	200
James Countice		pt. "Dublin"	150
John Culbreth		"Poplar Neck"	200
		pt. "Solomons Lott Addition"	35
		"Holly Neck Resurveyed"	415
		"Pearsons Delight" – for his daughter Mary	80
h/o Richard Chance		pt. "Boones Hope"	50
		"Littleworth"	100
		"Bear Point"	200
		"Littleworth Addition"	50
		pt. "Garden of Roses"	22¼
Henry Council		pt. "Hawkins Pharsalia"	162
John Collins, Jr.		pt. "Tottingham"	200
		pt. "Hackers Meadows"	100
William Cannon		pt. "Content"	100
Thomas Coleman		pt. "Tilghmans Discovery"	80
36:1754:15 ...			
John Commegys		pt. "Shepherds Forrest"	173
		pt. "Shepherds Redoubt"	200
John Clothier		"Clothiers Pharsalia"	150
		pt. "Hinesleys Plains"	64

Queen Anne's County - 1754

Robert Certain	"Jones's Delight"	200
	pt. "Levells" – for Margaret Collins	170
Mr. William Carmichall	pt. "Park"	500
	pt. "Allens Neck"	117
	pt. "Partnership"	36
	"Hannonton"	304
	"Allens Neck Outlett"	18¾
	pt. "Bennetts Choice"	212
	pt. "Stagwell"	526
	"Stagwell Addition"	129
Nicholas Clouds	pt. "Broad Creek Resurveyed"	200
Charles Conner	pt. "Woodward Thickett"	205
Richard Carter	pt. "Copartnership"	52
	pt. "Jones's Plott"	45
	pt. "Dunns Hazard"	75
	pt. "Carters Addition"	25
	pt. "Chance"	25
	pt. "Barnes Satisfaction"	50
Jacob Carter	"Oar Mine"	200
	pt. "Coppidges Range"	30
36:1754:16 ...		
Henry Carter	"Mattapax Neck"	98
Phillip Coppidge	"Indian Spring"	100
	pt. "Slaughterton"	200
h/o Henry Culley	pt. "Poplar Hill"	27
	5 lots in Kings Town – No. 1, No. 12, No. 13, No. 24, No. 25	5
Mr. Henry Casson	pt. "Large Range Addition"	124
	"Mistake"	20
	"Jumps Claims"	80
	pt. "Dudleys Desire"	100
	"Cassons Meadows"	490
	"Silvesters Discovery"	241
	"Mistakes Addition"	27
	pt. "Jumps Chance"	135

Nathaniel Cleave	"Mangy Pokey"	100
	"Troy"	100
	"Pocoyes Addition"	62
	"Wells's Park" – for his wife	110
Mr. William Clayton	"Prous's Park"	300
	pt. "Tryangle"	25
	"Winter House"	50
	"Hogg Pen Neck"	55
	"Hogg Hole"	50
	pt. "Bishopfields"	350
	"Claytons Chesterfields"	92
	"Chesterfield"	200
	"Claytons Landing"	20
	"Forrest"	100
James Clough	"Cloughs Fancy"	50
	"Cloughs Rambles"	100
36:1754:17 ...		
Richard Cook	pt. "Partnership"	20
Benjamin Covington	pt. "Toms Fancy Enlarged"	100
Mr. Edward Clayton	"Chesterfield Addition"	70
	pt. "Neglect"	200
	pt. "Park"	146
	pt. "Broad Neck"	100
John Covington	pt. "Providence"	100
	"Rowlands Hazard"	257
Elizabeth Coleman	pt. "Royston"	50
Robert Cooper	pt. "Peale Place"	32
	"Nimrods Pleasure"	100
William Covington	"Covingtons Necessity"	140
Sharpless Cooper	"Hills Outlett Resurveyed"	233
Nathaniel Curtice	pt. "Sarahs Fancy"	112
Henry Covington	"Rachels Desire"	508
	pt. "Hemsleys Plains"	140
36:1754:18 ...		
Charles Cockey (cnp)	pt. "Slaughterton" – for h/o John Elliott	100
	"Matthews Enlargement" – for h/o John Elliott	155

		pt. "Hogg Pen Neck", "Grose Hill", & pt. "Ridge"	95
Henry Council, Jr.		"Swine Range"	30
		"Widows Folly"	70
		pt. "Friendship"	25
		pt. "Friendship" – from (N) Atkinson	50
h/o Hercules Cook		pt. "Sandishwoods"	335
John Chaires		pt. "Wrenches Farme"	200
Thomas Carradine		"Commagys Hazard"	100
Benjamin Chaires		pt. "Warplesdon Addition" & pt. "Solomons Friendship"	100
Mr. John Council		"Hogg Pen Ridge"	150
John & Gias Bartus Comegys		"Salem"	360
Mr. Henry Callister		pt. "Crumpton"	200
		pt. "Sandy Hinst"	216
Daniel Cox		pt. "Coleraine"	525
36:1754:19 ...			
James & John Clayland		"Claylands Part of Trustram"	300
Anthony Cox		"Cox's Desire"	100
Elizabeth Clift		pt. "Stephens Fields" – for h/o Henry Clift	278
Mrs. Elizabeth Carter		pt. "Ridge"	62⅓
		pt. "Crawford" – for h/o Robert Willson	216
Mrs. Mary Cockey		pt. "Hogg Pen Neck", "Goose Hill", & pt. "Ridge"	95
Joseph Chaires		pt. "Lantley"	125
Martha Cohee		"Cohees Desire" – for h/o James Cohee	100
Mary Clough		"Cloughs Hope" – for h/o Nathaniel Clough	50
		pt. "Boones Hope" – by name of "Broom Hope", for h/o Nathaniel Clough	50
Dennis Carey		pt. "Coleraine" – for h/o John Burk	148
		"Locks Point" – for h/o John Burk	50
		pt. "Bennetts Out Lott" – for h/o John Burk, from Charles Seth	75
Joshua Clark		pt. "Lyford"	287
		pt. "Stephens Fields"	412
36:1754:20 ...			
Edward Cockey		pt. "Hogg Pen Neck", "Goose Hill", & pt. "Ridge"	95
George Cope		"Dennys Range"	100
William Curtis		"Curtices Lott"	50

William Countice	pt. "Dublin"	150
James Cassey	pt. "Connoway"	289
Edward Cahall	pt. "Hackton" – for his wife	50
James Callaghane	pt. "Hemsleys Arcadia"	70
William Croney	pt. "Colerain"	75
Francis Clymer	pt. "Shadwells Addition"	50
36:1754:21	**<blank>**	
36:1754:22	**...**	
Mr. John Downes, Jr.	"Wrights Plains"	100
	pt. "Wrights Reserve"	200
	"Wrights Reserve Addition"	50
	pt. "Security"	60
	pt. "Smeath"	106
	pt. "Stagwell"	42
	"Downes's Chance"	100
	pt. "Smeath on Resurvey" – for h/o John Beck	412
	pt. "Smeath on Resurvey" – for h/o John Beck, from (N) Barber	50
	pt. "Smeath on Resurvey" – for h/o John Beck, from (N) Hynson	175
Mr. William Dawson	pt. "Trustram"	300
Mrs. Henrietta Maria Dulany	"Loyds Insula"	1795
	"Purchase"	1000
	pt. "Willenlew"	682
	pt. "Brandfield"	228
	½ "Skinners Expectation"	240
Mr. Charles Downes	pt. "Fairplay"	116
	pt. "Macklinborough"	199
	"Highgate"	50
	pt. "Wrenches Adventure"	87
	"Mount Moluck" – for Charles Clayton	150
Thomas Dockery	pt. "Fishingham"	100
John Davis	pt. "Confusion"	220
	"Peters Lott"	150
	pt. "Content"	70

Matthew Dockery	pt. "Fishingham"	100
	"Fishingham Addition"	13
	"Matthews Fancy"	82
	"Dangerfield"	200
36:1754:23 ...		
Mr. John Downes	pt. "Nobles Range" & pt. "Hemsley Arcadia"	192
	pt. "Carters Forrest"	22
Mr. Hawkins Downes	pt. "Millford"	150
	pt. "Parkers Freshes"	87
	"Porters Folly"	100
	pt. "Millford" – from Richard Ragan	50
Mrs. Catherine Davis	"Clarkson Hill"	150
	"Clarkson Hill Addition"	80
Mr. Abner Dudley	"Sarahs Portion"	300
Mr. Henry Downes	pt. "Carters Forrest"	114
John Deford	"Chance"	284
Valentine Downey	"Pig Quarter Neck" – in corn	100
William Dockery	pt. "Hawkins's Farme"	8
	pt. "Moores Hope Addition"	20
William Durding	pt. "Powells Fancy"	50
Benjamin Denny	"Wootters's Choice"	100
	"Wootters's Choice Addition"	75
	"Outlett"	68
36:1754:24 ...		
h/o Dick (Negro)	pt. "Knowles's Range"	244
Hynson Downes	"Shore Ditch"	150
John Downes s/o John	"Downes's Chance"	150
James Downes	pt. "Nobles Range" & pt. "Hemsleys Arcadia"	100
Joseph Dodd	"Jamaica Addition"	50
	pt. "Jamaica"	59
Jacob Dodd	pt. "Rye Hall" – for George Ayres	184
John Duffey	"Batchelors Adventure" – for his wife	150
	"Storeys Park" – for his wife	100
Mrs. Rachel Duhamill	"Hynsons Lott"	199
	"Timber Swamp"	200

Mrs. Mary Dyre	pt. "Waltham"	16⅔
	pt. "Wilkinsons Addition"	16⅔
MM Phillip Davis, John Davis, & David Davis	"Partnership"	300
Thomas Davis	"Addy House"	68
36:1754:25 ...		
Thomas Doyle	pt. "Batchelors Hope"	20
	pt. "Neglect"	16⅓
	"Marshy Crook" – for Charles Brown (minor) s/o John	100
Lewis & Lewis Derochbrune, Jr.	"Friendship Resurveyed"	396
John Derochbrune	"Vaughans Kindness"	200
Lewis Derochbrune, Jr.	"Josephs Addition" – for his brother Joseph (minor)	60
Daniell Dulany	pt. "Vaughans Kindness"	200
Thomas Doyle (see above)	"Wexford"	100
36:1754:26 <blank>		
36:1754:27 ...		
John Emory, Jr.	"Emorys Resurvey"	537¾
Arthur Emory	"Welch Ridge"	500
	"Haphazard"	116
	"Haphazard Addition"	50
	"Moores Hope"	100
	pt. "Moores Hope Addition"	208
John Emory	"Emory's Chance"	110
	"Bee Tree"	500
	pt. "Partnership" – surveyed for John Emory	165
	pt. "Powells Fancy"	90
	"Batchelors Chance Resurveyed"	253
	"Hap Hazard"	17
	"Bee Tree Swamp"	76
Sarah Emory	pt. "Partnership" – surveyed for (N) Beck	100
William Elbert	½ "Reward"	200
	½ "Macklins Addition"	18
	"Lewis's Chance"	50
	pt. "Lambeth"	100

John Emerson	pt. "Addition"	100
Mary Eagle	"Lambeth Addition" – for h/o William	170
Benjamin Eadsworth	pt. "Brandfield & Sayers Addition" – for h/o John Willson	200
William Ewbanks	pt. "Ratcliffe"	140
36:1754:28 ...		
devisees of John Earle	pt. "Upperheathworth"	167
	"Heathworth"	533
John Errickson	pt. "Sarahs Portion"	96
William Elliott (KI)	"Forlorne Hope"	100
	"Elliotts Choice"	120
John Elliott, Jr.	pt. "Copartnership" – for h/o William Price	52
	pt. "Jones's Plott" – for h/o William Price	45
	pt. "Dunns Hazard" – for h/o William Price	75
	pt. "Carters Addition" – for h/o William Price	25
	pt. "Chance" – for h/o William Price	25
	pt. "Barnes's Satisfaction"	50
Joseph Elliott	pt. "Slaughterton"	100
	pt. "Williams Lott"	10
	"Newnams Hermitage"	50
	pt. "Sallisbury Plains"	100
	pt. "Sayers Range"	60
	pt. "Lowes Desire"	53
Elizabeth Errickson (widow)	pt. "Sarah's Portion"	54
	"Johnsons Lott" – escheat	46
Charles Errickson	"Stinton Errickson"	200
Richard Tilghman Earle	"Earles Beginning"	517
Lawrence Everitt	"Hunters Forrest"	200
	"Everitts Content"	100
36:1754:29 ...		
Michael Earle	"Emorys Fortune Addition"	270
	pt. "Partnership" – surveyed for (N) Emory	175
	pt. "Golden Grove"	20
Thomas Emory	"Emory Paxton"	100
	pt. "Partnership" – surveyed for (N) Beck	150
Rebeccah Elliott	pt. "Slaughterton"	100

Gidion Emory	pt. "Fortune"	90
	pt. "St. Pauls"	50
	pt. "Carmons Neck"	50
	pt. "McConnikins Fortune"	236
	pt. "McConnikins Fortune" – for his wife	143
	pt. "Woodridge" – for his wife	184
James Emory	pt. "Trustram"	196
Arthur Emory s/o John	pt. "Partnership" – surveyed for (N) Beck	90
	pt. "Partnership" – surveyed for (N) Emory	10
Joseph Elliott s/o George	"Clouds's Hermitage"	200
Tabitha Elliott	"Rawlings Chance" – for h/o William Elliott (Island Hundred)	100
Sarah Elston – devisee of Roger	1 lot in Kings Town – No. 7	1
36:1754:30 ...		
Thomas Emory s/o John	"Roberts Range"	150
	"Roberts Range Addition"	37
Joseph Everitt (Choptank)	"Roes Desire" – for h/o Thomas Roe	50
George Elliott	"Elliotts Luck"	125
George Edwards	"Edwards's Chance"	50
Henry Ellors	pt. "Smiths Range" – for his wife (N) daughter of Maurice McCarty	239
36:1754:31 ...		
Burton Francis Falconar & John	"Chesnutt Ridge"	200
Francis Foreman	pt. "Royston"	600
John Fouracres	pt. "Tullys Lott"	100
Winnefred Ford	pt. "Ashton" – for h/o William	142½
36:1754:32 ...		
Isaac Ford	pt. "Ashton"	82½
Andrew Finley	pt. "Rambles"	150
William Fisher	pt. "Large Range"	416⅔
	pt. "Codshead Manor"	384
Henry Feddeman	pt. "Hacketts Garden"	200
	pt. "Hacketts Garden" – more	400
	pt. "Long Range" – from W. Thomas	10
	pt. "Brandfield" – from (N) Willson	200

James Finley (wheelright)	pt. "Warplesdon Addition" & pt. "Solomons Friendship"	50
	"Nathan & Thomas's Beginning"	27
John Fisher	pt. "Suffolk"	300
Thomas Fisher	pt. "Suffolk"	300
	"Fishers Plains"	164
James Fisher	pt. "Fishers Meadows"	167
w/o Thomas Fisher	pt. "Fishers Meadows" – during her life, then to son Richard	167
36:1754:33 ...		
William Gregory	pt. "Benjamins Infancy" – take off	50
John Green	"Greens Adventure Upon Carpenters Square Resurveyed"	212
William Greenwood	"Miss Hitt" – for h/o Stephen Rich	250
Matthew Griffith	pt. "Park"	220
Benjamin Griffith	pt. "Park"	220
36:1754:34 ...		
Edward Garrett	"Sandy Hill"	50
Edward Godwin	pt. "White Marsh Addition"	338
	pt. "Parker Freshes"	8⅓
Michael Green	"Costins Hope"	200
William Godwin	pt. "Wrights Chance" a/s "Choice"	100
Richard Gould	pt. "Ripley"	266⅔
	pt. "Spread Eagle"	75
Mrs. Frances Gould	"Spring Branch"	100
	pt. "Ripley"	133⅓
	pt. "Sewells Fork"	500
Charles Gafford	"Macklins Beginning"	141
Charles Gafford, Jr.	pt. "Macklins Beginning"	118
	pt. "Smithfield"	40
Richard Gafford	pt. "Macklins Beginning"	141
	pt. "Smithfield"	10
36:1754:35 ...		
Marmaduke Goodhand (cnp)	pt. "Sillen"	200
	pt. "Point Love"	200
	"Broad Oak"	500
	"Poplar Neck"	300

Queen Anne's County - 1754

	pt. "Sillen" – more, for Nathaniel Brown	33⅓
	pt. "Woodyard Thickett" – for his wife	205
Philemon Green	"Greens Fortune"	80
	"Greens Fortune Addition"	75
	"St. Jones's Forrest"	100
	"Pratts Hope" – for Robert Pratt (minor)	100
Matthew Graves	"Graves's Beginning"	50
James Gould	pt. "Goulds Purchase"	195
William Green	"Bradford"	100
h/o John Granger	pt. "Conners Neck"	100
Elizabeth Gwinn	"Gunners Harbour" – for h/o John Gwin	100
Benjamin Gould	pt. "Camberwell"	100
Anne Gilbert	pt. "Isaac's Chance"	100
Boatswain Tom, Hannah, & Bess Gibbs (Negroes)	pt. "Killmanam Plains"	200
36:1754:36 <blank>		
36:1754:37 ...		
John Higgens	pt. "Dungarron"	150
Edward Hall	pt. "Vaughans Discovery" – for his wife Ellinor	100
	pt. "Hogg Harbour" – for his wife Ellinor	73¼
John Hall	pt. "Welch Poole" – for his wife	100
	pt. "Dancey"	300
	pt. "Hogg Harbour"	219¾
John Hill	"Green Hill"	100
William Hopper (cnp)	pt. "Chesterfield"	900
	pt. "Providence"	200
	"Bridge Water"	300
	pt. "Guilford"	200
	"Darkin"	210
	pt. "Courseys Point" or "Smiths Mistake"	200
	"Hoppers Industry"	213¼
	pt. "Smiths Mistake"	275
	pt. "Conquest"	256
	pt. "Green Spring"	100
	pt. "Camberwell"	300
	"Stephney"	300

Robert Hardcastle	"Dockeys Discovery"	73
	"Mount Hope"	150
	"Enewell"	164
h/o Joseph Hunter	"Jumps Lott"	50
	"Hunters Hazard"	50
	"Boones Ridge"	50
36:1754:38 ...		
William Harrington	pt. "Josephs Lott"	100
	pt. "Henrys Lott"	25
h/o David Harrington	"Hopewell"	100
	"Harringtons Desire"	50
	"Buck Bay"	100
	pt. "Beaver Dams"	50
Richard Harrington	"Solomons Lott"	100
	pt. "Solomons Lott Addition"	15
Richard Hynson	"Annes Portion"	150
Thomas Honey	"Spakes's Outlett"	114
Joseph Harriss	pt. "Crumps Chance"	50
Valentine Thomas Honey	pt. "Adventure"	100
	"Sparks's Own" – for h/o George Sparks	25
James Harriss	pt. "Crumps Chance"	50
	pt. "Toms Fancy Enlarg'd" – for his wife Rebecca	75
Mrs. Sarah Hollyday	"Readbourn Rectified" – for h/o James Hollyday	1440
	pt. "Macklinborough" – for h/o James Hollyday	114
36:1754:39 ...		
John Hambleton	pt. "Wrights Chance" a/s "Choice"	30
	pt. "Wrights Neglect"	50
	"Hambletons Range"	100
	"Mary Ann's Lott"	100
	"Hambletons Addition"	50
John Hollinsworth, Jr.	"Good Increase" – for h/o Thomas Crupper	200
Mary Hackett	pt. "Prices Hill" – for h/o John Hackett	200
Thomas Hackett	pt. "Prices Hill"	100
	pt. "Scotland"	50
	pt. "Providence"	330
	pt. "Shepherds Fortune" – for his wife	150

h/o John Harris	pt. "Contention"	150
	"Kilkenny"	200
John Hollinsworth	pt. "Hambletons Hermetage"	33⅓
Sarah Hollinsworth	"Refuge"	100
John Hadley	"Skinners Pleasure"	50
James Hutchins	"Wrights Fortune"	120
	pt. "Condone"	316
36:1754:40 ...		
Thomas Hutchins	"Castle Towne"	100
Charles Hynes	pt. "Spread Eagle" – for Thomas	33⅓
George Harrington	"Harringtons Venture"	103
Anthony Harrington	pt. "Warners Discovery Resurveyed" – for his wife (N) d/o William Vickers	193
James Hollyday	pt. "Macklinborough"	96
	pt. "Waterford"	18
	pt. "Macklin Borough" – from Edward Browne	134
James Harvey	"Harveys Discovery"	170
	pt. "Gould Hawks Enlargement"	35
James Hammond	pt. "Wrenches Adventure"	192
William Hopper & Christopher Cox	pt. "Jamaica"	1
Nathan Harrington	"Beaverdams Addition"	150
Robert Hawkins	pt. "Macklin Borough"	175
	pt. "Tullys Delight"	293
William Hunter	pt. "Chesnutt Meadow" – for Henry Price Williams	100
36:1754:41 ...		
Thomas Hamer	"Hamers Choice"	178
	pt. "White Hall" – for his wife	18
	pt. "Ratcliffs Part of Loyds Freshes"	19
Nathaniel Harrington	"Jadwins Folley"	44
John Higgins & James Sullyvant	pt. "Salsbury"	200
William & Thomas Hughlett	"Bakers Plains"	600
Matthew Hawkins	"Tullys Delight"	200
Andrew Hall	pt. "Spread Eagle"	184
John Holding (cnp)	"Nicholsons Fancy"	50
	pt. "Woodhouse"	61

	pt. "Woodhouse Addition"	14
William Horn	"Walnutt Neck Resurveyed" – for his wife	109
	"Barron Ridge" – for his wife	100
36:1754:42 ...		
Giles & James Hicks	pt. "Edmonsons Green Close"	200
MM Robert Hawkins & (N) Kelly (KE) in right of their wives (N) daughters & coheirs of Henry Jacobs	pt. "Sprigley"	300
	½ "Winchester"	125
Anna Maria Hemsley	"Hardest Fendoff"	150
h/o Mary Hemsley	"Towton Fields Addition"	140
	"Hemsleys Discovery"	91
Anna Maria & Mary Hemsley	pt. "Towton Fields"	400
Thomas Harriss	pt. "Ditteridge"	277
	pt. "Long Neck"	20½
	pt. "Coursey Upon Wye"	258½
	pt. "Reason"	35
	pt. "Mount Mills"	33
	"Standford"	105
	"Lawrences Delight"	100
	"Johnsons Addition"	100
Ernault Hawkins	pt. "Bramton"	126
Giles Hix	pt. "Killeray"	100
36:1754:43 <blank>		
36:1754:44 ...		
Francis Jackson	"Barbarahs Inlett"	263
Thomas Jackson s/o George	pt. "Winchester"	125
	"Barbarahs Choice"	80
	"Lanes Ridge" – for his wife	200
Stephen Jarman	pt. "Hogg Hole"	130
h/o Robert Jerman	"Newport"	284
	pt. "Brandford" – from William Diggs	211
John Jerman	pt. "St. Martins"	82
	pt. "Inclosure"	81
Joseph Jerman	pt. "Brandford"	140
Handcock Jones	pt. "Deluge"	80

Henry Jones	pt. "Nobles Range"	58
	pt. "Deluge"	50
William Jones	pt. "Deluge"	50
	"Jones's Chance"	100
devisees of James Jordan	pt. "Cold Raine"	216
36:1754:45 ...		
Mary Jadwin	pt. "Lyford" – for Robert Jadwin	70
Thomas Jumpe	"Horse Pasture"	200
	pt. "Jumps Chance"	100
Jeremiah Jadwin	"Timms Neglect"	50
	"Jadwins Project"	40
	"Cow Range"	100
Solomon Jumpe	pt. "Pocketty Ridge" pt. "Jump Chance"	89
	"Jumps Addition"	49
Edward Jones	"Beverdam Fork"	100
	"Hopewell"	100
	"Fords Parks"	30
	"Fords Folley"	20
	"Jones's Greenwood" – for his son William Kerby Jones	150
	"Jones's Safety"	59
	"Notingam"	89
Dorothy Isgate	"Fork"	200
John Johnson	"Cloudent"	200
	pt. "Notlars Delight"	80
Thomas Jackson	"Hopewell"	50
	"Nicholsons Chance"	50
William Joyner, Jr.	pt. "Parsons Neck"	60
36:1754:46 ...		
Jonathan Jolly	"Endeavour"	50
	"Nicholsons Adventure"	50
	"Burton"	50
	"Lester"	50
	"Lester Meadows"	50
Dr. John Jackson (cnp)	pt. "Providence"	213
	"Smithfield Addition"	327¼

	pt. "Lexton"	184
	pt. "Jamaica"	40
	pt. "Adventure Resurveyed"	27
Amos Jerman	"Blanford" a/s "Branford"	37
Thomas Jumpe, Jr.	"Jumps Lott"	34
Thomas Jones	"Sarahs Portion"	50
Inhabitants of Queen Anne's County	"Pierce Land" – whereon is Well's Warehouse	½
Joseph Jackson s/o Francis	pt. "Jasper's Lott"	200
James Jones	"Jones's Fancey"	100
Archebald Jackson	"Nodd"	113
	"Speedy Contract"	10
	pt. "Ratcliffe"	300
Anne Jolley	"Andever Meadows" tbc Thomas Roe (f. 113)	175
36:1754:47 ...		
h/o Richard Kieran	pt. "Confusion"	100
Nathaniel Knotts	"Knotts Addition"	50
	"Knotts Range"	235
	"Knotts Chance"	53
	"Turners Plains Addition" – for w/o & h/o James Bell	120
James Kentin	"Grevely Hoe"	150
	pt. "Upland"	100
36:1754:48 ...		
Solomon Kentin	"Upland"	200
	"Upland Addition"	50
James Kersey	pt. "Scotland"	100
Baldwin Kemp	pt. "Emorys Rich Land"	150
	pt. "Hinesleys Plains"	91
h/o James Knotts	pt. "Releaf"	55
	pt. "Emorys Rich Land"	95
	"Knotts's Chance"	302
William Kent	pt. "Toms Fancy Enlarged"	150
Thomas Kersey	pt. "Scotland"	50
h/o Walter Kerby	"Kerbys Hardship"	199

Queen Anne's County - 1754

Benjamin Kerby	"Clouds's Chance"	6
	"Bodys Neck"	200
	"Coopers Quarter"	50
	pt. "Sillen" – for h/o John Evans & Andrew Price	200
	pt. "Upper Deal" – for h/o John Evans & Andrew Price	500
James Kelley	pt. "Buckleys Delight" – for his wife	33⅓
Mary Kemp	pt. "Toms Fancy Enlarg'd"	75
h/o Thomas Kemp	pt. "Willinlew"	106
36:1754:49 <blank>		
36:1754:50 …		
Robert Lloyd	"Hemsleys Park" – for devisees of Phill. Hemsley	800
	"Clevefields" – for devisees of Phill. Hemsley	1622
	pt. "Trustram Wells" – for devisees of Phill. Hemsley	68
	"Hemsleys Adventure" – for devisees of Phill. Hemsley	200
	"Tilghmans Gift" – for William Hemsley	650
	"Tilghmans Meadows" – for his wife	270
	"Snodland" – for his wife	284
	"Friendship" – for h/o (N) Hemsley	175
Anne Loyd	pt. "Wrexamplaine" – for h/o Edward Lloyd	140
James London	"Kirkhams Lott"	200
James Lane	pt. "Worley's Outrange"	100
	"Lawes Addition"	175
h/o Joseph Longfellow	"Josephs Hopes"	50
Richard Lambert	pt. "Lowes Arcadia" – for Thomas Phillips s/o David	100
John Legg	pt. "Limrick" pt. "Leggs Beginning"	186
	pt. "Pentroby" – rightly called "Pentrogay"	14
Thomas Lee	pt. "Lee's Chance"	166
	pt. "Stratton"	52
	pt. "Hawkins's Pharsalia"	100
John Lee	pt. "Camberwell"	100
John Leith	"Horsependridge"	100
36:1754:51 …		

Bexley John Lambden	pt. "Swifts Outlett"	48
	pt. "Northumberland"	52
Mary Lane	"Lanes Folly" – for h/o Walter Lane	161
	pt. "Stephens Fields" – for h/o Walter Lane	110
Sarah Linsey	"Jadwins Hazard" – for her son Edward	61
John Legg, Jr.	pt. "Limrick" pt. "Leggs Beginning"	14
	⅓ "Woodland Neck"	16⅔
	⅓ "Oldsons Relief"	33⅓
Alexander Lee	"Knave Standoff"	50
	pt. "Whortons Addition"	19
John Loyd	pt. "Tom's Fancy Enlarg'd"	132
36:1754:52 ...		
Thomas Mooth	pt. "Friendship"	25
	"Watson's Delight"	50
	"Watsons Delight Addition"	30
	"Mooths Range"	105
William Merson	pt. "Middle Plantation"	66⅔
William Mansfield	pt. "Wattham" – in right of his wife	16⅔
	pt. "Wilkinson's Addition" – in right of his wife	16⅔
Rebecca Meeds	pt. "Brandford" – for h/o John Meeds; see f. 141	100
	pt. "Brandford" – from William Diggs for h/o John Meeds	141
William Meeds	pt. "Brandford"	100
	pt. "St. Martins"	100
John Meridith	"Trustram Ridge"	150
Thomas Merydith	pt. "Plain Dealing"	75
	pt. "Adventure"	100
36:1754:53 ...		
Anne Meridith	pt. "Shrewsbury"	150
	"Shrewsbury Addition"	100
	pt. "Middle Plantation"	100
David Mills	1 lot in Kings Town	1
John Mayne	"New London"	150
	"New London Addition"	114
Thomas Martindale (cnp)	pt. "Sylvesters Forrest"	100
	"Martindale's Range"	50

	"Martindales Hope"	316
Mary Merrick	"Merricks Delight" – for h/o Isaac Merrick	50
James Millis	"Campersons Choice" – for Samuel & William Cook (minors) in his care	100
William Winchester Mayson	"Ephraims Hope"	100
	pt. "Winchesters Folly Resurveyed"	273
William Mountague	pt. "Ratcliffe"	140
John Miller	pt. "Oaken Thorpe"	229
	pt. "Providence"	150
36:1754:54 ...		
Thomas Mountsieur	"Hacketts Delight"	150
James Massey	pt. "Friendship" – surveyed for (N) Tilghman	270
	pt. "Friendship" – from (N) Hadley	30
	"Masseys Addition"	23½
Patrick Mooney	⅓ "Nevils Delight"	16⅔
Daniel McConnikin	pt. "Woodridge"	16
	pt. "McConnikins Fortune"	20
	pt. "McConnikins Correar"	150
Thomas Marsh	"Little Thickett"	200
	"Marshes Forbearance"	150
	"Cabbin Neck"	350
	"Neglect"	200
	2 lot in Kings Town – No. 4, No. 5	2
	pt. "Shepherds Fortune"	150
	"Shepherds Fortune" – more	116
	1 lot in King Town – from (N) Maxwell	1
	pt. "Poplar Hill"	200
	"Clouds's Choice"	200
	"Lowthers Chance" – from (N) Swift	150
James McCoy	"Smiths Delight"	218½
	"Maccoy's Pleasure"	129
Thomas Meloy'd	pt. "Toms Fancy Enlarged"	100
Timothy Mannah	pt. "Mannahs Chance Resurveyed"	50
36:1754:55 ...		
Joseph Merchant (cnp)	"Jacks Purchase"	75
	"Musketo Ridge"	50

	"Josephs Own"	31
Thomas McClannahan	pt. "Fox Harbour"	100
	pt. "Collins's Lott"	56
	pt. "Brotherhood"	42½
Samuel McCosh	pt. "Upperheathworth"	88
	pt. "Collins's Refusal"	112
	pt. "Heaths Gift"	53
	pt. "Crumpton"	50
	pt. "Upperheathworth" – more from (N) Ruth	150
	pt. "Lanington"	119
William Matthews apprentice to William Pindar	pt. "Bridge North"	50
Charles Murphy	pt. "Hawkins's Pharsalia"	200
	"Murphys Chance Resurveyed"	99½
James Miller	"Forrest of Windsor"	250
Solomon Mayson	pt. "Winchesters Folly Resurveyed"	133
Richard Mayson	pt. "Winchesters Folly Resurveyed"	133
Henry Mayson	"Maysons Hazard"	192
Abraham McCustalow	"Forkalett"	62
36:1754:56 ...		
Anne Merridith (KI)	pt. "Connors Neck"	60
Abraham Milton	"Crumps Forrest"	150
James Massey, Jr.	pt. "Friendship" – surveyed for (N) Tilghman	50
William Maynor	pt. "Dispute" a/s "Brotherhood" – for h/o (N) Wright	47
	pt. "Dispute" a/s "Brotherhood" – for h/o Edward Wright, Jr.	351
	pt. "Notlars Delight"	33
	pt. "Brotherhood" – more, for h/o Edward Wright	200
John McConnakin	⅓ "Woodland Neck"	16⅔
	⅓ "Oldsons Relief"	33⅓
	"Georges Codd"	100
John Meeds	pt. "Beginning"	150
Thomas Meeds	pt. "Beginning"	150
John Mayson	⅔ "Nevills Delight" – for his wife	33⅓
Samuel Massey	pt. "Poplar Hill"	123
Peter Maxwell	"Hazard"	175

Queen Anne's County - 1754

36:1754:57 ...		
William Meredith (Tully's Neck)	"Meredith's Adventure"	100
36:1754:58 ...		
John Nabb	pt. "Tilghmans Addition"	100
	"Jones's Fortune"	100
	pt. "Adventure"	7
	pt. "Toms Fancy Enlarged"	150
Solomon Newnam	pt. "Williams Lott"	40
William Newnam	"Newnams Chance"	56
	pt. "Johns Meadows"	60
	pt. "Shaver"	107
	"Newnams Addition"	72
	"Addition" – for h/o Joseph Newnam	24
	pt. "Scottons Addition" – for h/o Joseph Newnam	10
	pt. "Johns Meadows" – for h/o Joseph Newnam	40
	"Shearing" – for h/o Joseph Newnam	100
	pt. "Devonishes Chance" – for h/o Joseph Newnam	16¾
Charles Nabb	pt. "Clouds Adventure"	200
	"Elizabeth Portion"	100
Thomas Newton	pt. "Toms Fancy Enlarged"	100
Mr. Edward Neale	pt. "Hawkins's Farme Resurveyed"	12
	pt. "Green Spring"	550
	"Neales's Residence"	899
Mr. Jonathan Nicols	pt. "Hackton"	200
	pt. "Redford"	150
	"Willsons Addition"	70
	pt. "Partnership"	250
	pt. "Partnership" – more	250
36:1754:59 ...		
Nathaniel Newnam	pt. "Shaver"	93
John Nevill s/o Walter	pt. "Barton"	40
	"Smiths Addition"	106
Mr. Charles Nicols	"Jones's Forrest"	500
	pt. "Brandfield" & pt. "Sayers Addition"	50

James William Nabb	pt. "Wrenches Farme" – for his wife	200
	pt. "Moores Hope Addition" – for his wife	172
John Nabb, Jr.	pt. "Batchelors Hope" – for John Brown (minor) s/o John	40
	pt. "Neglect" – for John Brown (minor) s/o John	32⅔
John Nevill s/o John	pt. "Whortons & Pindars Outrange"	75
	pt. "Sewalls Fork"	250
	"Nevills Outrange"	46½
	"Nevills Discovery"	3½
	pt. "Tilghmans Discovery"	200
	"Solomons Outlett"	50
	"Nevills Addition"	144
	"Farrington"	250
36:1754:60 ...		
Samuell Osburn	pt. "Addition"	133⅓
	pt. "Martins Neck Resurveyed"	78
	pt. "Addition" – more	66⅔
John Oldson s/o Henry	pt. "Hawkins's Pharsalia"	100
Abraham Oldson	pt. "Hawkins's Pharsalia"	50
	pt. "Hawkins Farm Resurveyed"	126
36:1754:61 ...		
John Oldson	pt. "Hawkins's Pharsalia"	50
Thomas OBryan	"Pleasant Spring Resurveyed"	418
	4 lots in Ogle Town – No. 22, No. 38, No. 39, No. 59	4
Robert Offley	pt. "Levells"	80
36:1754:62 ...		
William Pryor	"Pryors Chance"	271
Charles Price	"Lincoln"	200
	pt. "Broomley Lambeth"	247
Thomas Price	pt. "Brandford"	106
John Phillips	pt. "Vaughans Discovery"	230
William Pratt	pt. "Chaires's Addition"	54
	"Bucks Forrest"	187
Henry Pratt, Jr.	"Pleasant Park"	100
	"Pleasant Park Addition"	9½

Thomas Purnall	"Dudleys Chance"	200
Mr. Grundy Pemberton	pt. "Dawsons Neck"	142
	pt. "Partnership"	850
	pt. "Hawkins's Pharsalia"	600
	"Pembertons Resurvey"	969
	"Boston Addition"	150
	"Kingsale"	250
	"Kingsale Addition"	100
	"Change"	200
	pt. "Kelds Inheritance"	52
Mr. Vincent Price	"Andrew & Prudences Satisfaction"	696
	pt. "Lambert"	400
36:1754:63 ...		
John Powell	"Longs Desire"	50
	"Powells Fancy"	94
John Pickerin	pt. "Lowes Arcadia" – for his wife	66⅔
John Pondar	pt. "Smiths Delight"	81½
James Pondar s/o Richard	"Pondars Chance"	38
Margarett Pindar	pt. "Bishopton"	250
	pt. "Ashton"	75
	pt. "Collins's Lott"	116
	pt. "Whortons & Pindars Outrange"	67
Mary Perry	"Stafford"	100
Thomas Powell (Choptank)	"Powells Venture"	95½
Martha Primrose	pt. "Shepherds Fortune" – for h/o George Primrose	200
Morgan Pondar	pt. "Spread Eagle" – for his wife	16⅔
John Pratt	pt. "Vaughans Discovery" – for his wife	100
	"Wrights Park"	100
Henry Pollock	pt. "Colne Rectified"	284
36:1754:64 ...		
Mr. Thomas Price s/o Henry	"Goodhap"	126
	"Margaretts Hill"	200
Thomas Price s/o Thomas	pt. "Brandford"	23
	pt. "Conclusion"	64
Robert Pratt	"Pratts Choice"	100
Prudence Primrose	pt. "Kent Lott"	52

George Powell	"Longs Chance"	50
	"Tryangle"	50
William Price (KI)	pt. "Coppidge Range" – for h/o John Carter	190
	"Craney Neck" – for h/o John Carter	160
	pt. "Ridge" – for John Carter (minor)	124⅔
John Price	pt. "Toms Fancy Enlarged"	50
Thomas Price (KI)	pt. "Cloverfields"	100
h/p Thomas Powel (Double Creek)	pt. "Tilghman's Discovery"	1¼
36:1754:65 ...		
Quakers	"Land of Prophecy" – for a Meeting House	3
36:1754:66 ...		
Nathaniel Reed	pt. "Toms Fancy Enlarged"	400
	pt. "Wrights Square" – for his wife	100
Richard Ross	pt. "Coldraine"	125
William Roe	pt. "Dudleys Desire"	100
Benjamin Roe	"Clouds Range"	100
John Roe s/o Thomas	"Downes Forrest"	300
	"Roes Addition"	70
Abner Roe	"Hackers Adventure"	250
	"Abners Outlett"	125
	"Roes Choice"	64
Patrick Robertson	"Tully Barden"	50
	"Tully Bardens Inclosement"	150
Alexander Robertson	"Tully Bardens Addition"	62
	"Peith"	66
Peter Rich	"Bridge Town"	11
	3 lots in Bridge Town - No. 4, No. 5, No. 6	3
36:1754:67 ...		
William Ricketts s/o Edward	pt. "Hensleys Plains"	59
William Robinson	"Duns Lott"	100
	pt. "Elliotts Addition"	50
	pt. "Ridleys Chance"	96½
	pt. "Boltons Delight" & pt. "Parkers Lott" – for Daniel Bolton (minor)	140
James Reed	pt. "Providence"	100

Mr. Benjamin Roberts	pt. "Lowes Desire"	178
	pt. "Sayers Range"	200
	pt. "Shepherds Redoubt"	100
	"Dixons Gift" – for h/o James Roberts	100
	"Roberts Meadows" – for h/o James Roberts	100
	"Watsons Desire" – for h/o James Roberts	50
Francis Rochester	"Watry Plains"	150
	pt. "Tullys Lott"	200
	"Collins's Gift"	175
	pt. "Outrange"	80
	pt. "Ripley"	300
John Rochester	"Winchester"	200
	"John & Rachels Choice"	100
Henry Rochester	"Lowders Hazard"	77
	"Philadelphia"	50
John Railey	"Willsons Begining"	100
	"Raileys Begining"	62
36:1754:68 ...		
William Ridger	"Hope"	50
	"Small Hopes"	50
	"Ridgers Lott"	100
	"Ridgways Chance"	50
Benjamin Richardson	"Pascos Adventure"	150
	"Wading Place"	300
	"Ashburys Addition"	35
	pt. "Cloverfields"	335
David Register	pt. "Conquest"	138
	pt. "Turners Plains Addition"	120
	pt. "Bradburns Delight" a/s "Bailys Delight"	100
	pt. "Boagley"	60
Christopher Ruth	pt. "Chesnutt Meadows"	100
	pt. "Hawkins's Farm Resurveyed" – for h/o Peter Countice	120
	pt. "Conclusion"	86
	pt. "Baynards Pasture"	37
Thomas Robinson	pt. "Wrights Chance" a/s "Choice"	100

Queen Anne's County - 1754

Samuell Roe	pt. "Oakenthorp"	164
	"Tullys Addition"	300
	"Nedds Begining"	30
	"Roes Lane"	22
	pt. "Sarahs Fancy"	50
William Reed	"Newnothingham Rectified" – for his wife	169
Thomas Richardson Roe	pt. "Oakenthorpe"	226
	pt. "Sarahs Fancy"	30
36:1754:69 ...		
James Roe	"Begining"	85
	pt. "Sarahs Fancy"	540
William Ridgeway, Jr.	"Plain Dealing" – for h/o William Ferrell	100
John Roe s/o Edward	pt. "Narborough"	250
	"Hinesleys Choice"	100
	pt. "Oakenthorp"	40
	pt. "Sarahs Fancy"	111
Benjamin Ridgeway	"Long Delay"	150
John Roberts (minor) s/o (N)	"Roberts Desire"	150
Edward Rooke	"Revival"	1118
James Roberts	pt. "Sandy Hurst"	100
Theophilus Randall	"Bacon Neck" a/s "Barrow Neck"	227
	"Jones's" a/s "Janes Lott"	50
William Robinson	pt. "Tottingham" – for his wife	100
John Russam	"Clymores Chance" – for h/o Thomas Clymore	59
36:1754:70 ...		
Mr. Thomas Ringgold (KI)	"Coxes Neck" – in wheat	1000
William Robinson (Tuckahoe)	pt. "Todcaster"	500
William Roberts	"Roberts's Chance"	150
Charles Railey	pt. "Larrington"	31
	pt. "Bishops Outlett"	73½
John Roe	pt. "Woodland"	100
Thomas Robinson, Jr.	pt. "Lowes Arcadia"	100
John Ruth	pt. "Smiths Neglect"	150
Gilbert Reed	pt. "Spread Eagle"	1
36:1754:71 ...		
Patrick Sexton	pt. "Liberty"	100

John Seth	pt. "Mount Mill"	79¼
	pt. "Addition"	10
	pt. "Bennetts Outlett"	50
	pt. "Mount Mill" – for his brother Jacob	79¼
	pt. "Addition" – for his brother Jacob	10
	pt. "Bennetts Outlett" – for his brother Jacob	50
William Scandrett	pt. "Lexton"	235
	"Lott"	50
	pt. "Hinesleys Plains"	76
	pt. "Bristoll Marsh"	160
36:1754:72 ...		
John Sullivant	pt. "Ponderfield"	109
	pt. "Dungamon"	150
	pt. "Fossetts Plains" – for h/o John Hammond	150
Thomas Swann	pt. "Jumps Chance"	100
	pt. "Jumps Choice"	2½
Susanna Stewart	pt. "Kearys Discovery"	140
	pt. "Silvesters Forrest"	105
Emanuell Swift	"Swifts Forrest Addition"	50
James Slaughter	"Fern Ridge"	50
	pt. "Partnership" a/s "Ratcliffe"	50
	"Fairn Ridge Addition"	100
	"Golden Rod Ridge"	50
John Swift	"Swifts Forrest"	50
	"Bear Harbour"	50
Moses Swift	"Indian Tract"	50
James Silvester	pt. "Bear Garden"	123
	"Carmarthin"	100
h/o William Starkey	pt. "Oak Ridge"	175
	"Hickory Ridge"	150
	pt. "Codshead Manor"	116
36:1754:73 ...		
William Shepherd	pt. "Hinesleys Plains"	109
Solomon Sinnett	pt. "Hawkins's Pharsalia"	150
Thomas Shoobrook (cnp)	"Stoke"	100
	pt. "Crumps Forrest"	150

	pt. "Upperheathworth"	100
	"Wellow"	100
	"Stokes Addition Rectified"	60
Absalom Sparkes	pt. "Sparkes Own"	25
Robert Smith	"Toms Fancy Enlarged"	100
Caleb Sparkes	pt. "Sparkes Own"	25
Millington Sparkes	pt. "Sparkes Own"	25
Joseph Scrivner	pt. original of "Hackers Meadows"	14
	"Josephs Part of Hackers Meadows Enlarged"	325
Daniel Smith (planter)	pt. "Jones's Fancy"	75
Benjamin Smith	pt. "Jones's Fancy"	75
	"Mary's Chance"	30
	"Teats Desire"	35
36:1754:74 ...		
Daniel Smith (joyner)	"Mantons Addition"	5
	"Marys Portion"	100
John Spry	pt. "Friendship" – surveyed for (N) Tilghman	70
Thomas Spry	pt. "Friendship" – surveyed for (N) Tilghman	55
	pt. "Friendship" – another	15
Solomon Seney	pt. "Barton"	110
	"Bradfords Addition"	100
	pt. "Clouds Adventure"	187½
	pt. "Sewalls Fork" – for his wife (N) w/o John Nevill	250
	pt. "Tilghmans Discovery" – for his wife (N) w/o John Nevill	78¾
	pt. "Poplar Hill" – for his wife	150
Thomas Seward	"Outrange"	174
Thomas Sands	"Sands Outlett"	100
	"Dub Hen Ridge"	40
	"Timber Ridge"	70
	pt. "Swifts Outlett"	22
	"Long Swamp"	63
	"Lancaster"	119
	pt. "Northumberland"	48
James Sutton	pt. "Sandy Hurst"	100

Queen Anne's County - 1754

36:1754:75			
Mr. Gideon Swift	"Chance"		66
	pt. "Swifts Outlett"		70
	"Constantinople"		100
	pt. "James Choice"		50
	"Crumps Advice" – for his daughters Elizabeth & Mary		100
	"Mulberry Tract"		100
Christopher Spry	"Thief Keep Out"		100
	pt. "Friendship" – surveyed for (N) Tilghman		52
	pt. "Friendship" – another		29
	"Sprys Chance"		21
	"Thief Keep Out Addition"		150
	"Buck Range" – for your son Humphrey		50
Thomas Stanton	"Forrest of Sherwood"		200
	pt. "Security"		40
Mary Scotton	pt. "Sallisbury Plains" – for h/o Richard Scotton		50
	"Scottons Addition" – for h/o Richard Scotton		100
Mrs. Rebeccah Sudler	"Jones Hole Resurveyed" – for h/o James Sudler		276
	"Stent on Sudler" – for h/o James Sudler		173
Mr. Joseph Sudler	"Sledmore"		800
	pt. "Devonishes Chance"		15
	"Sudlers Purchase"		80
	"Sudlers Fortune"		186
	"Sudlers Island"		64
	pt. "Shepherds Forrest"		200
	pt. "Broad Creek Resurveyed" – for Anne Wells d/o & h/o John Wells		630
	½ "Cloaks Chance"		50
	"Tilbury"		50
	"Tilburys Addition"		50
36:1754:76			
Dr. John Smith (cnp)	"Smiths Neck"		128
	pt. "Spread Eagle"		346
	"Marys Portion"		150
	pt. "Martins Neck" – resurveyed by (N) Orsburn		39

	pt. "Spread Eagle" – for his mill	5
Susannah Stephens	"Derochbourns Neglect"	17½
	"Stephens's Adventure" – for h/o John Stephens	315
Robert Small	"Ship Point"	100
William Scott	pt. "Sayers Range"	40
Richard Smith	"Smiths Desire"	50
	"Smiths Outlett"	100
	"Long Ridge"	124
	"Indian Oldfield"	40
Thomas Scotton	"Scottons Forrest"	50
	"Scottons Desire"	100
Richard Swift	"Williams Pasture"	54
John Stent	pt. "Coldraine"	103
Richard Sparkes – grandson of Richard Collins	1 lot in Kings Town	1
36:1754:77 ...		
William Smith	pt. "Sallisbury Plains"	200
Francis Spry	pt. "Sprys Adventure"	75
William Spry	pt. "Friendship" – surveyed for (N) Spry	149
John Scott	pt. "Straton"	532½
Solomon Scott	pt. "Straton"	311
Aaron Saunders	"Purnalls Forrest" – for h/o William Purnall	500
	"Jumps Lane" – for h/o William Purnall	100
Lemon Swift	pt. "Soote Hill" – for h/o Fairclough Wright	200
Henry Storey	pt. "Todley"	193
James Silvester, Jr.	"Bear Garden Addition"	125
	pt. "Bear Garden"	80
Mr. John Seegar	"Johnsons Adventure"	100
	"Newnams Portion"	241½
	"Gwinns Hazard"	100
	pt. "Woodhouse"	39
	pt. "Woodhouse Addition"	11
	"McCleans Addition"	150
36:1754:78 ...		
Nathaniel Saterfield	"Saterfields Venture"	55

Francis Stephens	"Lanark"	86
	"Hunting Tower" – for his son Robertson	100
Joseph Slocum	pt. "Bishops Fields"	50
Charles Seth	pt. "Mount Mill"	158½
	pt. "Addition"	20
	pt. "Bennetts Outlett"	25
Richard Scotton	"Hazle Ridge"	65
Benjamin Silvester	"Bucks Range"	113
	"Silvesters Hazard"	189
Richard Small	"Coles Endeavour"	150
John Smith	"Sandy Hill"	100
Maurice Sliney	pt. "Pitts Gift"	85
	pt. "Timber Ridge" – see below	166⅔
	pt. "Timber Ridge" – more	83⅓
36:1754:79 ...		
George Smith	pt. "Smiths Forrest" – for Thomas Chaires (minor) s/o Joseph	61
	pt. "Confusion" – for Thomas Chaires (minor) s/o Joseph	159
Thomas Seward, Jr.	"Hawkins's Range"	90
Catherine Scotton	"Scottons Outlett"	50
Nathaniel Scotton	"Nathaniels Addition"	43
Mrs. Priscilla Sanders	pt. "Middle Plantation"	33⅓
Elizabeth Smith	"Jacksons Choice" – for h/o Thomas Jackson	100
Absalom Swift	pt. "Content"	50
Robert Scrivner	"Neglect"	190
James Smith	"Hemsleys Britland Rectified"	57
Josias Salloway	½ "Cloaks Chance"	50
David Silvester	pt. "Grubby Neck"	75
36:1754:80 ...		
Emory Sudler	"Little Neck"	55
Andrew Saunders	"Good Luck Range"	50
William Silvester	pt. "Grubby Neck"	75
John Sipple	pt. "Swifts Meadows" – for h/o William Swift	50
h/o Ralph Swift	pt. "Swifts Meadows"	50
Joseph Spry	pt. "Sprys Adventure"	75

h/o Nathaniel Scott	pt. "Toms Fancy Enlarg'd"	243
Samuel Swift	"Fosters Folly"	50
36:1754:81 ...		
Mr. Richard Tilghman	"Tilghmans Hermitage"	1843
	pt. "Bristoll Marsh"	50
	pt. "Forlone Hope"	1050
	pt. "Carpenter Outlett"	9
	pt. "Boagley"	75
	pt. "Park"	500
	"Wyatts Range"	50
	pt. "Confusion"	9
	pt. "Adventure" pt. "Confusion" – from (N) Alley	110
	pt. "Grays Inn"	75
	"Cheshire"	200
	pt. "Shrewsberry"	150
	"Sintra"	187
	"Tilghmans Recovery"	1050
	"Plains"	112
36:1754:82 ...		
Maj. William Tilghman	"Pauls Fort"	200
	pt. "Bristoll Marsh"	140
	pt. "Tilghmans Discovery"	490
	"Sallisbury"	500
	"Delmore End"	500
	1 lot in Ogle Town	1
	pt. "Poplar Plain"	191
	"Meadow"	28
	pt. "Smiths Mistake"	400
	"Andever"	500
MM Richard & William Tilghman	"Cove Point on Resurvey" – for h/o Mr. James Earle	200
	"Smiths Lott" – for h/o Mr. James Earle	100
	"Woodland Neck" – for h/o Mr. James Earle	200
Mr. Edward Tilghman (cnp)	pt. "Malton"	239
	1 lot in Ogle Town	1
	pt. "Porters Lodge"	200

Queen Anne's County - 1754

	"Tilghmans Landing"	68
	pt. "Resurvey of Forlone Hope Rectified"	2890
	"Tilghmans Resurvey of Long Neck"	539
	pt. "Union"	720
	"Scottons Folly"	50
	pt. "Long Neck"	2½
	pt. "Coursey Upon Wye"	321½
	"Pleasant Banks on Wye"	19
	pt. "Sparks Choice"	100
	pt. "Tully's Delight"	200
	"Just Design"	17½
	pt. "Discovery"	216
	pt. "Loyds Meadows & Loyds Meadows Addition"	655
	"Beaverdams"	50
	"Hollow Flatt"	50
	⅓ "Reviving Spring"	166⅔
Mr. James Tilghman	pt. "Adventure"	1030
	"Adventure Addition"	40
	"Tilghmans Freshes"	600
	pt. "Jerusalem"	200
	"Coles Bank Enlarged"	703
36:1754:83 ...		
Mr. Mattthew Tilghman	"Tilghmans Forrest"	1400
	"Rings End"	100
	"Notlars Enjoyment"	500
	1 lot in Ogle Town	1
	pt. "Poplar Plains"	191
	pt. "Glocester"	195
	½ "Timber Fork"	250
	½ "Negligence"	22½
	"Tilghmans Chance"	990
	"Ovall"	420
	pt. "Toms Fancy Enlarged"	162
Mr. Nathaniel Tucker	pt. "Adventure"	61
	"Jones's Addition"	200
	pt. "Batchelors Plains"	100

Trustram Thomas 3rd	"Trustram Thomas Part of Trustram"	127
Baynard Tillotson	pt. "Lords Gift on Resurvey"	270
	pt. "Todley"	170
	"Exchange"	100
	pt. "Lantley" – for his wife Margarett	325
Mr. John Tillotson	"Shepherds Fields on Resurvey"	140
	pt. "Todley"	150
	pt. "Lowes Arcadia"	100
	"Inkersell" – for h/o (N) Chatham	134
	"Timberland" – for h/o (N) Chatham	400
	"Pascalls Chance" – for h/o (N) Chatham	250
	pt. "Park" – for h/o (N) Chatham	354
	"Chethams Landing" – for h/o (N) Chatham	90
John Timm	"Society Hill"	50
	"Timms Arcadia"	50
	"Society Hills Addition"	75
36:1754:84 ...		
Stephen Thomas	pt. "Hawkins's Pharsalia"	80
	pt. "Alcocks Pharsalia"	33⅓
Philemon Thomas	pt. "Hawkins's Pharsalia"	120
	pt. "Lees Chance"	33
	pt. "Alcocks Pharsalia"	66⅔
Trustram Thomas (Long Neck)	"Grubby Neck"	50
	"Trustrams Ridge"	50
	"Trustrams Adventure"	150
Thomas Tanner	"Chance"	50
	"Tanners Advantage"	39
	"Providence"	100
	"Ashford" – for h/o Isaac Hudson	100
Alexander Toalson	pt. "Freshford"	140
	pt. "Partnership"	206½
Amia Toalson	pt. original of "Phillpotts Neck" – for h/o Alexander Toalson	233⅓
Mr. James Tuit	pt. "Youngs Chance"	270
	pt. "Lambeth Fields"	132
Richard Tickell	1 lot in Kings Town – No. 22	1

Queen Anne's County - 1754

Mary Thomas	"Forrest Plains" – for h/o Christopher Thomas	150
36:1754:85 ...		
Benjamin Toalson	pt. "Coppidges Range" – for h/o John	211
h/o or devisees of Mrs. Elizabeth Thompson	pt. "Cloverfields"	335
	"Kirbys Recovery"	52
Mr. Samuel Thompson	"Wilmores Range"	100
Mary Trickey	"Woodberry" – for h/o Thomas Trickey	100
John Tittle	1 lot in Kings Town – No. 1	1
Christopher Thomas, Jr.	pt. "Trustram Thomas Part of Trustram"	100
Mr. Dowdall Thompson	pt. "Prices Hill"	180
	pt. "Shepherds Discovery"	200
	"Parsons Marsh Addition"	10
	"Good Luck"	100
	pt. "Sparkes's Choice"	250
	pt. "Mount Pleasant"	102½
	pt. "Enjoyment"	50
	"Benfield" a/s "Bragholl"	200
	"Parsons Marsh"	34
	pt. "Shepherds Discovery" & pt. "Henfield"	218
	"Courseys Town Resurveyed"	394
	"Whortons Marsh" – as guardian of Arthur Holt	27
	"Highgate Lane" – as guardian of Arthur Holt	100
	"Holt" – as guardian of Arthur Holt	506
	"Holts Castle Hill Resurveyed" – as guardian of Arthur Holt	304½
	pt. "Mount Pleasant" a/s "Mount Pleasure" – as guardian to Arthur Holt	52½
	"Parsons Chance" – as guardian to Arthur Holt	115
	pt. "Mount Pleasure" a/s "Pleasant" – as guardian to Arthur Holt	80
36:1754:86 ...		
William Tarbutton	pt. "Codshead Manor"	100
James Toalson & John	"Partnership"	380
Joseph Toalson (cnp)	"Toalsons Desire"	193
	pt. original of "Philpotts Neck"	116⅔
	½ "Morgans Inclosure" – for h/o Andrew Toalson	218½

	pt. "Hogg Pen Neck", "Goose Hill", & pt. "Ridge" – as guardian to Edward Cockey (minor)	95
Edmond Thomas, Jr.	pt. "Trustram"	450
Joseph Thomas	"Trustram Thomas's Part of Trustram"	200
Tilden Thomas	"Addition"	227
John Taylor	pt. "Neglect"	51
	pt. "Batchelors Hope"	90
Philemon Tanner	⅓ "Woodland Neck"	16⅔
	⅓ "Oldsons Relief"	33⅓
Richard Taylor	"Alberts Delight" – for h/o William Mountsieur	200
Thomas Teet	"Bee Tree Ridge"	50
36:1754:87 ...		
Isaac Turner	pt. "Swann Brook"	170
36:1754:88 ...		
Visitors of Queen Anns County School	pt. "Forlone Hope"	100
Vestry of Saint Pauls Parish	pt. "Doctors Folly"	½
Richard Vanderford	pt. "Outrange" – in right of his wife	40
John Vanderford	pt. "Wrenches Farme"	200
	"Christophers Hazard"	100
Joshua Vincent	"Difficulty"	72
James Vanderford	pt. "Fox Hill"	28⅓
	pt. "Dispute" a/s "Brotherhood"	15⅔
John Vanderford s/o Rebecca	pt. "Fox Hill"	28⅓
	pt. "Dispute" a/s "Brotherhood"	15⅔
Vestry of Christs Church Parish	pt. "Little Ease" – a glebe	150
36:1754:89 ...		
h/o or devisees of John Walters	pt. "Smeath"	250
	"Barnstable Hill Resurveyed"	210
	"Westminster"	297
	pt. "Upperheathworth"	143
John Welch	pt. "Partnership"	200
	pt. "Ditteridge"	83
	pt. "Reason"	20
Henry Williams	pt. "Sallisbury Plains"	100
	"Williams's Fortune"	150

MM N. Samuel Turb. Wright & Thomas Wright	pt. "Wrights Reserve"	250
	pt. "Hemsleys Britland Rectified"	50
Mr. Thomas Wilkinson	"Barbadoes Hall"	350
36:1754:90 ...		
Daniel Wheatley	pt. "Welch Poole" tbc John Falconar	150
James Williams	pt. "Courseys Addition"	100
	pt. "Kendall"	100
Elizabeth Wootters	"Richard & Marys Forrest"	80
James Willson	"Willsons Chance"	100
	"Willsons Chance Addition"	200
Jacob Wootters	"New Buckley"	100
	"Cow Range"	38
John Wheatley	pt. "Wheatleys" a/s "Daniels Fields"	140
William Wheatley	"Wheatleys Park"	100
Thomas Wheeler	"Killmaiden"	100
	"Killmaiden Addition"	15
William Whitby	"Whitbys Forrest"	50
	"Buck Range"	100
36:1754:91 ...		
Mr. Nathaniel Wright	"Brotherhood"	50
	"Wrights Chance"	300
Daniel Willcox	pt. "Mount Hope"	250
	"Mount Hopes Addition"	100
John Woodall s/o John (KE)	pt. "Crumpton"	10
Matthew Weeks	pt. "Enjoyment"	79
	pt. "Woollverhamton"	120
Robert Wharton	"Whartons Adventure"	570
	pt. "Sayers Range Addition"	17
Benjamin Whittington	pt. "Hemsleys Britland" & pt. "Whittingtons Lott"	357
	pt. "Rattcliffe" pt. "Loyds Freshes"	171
	pt. "Poplar Hill"	34
Penelope Wright	pt. "Parsons Point"	100
Robert Wallters	"Dundee"	368
	"Jamaica"	150
	"Waltters Addition to Kirbys Prevention"	33

William White	"Workmans Hazard"	150
	"Sparkes Point"	50
36:1754:92 ...		
George Webb	"Wattsons Lott"	50
	"Webbs Plains"	50
John Willson (KI)	pt. "Eastern Island"	50
	"Willsons Adventure"	54
	"Erricksons Island"	20
Phinehas Willson	pt. "Sayers Addition" – for h/o John Jackerman	100
Thomas Walker	"Toms Adventure"	56
	"Toms Adventure Addition"	50
Mr. Nathan Wright	"White Marsh"	376
	pt. "White Marsh Addition"	250
	pt. "Smiths Reserve"	2½
	"Cork House"	590
	"Jones's Park Reserved"	340
John Wright	pt. "Narborough"	250
	"Narborough Addition"	100
	"Little Worth"	50
William Wallace	"Boothbys Fortune"	500
Jonathan Wootters	"Oak Ridge"	20
	"Oak Ridge Addition"	78
36:1754:93 ...		
h/o Littleton Ward	pt. "Colpe Rectified"	286
Nathan Wright s/o Edward	"Tullys Reserve"	300
	"Reserve Addition"	50
	"Marys Portion"	554
	pt. "Content"	400
John Willson, Jr.	"Willsons Adventure" – for his wife	262
h/o Humphrey Wells, Jr.	pt. "Jennys Begining"	22
	"Baths Meadows"	36
Peter Wrench	"Wrenches Chance"	35
	pt. "Wrenches Farme"	200
Samuel Walters	"Walters's Park"	150
James & Samuell Walters	pt. "Partnership"	217½

William Wrench	pt. "Guilford"	26
	pt. "Wrenches Lott"	100
	pt. "Hawkins's Farm Resurveyed"	326
Henry Wrench	pt. "Wrenches Lott"	354
	"Wrenches Reserve"	39
36:1754:94 ...		
Mr. Thomas Willson	"Sewals Range"	1120
	"Plain Dealing"	727
	"Jacksons Boggs"	46
	pt. "Bennetts Outlett" – for his wife	495
Zorobable Wells	"Teats Folly"	50
	"Buck Island"	100
John Whitby	"Batchelors Chance"	69
	"Bite the Biter"	78½
Josiah Whorton	"Fords Chance"	100
widow Woodall	pt. "James Choice" – for h/o Cornelius Comegys	150
	pt. "Crumps Chance" – for h/o Cornelius Comegys	50
Mrs. Elizabeth Wells	pt. "Bath"	255
Mr. George Wells	"Red Lion Point"	50
	pt. "Baths Addition"	150
Humphrey Wells s/o Humphrey	"Peirce Land Addition"	50
	"Crumps Fancy"	50
	"Landing"	30
	"Fancys Addition"	150
36:1754:95 ...		
John Wells s/o Humphrey	"Peirce Land"	199½
Benjamin Wells s/o Humphrey	"Low Lands"	45
	"Calebs Lott"	80
Joseph Whitby	"Buck Range"	100
Henry Ward	"Wards Flowers Fields"	50
Mr. William Wells	pt. "Bath"	100
	pt. "Baths Addition"	150
Richard Warner	pt. "Sayers Range Addition"	66
	"Alberts Desire" a/s "Abbotts Desire"	40
	"Alberts Desire" a/s "Abbotts Desire" – more	60
John Watson	"Baileys Delight on Resurvey" – for his wife Esther	100

Nathaniel Wright, Jr.	pt. "Sallisbury"	100
	½ "Skinners Expectation"	240
w/o Ambrose Wright	pt. "Wrights Chance"	100
	pt. "Hawkins's Farm Resurveyed"	41
	pt. "Guilford"	12
Mr. Nathaniel Wright s/o Edward	"Hazard"	100
	½ "Content"	100
	"Content Addition"	200
	"Content Outlett"	50
36:1754:96 ...		
Mr. N. Samuel Turbutt Wright	"New Hynson Town"	360
	pt. "Grays Inn"	75
	2 lots in Kings Town – No. 2, No. 27	2
	pt. "Wrights Square"	140
	pt. "Gould Hawks Enlargement" – as guardian to Elisha Brown	35
	"Claxton" – as guardian to Elisha Brown	100
	1 lot in Ogle Town – as guardian to Elisha Brown	1
	1 lot in Ogle Town	1
	pt. "Larrington" – as guardian to Elisha Brown	100
Mr. Thomas Wright	"New Reading"	300
	pt. "Grays Inn"	50
	pt. "Neglect"	45
	"Warplesdon"	300
	pt. "Warplesdon Addition" pt. "Solomons Friendship"	230
	pt. "Lowes Arcadia"	350
Mr. Edward Wright s/o Edward	pt. "Partnership"	250
	"Collonells Quarters"	100
Isaac Winchester	½ "Morgans Inclosure" – for h/o Alexander Toalson	218½
	"Purlivant"	180
	"Isaac Addition"	80
James Walters (KI)	pt. "Conners Neck" – for his wife	120
James Ware	pt. "Clouds Adventure"	112½
	pt. "Brotherhead"	67

h/o Ambrose Wright – one of which is a minor & has chosen John Tillotson as his guardian	pt. "Hawkins's Farme Resurveyed"	5
	pt. "Wrights Chance"	408
	pt. "Guilford"	40
36:1754:97 ...		
Rebecca Williams	"Millford" – for h/o Abraham Williams	123
Mary Webb (widow)	pt. "Lyford" – for h/o James Webb	643
Thomas Wilkinson s/o Henry	"Wattsons Chance"	50
Solomon Wright & Solomon Coursey Wright	"Guilford"	300
	"Guilford Addition"	150
	"Hogg Harbour"	100
Joshua Walleston	pt. "Condone"	10
	pt. "Crumpton"	10
Stephen Weeks	pt. "Mount Pleasant"	1½
	pt "Woollverhamton"	80
Richard Wells, Jr.	pt. "Bath"	145
Jacob Walters	"Kirbys Prevention"	50
James Walters	"Walters's Rambles"	150
Solomon Wright, Solomon Coursey Wright, & Sarah Wright	pt. "Narborough"	250
36:1754:98 <blank>		
36:1754:99 ...		
Solomon Yewell	"Purchase"	86
Stephen Yoe	pt. "Brandford"	100
John Young s/o William	pt. "Stratton"	50
Aaron Yoe	"Courseys Addition"	50
John Young	pt. "Stratton"	54½
36:1754:100 ...		
James Auld (DO)	1 lot in Kings Town – No. 19	1
John Andrews (in Jerseys)	"Mount Gilboa"	50
Andrew Abbington (CV)	"Abbington"	500
Thomas Adcock	"Wyatts Folly"	50
36:1754:101 ...		
Mr. Rizdon Bozman (TA) (cnp)	pt. "Killeray"	100
	pt. "Millford"	200
	"Point Landing"	5¼

	"Killerays Addition"	34¼
James Bartlett (TA)	"Partnership"	575
Benjamin Blackiston (KE)	pt. "Benjamins Park"	80
	"Upper Landing"	200
Daniel Bird (Biddeford)	1 lot in Kings Town – No. 8	1
James Benson (TA)	pt. "Spread Eagle" – for his wife	100
	"Collins's Own" – for his wife	92
James Baxter (CE)	"Beaver Neck Resurveyed" – for h/o Jo. Wicks	320
h/o William Brent (VA)	"Kent Fort Manor" – in corn	1000
Anne Brooke (widow) (TA)	pt. "Scarborough"	200
John Blackwell or Thomas Grace	pt. "Alcocks Pharsalia"	100
36:1754:102 ...		
Nathan Baggs	pt. "Bridge Town"	17
Benjamin Cleave (KE)	pt. "Cleaves Rambles" – for his son Nathaniel	110
Thomas Cockayne (TA)	"Betts Range"	400
Edward Clark (TA)	"Clarks Lott"	112
	"Clarks Delight"	76
	"Clarks Struggle"	65
Charles Carroll (Annapolis)	pt. "Tompsons Manor" a/s "Poplar Island"	1000
James Claypoole (KE)	pt. "Lambeth"	187½
	"Wells's Chance" – for his wife Elizabeth	100
	pt. "Lambeth" – more	62½
Johannah Carpenter (widow) (Duck Creek)	⅓ "Porters Lodge"	100
Elinor Carey	pt. "Silvesters Addition"	112
36:1754:103 ...		
Amy Carey	pt. "Silvesters Addition"	65
Peter Cummerford	"Mount Pleasure" – for h/o William Sharp	500
h/o James Dickinson (TA)	"Dickinsons Plains"	860
Samuell Dickinson (KEDE)	"Youghal"	175
	"Grouches Tryangle"	63
	"Poplar Ridge"	150
	"Poplar Ridge Addition"	200
William Dickinson	pt. "Scarborough"	200
Nathan Dobson	"Dobsons Westmoreland"	150

36:1754:104		
Susanna Douglass (CE)	"Macklyn's Fancy"	500
John Dixon (TA)	pt. "Jerusalem"	200
Henry Elbert	pt. "Davis's Range"	200
Abraham Falconar (KE)	"Grove"	150
	"Edenborough"	1074
Col. William Fitzhugh	"Morgans Neck" – for h/o Mr. John Rousby (CV)	400
	"Bluff Point" – for h/o Mr. John Rousby (CV)	496
36:1754:105		
Mr. Nicholas Gouldsborough (TA)	pt. "Old Town"	740
Mr. William Gouldsborough (TA)	"Walnutt Ridge" – for devisees of Mr. George Robins	600
	"Pearle" – for devisess of Mr. George Robins	1000
Mr. Robert Gouldsborough (TA)	"Controversey"	500
	pt. "Sandishwood" – for his wife	655
	pt. "Jaspers Lott"	570
Jeremiah Gresingham (TA)	pt. "Davis's Range" – for his wife	200
Peter Garon (TA)	pt. "Alcocks Pharsalia" – for h/o William Vickers	100
36:1754:106		
h/o John Gresham (KE)	"Pock. Hiccory Ridge"	1000
	"Sallisbury Meadows"	34
Edward Harding (TA)	pt. "Hemsleys Arcadia"	231
Mr. Samuell Hyde (London)	"Smiths Forrests"	2000
Patrick Hamilton (CE)	pt. "Point Love" – for his wife, in corn	400
h/o James Heath (CE)	pt. "Tottenham"	300
36:1754:107		
h/o Aquilla Johns	pt. "Cold Spring"	430
Alexander Kelly (KE)	pt. "Malton" – in right of his wife (N) one of d/o Maurice McCarty	150
36:1754:108		
John Lockerman, Jr.	"Bennetts Tolson Resurveyed"	930
William Lambden (TA)	pt. "Reviving Spring"	166⅔
	pt. "Reviving Spring" – for his son Williams	166⅔
Mr. Thomas Lane (TA)	pt. "Smiths Ridge"	300
	"Collins's Ridge" – for his wife	300
John Leeds (TA)	pt. "Scarborough"	200

Queen Anne's County - 1754

Edward Loyd, Esq.	"Ninevah"	600
	"Ninevahs Addition"	200
	pt. "Loyds Freshes"	810
	"Mill Range"	136
	"Chesnutt Neck"	300
	"Hoggs Hole"	50
	"Breek Nock"	100
	"Wilton"	650
	pt. "Addition to Wilton"	600
	"Hemsleys Reserve Rectified on Resurvey"	185
	pt. "Brandford"	186
	pt. "Saint Martins"	82
	pt. "Costins Park"	21
	"Scotts Chance"	100
	pt. "Oakenthorpe"	56
	"Nutwells Chance Resurveyed"	294
	"Courseys Range"	600
	pt. "Hemsleys Britland Rectified"	223
	pt. "Costins Chance"	32
	"Coopers Hill"	100
	pt. "Narborough"	250
	"Woolverton"	250
36:1754:109 ...		
Stead Lowe	"Addition"	500
	"Steads Go Between"	71
	pt. "Begining"	300
Rev. Mr. Richard Mollineaux (popish priest)	"Batchelors Plains"	216
	"Johns Forrest"	200
	"Lundy"	200
	pt. "Woodhouse"	200
	"Waterford"	200
Nicholas Massy (KE)	"Pacolett"	18
36:1754:110 ...		
Mr. George Millegin	"Edinkelley"	600
William Millington (TA)	pt. "Pitts Vineyard" – for h/o Thomas Baynard s/o Robert	166⅔

Francis Neale (TA)	"Shadwell" – for his son Francis	100
	pt. "Shadwell Addition" – for h/o Robert Jones	100
Edward Neale (TA)	pt. "Shadwells Addition"	100
Jonathan Neale (TA) – trustee for John Webb	"Webbs Chance"	150
	pt. "Silvesters Addition"	40
36:1754:111 ...		
h/o or devisee of Jeremiah Nicols (TA)	pt. "Partnership"	250
Jeremiah Neal (TA)	"Chance"	50
Mr. Edward Oldham (TA)	"Exchange"	470
	"Exchange" – amother	60
	pt. "Providence"	300
William Oxingham	pt. "Golden Lyon"	100
	"Mire Branch"	85
	"Turners Plains"	128
36:1754:112 ...		
Aaron Parrott (TA)	pt. "Cold Spring"	162
Mr. James Porter (KE)	pt. "Poplar Hill" – for his wife	50
	"Halls Harbour" – for his wife	500
Dr. Richard Porter (KE)	½ "Negligence" – for his wife's sister in Newfoundland	22½
	½ "Timber Fork" – for his wife's sister in Newfoundland	250
Edward Pamplilion (TA)	"Spryley"	200
36:1754:113 ...		
Mr. James Ringgold (KE)	pt. "Courseys Point" or "Smiths Mistake"	623
	pt. "Bishops Outlett"	400
	pt. "Bishops Addition" & pt. "Bishops Outlett" – from (N) Watson	100
Thomas Ruse (PA)	"Andever Meadows" – for his wife	175
John Robertson (SO)	"Athol"	500
h/o George Robotham	"Robothams Park"	500
Elizabeth Robrass (widow)	pt. "Providence"	150
36:1754:114 ...		
Mr. Tobias Stansbury (BA)	"Robinsons Farme" – for his wife	200
Mr. Jarvas Spencer (KE)	pt. "Connoway" – for h/o Christopher Williams	111
h/o Charles Stevens	pt. "Willenlew"	212

Thomas Spry	"Dodington"	200
36:1754:115 ...		
John Tharp	pt. "Coldraine"	50
Mr. William Thomas (TA)	pt. "Smiths Range"	61
	"Lampton"	135
Joseph Turner (TA)	"Turners Lane"	100
Abner Turner (TA)	"Abners Park"	130
	pt. "Turners Plains Addition"	58
36:1754:116 ...		
William Truelock (KE)	"Lower Fords"	200
h/o Mr. Lambert Willmore (KE)	1 lot in Kings Town	1
William Webb	pt. "Redford"	150
Park Webb (TA)	pt. "Shadwells Addition" – for h/o Samuel Neal	50
William Willson & wife (TA)	pt. "Bear Garden"	150

Queen Anne's County - 1756

36:1756:1 ...		Acres
Alice Allyband	"Allybands Hazard Inlarg'd" – for h/o Thomas Allyband	114
James Ayler	pt. "Inclosure"	50
Ellinor Anthony (widow)	pt. "Hackton"	100
William Austin	pt. "Waterford"	382
	"Rawlings Chance" – for h/o William Elliott	100
	"Smithfield"	150
John Atkinson	pt. "Rawlings Chance" – for h/o George Elliott	230
	pt. "Mount Hope" – for h/o George Elliott	50
	pt. "Elliotts Addition" – for h/o George Elliott	50
Samuel Austin	pt. "Courseys Point" a/s "Smiths Mistake"	22
	pt. "Bishops Outlett"	100
	pt. "Bishops Addition"	100
William All	pt. "Oakenthorpe" – for son James	100
Rebecca Ashbury	pt. "Pox Hill"	28⅓
	pt. "Dispute" a/s "Brotherhood"	15⅔
36:1756:2 ...		
John Atkinson, Jr.	pt. "Toms Fancy Enlarg'd"	332
Stephen Andrews	"Mount Gilboa"	50
36:1756:3 ...		
Edward Browning	pt. "Hope" – for his wife	33⅓
Mr. Phil. Charles Blake	"Blakeford"	555
	pt. "Loyds Meadows & Loyds Meadows Addition"	570
	"Bennetts Regulation"	1306
Mrs. Sarah Blake (cnp)	"Russendale" – for h/o Mr. John Sayer Blake	250
	"Coursey" – for h/o Mr. John Sayer Blake	250
	"Hoggs Hole" – for h/o Mr. John Sayer Blake	100
	"Jenkins's Neck" – for h/o Mr. John Sayer Blake	250
	"Cold Harbour" – for h/o Mr. John Sayer Blake	100
	"Sayers Forrest" – for h/o Mr. John Sayer Blake	2250
	"Gore" – for h/o Mr. John Sayer Blake	175
	"Jackson's Choice" – for h/o Mr. John Sayer Blake	100
	"Wading Place" – for her son John devised by Esq. Bennett	1000
	"Burton Upon Walsey" – for her son Charles devised by Esq. Bennett	388

	pt. "Neglect" – for her son Charles devised by Esq. Bennett	440
	"Ulthorpe" – for her son Charles devised by Esq. Bennett	100
	"Wrights Chance" – for her son Charles devised by Esq. Bennett	124
	pt. "Broomley Lambeth" – for her daughters Henrietta Maria & Mary Blake devised by Esq. Bennett	1503
John Burk s/o Thomas	pt. "Dawsons Neck"	172
	"Falconars Lott"	50
36:1756:4 ...		
William Banning	pt. "Golden Lyon"	100
	"Clarks Venture"	35
	"Bannings Discovery"	48
George Baynard	pt. "Relief"	500
	pt. "Relief" – more & "Hawkins's Pharsalia" – from (N) Hussy	185
	"Baynard's Pasture"	202
	"Roes Chance"	247
	"Hogg Harbour"	125
	pt. "Cods Head Manor"	100
Margaret Banning	"Bells Venture" – for h/o John Banning	50
	"Purnalls Addition" – for h/o John Banning	300
	"Widows Choice" – for h/o John Banning	83
Thomas Bostick	"Hinesly Fancy"	50
	"Bosticks Chance"	50
	"Addition"	100
Charles Bradley	"Aylers Hope"	100
James Blades	"Good Will"	50
John Baggs	"Hackers Adventure" – for h/o Abner Roe	200
	"Abners Outlett" – for h/o Abner Roe	125
	"Roes Choice" – for h/o Abner Roe	64
Thomas Baggs	pt. "Old Town"	60
	"Chance Hitt"	50
	"Hunters Hope"	50
	pt. "Ratcliffe" – from (N) Montaque	<n/g>

Queen Anne's County - 1756

36:1756:5	...		
Henry Burt	"Burts Fancy"		50
	"Burts Delight"		100
	"Doggwood Ridge"		100
	"Casbury"		33
Jacob Boone	"Boones Park"		240
	"Boones Hazard"		120
	"Boones Struggle"		30
	"Boones Hazard Addition"		46
	pt. "Sayers Addition & Brandfield" – for his wife (N) w/o James Andrew		120
Isaac Boone	pt. "Haddon"		200
	"Boons Venture"		130
	pt. "Garden of Roses"		92
Joseph Boone	pt. "Boones Pleasure"		160
	"Boones Addition"		39
Abraham Boone	pt. "Boones Pleasure"		90
	"Boones Covett"		75
James Barwick	pt. "Oakenthorpe"		185
William Bolton	pt. "Spread Eagle" – for his wife		100
	pt. "Carman & Burton" – for his wife		75
	"Littleworth" – for his wife		100
John Bolton	pt. "Tully's Delight"		100
36:1756:6	...		
Thomas Baily s/o Jacob	pt. "Todley"		187
	pt. "Bishops Outlett"		26½
Thomas Baily	pt. "Baily's Delight"		156
Thomas Peo. Betts	pt. "Providence"		200
	"Come by Chance"		50
h/o Mr. James Brown	pt. "Hambletons Hermitage"		33⅓
	"Ripley Resurveyed"		265
Robert Basnett	pt. "Mannahs Chance" – for h/o Timothy Mannah		100
Nicholas Broadaway	pt. "Whittabl"		82
	pt. "Cottington"		100
	pt. "Notlars Desire"		38
	pt. "Carman & Burton"		75

Katharine Buckley (widow)	pt. "Buckleys Delight"	16⅔
Charles Bermingham	"Berminghams Fortune"	100
Fran. Bright	"Stoopley Gibson"	200
	"Brights Island"	28
36:1756:7 ...		
Robert Blunt	pt. "Blunts Marsh" a/s "Great Neck"	220
	"Copartnership"	373
	pt. "Parsons Point"	400
Samuel Blunt	pt. "Blunts Marsh" a/s "Great Neck"	110
Thomas Benton	pt. "Pentrogay"	186
	"Pentrovay"	50
Thomas Barnes	pt. "Barnes's Satisfaction"	223
Edward Brown	pt. "Pascos Lott" – for h/o John Griffith	50
	pt. "Eastern Island" – for h/o John Griffith	25
	pt. "Addition" – for h/o John Griffith	90
	pt. "Primus" – for h/o John Griffith	48
	pt. "Bonadventure" – for h/o John Griffith	37½
	pt. "Rotterdam" – for h/o John Griffith	25
	pt. "Tully's Delight"	107
	3 lots in Ogle Town – from John Hawkins	3
Vincent Benton	pt. "Contention"	50
	"Bentons Hazard"	87
	pt. "Saspers Lott"	200
h/o George Burroughs	"Georges Hazard"	50
36:1756:8 ...		
William Barkhust	"Pensylvania Border"	50
	"Golden Ridge"	80
James Baily	pt. "Bailys Addition"	70
	pt. "Cleaves's Addition" – for his wife (N) d/o N. Cleave	120
	"Tryangle"	50
William Baxter (cnp)	"Upper Blunt Point"	324
	pt. "Parsons Neck" – as guardian to T. Price	60
	pt. "Pascos Lott" – as guardian to T. Price	50
	pt. "Eastern Island" – as guardian to T. Price	25
	pt. "Addition" – as guardian to T. Price	90

		pt. "Primus" – as guardian to T. Price	48
		pt. "Bonadventure" – as guardian to T. Price	37½
		pt. "Rotterdam" – as guardian to T. Price	25
Sweat. Burn		pt. "Royston"	525
Nathan Baynard		pt. "Relief"	476
h/o James Boone		pt. "Haddon"	160
		pt. "Garden of Roses"	48
		"Garden of Roses" – more	200
		"Haddon" – more	40
George, Thomas, & John Burroughs		"Buck Road"	100
36:1756:9 ...			
Mr. Charles Brown		"Meaguholm"	608
		pt. "Bennetts Choice" – for his wife	1180
		pt. "Neglect" – for his wife	100
		"Halls Discovery"	150
		"Burks Expectation"	150
		"Butlers Own"	164
		"Piney Swamp Tract"	50
		"Canaan"	50
		"Alder Branch"	100
		"Watry Plains"	50
		pt. "Long Marsh Ridge Enlarg'd"	33½
		"Hobbs Venture"	281
William Bancks		pt. "Pitts's Vineyard"	166⅔
		"Godfrey's Folly"	50
		pt. "Sokely Ridge & Jumps Chance"	126
		"Hunters Chance"	100
		"Bancks's Addition"	665
		"Aylers Outlett"	97
		"James's Park"	50
		"Bancks's Delight"	773½
		pt. "Jumps Chance"	50
		"Merricks Delight"	50
Edward Brown, Jr. (KI)		pt. "Sillin"	100
		pt. "Belcher"	100

Thomas Butler	pt. "Chesterfield"	200
	pt. "Tryangle"	25
John Brown	pt. "Hambletons Hermitage"	33⅓
	"Sedge Harbour"	167
	"Huntly"	251
36:1756:10 ...		
Thomas Buroughs	"Scottons Inclosure"	55
John Bracco	"Bracco"	393
	"Bracco Addition"	98¼
	"Rattle Snake Ridge"	151
	pt. "Long Marsh Ridge Enlarg'd"	724
John Bostick	"Haysell Point"	75
Samuel Blunt, Jr.	pt. "Fox Harbour" – for his wife	50
	pt. "Bishopton" – for his wife	32
	pt. "Notlars Desire" – for his wife	80
	pt. "Brotherhood" – for his wife	45
William Bennett	"Bennetts Chance"	281
	"Lambdens Adventure"	100
Hannah Burroughs	pt. "Adventure"	50
36:1756:11 ...		
Turbutt Betton	pt. "Waltham"	21
	pt. "Wilkinsons Addition"	45
Robert Broady	pt. "Henrys Lott"	50
	"Roberts Outlett"	150
	"Society Hill"	50
	pt. "Society Hills Addition"	25
James Butler	pt. "Fox Hill"	85
	pt. "Notlars Delight"	37
Edward Brown (Chester)	pt. "Brampton"	124
Charles Baker	pt. "Sallisbury Plains" – for h/o John Walker	100
Nathan Baggs	"Ingrams Desire" – in DO, for his wife	<n/g>
	pt. "Bridge Town" – for his wife	17
h/o William Bishop	"Parsons Neck"	64
James Broadaway	pt. "Sallisbury Plains" – for h/o Richard Scotton	50
	pt. "Scottons Addition" – for h/o Richard Scotton	100
	"Nathaniels Addition" – for Nathaniel Scotton	43

36:1756:12 ...		
Mary Baggs w/o John Baggs	"Hazard"	50
	pt. "Controversye"	22
Darias Burn	"Jacksons Choice" – for h/o Thomas Jackson	100
John Brown s/o Edward	"Stoke" – for his wife	100
	pt. "Crumps Forrest" – for his wife	135
	"Wellow" – for his wife	100
	"Stokes Addition Rectified" – for his wife	60
36:1756:13 ...		
John Carradine	pt. "Forlorne Hope"	50
William Campbell	pt. "Ditteridge"	166
	pt. "Anthorpe"	197
	pt. "Hambletons Hermitage"	250
	pt. "Bishopton"	68
	"Walkers Square"	260
	pt. "Davis's Range"	185
	pt. "Reason"	74
	pt. "Loyds Meadows"	66
	pt. "Anthorpe"	203
	"Churnells Neck"	200
	"Adventure"	30
	"Hambletons Hermitage" – more	150
John Clemments	pt. "Edmondsons Green Close"	200
	pt. "Smiths Clifts"	100
	"Range"	200
36:1756:14 ...		
Christopher Cox	pt. "Smiths Ridge"	300
	pt. "Prophecy"	217
	pt. "Heaths Discovery"	23
	pt. "Adventure"	39
	"Coxes Necessity"	½
	pt. "Partnership"	500
	pt. "Lowes Arcadia"	233⅓
	"Plain Dealing Resurveyd" – for his son Christopher	350
	pt "Walkers Square"	40

Queen Anne's County - 1756

John Coursey	½ "Steward" – same as charged to Edward Lloyd (p. 115)	200
	½ "Macklyns Addition" – same as charged to Edward Lloyd (p. 115	18
Mr. William Coursey	"Cheston"	800
	"Coursey Upon Wye"	290
	"Lords Gift"	1050
	pt. "Smeath"	25
	"Sleeford" – for his wife	200
	"Shepherd's Hook" – for his wife	200
	"Solomons Fancy" – for Solomon Clayton	50
James Clayland	pt. "Costin's Park" – for h/o James Costin	279
John Cooper, Jr.	pt. "Kearys Discovery"	60
	"Grime's Folly"	40
Matthew Chilton	"New Cunningham"	100
36:1756:15 ...		
Richard Costin	"Newington"	80
	"Newington Addition"	50
	pt. "Carters Forrest"	22
	pt. "Toms Fancy Enlarg'd"	100
Phil. Croney	pt. "Cold Raine"	75
h/o James Croney	pt. "Cold Raine"	75
John Cahall	pt. "Wheatly" a/s "Daniels Fields" – for h/o Edward Cahall	60
John Cooper	"Taylors Chance"	200
James Countice	pt. "Dublin"	150
h/o William Countice	pt. "Dublin"	150
John Culbreath	pt. "Poplar Neck"	200
	pt. "Solomons Lott Addition"	35
	"Holly Neck Resurveyed"	415
	"Poplar Neck Addition"	70
	"Buck Range"	100
	"Parsons Delight" – for his daughter Mary	80
36:1756:16 ...		
Elijah Chance	pt. "Bear Point"	100
Batchelor Chance	pt. "Bear Point"	100
John Chance	pt. "Littleworth"	50

Ellinor Chance	pt. "Littleworth"	50
	pt. "Littleworth Addition"	50
	pt. "Garden of Roses"	22¼
Henry Councill	pt. "Hawkins's Pharsalia"	162
John Collins	pt. "Tottingham"	200
	pt. "Hackers Meadows" – for his wife	100
	"Freshford Addition"	100
William Cannon	pt. "Content"	100
Thomas Coleman	pt. "Tilghmans Discovery"	80
John Commegys	pt. "Shepherds Forrest"	173
	pt. "Shepherds Redoubt"	200
36:1756:17 ...		
John Clothier	"Clothiers Pharsalia"	150
	pt. "Hinesleys Plains"	64
Robert Certain	"Jones's Delight"	200
	pt. "Levells" – for Margaret Collins (minor)	170
James Cassey	pt. "Connaway"	289
Mr. William Carmichall	pt. "Park"	500
	pt. "Allens Neck"	117
	pt. "Partnership"	36
	"Harmonton" a/s "Harmions Lott"	304
	"Allens Neck Outlett"	18¾
	pt. "Bennetts Choice"	212
	pt. "Stagwell"	526
	"Stagwell Addition"	129
Nicholas Clouds	pt. "Broad Creek Resurveyed"	200
Charles Conner	pt. "Woodyard Thickett"	205
Richard Carter	pt. "Copartnership"	52
	pt. "Jones's Plott"	45
	pt. "Dunns Hazard"	75
	pt. "Carters Addition"	25
	pt. "Chance"	25
	pt. "Barns's Satisfaction"	50
36:1756:18 ...		
Jacob Carter	"Oar Mine"	200
	pt. "Coppidges Range"	30

Queen Anne's County - 1756

Henry Carter	"Mattapax Neck"	98
Phillip Coppidge	"Indian Spring"	100
	pt. "Slaughterton"	200
	pt. "Coppidges Range"	13
Henry Casson	pt. "Large Range Addition"	124
	"Mistake"	20
	"Jumps Claims"	80
	pt. "Dudley's Desire"	100
	"Cassons Meadows"	490
	"Silvesters Discovery"	241
	"Mistakes Addition"	27
	pt. "Jumps Chance"	135
	pt. "Pitts's Vineyard"	166⅔
	"Bakers Chance"	127
h/o Henry Culley	pt. "Poplar Hill"	27
	5 lots in Kings Town – No. 1, No. 12, No. 13, No. 24, No. 25	5
William Clayton	"Rous's Park"	300
	pt. "Tryangle"	25
	"Winter House"	50
	"Hogg Pen Neck"	55
	"Hogg Hole"	50
	pt. "Bishops Fields"	350
	"Claytons Chesterfield"	92
	"Chesterfield"	200
	"Claytons Landing"	20
	"Forrest"	100
36:1756:19 ...		
Nathaniel Cleave	"Mangy Pocky"	100
	"Troy"	100
	"Poccoyes Addition"	62
	"Wells's Park" – for his wife	110
James Clough	"Cloughs Fancy"	50
	"Cloughs Rambles"	100
Fran. Climer	pt. "Shadwells Addition"	50
Richard Cook s/o Hercules	pt. "Partnership"	20

Benjamin Covington	pt. "Toms Fancy Enlarg'd"	100
Edward Cahall	pt. "Hackton" – for his wife	50
	pt. "Hackton" – for his wife [!]	50
Edward Clayton	"Chesterfield Addition"	70
	pt. "Neglect"	200
	"Broad Neck"	100
	pt. "Park" – for his wife	146
	"Broad Neck" – more	13
John Covington	pt. "Providence"	100
	"Rowlands Hazard"	257
	pt. "Providence"	81
36:1756:20 ...		
Elizabeth Coleman	pt. "Royston"	50
Robert Cooper	"Peale Place"	32
	"Nimrods Pleasure"	100
William Covington	pt. "Hemsly's Plains"	91
James Callaghane	pt. "Hemsly's Arcadia"	70
Sharpless Cooper	"Hills Outlett Resurveyed"	233
Nathaniel Curtice	pt. "Sarahs Fancy"	112
Henry Covington	pt. "Rachels Desire"	471
	pt. "Hinesly's Plains"	140
Charles Cockey	pt. "Slaughterton" – for h/o John Elliott	100
	"Matthew's Enlargement" – for h/o John Elliott	155
	"Hogg Pen Neck", "Goose Hill", & pt. "Ridge"	95
36:1756:21 ...		
Henry Councill, Jr.	"Swine Range" – for wife	30
	"Widow's Folly" – for wife	70
	pt. "Friendship" – for wife	25
	pt. "Friendship" – for wife, more	50
h/o Hercules Cook	pt. "Sandish Woods"	335
John Chaires	pt. "Wrenches Farm"	200
	pt. "Chaires's Addition"	46
Thomas Carradine (cnp)	"Commegy's Hazard"	100
	pt. "Lexton"	235
	"Lott"	50
	pt. "Hemsly's Plains"	76

	pt. "Bristol Marsh"	160
Benjamin Chaires	pt. "Warplesdon Addition & Solomons Friendship"	100
John Councill	"Hogg Pen Ridge"	150
John & Gias Bartus Commegys	"Salem"	300
36:1756:22 ...		
Henry Collister	pt. "Crumpton"	200
	pt. "Sandy Hurst"	216
Daniel Cox	pt. "Coleraine"	525
James & John Clayland	pt. "Trusham"	300
Anthony Cox	"Coxs Desire"	100
Mary Cockey	pt. "Hogg Pen Neck", "Goose Hill", & pt. "Ridge"	95
Joseph Chaires	pt. "Lantly"	125
Mary Clough	"Cloughs Hope" – for h/o Nathaniel Clough	50
	"Boones Hope" – by name of "Broomhope"	100
Dennis Carey	pt. "Coleraine" – for h/o John Burk	148
	"Locks Point" – for h/o John Burk	50
	pt. "Bennetts Outlett"	75
	"Middle Plantation"	100
36:1756:23 ...		
Joshua Clark	pt. "Lyford"	287
	pt. "Stephen's Fields"	412
Edward Cockey	pt. "Hogg Pen Neck", "Goose Hill", & pt. "Ridge"	95
George Cope	"Dennys Range"	100
	"Coxes Range"	250
	"Cohees Desire" – for h/o James Cohee	100
William Curtis	"Curtices Lott"	50
Nathaniel Covington	"Covingtons Necessity"	140
	pt. "Rachels Desire"	37
Samuel Cocklin	"Wyatts Lott" – for h/o (N) Wyatt	150
Thomas Clayland	pt. "Dungarnon"	116¼
36:1756:24 ...		
Mr. John Downes, Jr. (cnp)	"Wrights Plains"	100
	pt. "Wrights Reserve"	200
	"Wrights Reserve Addition"	50
	pt. "Security"	60

	pt. "Smeath"	106
	pt. "Stagwell"	42
	"Downes's Chance"	100
	pt. "Smeath on Resurvey" – for h/o John Beck	412
	pt. "Smeath on Resurvey" – from (N) Barber, for h/o John Beck	50
	pt. "Smeath on Resurvey" – from (N) Hynson, for h/o John Beck	175
William Dawson	pt. "Trusham"	300
Mrs. Henrietta Maria Dulany	"Lloyds Insula"	1795
	"Purchase"	1000
	pt. "Willenlew"	682
	pt. "Brandfield"	228
	½ "Skinners Expectation"	240
Mr. Charles Downes	pt. "Fair Play"	116
	pt. "Macklinborough"	199
	"High Gale"	50
	pt. "Wrenches Adventure"	87
	"Mount Moluck" – for Charles Clayton	150
Thomas Dockery	pt. "Fishingham"	100
	"Dockerys Meadow"	142
36:1756:25 ...		
John Davis	pt. "Confusion"	220
	"Peters Lott"	150
	pt. "Content"	70
Matthew Dockery	pt. "Fishingham"	100
	"Fishinghams Addition"	13
	"Matthew's Fancy"	8½
	"Dangerfield"	200
John Downes	pt. "Nobles Range" & pt. "Hemslys Arcadia"	192
	pt. "Carters Forrest"	22
Hawkins Downes	pt. "Mittford"	200
	pt. "Parkers Freshes"	87
	"Porters Folly"	100
Henry Downes	pt. "Carters Forrest"	114

Queen Anne's County - 1756

Mrs. Catharine Davis	"Clarkson Hill"	150
	"Clarkson Hill Addition"	80
36:1756:26 ...		
William Dockery	pt. "Hawkins's Farm"	8
	pt. "Moores Hope Addition"	20
William Durding	pt. "Powells Fancy"	50
Benjamin Denny	"Wootters's Choice"	100
	"Wootters's Choice Addition"	75
	"Outlett"	68
Hynson Downes	"Shore Ditch"	150
John Downes s/o John	"Downes's Chance"	150
James Downes	pt. "Nobles Range & Hemsleys Arcadia"	100
Jo. Dodd	"Jamaica Addition" – for wife	50
	pt. "Jamaica" – for wife	59
Jacob Dodd	pt. "Rye Hall" – for George Ayres	184
36:1756:27 ...		
John Duffey	"Batchelors Adventure" – for wife	150
	"Storeys Park" – for wife	100
Rachell Duhamill	"Hynsons Lott"	199
	"Timber Swamp" – for h/o Dr. (N) Duhamill	200
Mary Dyre	pt. "Waltham"	16⅔
	pt. "Wilkinsons Addition"	16⅔
Thomas Davis	"Addy House"	68
Abner Dudley	"Sarahs Portion"	300
Thomas Doyle	pt. "Batchelors Hope" – for his wife	20
	pt. "Neglect" – for his wife	16⅓
	"Marshy Crook" – for Charles Brown (minor) s/o John	100
	"Wexford"	100
Lewis & Lewis Derochbrune, Jr.	"Friendship Resurveyed"	396
John Derochbrune	pt. "Vaughans Kindness"	200
Lewis Derochbrune, Jr.	"Josephs Addition" – for his brother Joseph (minor)	60
36:1756:28 ...		

William Dames	"Danby Resurveyed" – for devisess of Rev. James Cox	275
	"Discovery" – for devisees of Rev. James Cox	100
	pt. "Adventure Resurveyed" – for devisees of Rev. James Cox	124
	pt. "Bridge North" – for devisees of Rev. James Cox	100
Daniel Dulany	pt. "Vaughans Kindness"	200
36:1756:29 ...		
Mr. Arthur Emory	"Welch Ridge"	500
	"Hap Hazard"	116
	"Hap Hazard Addition"	100
	"Moores Hope"	100
	pt. "Moores Hope Addition"	208
Mr. John Emory	"Bee Tree"	500
	pt. "Partnership"	165
	pt. "Powells Fancy"	90
	"Batchelors Chance Resurveyed"	253
	"Hap Hazard"	17
	"Emorys Chance"	110
	"Bee Tree Swamp"	76
Mr. John Emory, Jr.	"Emorys Resurvey"	537¾
	"Emory's Fortune"	190
36:1756:30 ...		
Sarah Emory	pt. "Partnership" – surveyed for (N) Beck	100
Mr. William Elbert	½ "Reward"	200
	½ "Macklyns Addition"	18
	"Lewis's Chance"	50
	pt. "Lambeth"	100
	pt. "Lambeth" – more	29½
John Emerson	pt. "Addition"	100
Mary Eagle	"Lambeth Addition" – for h/o William	170
Benjamin Endsworth	pt. "Brandfield & Sayers Addition" – for h/o John Willson	200
w/o William Ewbanks	pt. "Rattcliffe" – for h/o said Ewbanks	140
	pt. "Outrange" – for h/o said Ewbanks	50

devisees of John Earle	pt. "Upperheathworth"	167
	"Heathworth"	533
John Errickson	pt. "Sarahs Portion"	96
36:1756:31 ...		
William Elliott (KI)	"Forlorne Hope"	100
	"Elliotts Choice"	120
John Elliott, Jr.	pt. "Copartnership" – for h/o William Price	52
	pt. "Jones's Plott" – for h/o William Price	45
	pt. "Hunns Hazard" – for h/o William Price	75
	pt. "Carters Addition" – for h/o William Price	25
	pt. "Chance" – for h/o William Price	25
	pt. "Barns's Satisfaction" – for h/o William Price	50
Elizabeth Errickson (widow)	pt. "Sarahs Portion"	54
	"Johnson Lott"	46
Jos. Elliott	pt. "Slaughterton"	100
	"Williams Lott"	10
	"Newnams Hermitage"	50
	pt. "Sallisbury Plains"	100
	pt. "Sayers Range"	60
	pt. "Lowes Desire"	53
Charles Errickson	"Stinton Errickson"	200
Mr. Richard Tilghman Earle	"Earles Beginning"	517
36:1756:32 ...		
Law. Everett	"Hunters Forrest"	200
Mr. Michael Earle (CE)	"Emorys Fortune Addition"	270
	pt. "Partnership" – surveyed for (N) Emory	175
	"Golden Grove"	20
	pt. "Sprigley"	65
Thomas Emory	"Emory Paxton"	100
	pt. "Partnership" – surveyed for (N) Beck	150
Gideon Emory	pt. "Fortune"	90
	pt. "St. Pauls"	50
	pt. "Carmans Neck"	50
	pt. "McConnickins Fortune"	236
	pt. "McConnickins Fortune" – more, for wife	143
	pt. "Woodridge" – for wife	184

James Emory	"Emorys Part of Trustram"	196
	pt. "Trustram"	170
	pt. "Coursey Upon Wye"	30
Arthur Emory s/o John	pt. "Partnership" – surveyed for (N) Beck	90
	pt. "Partnership" – surveyed for (N) Emory	10
Jo. Elliott s/o George	"Clouds's Hermitage"	200
36:1756:33 ...		
Sarah Elston (widow)	1 lot in Kings Town – No. 7	1
Thomas Emory s/o John	"Roberts Range"	150
	"Roberts Range Addition"	37
Jo. Everett	"Roes Desire" – for h/o Thomas Roe, Jr. (Choptank)	50
	pt. "Hackers Adventure" – for h/o Thomas Roe, Jr. (Choptank)	50
George Elliott	"Elliotts Luck"	125
George Edwards	"Edwards's Chance"	50
Mr. James Earle	"Cove Point on Resurvey"	200
	"Smiths Lott"	100
	"Wood Land Neck"	200
Jonathan Evans	pt. "Winfield"	55
Law. Everett, Jr.	pt. "Everetts Content"	100
36:1756:34 ...		
Burton F. Falconar & John	"Chesutt Ridge"	200
Fran. Foreman	pt. "Royston"	500
Thomas Ford	pt. "Ashton"	142½
Isaac Ford	pt. "Ashton"	82½
James Finley	pt. "Rambles"	150
William Fisher	pt. "Large Range"	416⅔
	pt. "Codshead Manor"	384
	pt. "Codshead Manor" – for his sister	100
	"Codshead Manor" – surveyed in DO	366
Henry Fiddeman	pt. "Hacketts Garden"	600
	pt. "Brandfield"	200
	pt. "Large Range" – from W. Thomas	10
John Fouracres	pt. "Tullys Lott"	100

James Finley (wheelright)	pt. "Warplesdon Addition" & pt. "Slomans Friendship"	50
	"Nathan & Thomas's Beginning"	27
36:1756:35 ...		
John Fisher	pt. "Suffolk"	300
Lidia Fisher (widow)	pt. "Suffolk" – for William Fisher (minor)	300
	"Fishers Plains" – for William Fisher (minor)	164
James Fisher	pt. "Fishers Meadows"	167
w/o Thomas Fisher – during her lifetime, & afterward to her son Richard	pt. "Fishers Meadows"	167
John Falconar	"Falconars Hope" tbc John Hall	\<unr\>
	"Falconars Chance"	12
	pt. "Welch Pool" – as tenant under Daniel Wheatly	150
John Foreman s/o Fran.	pt. "Royston"	100
36:1756:36 ...		
John Green	"Greens Adventure Upon Carpenters Square"	212
William Greenwood	"Miss Hitt" – for h/o Stephen Ritch	250
Matthew Griffith	pt. "Park"	220
Edward Garrett	"Sandy Hill"	50
Edward Godwin	pt. "White Marsh Addition"	338
	pt. "Parkers Freshes"	8⅓
Michael Green	"Costins Hope"	200
William Godwin	pt. "Wrights Chance" a/s "Choice"	100
Richard Gould	pt. "Ripley"	266⅔
	pt. "Spread Eagle"	75
Charles Gafford, Jr.	pt. "Macklyns Beginning"	118
	pt. "Smithfield"	40
Richard Gafford	pt. "Macklyns Beginning"	141
	pt. "Smithfield"	17
36:1756:37 ...		
Marmaduke Goodhand	pt. "Sillen"	200
	"Broad Neck"	500
	"Poplar Neck"	300
	pt. "Sillen" – more, for Nathaniel Brown	100
	"Woodyard Thickett" – for his wife	205
	pt. "Point Love" – in corn	200

Queen Anne's County - 1756

Philemon Green	"Greens Fortune"	80
	"Greens Fortune Addition"	75
	"Jones's Forrest"	100
	"Pratts Hope" – for Robert Pratt (minor)	100
Matthew Graves	"Graves's Beginning"	50
Fran. Gould	"Spring Branch"	100
	pt. "Ripley"	133⅓
	pt. "Sewalls Fork"	500
James Gould	"Goulds Purchase"	195
William Green	"Bradford"	100
36:1756:38 ...		
Elizabeth Gwinn	"Gunners Harbour" – for h/o John Gwin	100
Benjamin Gould	pt. "Camberwell"	100
Anne Gilbert	"Isaacs Chance"	100
Boatswain Tom, etc. Gibbs (Negroes)	pt. "Killmanam Plains"	200
James Ginn	pt. "Bakers Plains"	200
Charles Gafford	pt. "Macklyns Beginning"	141
John Gafford & James Roseberry	pt. "Brotherhood" – for their wives	317½
John Gilbert & John Daily or heirs	"Ralphs Frollick"	67
36:1756:39 ...		
John Higgens	pt. "Dungarnon"	150
Edward Hall	pt. "Vaughans Discovery" – for wife Ellinor	100
	pt. "Hogg Harbour" – for wife Ellinor	73¼
	pt. "Hogg Harbour" – more, for wife Ellinor	1¾
William Hopper, Esq. (cnp)	"Chesterfield"	900
	pt. "Providence"	200
	"Bridge Water"	300
	pt. "Guilford"	200
	"Darkin"	210
	pt. "Coursey's Point" or "Smiths Mistake"	200
	"Hoppers Industry"	213¼
	pt. "Smiths Mistake"	275
	pt. "Conquest"	256
	pt. "Green Spring"	100

		pt. "Camberwell"	272
		pt. "Stepney"	255½
		"Dockerys Discovery"	73
		pt. "Paxtons Lott"	20
		pt. "Paxtons Lott" – more	80
		pt. "Camberwell" – more	28
		pt. "Stepney" – more	44½
	John Hall	pt. "Welch Poole" – for his wife	100
		pt. "Duney"	300
		pt. "Hogg Harbour"	219¾
		pt. "Hogg Harbour" – more	1¾
		"Falconars Hope"	21½
36:1756:40 ...			
	John Hill	"Green Hill"	100
	Robert Hardcastle	"Mount Hope"	150
		"Stenewell"	154
		pt. "Newington"	120
	Ezekiel Hunter	"Boones Ridge"	50
	Mary Hunter	"Jumps Lott"	50
		"Hunters Hazard"	50
	William Harrington	pt. "Josephs Lott"	100
		pt. "Henrys Lott"	25
	h/o David Harrington	"Hopewell"	100
		"Harringtons Desire"	50
		"Buck Bay"	100
		"Beaver Dams"	50
	Richard Harrington	"Solomons Lott"	100
		pt. "Solomons Lott Addition"	15
		pt. "Fishers Chance"	50
36:1756:41 ...			
	Ernault Hawkins	pt. "Brampton"	126
	Richard Hynson	"Anns Portion"	150
	Thomas Honey	"Sparks Outlett"	114
	Val. Tho. Honey	pt. "Mitchells Adventure" a/s "Adventure"	100
		pt. "Sparks's Own"	25
		"Mitchels Adventure & Adventure" – more	100

Jos. Harris	pt. "Crumps Chance"	50
	pt. "Upper Heathworth"	100
	pt. "Crumps Forrest"	15
James Harris	pt. "Crumps Chance"	50
	pt. "Toms Fancy Enlarg'd" – for his wife	75
Mrs. Sarah Hollyday	"Readburn Rectified" – for h/o James Hollyday, Esq.	1440
	pt. "Macklinborough" – for h/o James Hollyday, Esq.	114
	"Bremington" – for h/o James Hollyday, Esq.	300
John Hollingsworth, Jr.	"Good Increase" – for h/o Thomas Crupper	200
36:1756:42 ...		
John Hambleton	pt. "Neglect"	50
	"Hambletons Range"	100
	"Mary Anns Lott"	100
	"Hambletons Addition"	50
	"Hambletons Luck"	100
Mary Hackett	pt. "Prices Hill" – for h/o John Hackett	200
Thomas Hackett	pt. "Prices Hill"	100
	pt. "Scottland"	50
	pt. "Providence"	330
	pt. "Shepherds Fortune" – for his wife	150
h/o John Harris	pt. "Contention"	150
John Hollingsworth	pt. "Hambletons Hermitage"	33⅓
Sarah Hollingsworth	"Refuse"	100
John Hadley	"Skinner's Pleasure"	50
36:1756:43 ...		
James Hutchings	"Wrights Fortune"	120
	pt. "Condon"	316
	"James's Camp"	1000
	"Little Thickett"	453
Thomas Hutchings	"Lanes Ridge"	200
Giles Hix	pt. "Killeray"	100
Charles Hines	pt. "Spread Eagle" – for Thomas	33⅓
George Harrington	"Harringtons Venture"	100
Anthony Harrington	pt. "Warners Discovery" – for his wife (N) d/o William Vickers	195

Mr. James Hollyday (London)	pt. "Macklynborough"	230
	pt. "Waterford"	18
James Harvey	"Harveys Discovery"	170
	pt. "Gould Hawks Enlargement"	35
36:1756:44 ...		
MM William Hopper & Christopher Cox	pt. "Jamaica"	1
Nathan Harrington	"Beaverdams Addition"	150
	½ "Ingram's Desire" – for his wife Sedney	<n/g>
Robert Hawkins	pt. "Macklinborough"	175
	pt. "Tullys Delight"	293
William Hunter	pt. "Chesnutt Meadows" – for h/o Price Williams	100
Thomas Hamer	"Hamers Chance"	178
	pt. "Whitall" – for his wife	18
	pt. "Rattcliffs Part of Lloyd's Freshes"	19
Nathaniel Harrington	"Jadwins Folly"	44
John Higgens & James Sullivane	pt. "Sallisbury"	200
William & Thomas Hughlett	pt. "Bakers Plains"	400
36:1756:45 ...		
Matthew Hawkins	pt. "Tullys Delight"	200
Andrew Hall	pt. "Spread Eagle"	149
	pt. "Spread Eagle" – more	35
	pt. "Brotherhood"	234
John Holding	"Nicholsons Fancy"	50
	pt. "Wood House"	61
	pt. "Wood House Addition"	14
William Horne	"Walnutt Neck Resurveyed" – for his wife	109
	"Barron Ridge" – for his wife	100
Mark Hargadine, Jr.	pt. "Smiths Neglect" – for his wife's daughter-in-law Mary Downs	150
Giles & James Hix	pt. "Edmundsons Green Close"	200
MM Robert Hawkins & (N) Kendall (KE)	pt. "Sprigley" – in right of their wives (N) d/o & co-heiresses of Henry Jacob	300
	pt. "Winchester" – in right of their wives (N) d/o & co-heiresses of Henry Jacob	125
36:1756:46 ...		

Queen Anne's County - 1756

Mrs. Anna Maria Hemsley	"Hardest Fend Off"	150
h/o Mrs. Mary Hemsley	"Towton Fields Addition"	140
	"Hemsley's Discovery"	91
Mrs. Anna Maria Hemsley & h/o Mary Hemsley	pt. "Towton Fields"	460
Mr. Henry Hollyday	pt. "Turners Plains Addition"	120
James Hammond	pt. "Wrenches Adventure"	192
Thomas Harris	"Addition"	500
	"Steads Go Between"	71
	pt. "Beginning"	429
	pt. "Standford"	114
	pt. "Ditteridge"	251
	pt. "Long Neck Addition"	20½
	pt. "Coursey Upon Wye"	258½
	pt. "Reason"	35
	pt. "Mount Mill"	33
	"Lawrences Delight"	100
	"Johnson Addition"	100
	pt. "Standford" – more	86
	pt. "Ditteridge" – more	26
36:1756:47 <blank>		
36:1756:48 ...		
Francis Jackson	"Barbarahs Inlett"	263
Thomas Jackson s/o George	pt. "Winchester"	125
	"Barbarahs Choice"	80
	"Castle Towne"	100
Stephen Jerman	pt. "Hogg Hole"	130
h/o Robert Jerman	"Newport"	284
	pt. "Brandford" – from (N) Diggs	211
	pt. "Saint Martins"	136
John Jerman	pt. "St. Martins"	82
	pt. "Inclosure"	81
Handcock Jones	pt. "Deluge"	80
Henry Jones	pt. "Nobles Range"	58
	pt. "Deluge"	50
36:1756:49 ...		

William Jones	pt. "Deluge"	50
Mary Jadwin	pt. "Lyford" – for h/o Robert	70
Peter Jumpe	pt. "Horse Pasture"	100
Isaac Jumpe	pt. "Horse Pasture"	50
Abraham Jumpe	pt. "Jumps Chance"	100
Volentine Jumpe	pt. "Pokely Ridge"	45
Solomon Jumpe	pt. "Jumps Chance"	44
	"Jumps Addition"	49
Jere. Jadwin	"Cow Range"	100
	"Tom's Neglect"	50
	"Jadwins Project"	40
	"Scarborough"	200
William Jones – I think the s/o Edward [!]	"Jones's Chance"	100
36:1756:50 ...		
Edward Jones	"Beaverdam Fork"	100
	"Hopewell"	100
	"Fords Park"	30
	"Fords Folly"	20
	"Jones's Greenwood" – for his son William K. Jones	150
	"Jones's Safty"	59
	"Nottingham"	89
Dorothy Isgate	"Fork"	200
John Johnson	"Cloudent"	200
	"Notlars Delight"	80
Thomas Jackson	"Hopewell"	50
	"Nicholsons Chance"	50
William Joyner, Jr.	pt. "Parsons Neck"	60
Jonathan Jolly	"Andeaver"	50
	"Nicholsons Adventure"	50
	"Burton"	50
	"Lester"	50
	"Lester Meadows"	50
Amos Jerman	pt. "Blandford" a/s "Brandford"	37
36:1756:51 ...		

Dr. John Jackson	pt. "Providence"	213
	"Smithfield Addition"	327¼
	pt. "Lexton"	184
	pt. "Jamaica"	40
	pt. "Adventure Resurveyed"	27
	pt. "Smithfield"	100
Thomas Jumpe, Jr.	"Jumps Lott"	34
Thomas Jones	"Sarah's Portion"	50
Inhabitants of Queen Ann's County	pt. "Price Land" – whereon Wells Inspection House stands	½
Jo. Jackson s/o Fra.	"Jaspers Lott" tbc Vincon Benton (f. 7)	<n/g>
James Jones	"Jones's Fancy"	100
Archibald Jackson	"Speedy Contract"	10
	pt. "Rattcliffe"	100
36:1756:52 ...		
Samuel Jackson	pt. "Oak Ridge" – for h/o Benjamin Boone	175
	pt. "Garden of Roses" – for h/o Benjamin Boone	177¾
Thomas Jumpe s/o Thomas	pt. "Horse Pasture"	50
Archibald Jackson, Jr.	"Nodd"	113
James Jackson	pt. "Ratcliffe"	100
Obednego Jackson	pt. "Ratcliffe"	100
36:1756:53 ...		
h/o Richard Kieron	pt. "Confusion"	100
Nath. Knotts	"Knotts Addition"	50
	"Knotts Range"	235
	"Knotts Chance"	53
	"Turners Plains Addition" – for h/o James Bell	120
James Kentin	pt. "Grovely Hoe"	150
	pt. "Upland"	100
36:1756:54 ...		
Solomon Kentin	pt. "Upland"	200
	"Upland Addition"	50
James Kersey	pt. "Scotland"	100
Baldwin Kemp	pt. "Emorys Rich Land"	150
James Knotts	pt. "Knotts Chance"	200
John Knotts	pt. "Knotts Chance"	102

Ann Knotts (widow)	pt. "Emory's Rich Land"	95
	pt. "Relief"	55
William Kent	pt. "Toms Fancy Enlarg'd"	150
36:1756:55 ...		
Thomas Kersey	pt. "Scotland"	50
Susanna Kirby (widow)	"Kerbys Hardship" – for h/o Walter Kirby	199
	"Kirbys Addition" – for h/o Walter Kirby	50
Benjamin Kirby	"Clouds's Chance"	6
	"Bodys Neck"	200
	"Coopers Quarter"	50
	pt. "Sillen" – for h/o John Evans & Andrew Price	200
	pt. "Upper Deal" – for h/o John Evans & Andrew Price	500
James Kelly or Jo. Buckley	pt. "Buckleys Delight" – for his wife	33⅓
Mary Kemp	pt. "Toms Fancy Enlarg'd"	75
h/o Thomas Kemp	pt. "Wellenlew"	106
36:1756:56 ...		
Robert Kent	pt. "Batchelor's Plains"	200
William Kirkham	pt. "Stephens Fields" – for h/o Henry Clift	278
36:1756:57 ...		
Mr. Robert Lloyd	"Hemsley's Park" – for devisees of Phil. Hemsley	800
	"Cloverfields" – for devisees of Phil. Hemsley	1622
	pt. "Trustram Wells" – for devisees of Phil. Hemsley	68
	"Hemsleys Adventure" – for devisees of Phil. Hemsley	200
	"Tilghmans Gift" – for William Hemsley	650
	"Tilghmans Meadow's" – fro his wife	270
	"Snodland" – for his wife	284
	"Friendship"	175
	"Friendship"	89
	"Plain Dealing"	600
James London	"Kirkhams Lott"	200
James Lane	pt. "Worleys Outrange"	100
	"Lanes Addition"	75
Elizabeth Longfellow	"Josephs Hope" – for h/o Jo. Longfellow	50

Richard Lambert	pt. "Lowes Arcadia" – for h/o Thomas Phillips s/o David	100
Thomas Lee	pt. "Lees Chance"	166
	pt. "Stratton"	52
	pt. "Hawkins's Pharsalia"	100
36:1756:58 ...		
John Legg	pt. "Limrick & Leggs Beginning"	186
	pt. "Pentroby" – rightly called "Pentrogy"	14
John Lee	pt. "Camberwell"	100
John Leith	"Horse Pen Ridge"	100
Bexly John Lambden	pt. "Swifts Outlett"	48
	pt. "Northumberland"	52
Mary Lane	"Lanes Folly" – for h/o Walter Lane	161
	pt. "Stevens's Fields" – for h/o Walter Lane	110
Sarh Linsey	"Jadwins Hazard" – for her son Edward	61
John Legg, Jr.	pt. "Limrick & Leggs Beginning"	14
	⅓ "Wood Land Neck"	16⅔
	⅓ "Oldsons Relief"	33⅓
John Lookerman, Jr.	"Bennetts Tolson Rest"	930
Alexander Lee	"Knave Stand Off" – for wife	50
	pt. "Whartons Addition" – for wife	19
36:1756:59 ...		
Thomas Mooth	pt. "Friendship"	25
	"Wattsons Delight"	50
	"Wattsons Delight Addition"	30
	"Mooths Range"	105
William Merson	pt. "Middle Plantation"	66⅔
William Manfield	pt. "Waltham" – in right of his wife	16⅔
	pt. "Wilkinsons Addition" – in right of his wife	16⅔
Rebecca Meeds	pt. "Brandford" – from William Diggs, for h/o John Meeds	141
William Meeds	pt. "Brandford"	100
	pt. "Saint Martins"	100
John Meridith	"Trustram Ridge"	150
Thomas Meridith	pt. "Plain Dealing"	75
	pt. "Adventure"	100

Ann Merridith	pt. "Shrewsbury" – for h/o William	150
	"Shrewsberry Addition" – for h/o William	100
David Mills	1 lot in Kings Town	1
John Mayne	"New London"	150
	"New London Addition"	114
Thomas Martindale	pt. "Silvesters Forrest"	100
	"Martindales Range"	50
	"Martindales Hope"	316
36:1756:60 ...		
h/o James Millis	"Campersons Choice" – for Samuel & James Cook (minors)	100
	pt. "Codshead Manor"	20
	pt. "Fishers Chance"	50
	"Hitt or Miss"	50
William Winchester Mason	"Ephraims Hope"	100
	pt. "Winchesters Folly Resurveyed"	273
William Mountague	pt. "Rattcliffe"	140
	"Mountagues Luck"	40
John Miller	pt. "Oakenthorpe"	229
	pt. "Providence"	150
Thomas Mountsieur	"Hacketts Delight"	150
James Massy	pt. "Friendship"	300
	pt. "Massys Addition"	23½
Patrick Mooney	⅓ "Nevells Delight"	16⅔
	"Mooneys Luck"	75
Daniel McConnikin	"McConnikins Correar"	150
	pt. "McConnikins Fortune"	20
	pt. "Wood Ridge"	16
Mr. Thomas Marsh (cnp)	"Little Thickett"	200
	"Marshes Forbearance"	150
	"Cabbin Neck"	350
	"Neglect"	200
	2 lots in Kings Town – No. 4, No. 5	2
	pt. "Shepherd's Fortune"	266
	1 lot in Kings Town – for (N) Maxwell	1
	pt. "Poplar Hill"	200

Queen Anne's County - 1756

		"Clouds's Choice"	200
		"Lowthers Chance"	150
36:1756:61 ...			
James McCoy		pt. "Smiths Delight"	218½
		"McCoys Pleasure"	129
		pt. "Hamers Addition"	18½
Thomas Meloyd		pt. "Toms Fancy Enlarg'd"	100
Timothy Mannah		"Mannahs Chance Resurveyed"	50
Jo. Merchant		"Jacks Purchase"	75
		"Musketo Ridge"	50
		"Josephs Own"	30
Thomas McClannahan		pt. "Fox Harbour"	100
		pt. "Collins's Lott"	56
		pt. "Brotherhood"	42½
Samuel McCosh		pt. "Upper Heathworth"	238
		pt. "Collins's Refusall"	112
		pt. "Heaths Forrest"	50
		"Heaths Gift"	53
		pt. "Larrington"	119
		"Crumpton"	50
William Matthews		pt. "Bridge North"	50
Charles Murphey		pt. "Hawkins's Pharsalia"	200
		"Murphys Chance Resurveyed"	99½
James Miller		"Forrest of Windsor"	250
36:1756:62 ...			
Solomon Mason		pt. "Winchesters Folly Resurveyed"	133
Richard Mason		pt. "Winchesters Folly Resurveyed"	133
Henry Mason		"Masons Hazard"	192
Abraham McCastelow		"Forkalett"	62
Anne Meridith (KI)		pt. "Conners Neck"	60
Abraham Milton (KE)		"Crumps Forrest"	150
James Massy, Jr.		pt. "Friendship" – surveyed for (N) Tilghman	50
William Mayner		pt. "Dispute" a/s "Brotherhood" – for his wife	47
		"Notlars Delight" – for his wife	33
John Meeds		pt. "Beginning" – on TA Rent Roll	150
Thomas Meeds		pt. "Beginning" – on TA Rent Roll	150

John Mason	⅔ "Nevills Delight" – for his wife	33⅓
John McConnikin	"Georges Codd"	100
	⅓ "Wood Land Neck" – for his wife	16⅔
	⅓ "Oldsons Relief" – for his wife	33⅓
36:1756:63 ...		
Samuel Massy	pt. "Poplar Hill"	123
	"Massys Addition"	49½
William Meridith (Tully's Neck)	"Meridith's Adventure"	100
Nathaniel Moore	pt. "Clouds's Adventure" – for h/o James Ware	112½
	pt. "Brotherhood" – from (N) Roseberry & his wife	67
h/o Edward McDaniel	"Emory Paxton"	272
William Mason	"Ephraims Hope"	100
Peter Massy, Jr.	"Massys Hazard"	50
Charles Mooney	pt. "Southampton" – for his wife	75
36:1756:64 ...		
James Meanor	pt. "Teagues Hazard"	60
John Nabb	pt. "Tilghmans Addition"	100
	"Jones's Fortune"	100
	pt. "Adventure"	7
	pt. "Toms Fancy Enlarg'd"	150
Solomon Newnam	pt. "Williams Lott"	40
William Newnam	"Newnam's Chance"	56
	pt. "John's Meadows"	60
	pt. "Shaver"	107
	"Newnams Addition"	72
	"Addition" – for h/o Jos. Newnam	24
	pt. "Scottons Addition" – for h/o Jos. Newnam	10
	pt. "Johns Meadows" – for h/o Jos. Newnam	40
	"Shearing" – for h/o Jos. Newnam	100
	pt. "Devonishes Chance" – for h/o Jos. Newnam	16¾
	"Devonishes Chance" – more, for h/o Jos. Newnam	133¼
36:1756:65 ...		
Charles Nabb (cnp)	pt. "Clouds's Adventure"	200
	"Elizabeths Portion" – not patented	100
	pt. "Manton" – not patented	75

	"Clockerton" – not patented	50
Thomas Newton	pt. "Toms Fancy Enlarg'd"	100
Mr. Edward Neale	pt. "Hawkins Farm Resurveyed"	12
	pt. "Green Spring"	550
	"Neales Residence"	899
	pt. "Hawkins's Pharsalia"	8
	pt. "Knowles's Range"	256
	"Partnership"	400
Mr. Jonathan Nicols	pt. "Hackton" – for his wife	200
	pt. "Redford" – for his wife	150
	"Willsons Addition" – for his wife	70
	pt. "Partnership"	500
Nathaniel Newnam	pt. "Shaver"	93
Rachell Nevell	pt. "Barton" – for h/o John Nevell	40
	"Smiths Addition" – for h/o John Nevell	106
	pt. "Southampton" – for h/o John Nevell	75
Mr. Charles Nicols	"Jones's Forrest"	500
	pt. "Brandfield & Sayers Addition"	50
36:1756:66 ...		
James Williams Nabb	pt. "Wrenches Farm" – for his wife	200
	"Moores Hope Addition" – for his wife	172
John Nabb, Jr.	pt. "Batchelors Hope" – for John Brown (minor) s/o John	40
	pt. "Neglect" – for John Brown (minor) s/o John	32⅔
John Nevell s/o John	pt. "Whortons & Pinders Outrange"	75
	pt. "Sewalls Fork"	250
	"Nevells Outrange"	3½
	pt. "Tilghmans Discovery"	200
	"Solomons Outlett"	50
	"Nevells Addition"	144
	"Farrington"	250
h/o Negro Dick	pt. "Knowles Range"	244
36:1756:67 ...		
John Oldson	pt. "Hawkins's Pharsalia"	150

Thomas OBryan	"Pleasant Spring Resurveyed"	418
	4 lots in Ogle Town – No. 22, No. 38, No. 39, No. 59	4
Robert Offley	pt. "Levells"	80
Samuel Osburn	"Addition"	200
	pt. "Martins Neck Resurveyed"	78
Abraham Oldson	pt. "Hawkins's Pharsalia"	50
	pt. "Hawkins's Farme Resurveyed"	126
William Oxenham	pt. "Golden Lyon"	100
	"Mire Branch"	85
	"Turners Plains"	128
36:1756:68 ...		
William Pryor	"Pryors Chance"	271
Charles Price	"Lincoln"	200
	pt. "Broomley Lambeth"	247
Thomas Price	pt. "Brandford" – from William Diggs	106
John Phillips	pt. "Vaughans Discovery"	230
William Pratt	pt. "Chaires's Addition"	54
	"Bucks Forrest"	187
Henry Pratt, Jr.	"Pleasant Park"	100
	"Pleasant Park Addition"	9½
Thomas Purnall	"Dudleys Chance"	200
Mr. Grundy Pemberton	pt. "Dawsons Neck"	142
	pt. "Partnership"	850
	pt. "Hawkins's Pharsalia"	600
	"Pembertons Resurvey"	969
	"Bostons Addition"	150
	"Kingsale"	250
	"Kingsale Addition"	100
	"Change"	200
	pt. "Kelds Inheritance"	52
Vincent Price	"Andrew & Prudences Satisfaction"	696
	pt. "Lambert" – for h/o Timothy Lane	400
36:1756:69 ...		
John Powell	"Longs Desire"	50
	"Powells Fancy"	94

Queen Anne's County - 1756

John Pickering	pt. "Lowes Arcadia" – for wife	66⅔
John Ponder	pt. "Smiths Delight"	81½
James Ponder s/o Richard	"Ponders Chance"	38
Margaret Pinder	pt. "Bishopton"	250
	pt. "Ashton"	75
	pt. "Collins's Lott"	116
	pt. "Wharton's & Pinders Outrange"	67
Mary Perry (widow)	"Stafford"	100
Martha Primrose	pt. "Shepherd Fortune" – for h/o George Primrose	200
Thomas Powell (Choptank)	"Powells Venture"	95½
Morgan Ponder	pt. "Spread Eagle" – for wife	16⅔
36:1756:70 ...		
John Pratt	"Wrights Park"	100
	"Vaughans Discovery" – for wife	100
Henry Pollock	pt. "Colne Rectified"	284
Thomas Price s/o Henry	"Good Hap"	126
	"Margaretts Hill"	200
Thomas Price s/o Thomas	pt. "Brandford"	23
	pt. "Conclusion"	64
Robert Pratt	"Pratts Choice"	100
Prudence Primrose	pt. "Kent Lott"	52
George Powell	"Longs Chance"	50
	"Tryangle"	50
William Price (KI)	pt. "Coppidges Range" – for h/o John Carter	198
	"Craney Neck" – for h/o John Carter	160
	pt. "Ridge" – for John Carter (minor)	124⅔
John Price	pt. "Toms Fancy Enlarg'd"	50
36:1756:71 ...		
Thomas Powell (Double Creek)	pt. "Tilghmans Discovery"	1¼
Thomas Price (KI)	pt. "Cloverfields"	100
John Primrose	pt. "Whittingtons Lott & Hemsleys Britland Resurveyed" – for h/o John Whittington	178½
George Personate	"Smiths Range" – as tenant under William Thomas	220
	"Smiths Range" – more	80
Thomas Priest	"Wigg Moore"	61

Oneal Price	pt. "Winfield"	111
36:1756:72 ...		
Quakers	pt. "Land of Prophesy" – for a Meeting House	3
Nathaniel Reed	pt. "Toms Fancy Enlarg'd"	400
	pt. "Wrights Square" – for wife	100
Richard Ross	pt. "Coldraine"	125
	pt. "Coldraine" – for Andrew Jordan (minor)	183
William Roe	pt. "Dudleys Desire"	100
John Roe	"Wood Land"	100
36:1756:73 ...		
Benjamin Roe	"Clouds's Range"	100
John Roe s/o Thomas	"Downes's Forrest"	300
	"Roes Addition"	70
Patrick Robertson	"Tully Barden"	50
	"Tully Barden's Inclosement"	150
	"Blair Creisk"	200
Alexander Robertson	"Tully Barden's Addition"	62
	"Peith"	66
Peter Rich	pt. "Bridge Town"	11
	3 lots in Bridge Town – No. 4, No. 5, No. 6	3
William Ricketts s/o Edward	pt. "Hineslys Plains"	59
William Robinson	"Anns Lott"	100
	pt. "Elliotts Addition"	50
	pt. "Ridley's Chance"	96½
	pt. "Parkers Lott" & pt. "Boltons Delight" – for Daniel Bolton (minor)	140
	pt. "Ridleys Chance"	103½
James Reed	pt. "Providence"	100
36:1756:74 ...		
Benjamin Roberts	pt. "Lowes Desire"	178
	pt. "Sayers Range"	200
	pt. "Shepherd's Redoubt"	100
	"Dixon's Gift" – for h/o James Roberts	100
	"Roberts Meadow's" – for h/o James Roberts	100
	"Watsons Desire"	50

Fran. Rochester	"Watery Plains"	150
	pt. "Tully Lott"	200
	"Collins's Gift"	175
	pt. "Outrange"	80
	pt. "Ripley"	300
John Rochester	"Winchester"	200
	"John & Rachells Choice"	100
Henry Rochester	"Lowders Hazard"	77
	"Philadelphia"	50
h/o John Railey	pt. "Willsons Beginning"	100
	"Raily's Beginning"	62
William Ridger	"Hope"	50
	"Small Hopes"	50
	"Ridgers Lott"	100
	"Ridgeways Chance"	50
36:1756:75 ...		
Benjamin Richardson	pt. "Cloverfields"	335
	"Pascoes Adventure"	150
	"Wading Place"	300
	"Ashburys Addition"	35
	pt. "Cloverfields" – more	335
h/o John Ruth	pt. "Smiths Neglect"	150
David Register	pt. "Conquest"	138
	"Bradburns Delight" a/s "Bradys Delight"	100
	pt. "Boagly"	60
Christopher Ruth	pt. "Chesnutt Meadows"	100
	pt. "Conclusion"	86
	pt. "Hawkins Farm Resurveyed" – for h/o Peter Countis	120
	pt. "Baynards Pasture"	37
	pt. "Conclusion" – more	4
Thomas Robinson	"Wrights Chance" a/s "Choice"	100
Samuel Roe (cnp)	pt. "Oaken Thorpe"	164
	"Tullys Addition"	300
	"Nedds Beginning"	30
	"Roes Lane"	20

	pt. "Sarahs Fancy"	50
William Reed	"New Nothingham Rectified" – for his wife	169
Thomas Richardson Roe	pt. "Oaken Thorpe"	226
	pt. "Sarahs Fancy"	30
36:1756:76 ...		
James Roe	"Beginning"	85
	pt. "Sarahs Fancy"	540
William Ridgeway, Jr.	"Plain Dealing" – for h/o William Ferrell	100
John Roe s/o Edward	pt. "Narborough"	250
	"Hineslys Choice"	100
	pt. "Oaken Thorpe"	40
	pt. "Sarahs Fancy"	111
Benjamin Ridgeway	"Long Delay"	150
John Roberts (minor) s/o John	"Roberts Desire"	150
Edward Rooke	pt. "Revivall"	1118
	"Chance"	100
Gilbert Reed	pt. "Spread Eagle"	1
Theophilus Randall (KE)	"Bacon Neck" a/s "Barren Neck"	227
	"Jones's" a/s "James Lott"	50
James Roberts	pt. "Sandy Hurst"	100
36:1756:77 ...		
William Robinson, Jr.	pt. "Tottingham" – for his wife (N) d/o Samuel Sallisbury	100
John Russum	"Clymores Chance" – for h/o Thomas Clymore	59
Thomas Ringgold (KI)	"Cox's Neck"	1000
William Robinson (Tuckahoe)	"Todcaster"	500
William Roberts	"Roberts Chance"	150
Thomas Robinson, Jr.	pt. "Lower Arcadia" – for his wife	100
Damsel Railey	pt. "Larrington" – for h/o Charles Railey	31
	pt. "Bishops Outlett" – for h/o Charles Railey	73½
36:1756:78 ...		
Patrick Sexton	"Liberty"	100
36:1756:79 ...		
John Seth (cnp)	pt. "Mount Mill"	79¼
	pt. "Addition"	10
	pt. "Bennetts Outlett"	50

Queen Anne's County - 1756

	pt. "Mount Mill" – for his brother Jacob	79¼
	pt. "Addition" – for his brother Jacob	10
	pt. "Bennetts Outlett" – for his brother Jacob	50
John Sullivant	pt. "Ponderfield"	109
	pt. "Dungamon"	133¾
	pt. "Fossetts Plains" – for h/o John Hammond	150
	"Sullivants Chance"	66
Andrew Sanders	"Good Luck Range"	50
Thomas Swann	pt. "Jumps Chance"	100
	pt. "Jumps Choice"	2½
	pt. "Sayers Addition & Brandfield"	100
Susanna Steward	pt. "Kearys Discovery" – for h/o Thomas Steward	140
	pt. "Silvesters Forrest" – for h/o Thomas Steward	105
Emanuel Swift	"Swifts Forrest Addition"	50
James Slaughter	"Fern Ridge"	50
	pt. "Partnership" a/s "Ratcliffe"	50
	"Fairn Ridge Addition"	100
	"Golden Rod Ridge"	50
John Swift	"Swifts Forrest"	50
	"Bear Harbour"	50
36:1756:80 ...		
Moses Swift	"Indian Tract"	50
	"Swifts Meadows"	100
James Silvester	pt. "Bear Garden"	123
	"Carmarthan"	100
	"Mischief"	100
	pt. "Parkers Freshes"	33
h/o William Starkey	pt. "Oak Ridge"	175
	pt. "Hickory Ridge"	150
	pt. "Cods Head Manor"	116
William Shepherd	pt. "Hineslys Plains"	109
Solomon Sinnott	pt. "Hawkins's Pharsalia"	150
Robert Smith	pt. "Toms Fancy Enlarg'd"	100
Joseph Scrivner	pt. "Hackers Meadows's"	14
	"Josephs Part of Hackers Meadows Inlarg'd"	325

Daniel Smith (planter)	pt. "Jones's Fancy"	75
	pt. "Jones's Fancy" – more	24
Benjamin Smith	pt. "Jones's Fancy"	75
	"Marys Chance"	30
	"Teass Desire"	35
	pt. "Jones Fancy" – more	24
36:1756:81 ...		
John Spry	pt. "Friendship" – surveyed for (N) Sprye	70
Thomas Spry	pt. "Friendship" – surveyed for (N) Tilghman	55
	pt. "Friendship" – more	15
Solomon Seney	pt. "Barton"	110
	"Bradfords Addition"	100
	pt. "Clouds's Adventure"	187½
	pt. "Sewalls Fork" – for his wife (N) w/o John Nevell	250
	pt. "Tilghmans Discovery" – for his wife (N) w/o (N) Nevell	78¾
	pt. "Poplar Hill"	150
Thomas Seward	"Outrange"	174
Thomas Sands	"Sands Outlett"	100
	"Dub Hen Ridge"	40
	"Timber Ridge"	70
	pt. "Swifts Outlett"	22
	"Long Swamp"	63
	"Lancaster"	119
	pt. "Northumberland"	48
	pt. "Lowes Desire"	122
Gideon Swift	"Chance"	66
	pt. "Swifts Outlett"	70
	"Constantinople"	100
	"Mulberry Tract"	100
	"Crump's Advice" – for his daughters Elizabeth & Mary	100
	pt. "Lowes Desire"	47
James Sutton	pt. "Sandy Hurst"	100
Absolam Sparks	pt. "Sparkes Own"	25
36:1756:82 ...		

Christopher Spry	"Thief Keep Out"	100
	pt. "Friendship" – surveyed for (N) Tilghman	52
	pt. "Friendship" – another	29
	"Sprys Chance"	21
	"Thief Keep Out Addition"	150
	"Buck Range" – for you son Humphrey	50
Thomas Shenton	"Forrest of Sherwood"	200
	pt. "Security"	40
Rebecca Sudler	"Johns Hole Resurveyed" – for h/o James Sudler	276
	"Stint on Sudler"	173
Mr. Jos. Sudler	"Sledmore"	800
	pt. "Devonishes Chance"	15
	"Sudlers Purchase"	80
	"Sudlers Fortune"	186
	"Sudlers Island"	64
	pt. "Shepherds Forrest"	200
	"Broad Creek Resurveyed" – for Anne Wells d/o & heiress of John Wells	630
	½ "Cloaks Chance"	50
	"Tilbury"	50
	"Tilburys Addition"	50
Dr. John Smith	"Smith's Neck"	128
	pt. "Spread Eagle"	346
	"Marys Portion"	150
	pt. "Martins Neck"	39
	pt. "Spread Eagle" – more, for mill land	5
	"Timber Neck"	100
Susanna Stevens	"Derochbourns Neglect"	17½
	"Stephens's Range" – for h/o John Stevens	315
36:1756:83 ...		
Robert Small	"Ship Point"	100
William Scott	pt. "Sayers Range"	40
	"Scotts Outrange"	304
Nathaniel Smith (cnp)	"Smiths Desire"	50
	"Smiths Outlett"	100
	"Long Ridge"	124

	"Indian Oldfield"	40
Thomas Scotton	"Scottons Forrest"	50
	"Scottons Desire"	100
Richard Swift	"Williams Pasture"	54
John Stent	pt. "Coldraine"	103
Richard Sparks – grandson of Richard Collins	1 lot in Kings Town	1
Samuel Swift	"Fosters Folly"	50
William Smith	pt. "Sallisbury Plains"	200
Caleb Sparkes	pt. "Sparkes Own"	25
36:1756:84 ...		
Fran. Spry	pt. "Spry's Adventure"	75
William Spry	pt. "Friendship" – surveyed for (N) Spry	149
John Scott	pt. "Stratton"	532½
Solomon Scott	pt. "Stratton"	311
Aron Sanders	"Purnalls Forrest" – for h/o William Purnell	500
	"Jumps Lane"	100
Moses Swift	"Swifts Meadows" tbc Moses Swift (f. 80)	100
Lemon Swift	"Toole Hill" – for h/o Fair. Wright	200
Henry Storey	pt. "Todley" – for wife	190
James Silvester, Jr.	"Beargarden Addition"	125
	pt. "Bear Garden"	80
	pt. "Silvesters Forrest"	45
Mr. John Segarr	"Johnsons Adventure"	100
	"Newnams Portion"	241½
	"Gwinns Hazard"	100
	pt. "Wood House"	39
	pt. "Wood House Addition"	11
	pt. "Cleans Addition"	150
	pt. "Seegars Hazard"	<n/g>
36:1756:85 ...		
Nathaniel Saterfield	"Saterfields Venture"	55
Fran. Stephens	"Lanark"	86
	"Hunting Tower" – for his son Robertson	100
Joseph Slocum	pt. "Bishops Fields" – for wife	50

Queen Anne's County - 1756

Charles Seth	pt. "Mount Mill"	158½
	pt. "Addition"	20
	pt. "Bennetts Outlett"	25
Richard Scotton	"Hazle Ridge"	65
Benjamin Silvester	"Bucks Range"	113
	"Silvesters Hazard"	189
	"Hemsleys Dispute"	76
Richard Small	"Coles Endeavour"	150
Maurice Sliney	pt. "Pitts Gift"	85
	"Timber Ridge"	250
John Smith	"Sandy Hill"	100
Thomas Seward, Jr.	"Hawkins's Range"	90
Millington Sparkes	pt. "Sparks Own"	25
36:1756:86 ...		
George Smith	pt. "Smiths Forrest" – for Thomas Chaires (minor) s/o John	61
	pt. "Confusion" – for Thomas Chaires (minor) s/o John	159
Catherine Scotton	"Scottons Outlett"	50
Priscilla Sanders	pt. "Middle Plantation"	33⅓
Absolam Swift	"Content"	50
Robert Scrivner	"Neglect"	190
James Smith (Wye)	pt. "Hemsleys Britland Rectified"	57
Jo. Spry	pt. "Sprys Adventure"	75
Josias Salloway	½ "Cloaks Chance"	50
David Silvester	pt. "Grubby Neck"	75
Emory Sudler	"Sudlers Chance" – for James Sudler (minor)	87½
	"Little Neck" – for James Sudler (minor)	55
William Silvester	pt. "Grubby Neck"	75
36:1756:87 ...		
John Sweat, Jr.	pt. "Park" – for h/o Benjamin Griffith	220
Daniel Smith (joyner)	"Marys Portion"	100
	"Mantons Addition"	5
Nathaniel Scott, Jr.	pt. "Stratton"	54½
h/o Nathaniel Scott	"Toms Fancy Enlarg'd"	243
Christopher Spry (TA)	"Dodlington"	200

Queen Anne's County - 1756

William Saterfield	pt. "Winfield"	100
36:1756:88 ...		
Col. Richard Tilghman	"Tilghmans Hermitage"	1843
	pt. "Bristol Marsh"	50
	pt. "Forlorne Hope"	1050
	pt. "Carpenters Outlett"	9
	pt. "Boadley"	75
	pt. "Park"	500
	"Wyatts Range"	50
	pt. "Confusion"	9
	pt. "Adventure & Confusion" – from (N) Alley	110
	pt. "Gray's Inn"	75
	"Cheshire"	200
	pt. "Shrewsberry"	150
	"Sintia"	187
	"Tilghmans Recovery"	1050
	"Plains"	112
	"Adventure"	160
36:1756:89 ...		
Maj. William Tilghman	"Pauls Fort"	200
	pt. "Bristol Marsh"	1110
	pt. "Tilghmans Discovery"	490
	"Sallisbury"	500
	"Delmore End"	350
	1 lot in Ogle Town	1
	"Poplar Plain" tbc Mr. Matthew Tilghman (f. 90)	191
	"Meadows"	28
	pt. "Smiths Mistake"	400
	"Andevour"	500
Col. Edward Tilghman (cnp)	pt. "Malton"	239
	1 lot in Ogle Town	1
	pt. "Porters Lodge"	200
	"Tilghmans Landing"	68
	pt. "Resurvey of Forlorne Hope Rectified"	2890
	"Tilghmans Resurvey of Long Neck"	539
	pt. "Union"	720

	"Scottons Folly"	50
	pt. "Long Neck Addition"	2½
	pt. "Coursey Upon Wye"	321½
	"Pleasant Bank on Wye"	19
	pt. "Sparkers Choice"	100
	pt. "Tully's Delight"	200
	"Just Design"	17½
	pt. "Lloyds Meadows & Lloyds Meadows Addition"	655
	"Beaver Dams"	50
	"Hollow Flatt"	50
	pt. "Reviving Spring"	166⅔
	pt. "Discovery"	216
	"Tully's Delight" – more	100
Nathaniel Tucker	pt. "Adventure"	61
	"Jones's Addition"	200
	pt. "Batchelors Plains"	100
36:1756:90 ...		
James Tilghman, Esq.	pt. "Adventure"	1030
	"Adventure Addition"	40
	"Tilghmans Freshes"	600
	pt. "Jerusalem"	200
	"Cow Bank Enlarg'd"	700
	"Kilkenney"	200
	"Gloscoster"	255
Mr. Matthew Tilghman (cnp)	"Tilghmans Forrest"	1400
	"Ring's End"	100
	"Notlars Enjoyment"	500
	1 lot in Ogle Town	1
	pt. "Poplar Plains"	191
	pt. "Closcester"	195
	½ "Timber Fork"	250
	½ "Negligence"	22½
	"Tilghmans Chance"	990
	"Wall"	420
	pt. "Toms Fancy Enlarg'd"	162

	"Poplar Plain"	191
	pt. "Delmore End"	150
Trustram Thomas 3rd	"Trustram Thomas's Part of Trustram"	127
Baynard Tillottson	pt. "Lords Gift on Resurvey"	270
	pt. "Todley"	170
	"Exchange"	100
	"Lantley" – for his wife Margaret	325
Mr. John Tillottson	"Shepherd's Folds on Resurvey"	140
	pt. "Todley"	150
	pt. "Lowes Arcadia"	100
	"Inkersell" – for h/o (N) Chettham	134
	"Timber Land" – for h/o (N) Chettham	400
	"Pascalls Chance" – for h/o (N) Chettham	250
	pt. "Park" – for James Chetham	354
	"Chethams Landing" – for h/o (N) Chettham	90
36:1756:91 ...		
h/o John Timm	"Society Hill" tbc Robert Breday	<n/g>
	"Timms Arcadia" tbc George Tote	<n/g>
	"Society Hills Addition"	50
Stephen Thomas	pt. "Hawkins's Pharsalia"	80
	pt. "Alcocks Pharsalia"	33⅓
Philemon Thomas	pt. "Hawkins's Pharsalia"	120
	pt. "Lees Chance"	33
	pt. "Alcocks Pharsalia"	66⅔
Trustram Thomas (Long Neck)	"Grubby Neck"	50
	"Trustrams Ridge"	50
	"Trustrams Adventure"	150
Thomas Tanner	"Chance"	50
	"Tanners Advantage"	39
	"Providence"	100
	"Ashford" – for h/o Isaac Hudson	100
Alexander Toalson	pt. "Freshford"	140
	pt. "Partnership"	206½
Anna Toalson	pt. "Philpotts Neck" – for h/o Alexander Toalson	233⅓
James Tuit	pt. "Youngs Chance"	270
	pt. "Lambeth Fields"	132

36:1756:92	...		
Richard Tickell		1 lot in Kings Town – No. 22	1
Mary Thomas		"Forrest Plains" – for h/o Charles Thomas	150
Benjamin Toalson		pt. "Coppidges Range"	211
		pt. "Slaughterton" – for wife	100
Samuel Thompson		"Kirbys Recovery"	52
		"Willmores Range"	1000
Mary Trickey		"Woodberry" – for h/o Thomas Trickey	100
w/o Dowdall Thompson		pt. "Price's Hill"	180
		pt. "Shepherds Discovery"	200
		"Parsons Marsh Addition"	10
		"Good Luck"	100
		"Sparkes Choice"	250
		pt. "Mount Pleasant"	102½
		pt. "Enjoyment"	50
		"Barefield" a/s "Barghold"	200
		"Parsons Marsh"	34
		pt. "Shepherds Discovery" & pt. "Henfield"	218
		"Courseys Town Resurveyed"	394
		pt. "Mount Pleasant" a/s "Mount Pleasure"	52½
		"Parsons Chance"	115
		pt. "Mount Pleasure"	80
		pt. "Enjoyment"	79
		"Whartons Marsh" – as guardian to Arthur Holt	27
		"Highgate Lane" – as guardian to Arthur Holt	100
		"Holt" – as guardian to Arthur Holt	506
		"Holts Castle Hill Resurveyed" – as guardian to Arthur Holt	304½
Isaac Tharp		pt. "Cole Raine"	83
36:1756:93	...		
John Tittle		1 lot in Kings Town – No. 7	1
Christopher Thomas, Jr.		pt. "Trustram Thomas's Part of Trustram"	100
Joseph Toalson		"Toalsons Desire"	193
		pt. "Phillips Neck"	116⅓
		½ "Morgans Inclosure" – for h/o Andrew Toalson	218½
Edm. Thomas, Jr.		pt. "Trustram"	458

Jo. Thomas	pt. "Trustram Thomas's Part of Trustram"	200
John Taylor	pt. "Neglect"	51
	pt. "Batchelors Hope"	90
Tilden Thomas	"Addition"	227
Phil. Tanner	⅓ "Wood Land Neck"	16⅔
	⅓ "Oldsons Relief"	33⅓
Richard Taylor	"Alberts Delight" – for h/o William Moun	200
John & James Toalson	"Partnership"	380
Thomas Teate	"Bee Tree Ridge"	50
36:1756:94 ...		
Henry Thompson	"Baynards Large Range Addition" – for h/o John Baynard	505
	"Vineyard Addition" – for h/o John Baynard	28½
	"Baynards Chance"	54
	pt. "Pitts Vineyard"	166⅔
	"Joans Plackett"	100
Isaac Turner	"Swann Brook"	770
36:1756:95 ...		
Visitors of Queen Ann's County School	pt. "Forlorne Hope"	100
Vestry of St. Pauls Parish	pt. "Doctors Folly"	½
Richard Vanderford	pt. "Outrange" – in right of his wife Hannah d/o Robert Green	40
John Vanderford	pt. "Wrenches Farm"	200
	"Christophers Hazard"	100
	pt. "Wrenches Farm" – more, from John Chaires	\<n/g\>
Joshua Vansant (KE)	"Difficulty"	72
James Vanderford	"Fox Hill"	28⅓
	pt. "Dispute" a/s "Brotherhood"	15⅔
John Vanderford s/o Robert	pt. "Fox Hill"	28⅓
	pt. "Dispute" a/s "Brotherhood"	15⅔
Vestry of Christ Church Parish	pt. "Little Ease" – glebe land	150
36:1756:96 ...		
devisees of or h/o John Walter (cnp)	pt. "Smeath"	250
	"Barnstable Hill Resurveyed"	210
	"Westminster"	297

h/o John Welch	pt. "Upperheathworth"	140
	pt. "Partnership"	200
	pt. "Ditteridge"	83
	pt. "Reason"	20
	"Ring Hammer"	99
Henry Williams	pt. "Sallisbury Plains"	100
	"Williams Fortune"	150
MM N. S. T. Wright & Thomas Wright	pt. "Hemsleys Britland Rectified"	50
	pt. "Wrights Reserve"	250
	pt. "Fair Play"	40
	"Fool Play"	500
	pt. "Fair Play" – more	14
Mr. Thomas Wilkinson	"Barbadoes Hall"	350
36:1756:97 ...		
James Williams	pt. "Courseys Addition"	100
	pt. "Kendall"	100
Elizabeth Wootters	"Richard & Marys Forrest"	80
James Willson	"Willsons Chance"	100
	"Willsons Chance Addition"	200
Jacob Wootters	"New Buckley"	100
	"Cow Range"	38
John Wheatly	"Wheatlys" a/s "Daniels Fields"	140
William Wheatly	"Wheatlys Park"	100
Thomas Wheeler	"Killmaiden"	100
	"Killmaiden Addition"	15
William Whitby	"Whitbys Forrest"	50
Nathaniel Wright	"Brotherhood"	50
	"Wrights Chance"	300
36:1756:98 ...		
Daniel Willcox	pt. "Mount Hope"	250
	"Mount Hopes Addition"	100
John Woodall (KE) s/o John	pt. "Crumpton"	10
Matthew Wicks	"Woolverhampton"	120
William Wharton	"Whartons Adventure"	570
	"Sayers Range Addition"	17

Benjamin Whittington	pt. "Hemsleys Britland"	300
	pt. "Whittingtons Lott"	400
	"Whittingtons Lott Resurveyed"	178½
	pt. "Poplar Hill"	34
	"Rattcliffs Part of Lloyds Freshes"	171
	"Recovery"	100
	"Whittingtons Luck"	200
Penelope Wright	pt. "Parsons Point"	100
Robert Walters	"Dundee"	368
	"Jamaica"	150
	"Walters Addition to Kirbys Prevention"	33
	pt. "Hope"	50
William White	"Workmans Hazard"	150
	"Sparks's Point"	50
36:1756:99 ...		
Jonathan Wootters	"Oak Ridge"	20
	"Oak Ridge Addition"	78
h/o Littleton Ward	pt. "Colne Rectified"	286
Nathaniel Wright s/o Edward	"Tullys Reserve"	300
	"Reserve Addition"	50
	"Marys Portion"	554
	pt. "Content"	400
John Willson, Jr.	"Willsons Adventure" – for his wife	262
h/o Hum. Wells, Jr.	pt. "Jennys Beginning"	22
	"Baths Meadows"	36
	"Jennys Beginning" – more	78
Peter Wrench	"Wrenches Chance"	35
	"Wrenches Farme"	200
Samuel & James Walters	pt. "Partnership"	217½
Samuel Walters	"Walters's Park"	150
James Walters	"Walters's Rambles"	150
36:1756:100 ...		
William Wrench	pt. "Guilford"	26
	pt. "Wrenches Lott"	100
	pt. "Hawkins's Farm Resurveyed"	326

Queen Anne's County - 1756

Henry Wrench	pt. "Wrenches Lott"	354
	"Wrenches Reserve"	39
Thomas Willson	"Sewalls Range"	1120
	"Plain Dealing"	727
	"Jacksons Boggs"	46
	pt. "Bennetts Outlett"	495
Josias Wharton	"Fords Chance"	100
Zorob. Wells	"Teats Folly"	50
	"Buck Island"	100
John Whitby	"Batchelors Chance"	69
	"Bite the Biter"	78½
	"Clarks Lott"	112
widow Woodall	pt. "James's Choice" – for h/o Cornelius Comegys	150
	pt. "Crumps Chance" – for h/o Cornelius Comegys	50
	pt. "Hope" – for h/o Cornelius Comegys	228⅔
Elizabeth Wells	pt. "Bath"	255
36:1756:101 ...		
George Wells	"Red Lyon Point"	50
	pt. "Baths Addition"	150
Hum. Wells s/o Hum.	"Price Land Addition"	50
	"Crump's Fancy"	50
	"Landing"	30
	"Fancys Addition"	150
Ben. Wells s/o Hum.	"Low Lands"	45
	"Caleb's Lott"	80
John Wells s/o Hum.	pt. "Price Land"	199½
Jo. Whitby	"Buck Range"	100
h/o Henry Ward	"Wards Flower Fields"	50
William Walls (KE)	pt. "Bath"	100
	pt. "Baths Addition"	150
Richard Warner	pt. "Sayers Range Addition"	66
	"Alberts Desire" a/s "Abbotts Desire" a/s "Delight"	100
John Wattson	pt. "Bailys Delight" – for his wife Esther	100
36:1756:102 ...		
Nathaniel Wright, Jr.	pt. "Sallisbury"	100
	½ "Skinners Expectation"	240

w/o Ambrose Wright	pt. "Wrights Chance"	100
	pt. "Hawkins's Farm Resurveyed"	41
	pt. "Guilford"	12
Mr. N. Samuel T. Wright	"New Hynson Town"	360
	pt. "Grays Inn"	75
	pt. "Larrington"	100
	2 lots in Kings Town – No. 2, No. 27	2
	1 more lot in Kings Town	1
	pt. "Wrights Square"	140
	pt. "Gould Hawks Enlargement" – as guardian to Elisha Brown	35
	"Claxton" – as guardian to Elisha Brown	100
	1 lot in Ogle Town – as guardian to Elisha Brown	1
Mr. Thomas Wright	"New Reading"	300
	pt. "Grays Inn"	50
	pt. "Neglect"	45
	"Warplesdon"	300
	pt. "Warplesdon Addition" & pt. "Solomons Friendship"	230
	pt. "Lowes Arcadia"	350
Mr. Nathaniel Wright s/o Edward	"Hazard"	100
	½ "Content"	100
	"Content Addition"	200
	"Content Outlett"	50
36:1756:103 ...		
Edward Wright s/o Edward	pt. "Partnership"	250
	"Colonells Quarters"	100
Isaac Winchester	½ "Morgains Inclosure" – for h/o Alexander Toalson	218½
	"Purlivant"	180
	"Isaacs Addition"	80
James Walters (KI)	pt. "Conners Neck" – for his wife (N) d/o Phil. Conner	120
Elizabeth White	pt. "Crawford" – for h/o Robert Willson	216
	pt. "Ridge"	62⅓

h/o Ambrose Wright – one of which is a minor under guardianship of Mr. J. Tillottson	pt. "Hawkins's Farm Resurveyed"	5
	"Wrights Chance"	408
	"Guilford"	40
Rebecca Williams	"Millford" – for h/o Abraham Williams	123
Mary Webb (widow)	pt. "Lyford" – for h/o James Webb	643
Thomas Wilkinson s/o Henry	"Wattsons Chance"	50
Mr. Solomon Wright	"Guilford"	300
	"Guilford Addition"	150
	"Hogg Harbour"	100
	pt. "Narborough"	250
36:1756:104 ...		
Stephen Weeks	pt. "Woolverhampton"	80
	pt. "Mount Pleasant" & pt. "Lillingstons Enjoyment"	1½
Joshua Walliston	pt. "Condone"	10
	pt. "Crumpton"	10
George Webb	"Wattsons Lott"	50
	"Webbs Plains"	50
John Willson (KI)	pt. "Eastern Island"	50
	"Willson's Adventure"	54
	"Erricksons Island"	20
Thomas Walker	"Toms Adventure"	56
	"Toms Adventure Addition"	50
Richard Wells, Jr.	pt. "Bath"	145
	"Williams Adventure"	50
Mr. Nathan Wright	"White Marsh on Resurvey"	376
	pt. "White Marsh Addition"	250
	pt. "Smiths Reserve"	2½
	"Cork House"	590
	"Jones's Park"	340
	pt. "Smiths Reserve"	31¼
John Wright	pt. "Narborough"	250
	"Narborough Addition"	100
	"Littleworth"	50
William Wallace	"Boothbys Fortune"	500

Jacob Walters	"Kirbys Prevention"	50
	pt. "Allens Deceit"	40
36:1756:105 ...		
Solomon Yewell	"Purchase"	86
Stephen Yoe	pt. "Brandford"	100
John Young s/o William	pt. "Stratton"	50
Aaron Yoe	pt. "Courseys Addition"	50
36:1756:106 <blank>		
36:1756:107 ...		
Dr. James Anderson (Chestertown)	pt. "Providence" – in right of his wife	200
	"Ashford" – in right of his wife	200
	pt. "Rambles" – in right of his wife	200
	"Shepherds Fields" a/s "Forrest"	200
James Aud (DO)	1 lot in Kings Town – No. 19	1
Thomas Adcock (TA)	"Wyatts Folly"	50
Stephens Andrews (Jerseys)	"Mount Gilboa" – see f. 2	50
Mr. William Anderson (London)	"Darland Resurveyed"	1750
	"Lloyds Town"	1000
36:1756:108 ...		
Mr. Rizdon Bozman (TA)	pt. "Killeray"	100
	pt. "Millford"	200
	"Point Landing"	5¼
	"Killerays Addition"	34¾
James Bartlett (TA)	"Partnership"	575
Benjamin Blackiston (KE)	"Benjamins Park"	80
	"Upper Landing"	200
Daniel Bird (Biddeford)	1 lot in Kings Town – No. 8	1
James Benson (TA)	pt. "Spread Eagle" – for wife	100
	"Collins's Own" – for wife	92
James Baxter (CE)	"Beaver Neck Resurveyed" – for h/o John Roles	320
	"Widows Lott" – for h/o John Roles	287
h/o William Brent (VA)	"Kent Fort Manor"	1000
John Blackwell or Thomas Grace	pt. "Alcocks Pharsalia"	100
Anne Brooke (widow, TA)	pt. "Scarborough"	200
John Barwick	pt. "Jump's Choice"	97½

36:1756:109 ...		
John Buck, Esq.	pt. "Poplar Hill"	100
	2 lots in Ogle Town	2
Fran. Bullock	"Chance"	200
John Blackiston	"Robass Mill & Land"	<n/g>
Edward Clark	"Clarks Delight" – for h/o Caleb Clark (TA)	76
	"Clarks Struggle" – for h/o Caleb Clark (TA)	65
Charles Carroll (Annapolis)	pt. "Thompsons Manor" a/s "Poplar Island"	1000
James Claypole (KE)	pt. "Lambeth"	187½
	pt. "Wells Chance" – for wife	100
	pt. "Lambeth" – more	62½
Johannah Carpenter (widow, Duck Creek)	⅓ "Porters Lodge"	100
36:1756:110 ...		
Ellionor Carey	pt. "Silvesters Addition"	112
Amia Carey	pt. "Silvesters Addition"	65
Peter Cummerford	"Mount Pleasure" – for h/o (N) Sharp	500
Benjamin Cleave (KE)	"Cleaves Rambles" – for his son Nathaniel	110
36:1756:111 ...		
h/o James Dickinson (TA)	"Dickensons Plains"	860
Samuel Dickenson (KEDE)	"Yough Hall"	175
	"Gorsuches Tryangle"	63
	"Poplar Ridge"	150
	"Poplar Ridge Addition"	200
	"Tuttle Fields"	200
Susanna Douglass (CE)	"Macklyns Fancy"	500
	"Poplar Ridge"	500
John Dixon (TA)	pt. "Jerusaley"	200
William Dickenson (TA)	pt. "Scarborough" – for h/o John Dickenson	200
Phillip Davis, John Davis, & David Davis	"Partnership"	300
36:1756:112 ...		
Henry Elbert	pt. "Davis's Range"	200
h/o Abraham Falconar (KE)	"Grove"	150
	"Edinborough"	1074

Queen Anne's County - 1756

Col. William Fitzhugh (CV)	"Morgans Neck" – for h/o John Rousby	400
	"Bluff Point" – for h/o John Rousby	496
Thomas Flemming (Annapolis)	pt. "Conners Neck" – for h/o John Granger	100
36:1756:113 ...		
Mr. Nicholas Goldsborough (TA)	pt. "Old Town"	740
Mr. William Goldsborough (TA)	"Walnutt Ridge" – for devisees of Mr. G. Robins	600
	"Pearle" – for devisees of Mr. G. Robins	1000
Mr. Robert Goldsborough (TA)	pt. "Controversey"	500
	pt. "Jaspers Lott"	570
	pt. "Sandish Wood" – for wife	665
Jere Grisingham (TA)	pt. "Davis's Range" – for wife	200
	pt. "Davis's Range" – more, for wife	15
Peter Garron	pt. "Alcocks Pharsalia" – for wife (N) w/o William Vickers	100
h/o John Gresham (KE)	"Sallisbury Meadow"	34
	"Pochickory Ridge"	1000
36:1756:114 ...		
Edward Harding (TA)	pt. "Hemsleys Arcadia"	231
Mr. Samuel Hyde (London)	"Smiths Forrest"	2000
Patrick Hamilton (CE)	pt. "Point Love" – for his wife (N) d/o Jo. Wicks	400
Nehemiah Jones	pt. "Outrange" – for wife	40
h/o Aquilla Johns	pt. "Cold Spring"	438
Alexander Kelly (KE)	pt. "Malton" – for his wife (N) d/o Maurice McCarty	150
36:1756:115 ...		
William Lambden (TA)	pt. "Reviving Spring"	333⅓
Mr. Thomas Lane (TA)	pt. "Smiths Ridge" – for wife	300
	"Collins's Range" – for wife	300
Mr. John Leeds (TA)	pt. "Scarborough"	200
Edward Lloyd, Esq. (TA) (cnp)	"Nineveh"	600
	"Ninevehs Addition"	200
	pt. "Lloyds Freshes"	810
	"Mill Range"	136
	"Chesnutt Neck"	300
	"Hoggs Hole"	50

Queen Anne's County - 1756

	"Break Neck"	100	
	"Wilton"	650	
	"Addition to Wilton"	600	
	"Hemsleys Reserve Rectified on Resurvey"	185	
	pt. "Brandford"	186	
	pt. "St. Martins"	82	
	pt. "Costins Park"	24	
	"Scotts Chance"	100	
	pt. "Oaken Thorpe"	56	
	"Nutwells Chance Resurveyed"	294	
	pt. "Hemsleys Britland Rectified"	223	
	"Courseys Range"	600	
	pt. "Costins Chance"	32	
	"Coopers Hill"	100	
	"Woolverton"	250	
	"Narborough"	250	
	½ "Reward" – for John Coursey	200	
	½ "Macklins Addition" – for John Coursey	18	
	pt. "Poplar Plains"	118	
36:1756:116 ...			
Richard Molineaux (popish priest) or his successor	"Batchelors Plains"	151¼	
	"Johns Forrest"	200	
	"Lundy"	200	
	pt. "Wood House"	200	
	"Waterford"	200	
	pt. "Batchelors Plains"	64¼	
Nicholas Massy (KE)	"Pacolett"	18	
Mr. George Millican (CE)	"Edinkelly"	600	
36:1756:117 ...			
Fran. Neale (TA)	"Shadwell" – for his son Fran.	100	
	pt. "Shadwells Addition" – for h/o Robert Jones	100	
	"Fairfield"	200	
Edward Neale (TA)	"Shadwells Addition"	100	
Jonathan Neale (TA) as trustee for John Webb	"Webbs Chance"	150	
	"Silvesters Addition"	40	
Mrs. Deborah Nicols	pt. "Partnership" – for devisees of Jere Nicols	250	

Mr. Edward Oldham (TA)	"Exchange"	470
	"Exchange" – another	60
	pt. "Providence"	300
36:1756:118 ...		
Aaron Parrott (TA)	pt. "Cold Spring"	162
John & James Porter (KE)	"Halls Harbour" – for their wives (N) d/o Capt. Henry Rippon	500
	pt. "Poplar Hill" – for their wives (N) d/o Capt. Henry Rippon	50
old Dr. Porter (TA)	½ "Negligence" – for his wife's sister in Newfoundland	22½
	½ "Timber Fork" – for his wife's sister in Newfoundland	250
36:1756:119 ...		
Thomas Reese (PA)	"Andever Meadows" – for his wife	175
Mr. James Ringgold (KE)	"Courseys Point" or "Smiths Mistake"	623
	pt. "Bishops Outlett"	400
	pt. "Bishops Addition" & pt. "Bishops Outlett"	100
John Robertson (SO)	"Athol"	500
h/o George Robotham	"Robathams Park"	500
Elizabeth Robass	pt. "Providence"	150
36:1756:120 ...		
Tobias Stansbury (BA)	"Robinsons Farm" – for his wife	200
Mr. Jarvis Spencer (KE)	pt. "Connoway" – for h/o Christopher Williams	111
h/o Charles Stevens (TA)	pt. "Willenlew"	212
Jo. Turner (TA)	"Turners Lane"	100
Abner Turner	"Abners Park"	130
	pt. "Turners Plains Addition"	58
36:1756:121 ...		
h/o Lambert Wilmore (KE)	1 lot in Kings Town	1
William Webb	pt. "Redford"	150
Park Webb	pt. "Shadwells Addition" – for h/o Samuel Neale	50
William Willson & wife (TA)	pt. "Bear Garden"	150
36:1756:122 <blank>		
36:1756:123 ...		
h/o James Ross (Bristoll)	pt. "Codshead Manor"	904
h/o Daniel Mullikin (TA)	"Mullikins Delight"	150

Presley Raymond (KEDE)	"Raymond's Travells"	100
Weightman Sipple (KEDE)	"Spicie Grove"	250
	"Tappahannah"	1375
	"Land of Benjamin"	275
George Whitehead & Co.	"Tappahannah"	1000
	"Addition to Frieth"	725
	"Winterfields"	50
William & Isaac Broadway	pt. "Tounton Fields"	250
Samuel Broadway	pt. "Tounton Fields"	210
36:1756:124 ...		
William Thomas (TA)	"Allens Neck"	83
	"Lampton"	135
h/o John Alley	pt. "Adventure"	31
h/o Matthew Mason	pt. "Bishops Outlett"	150
William Wrench & h/o Robert Grundy	pt. "Briglin & Briglins Addition"	86
Stead Lowe or Thomas Harris	pt. "Beginning"	71
h/o John Thomas	pt. "Brandfield"	102
36:1756:125 ...		
Michael Earle & h/o John Lillingston	pt. "Carpenters Outlett"	127
h/o Richard Carter (ENG)	pt. "Carters Forrest"	168
	"Collins Chance"	109
	"Lambeth Fields"	68
	"Stevens's Fields"	200
Robert Smith or h/o (N) Ivey (cnp)	pt. "Confusion"	55
	"Double Kill"	60
	pt. "Enjoyment" & pt. "Mount Pleasant"	321
	"Mount Pleasant" & pt. "Enjoyment"	234
	pt. "Smiths Forrest"	29
	"Smiths Reserve"	66
	pt. "Wrexam Plains"	130
	"Chance"	200
	"Smiths Forrest Addition"	140
	"Smiths Reserve"	84
	pt. "Tryangle Addition"	60

	"Tell Tales Loss"	100
	"Adventure"	160
	pt. "Mount Pleasant & Enjoyment"	171½
	pt. "Reason"	231
h/o Samuel Turbutt	pt. "Controversie"	178
h/o Edward Chetham	pt. "Collins's Lott"	28
36:1756:126 ...		
Charles Lowther	pt. "Connaway"	70
h/o John Pitts	pt. "Colerain"	183
Pere Frisby (KE)	pt. "Crawford"	48
	"Coopers Freehold"	80
h/o James Heath	pt. "Collins's Refusall"	17
h/o Anthony Cox	pt. "Devonishes Chance"	200
David Mills	"Davids Prospect"	75
h/o Charles Ferress	pt. "Daney"	100
	"Maxfield"	100
36:1756:127 ...		
h/o William Sidly	pt. "Double Kill"	100
	pt. "Mount Pleasant"	100
h/o Henry Ayler (Carolina)	pt. "Dawsons Neck"	86
	pt. "Inclosure"	169
William Calvin	pt. "Freshford"	50
h/o Charles Vanderford	pt. "Fortune"	10
	"Vanderfords Agreement"	100
Thomas Whittington (TA)	pt. "Freshford"	30
	"Burroughs Ridge"	100
Hynson Wright	"Guilford"	22
h/o Christopher St. Tee	pt. "Golden Grove"	96
Anthony Bacon (TA)	pt. "Hacketts Garden" – for h/o Anthony Richardson	300
	"Limrick" – for h/o Anthony Richardson	50
	"Richardsons Adventure" – for h/o Anthony Richardson	80
36:1756:128 ...		

h/o James Heath (CE)	pt. "Heaths Forrest"	100
	pt. "Park"	50
	"Tottenham"	300
	"Upperheathworth"	42
h/o Joseph Rawlings (DO)	pt. "Josephs Lott"	50
Timothy Tool	pt. "Kendall"	88
h/o George Bows	pt. "Kendall"	100
Stead Lowe	pt. "Lowes Desire"	1000
	"Expectation"	300
h/o old Thomas Fisher	"Large Range"	300
	"Long Range"	147
h/o Richard Fisher	pt. "Large Range Addition"	26
John Lane	"Lambert"	100
	"Lowes Birmington"	250
	"Lanes Folly Addition"	150
h/o John Woodall	pt. "Lexton"	81
36:1756:129 ...		
h/o John Carr	"Lanes Forrest"	127
Thomas Haddaway	pt. "Lowes Desire"	100
h/o Henry Costin	"Lambeth"	39
Samuel Taylor	pt. "Lowes Arcadia"	50
John Hawkins	pt. "Macklinborough"	90
h/o John Powers	pt. "Macklinborough"	26
h/o Nicholas Clouds	pt. "Notlars Desire"	80
	"Willsons Beginning"	250
h/o Robert Kent	pt. "Neglect"	55
h/o John Lang	"New Hall"	90
36:1756:130 ...		
John Nemo (KE)	pt. "Outrange"	40
Henry Short	pt. "Outrange"	200
h/o George Powell	"Partnership"	194
h/o Nathaniel Scott	pt. "Partnership"	250
	pt. "Sayers Range Addition"	41
	"Scotts Inclosure"	150
h/o John Ponder	"Ponderfield"	91
h/o John Sutton	"Pascos Lott"	100

Thomas Cooper	"Parsons Neck"	80
Phil. Lloyd & h/o Henry Costin	"Park"	10
John & George Gale	pt. "Rattcliffe"	370
36:1756:131 ...		
Edward Crew	"Rye Hall"	40
h/o Richard Royston	pt. "Royston"	25
h/o John Long	"Sandy Hurst"	50
h/o John Sparks	pt. "Sparks's Choice"	100
h/o John Carridine	pt. "Smiths Addition"	50
h/o old Edward Jones	pt. "Sandy Hurst"	34
h/o Albert Johnson	"Sayers Range Addition"	34
h/o Daniel Newnam	pt. "Scottons Addition"	6
h/o William Harrisson	pt. "Scarborough"	600
36:1756:132 ...		
Anne Lloyd	pt. "Wrexham Plains"	140
h/o old William Swift	"Williams Hazard"	50
Richard Wells the elder	"Welch Ridge Addition"	300
h/o Thomas Allen	"Allen's Neck"	66
Christopher Granger	"Adventure"	50
h/o Edm. Pryor	"Arthurs Chance"	300
William Ailward	"Ailward Town"	500
Richard Hopewell (SM)	"Bloomsberry"	400
	"Irish Discovery"	350
h/o old Thomas Butler	"Butlers Marsh"	50
	"Butlers Neck"	200
36:1756:133 ...		
h/o Edm. Burton	"Burtons Lott"	200
h/o Anthony Workman	"Barren Ridge Addition"	60
Nicholas Banks	"Banks's Fork"	200
	"Banks's Addition"	200
John Clayland	"Claylands Purchase"	200
h/o Henry Martin	"Contention"	50
Thomas Phillips	"Cabbin Branch"	200
h/o John Reynolds	"Chesterton"	150
h/o David Rogers	"Chance"	100

Queen Anne's County - 1756

h/o Thomas Cockayne	"Carters Addition"	191
	"Betts Range"	400
36:1756:134 ...		
h/o Dennis Connerly	"Connally's Park"	200
Richard Cheshire	"Cheshires Delight"	600
h/o Gabriel Johnson	"Chichester"	50
John Dobbs	"Dobb's Adventure"	36
Maurice Woollahand	"Dunnington"	100
Daniel Cornelius	"Daniels Fancy"	100
h/o John Davis (TA)	"Davis's Pharsalia"	350
h/o William Dobson	"Dobsons Westmoreland"	150
h/o John Parsons	"Frankford"	200
	"Killmanam Plains Addition"	500
36:1756:135 ...		
James Smith (KE)	"Fresh Run"	160
Martha Burn (SM)	"Gwythers Range"	500
h/o William Clayland (TA)	"Glocester"	300
h/o Thomas Gwyther	"Gwythers Lott"	250
h/o William Darvill	"Hills Addition"	50
h/o Nicholas Massy (KE)	"Hazard"	100
	"Massys Hazard"	40
John Jones	"Jones's Tryangle"	50
James Dawson	"Kniver Heath"	500
	"Padan Aran"	500
John Holloway	"Little Ease"	400
36:1756:136 ...		
Thomas Maynard (AA)	"Lillingstons Castle"	500
	"Lillingstons Addition"	350
h/o Robert Broadway	"Musketo Range"	51
	"Plains"	110
h/o Michael Fling	"Mill Land"	60
h/o William Nuthead	"Nutheads Choice"	300
h/o Christopher Wise	"Naseby"	100
h/o John Harrington	"Purnalls Chance"	100
h/o Edward Day	"Providence"	1100
Ralph Distance	"Ralphs Frolick"	67

h/o John Starkey	"Randon"	100
h/o Richard Bruff (TA)	"Ramseys Folly"	200
36:1756:137 ...		
h/o Christopher Rousby	"Rousby"	500
h/o Stephen Tully	"Sandwich"	150
	"Tullington"	300
h/o Simon West	"Stepney"	200
William Firth	"Smiths Beginning"	200
h/o Charles Edgerton (SM)	"Sebergham"	800
h/o William Sudborough	"Sudborough Hills"	200
h/o Thomas Carman	"Tilghmans Lott"	500
h/o Daniel Glover	"Hope"	200
h/o Thomas Gadd	"Addition"	50
h/o Nicholas Painter	"Kindness"	400
36:1756:138 ...		
h/o John Wright	"Wrights Choice"	200
h/o Robert Betts	"Westberry"	100
h/o John Winchester	"Winchester"	250
John Coursey & William Elbert	"Yarmouth"	100
James Hurlock (TA)	"Yarpton"	200
h/o Richard Jones (KEDE)	"Youngs Chance"	100
h/o Augustine Thompson	"Addition"	250
Andrew Abbington	"Abbingtons Square"	300
	"Abbington"	500
h/o William Hollingsworth	"Beginning"	100
h/o Edm. Cary	"Baynards Discovery"	50
36:1756:139 ...		
William Gregory	pt. "Benjamin's Infancy"	50
h/o Caleb Clark (TA)	"Clarks Adventure"	12
h/o Matthew Griffith	"Griffiths Adventure"	220
h/o Thomas Hinesley	"Hinesleys Addition"	50
Anne Morriss	"Morris's Chance"	100
Renatus Smith	"Malden"	283
h/o John Norward	"Norwood"	1000
h/o John Oldson	"Oldsons Pasture"	20

Joseph Willson	"Poplar Neck"	150
John Briscoe	"Pleasant Springs"	500
36:1756:140 ...		
Richard Smith	"Panther Point"	50
James Williams (VA)	"Williams Fancy"	40
William Elliott (KI)	"Addition"	200
Thomas Spry (TA)	pt. "Devonishes Chance"	85
John Offley Collins	pt. "Spread Eagle"	39
h/o Jacob Seth	"Shepherds Discovery" & pt. "Hinfield"	182
h/o Nathaniel Smith	"Taylerton"	800
John Wallace (Chester Town)	pt. "Tryangle Addition"	300
	"Tryangle"	100
h/o Richard Chance	pt. "Boones Hope"	7¾
William Diggs (PG)	pt. "Brandford"	146
36:1756:141 ...		
George Lewis	pt. "Boagley"	40
h/o William Shepherd	pt. "Shepherd's Forrest"	27
William Hall	pt. "Hogg Harbour"	1¾
Lawrence Hall	pt. "Hogg Harbour"	1¾
John Hamer, Jr.	"Hamers Lott"	200
Peter Froom (VA)	pt. "Land of Prophecy"	280
Martin Morgan	"Morgans Hope"	400
William Driskell	pt. "Newington"	120
h/o Thomas Pett	"Petts Neck"	100
Giles Bashaw	"Pear Plantation"	75
36:1756:142 ...		
h/o Jere. Neale	"Chance"	50
h/o Thomas Pamphilion (TA)	"Sprigley"	200
h/o William Trulock	"Lowerford's"	200
36:1756:<unnumbered>	Corrections	
36:1756:<unnumbered>	Recapitulation – Part 2	
36:1756:<unnumbered>	<blank>	
36:1756:<unnumbered>	Recapitulation – Part 1	
36:1756:<unnumbered>	<blank>	

Queen Anne's County - 1756 – 2nd Set

37:1756:<unnumbered>	Certification	Acres
37:1756:<unnumbered>	<blank>	
37:1756:1 ...		
Alice Allyband	"Allybands Hazard Inlarged" – for h/o Thomas Allyband	114
James Ayler	pt. "Inclosure"	50
Ellinor Anthony (widow)	pt. "Hacton"	100
William Austin	pt. "Waterford"	382
	"Rawlings Chance" – for h/o William Elliott	100
John Atkinson	pt. "Rawlings Chance" – for h/o George Elliott	230
	pt. "Mounthope" – for h/o George Elliott	50
	pt. "Elliotts Addition" – for h/o George Elliott	50
Samuel Austin	pt. "Courseys Point" a/s "Smiths Mistake"	22
	pt. "Bishops Outlett"	100
	pt. "Bishops Addition"	100
William All	pt. "Oakenthorpe" – for his son James	100
Rebecca Ashbury	pt. "Fox Hill"	28⅓
	pt. "Dispute" a/s "Brotherhood"	15⅔
37:1756:2 ...		
John Atkinson, Jr.	"Toms Fancy Enlarged"	332
Edward Browning	pt. "Hope" – for his wife	33⅓
Mr. Philemon Charles Blake	"Blakeford"	555
	pt. "Loyds Meadows & Loyds Meadows Addition"	570
	"Bennetts Regulation"	1306
Mrs. Sarah Blake (cnp)	"Russendale" – for h/o John Blake	250
	"Coursey" – for h/o John Blake	250
	"Hoggs Hole" – for h/o John Blake	100
	"Jenkins's Neck" – for h/o John Blake	250
	"Cold Harbour" – for h/o John Blake	100
	"Sayers Forrest" – for h/o John Blake	2250
	"Gore" – for h/o John Blake	175
	"Jacksons Choice" – for h/o John Blake	100
	"Wading Place" – devised by Esq. Bennett for her son John	12000
	"Burton Upon Walsey" – devised by Esq. Bennett for her son Charles	388

	pt. "Neglect" – devised by Esq. Bennett for her son Charles	440
	"Ulthorpe" – devised by Esq. Bennett for her son Charles	124
	"Wrights Chance" – devised by Esq. Bennett for her son Charles	124
	pt. "Broomley" – devised by Esq. Bennett for her daughters Henrietta Maria & M.	1503
John Burk s/o Thomas	pt. "Dawsons Neck"	172
	"Falconars Lott"	50
37:1756:3 ...		
William Banning	pt. "Golden Lion"	100
	"Clarks Venture"	35
	"Bannings Discovery"	48
Mr. George Baynard	pt. "Relief"	500
	pt. "Relief" & pt. "Hawkins's Pharsalia" – from (N) Hussey	135
	"Baynards Pasture"	200
	"Roes Chance"	247
	"Hogg Harbour"	125
	pt. "Codshead Manor"	100
Margarett Banning	"Bells Venture" – for h/o John Banning	50
	"Purnalls Addition" – for h/o John Banning	300
	"Widows Choice" – for h/o John Banning	83
Thomas Bostick	"Hinsleys Fancy"	50
	"Bosticks Chance"	50
	"Addition"	100
Charles Bradley	"Aylers Hope"	100
James Blades	"Goodwill"	50
John Baggs	"Hackers Adventure" – for h/o Abner Roe	200
	"Abners Outlett" – for h/o Abner Roe	125
	"Roes Choice" – for h/o Abner Roe	64
Thomas Baggs	pt. "Old Town"	60
	"Chance Hill"	50
	"Hunters Hope"	50
37:1756:4 ...		

Henry Burt	"Burts Fancy"	50
	"Burts Delight"	100
	"Dogwood Ridge"	100
	"Elisbury"	33
Jacob Boone	"Boones Park"	240
	"Boones Hazard"	120
	"Boones Struggle"	30
	"Boones Hazard Addition"	46
	pt. "Brandford" & pt. "Sayers Addition" – for his wife (N) w/o James Anderson	120
Isaac Boone	pt. "Haddon"	200
	"Boons Venture"	130
Joseph Boone	pt. "Boones Pleasure"	160
	"Boones Addition"	'39
Abraham Boone	pt. "Boones Pleasure"	90
	"Boones Covett"	75
James Barwick	pt. "Oakenthorpe"	185
William Bolton	pt. "Spread Eagle" – for his wife	100
	pt. "Carman & Burton" – for his wife	75
	"Littleworth" – for his wife	100
John Bolton	pt. "Tullys Delight"	100
37:1756:5 ...		
Thomas Baily s/o Jacob	pt. "Todley"	187
Thomas Baily	pt. "Bailys Delight on Resurvey"	156
Thomas Peacock Betts	pt. "Providence"	200
	"Come by Chance"	50
Mr. James Brown	pt. "Hambletons Hermitage"	33⅓
	"Ripley Resurveyed"	265
Robert Basnett	pt. "Mannahs Chance" – for h/o Timothy Mannah	100
Nicholas Broadaway	pt. "White Hall"	82
	pt. "Collington"	100
	pt. "Notlars Desire"	38
	pt. "Carman & Burton"	75
Katherine Buckley (widow)	pt. "Buckleys Delight"	16⅔
Charles Bermingham	"Berminghams Fortune"	100

Queen Anne's County - 1756 – 2nd Set

Francis Bright	"Stoopley Gibson"	200
	"Brights Island"	28
37:1756:6 ...		
Robert Blunt	pt. "Blunts Marsh" a/s "Great Neck"	220
	"Copartnership"	373
	pt. "Parsons Point"	400
Samuel Blunt	pt. "Blunts Marsh" a/s "Great Neck"	110
Thomas Benton	pt. "Pentrogay"	186
	"Pentrovey"	50
Thomas Barnes	pt. "Barnes's Satisfaction"	223
Edward Brown	pt. "Pascos Lott" – for h/o John Griffith	50
	pt. "Eastern Island" – for h/o John Griffith	25
	pt. "Addition" – for h/o John Griffith	90
	pt. "Primus" – for h/o John Griffith	48
	pt. "Bonadventure" – for h/o John Griffith	37½
	pt. "Rotterdam" – for h/o John Griffith	25
	pt. "Tullys Delight"	107
	3 lots in Ogle Town – from John Hawkins	3
Vincent Benton	pt. "Contention"	50
	"Bentons Hazard"	87
George Burroughs	"Georges Hazard"	50
37:1756:7 ...		
William Burkhust	"Pensylvania Border"	50
	"Golden Ridge"	80
James Baily	pt. "Cleaves's Rambles" – for his wife (N) d/o Nathaniel Cleaves	120
	"Bailys Addition"	70
William Baxter	"Parsons Neck" – as guardian to Thomas Price	60
	pt. "Pascoes Lott" – as guardian to Thomas Price	50
	pt. "Eastern Island" – as guardian to Thomas Price	25
	pt. "Addition" – as guardian to Thomas Price	90
	pt. "Primus" – as guardian to Thomas Price	48
	pt. "Bonadventure" – as guardian to Thomas Price	37½
	pt. "Rotterdam" – as guardian to Thomas Price	25
	"Upper Blunt Point Resurveyed"	324
Sweatnam Burn	pt. "Royston"	525

Nathan Baynard	pt. "Reliefe"	476
h/o James Boone	pt. "Hadden"	160
	pt. "Garden of Roses"	48
	pt. "Garden of Roses"	200
	pt. "Hadden"	40
George, Thomas, & John Burroughs	"Buck Road"	100
37:1756:8 ...		
Mr. Charles Brown	"Meagreholm"	608
	pt. "Bennetts Choice" – for his wife	1180
	pt. "Neglect" – for his wife	100
	"Halls Discovery"	150
	"Bucks Expectation"	150
	"Butlers Own Resurveyed"	164
	"Piney Swamp Tract"	50
	"Canaan"	50
	"Older Branch"	100
	"Watry Plains"	50
	pt. "Long Marsh Ridge Enlarged"	33½
	"Hobbs Venture"	281
William Banckes	pt. "Pitts's Vineyard"	166⅔
	"Godfreys Folly"	50
	pt. "Pokety Ridge" & pt. "Jumps Chance"	126
	"Hunters Chance"	100
	"Bancks's Addition"	665
	"Aylers Outlett"	97
	"James's Park"	50
	"Banckes's Delight"	773½
	pt. "Jumps Chance"	50
Edward Brown, Jr. (KI)	pt. "Sillen"	100
	pt. "Belcher"	100
Thomas Butler	pt. "Chesterfield"	200
	pt. "Tryangle"	25
Mr. John Brown	pt. "Hambletons Hermitage"	33⅓
	"Sedge Harbour"	167
	"Huntley"	251

37:1756:9 ...		
Thomas Burroughs	"Scottens Inclosure"	55
Mr. John Bracco	"Bracco"	393
	"Bracco Addition"	98¾
	"Rattle Snake Ridge"	151
	pt. "Long Marsh Ridge Enlarged"	724
John Bostick	"Haysel Point"	75
Samuel Blunt, Jr.	pt. "Fox Harbour" – for his wife	50
	pt. "Bishopton" – for his wife	32
	pt. "Notlars Desire" – for his wife	80
	pt. "Brotherhood" – for his wife	45
William Bennett	"Bennetts Chance"	281
	"Lambdens Adventure"	100
Nathaniel Brown	pt. "Sillen" tbc Mar. Goodhand (f. 34)	<n/g>
Hannah Burroughs	pt. "Adventure"	50
37:1756:10 ...		
Turbutt Betton	pt. "Waltham"	21
	pt. "Wilkinsons Addition"	45
Robert Broady	pt. "Henrys Lott"	50
	"Roberts Outlett"	150
James Butler	pt. "Fox Hill"	85
	pt. "Notlars Delight"	37
Edward Brown (Chester)	pt. "Brampton"	124
Charles Baker	pt. "Salisbury Plains" – for h/o John Walker	100
Nathan Baggs	pt. "Ingrams Desire" & pt. "Bridge Town"	17
h/o William Bishop	"Parsons Neck"	64
James Broadway	pt. "Salisbury Plains" – for h/o Richard Scotton	50
	"Scottens Addition" – for h/o Richard Scotton	100
	"Nathaniels Addition" – for Nathaniel Scotton	43
37:1756:11 ...		
Mary Baggs w/o John Baggs	"Hazard"	50
	pt. "Controversey"	22
Daris Burn	"Jacksons Choice" – for h/o Thomas Jackson	100
John Brown s/o Edward (cnp)	"Stoke"	100
	pt. "Crums Forrest"	135
	"Wellow"	100

		"Stokes Addition Rectified"	60
John Carradine		pt. "Forlorne Hope"	50
Mr. William Campbell		pt. "Ditteridge"	166
		pt. "Anthorpe"	197
		pt. "Hambletons Hermitage"	250
		pt. "Bishopton"	68
		"Walkers Square"	300
		pt. "Davis's Range"	185
		pt. "Reason"	74
		pt. "Loyds Meadows"	66
		pt. "Anthorpe"	203
		"Churnells Neck"	200
		"Adventure" – from (N) Primrose	30
		pt. "Hambletons Hermitage" – from (N) Primrose	150
John Clemments		pt. "Edmonsons Green Close"	200
		pt. "Smiths Ridge"	100
37:1756:12 ...			
Mr. Christopher Cox		pt. "Smiths Ridge"	300
		pt. "Prophecy"	217
		pt. "Heaths Discovery"	23
		pt. "Adventure"	39
		"Cox's Necessity"	½
		pt. "Partnership"	500
		pt. "Lowes Arcadia"	233⅓
		"Plain Dealing Resurveyed" – for his son Christopher	350
Mr. John Coursey		½ "Reward"	200
		½ "Mackleys Addition"	18
Mr. William Coursey		"Cheston"	800
		pt. "Coursey Upon Wye"	290
		"Lords Gift"	1050
		pt. "Smeath"	25
		"Sleeford" – for his wife	200
		"Shepherds Hook" – for his wife	200
		pt. "Solomons Fancy" – for Solomon Clayton	50
James Clayland		pt. "Costins Park" – for h/o James Costin	279

John Cooper, Jr.	pt. "Kearys Discovery"	60
	"Grimes's Folly"	40
Mathew Chilton	"New Cunningham"	100
37:1756:13 ...		
Richard Costin	"Newington"	80
	"Newington Addition"	50
	pt. "Carters Forrest"	22
	pt. "Toms Fancy Enlarged"	100
Phill. Croney	pt. "Coldraine"	75
h/o James Croney	pt. "Coldraine"	75
John Cahall	pt. "Wheatlys" a/s "Daniels Field" – for h/o Edward Cahall	60
John Cooper	"Taylors Chance"	200
James Countice	pt. "Dublin"	150
h/o William Countice	pt. "Dublin"	150
John Culbreth	"Poplar Neck"	200
	pt. "Solomons Lott Addition"	35
	"Holly Neck Resurveyed"	415
	"Parsons Delight" – for Mary	80
	"Poplar Neck Addition"	70
	"Buck Range"	100
37:1756:14 ...		
Elijah Chance	pt. "Bearpoint"	100
Batchelor Chance	pt. "Bearpoint"	100
John Chance	pt. "Littleworth"	50
Elinor Chance	pt. "Littleworth"	50
	pt. "Littleworth Addition"	50
	pt. "Garden of Roses"	22¼
Henry Council	pt. "Hawkins's Pharsalia"	162
John Collins, Jr.	pt. "Tottingham"	200
	pt. "Hackers Meadow" – for his wife	100
William Cannon	pt. "Content"	100
Thomas Coleman	pt. "Tilghmans Discovery"	80
John Commegys	pt. "Shepherds Forrest"	173
	pt. "Shepherds Redoubt"	200
37:1756:15 ...		

John Clothier	"Clothiers Pharsalia"	150
	pt. "Hinsleys Plains"	64
Robert Certain	"Jones's Delight"	200
	pt. "Levells" – for Margaret d/o Thomas Collins	170
James Cassey	pt. "Connoway"	289
Mr. William Carmichall	pt. "Park"	500
	pt. "Allens Neck"	117
	pt. "Partnership"	36
	"Hannonton"	304
	"Allens Neck Outlett"	18¾
	pt. "Bennetts Choice"	212
	pt. "Stagwell"	526
	"Stagwell Addition"	129
Nicholas Clouds	pt. "Broad Creek Resurveyed"	200
Charles Conner	pt. "Woodyard Thickett"	205
Richard Carter	pt. "Copartnership"	52
	pt. "Jones's Plott"	45
	pt. "Dunns Hazard"	75
	pt. "Carters Addition"	25
	pt. "Chance"	25
	pt. "Barnes's Satisfaction"	50
37:1756:16 ...		
Jacob Carter	"Oar Mine"	200
	pt. "Coppidges Range"	30
Henry Carter	"Mattapox Neck"	98
Phillip Coppidge	"Indian Spring"	100
	pt. "Slaughterton"	200
Mr. Henry Casson (cnp)	pt. "Large Range Addition"	124
	"Mistake"	20
	"Jumps Claims"	80
	pt. "Dudleys Desire"	100
	"Cassons Meadows"	490
	"Silvesters Discovery"	241
	"Mistakes Addition"	27
	pt. "Jumps Chance"	135
	pt. "Pitts's Vineyard"	166⅔

Queen Anne's County - 1756 – 2nd Set

	"Bakers Chance"	127
h/o Henry Culley	pt. "Poplar Hill"	27
	5 lots in Kings Town – No. 1, No. 12, No. 13, No. 24, No. 25	5
Mr. William Clayton	"Prouss's Park"	300
	pt. "Tryangle"	25
	"Winter House"	50
	"Hogg Pen Neck"	55
	"Hogg Hole"	50
	pt. "Bishops Fields"	350
	"Claytons Chesterfields"	92
	"Chesterfield"	200
	"Claytons Landing"	20
37:1756:17 ...		
Nathaniel Cleave	"Mangy Pokey"	100
	"Troy"	100
	"Pocayes Addition"	62
	"Wells's Park" – for his wife	110
James Clough	"Cloughs Fancy"	50
	"Cloughs Rambles"	100
Francis Climer	pt. "Shadwells Addition"	50
Richard Cook s/o Hercules	pt. "Partnership"	20
Benjamin Covinton	pt. "Toms Fancy Enlarged"	100
Edward Cahall	pt. "Hacton" – for his wife	50
Mr. Edward Clayton	"Chesterfield Addition"	70
	pt. "Neglect"	200
	"Broad Neck"	100
	pt. "Park" – for his wife	146
John Covinton	pt. "Providence"	100
	"Rowlands Hazard"	257
37:1756:18 ...		
Elizabeth Coleman	pt. "Royston"	50
Robert Cooper	"Peale Place"	32
	"Nimrods Pleasure"	100
William Covinton	pt. "Hinsleys Plains"	91
James Callaghane	pt. "Hemsleys Arcadia"	70

Sharpless Cooper	"Hills Outlett Resurveyed"	233
Nathaniel Curtice	pt. "Sarahs Fancy"	112
Henry Covington	pt. "Rachels Desire"	471
	pt. "Hinesleys Plains" – for his wife	140
Charles Cockey	pt. "Slaughterton" – for h/o John Elliott	100
	"Matthews Enlargement" – for h/o John Elliott	155
	pt. "Hogg Pen Neck", "Goose Hill", & pt. "Ridge"	95
37:1756:19 ...		
Henry Council, Jr.	"Swine Range" – for his wife	30
	"Widows Folly" – for his wife	70
	pt. "Friendship" – for his wife	25
	pt. "Friendship" – from (N) Atkinson	50
h/o Hercules Cook	pt. "Sandishwoods"	335
John Chaires	pt. "Wrenches Farme"	200
Thomas Carradine	"Commegys Hazard"	100
	pt. "Lexton"	235
	"Lott"	50
	pt. "Hinesleys Plains"	76
Benjamin Chaires	pt. "Waplesdon Addition" & pt. "Solomons Friendship"	100
Mr. John Councill	"Hoggpen Ridge"	150
John & Gias Bartus Commegys	"Salem"	360
37:1756:20 ...		
Mr. Henry Callister	pt. "Crumpton"	200
	pt. "Sandy Hurst"	216
Daniel Cox	pt. "Coleraine"	525
James & John Clayland	pt. "Trustram"	300
Anthony Cox	"Cox's Desire"	100
Mrs. Mary Cockey	pt. "Hoggpen Neck", "Goose Hill", & pt. "Ridge"	95
Joseph Chaires	pt. "Lantley"	125
Mary Clough	"Cloughs Hope" – for h/o Nathaniel Clough	50
	"Boones Hope" – by name of "Broomhope", for h/o Nathaniel Clough	100
Dennis Carey (cnp)	pt. "Coleraine" – for h/o John Burk	148
	"Locks Point" – for h/o John Burk	50
	pt. "Bennetts Outlett" – from Charles Seth	75

Queen Anne's County - 1756 – 2nd Set

		pt. "Middle Plantation" – from Charles Seth	100
37:1756:21	...		
Joshua Clark		pt. "Lyford"	281
		pt. "Stephens Fields"	412
Edward Cockey		pt. "Hoggpen Neck", "Goose Hill", & pt. "Ridge"	95
George Cope		"Dennys Range"	100
		"Cohees Desire" – for h/o James Cohee	100
		"Copes Range"	250
William Curtis		"Curtices Lott"	50
Nathaniel Covinton		"Covintons Necessity"	140
		pt. "Rachels Desire"	37
37:1756:22	...		
Mr. John Downes, Jr.		"Wrights Plains"	100
		pt. "Wrights Reserve"	200
		"Wrights Reserve Addition"	50
		pt. "Security"	60
		pt. "Smeath"	106
		pt. "Stagwell"	42
		"Downes's Chance"	100
		pt. "Smeath on Resurvey" – for h/o John Beck	412
		pt. "Smeath on Resurvey" – from (N) Barber, for h/o John Beck	50
		pt. "Smeath on Resurvey" – from (N) Hynson, for h/o John Beck	175
Mr. William Dawson		pt. "Trustram"	300
Mrs. Dulany		"Loyds Insula"	1795
		"Purchase"	1000
		pt. "Willenlew"	682
		pt. "Brandfield"	228
		½ "Skinners Expectation"	240
Mr. Charles Downes		pt. "Fairplay"	116
		pt. "Macklinborough"	199
		"Highgate"	50
		pt. "Wrenches Adventure"	87
		"Mount Moluck" – for Charles Clayton	150

Thomas Dockery	pt. "Fishingham"	100
	"Dockerys Meadow"	142
37:1756:23 ...		
John Davis	pt. "Confusion"	220
	"Peter's Lott"	150
	pt. "Content"	70
Matthew Dockery	pt. "Fishingham"	100
	"Fishingham Addition"	13
	"Matthews Fancy"	8½
Mr. John Downes	pt. "Nobles Range" & pt. "Hemsleys Arcadia"	192
	pt. "Carters Forrest"	22
Mr. Hawkins Downes	pt. "Millford"	200
	pt. "Parkers Freshes"	87
	"Porters Folly"	100
Mr. Henry Downes	pt. "Carters Forrest"	114
Mrs. Catharine Davis	"Clarkson Hill"	150
	"Clarksons Hill Addition"	80
John Deford	"Chance" – for his wife	284
Valentine Downey	"Pig Quarter Neck"	100
37:1756:24 ...		
William Dockery	pt. "Hawkins's Farm"	8
	pt. "Moores Hope Addition"	20
William Durding	pt. "Powells Fancy"	50
Benjamin Denny	"Wootters's Choice"	100
	"Wootters's Choice Addition"	75
	"Outlett"	68
Hynson Downes	"Shore Ditch"	150
John Downes s/o John	"Downes's Chance"	150
James Downes	pt. "Nobles Range" & pt. "Hemsleys Arcadia"	100
Joseph Dodd	"Jamaica Addition" – for his wife	50
	pt. "Jamaica" – for his wife	59
Jacob Dodd	pt. "Rye Hall" – for George Ayres	184
37:1756:25 ...		
John Duffey	"Batchelors Adventure" – for his wife	150
	"Storeys Park" – for his wife	100

Queen Anne's County - 1756 – 2nd Set

Mrs. Rachell Duhamill	"Hynsons Lott"	199
	"Timber Swamp" – for Peter Duhamil	200
Mrs. Mary Dyre	pt. "Waltham"	16⅔
	pt. "Wilkinsons Addition"	16⅔
Thomas Davis	"Addy House"	68
Mr. Abner Dudley	"Sarahs Portion"	300
Thomas Doyle	pt. "Batchelors Hope" – for his wife	20
	pt. "Neglect" – for his wife	16⅓
	"Marshy Crook" – for Charles Brown (minor) s/o John	100
Lewis & Lewis Derochbrune, Jr.	"Friendship Resurveyed"	396
John Derochbrune	"Vaughans Kindness"	200
Lewis Derochbrune, Jr.	"Josephs Addition" – for his brother Jos. (minor)	60
37:1756:26 ...		
William Dames	"Denley Resurveyed" – for h/o Rev. Mr. James Cox	275
	"Discovery" – for h/o Rev. Mr. James Cox	100
	pt. "Adventure Resurveyed" – for h/o Rev. Mr. James Cox	124
	pt. "Bridge North" – for h/o Rev. Mr. James Cox	100
Daniel Dulany	pt. "Vaughans Kindness"	200
Mr. Arthur Emory	"Welch Ridge"	500
	"Haphazard"	116
	"Haphazard Addition"	50
	"Moores Hope"	100
	pt. "Moores Hope Addition"	208
Mr. John Emory	"Bee Tree"	500
	pt. "Partnership"	165
	pt. "Powells Fancy"	90
	"Batchelors Chance Resurveyed"	253
	"Haphazard"	17
	"Emory Chance"	110
	"Bee Tree Swamp"	76
Mr. John Emory, Jr.	"Emorys Resurvey"	537¾
37:1756:27 ...		
Mrs. Sarah Emory	pt. "Partnership" – surveyed for (N) Beck	100

Queen Anne's County - 1756 – 2nd Set

Mr. William Elbert	½ "Reward"	200
	½ "Macklins Addition"	18
	"Lewis's Chance"	50
	pt. "Lambeth"	100
John Emerson	pt. "Addition"	100
Mary Eagle	"Lambeth Addition" – for h/o William	170
Benjamin Endsworth	pt. "Brandfield & Sayers Addition" – for h/o John Willson	200
widow Ewbanks	pt. "Ratcliffe" – for h/o William Ewbanks	140
devisees of John Earle	pt. "Upperheathworth"	167
	"Heathworth"	533
John Errickson	pt. "Sarahs Portion"	96
37:1756:28 ...		
Mr. William Elliott (KI)	"Forlorne Hope"	100
	"Elliotts Choice"	120
John Elliott, Jr.	pt. "Copartnership" – for h/o William Price	52
	pt. "Jones's Plott" – for h/o William Price	45
	pt. "Dunns Hazard" – for h/o William Price	75
	pt. "Carters Addition" – for h/o William Price	25
	pt. "Chance" – for h/o William Price	25
	pt. "Barnes's Satisfaction" – for h/o William Price	50
Elizabeth Errickson (widow)	pt. "Sarahs Portion"	54
	"Johnsons Lott" – escheat	46
Mr. Joseph Elliott	pt. "Slaughterton"	100
	"Williams Lott"	10
	"Newnams Hermitage"	50
	pt. "Salisbury Plains"	100
	pt. "Sayers Range"	60
	pt. "Lowes Desire"	53
Charles Errickson	"Stinton Errickson"	200
Mr. Richard Tilghman Earle	"Earles Beginning"	517
37:1756:29 ...		
Lawrance Everett	"Hunters Forrest"	200
	"Everetts Content"	100
Mr. Michael Earle (cnp)	"Emorys Fortune Addition"	270
	pt. "Partnership" – surveyed for (N) Emory	175

Queen Anne's County - 1756 – 2nd Set

	pt. "Golden Grove"	20
Thomas Emory	"Emory Paxton"	100
	pt. "Partnership" – surveyed for (N) Beck	150
Mr. Gideon Emory	pt. "Fortune"	90
	pt. "St. Pauls"	50
	pt. "Carmans Neck"	50
	pt. "McConnikins Fortune"	236
	pt. "McConnikins Fortune" – for his wife	143
	pt. "Woodridge" – for his wife	184
Mr. James Emory	pt. "Trustram"	196
Arthur Emory s/o John	pt. "Partnership" – surveyed for (N) Beck	90
	pt. "Partnership" – surveyed for (N) Emory	10
Joseph Elliott s/o George	"Clouds's Hermitage"	200
37:1756:30 ...		
Sarah Elston – devisee of Roger	1 lot in Kings Town – No. 7	1
Thomas Emory s/o John	"Roberts Range"	150
	"Roberts's Range Addition"	37
Joseph Everett (Choptank)	"Roes Desire" – for h/o Thomas Roe, Jr.	50
	pt. "Hackers Adventure" – for h/o Thomas Roe, Jr.	50
George Elliott	"Elliotts Luck"	125
George Edwards	"Edwards's Chance"	50
Mr. James Earle	"Cove Point on Resurvey"	200
	"Smiths Lott"	100
	"Woodland Neck"	200
Burton Francis Falconer & John	"Chesnutt Ridge"	200
Francis Foreman	pt. "Royston"	600
37:1756:31 ...		
Thomas Ford	pt. "Ashton"	142½
Isaac Ford	pt. "Ashton"	82½
James Finley	pt. "Rambles"	150
William Fisher	pt. "Large Range"	416⅔
	pt. "Codshead Mannor"	384
Henry Fiddeman (cnp)	pt. "Hacketts Garden"	200
	pt. "Hacketts Garden" – more	400

	pt. "Large Range" – from W. Thomas	10
	pt. "Brandfield" – from (N) Willson	200
	pt. "Large Range" – from W. Thomas	<n/g>
	pt. "Hacketts Garden" – from W. Thomas	<n/g>
John Fouracres -- -	pt. "Tullys Lott"	100
James Finley (wheelright)	pt. "Warplesdon Addition" & pt. "Solomons Friendship"	50
	"Nathan & Thomas's Beginning"	27
37:1756:32 ...		
John Fisher	pt. "Suffolk"	300
Ladia Fisher (widow)	pt. "Suffolk" – for William Fisher (minor)	300
	"Fishers Plains" – for William Fisher (minor)	164
James Fisher	pt. "Fishers Meadows"	167
w/o Thomas Fisher – during life & after to son Richard	pt. "Fishers Meadows"	167
John Falconer	"Falconers Hope"	21½
	"Falconers Chance"	12
	pt. "Welch Pool"	150
John Green	"Greens Adventure Upon Carpenters Square Resurveyed"	212
William Greenwood	"Miss Hitt" – for h/o Stephen Riche	250
37:1756:33 ...		
Matthew Griffith	pt. "Park"	220
Edward Garrett	"Sandy Hill"	50
Edward Godwin	pt. "White Marsh Addition"	330
	pt. "Parkers Freshes"	8⅓
Michael Green	"Costins Hope"	200
William Godwin	pt. "Wrights Chance" a/s "Choice"	100
Mr. Richard Gould	pt. "Ripley"	266⅔
	pt. "Spread Eagle"	75
Charles Gafford, Jr.	pt. "Macklins Beginning"	118
	pt. "Smithfield"	40
Richard Gafford	pt. "Macklins Beginning"	141
	pt. "Smithfield"	17
37:1756:34 ...		
Marmaduke Goodhand (cnp)	pt. "Sillen"	200
	"Broad Oak"	500

	"Poplar Neck"	300
	pt. "Sillen" – more, Nathaniel Brown	33⅓
	pt. "Woodyard Thickett" – for his wife	205
	pt. "Sillen Chance" – for Nathaniel Brown	66⅔
	pt. "Point Love"	200
Philemon Green	"Greens Fortune"	80
	"Greens Fortune Addition"	75
	pt. "Jones's Forrest"	45
	"Pratts Hope" – for Robert Pratt (minor)	100
	pt. "Jones's Forrest" – from h/o David Herrington	55
Matthew Graves	"Graves's Beginning"	50
Mrs. Frances Gould	"Spring Branch"	100
	pt. "Ripley"	133⅓
	pt. "Sewalls Fork"	500
James Gould	pt. "Goulds Purchase"	195
William Green	"Bradford"	100
37:1756:35 ...		
Elizabeth Gwinn	"Gunners Harbour" – for h/o John Gwinn	100
Benjamin Gould	pt. "Dambewell"	100
Anne Gilbert	"Isaacs Chance"	100
Boatswain Thomas, Hannah, & Bess Gibbs (Negroes)	pt. "Killmanam Plains"	200
James Ginn	pt. "Bakers Plains"	200
Charles Gafford	pt. "Macklins Beginning"	141
John Gafford & James Roseberry	pt. "Brotherhood" – for their wives	317
37:1756:36 ...		
John Higgens	pt. "Dungarnon"	150
Edward Hall	pt. "Vaughans Discovery" – for his wife Ellinor	100
	pt. "Hogg Harbour" – for his wife Ellinor	73¼
Mr. William Hopper (cnp)	pt. "Chesterfield"	900
	pt. "Providence"	200
	"Bridge Water"	300
	pt. "Guilford"	200
	"Darkin"	210
	pt. "Courseys Point" or "Smiths Mistake"	200

	"Hoppers Industry"	213¼
	pt. "Smiths Mistake"	275
	pt. "Conquest"	256
	pt. "Green Spring"	100
	pt. "Camberwell"	272
	"Stepney"	255½
	"Dockerys Discovery"	73
	pt. "Paxtons Lott"	20
John Hall	pt. "Welch Poole" – for his wife	100
	pt. "Dancey"	300
	pt. "Hogg Harbour"	219¾
37:1756:37 ...		
John Hill	"Green Hill"	100
Robert Hardcastle	"Mount Hope"	150
	"Benewell"	164
Ezekiel Hunter	"Boones Ridge"	50
Mary Hunter	"Jumps Lott"	50
	"Hunters Hazard"	50
William Harrington	pt. "Josephs Lott"	100
	pt. "Henrys Lott"	25
h/o David Herrington	"Hopewell"	100
	"Harringtons Desire"	50
	"Buck Bay"	100
	pt. "Beaverdams"	50
Richard Harrington	"Solomons Lott"	100
	pt. "Solomons Lott Addition"	15
37:1756:38 ...		
Mr. Ernault Hawkins	pt. "Brampton"	126
Richard Hynson	"Anns Portion"	150
Thomas Honey	"Sparks's Outlett"	114
Valentine & Thomas Honey	pt. "Mitchels Adventure" – from Samuell Sparks	100
	pt. "Sparks's Own"	25
Joseph Harris	pt. "Crumps Chance"	50
	pt. "Upperheathworth"	100
	pt. "Crumps Forrest"	15

Queen Anne's County - 1756 – 2nd Set

James Harris	pt. "Crumps Chance"	50
	pt. "Toms Fancy Enlarged" – for his wife Rebecca	75
Mrs. Sarah Hollyday	"Readburn Rectified" – for h/o James Hollyday, Esq.	1440
	pt. "Macklinborough" – for h/o James Hollyday, Esq.	114
John Hollingsworth, Jr.	"Good Increase" – for h/o Thomas Crupper	200
37:1756:39 ...		
John Hambleton	pt. "Neglect"	50
	"Hambletons Range"	100
	"Mary Anns Lott"	100
	"Hambletons Addition"	50
	"Hambletons Luck"	100
Mary Hackett	pt. "Prices Hill" – for h/o John Hackett	200
Thomas Hackett	pt. "Prices Hill"	100
	pt. "Scottland"	50
	pt. "Providence"	330
	pt. "Shepherds Fortune" – for his wife	150
h/o John Harris	pt. "Contention"	150
John Hollingsworth	pt. "Hambletons Hermitage"	33⅓
Sarah Hollingsworth	"Refuse"	100
John Hadley	"Skinners Pleasure"	50
37:1756:40 ...		
James Hutchins	"Wrights Fortune"	120
	pt. "Condone"	316
Thomas Hutchins	"Lanes Ridge"	200
Giles Hix	pt. "Killeray"	100
Charles Hines	pt. "Spread Eagle" – for Thomas	33⅓
George Harrington	"Harringtons Venture"	100
Anthony Harrington	pt. "Warners Discovery Resurveyed" – for his wife (N) d/o William Vickers	195
Mr. James Hollyday	pt. "Macklinborough"	230
	pt. "Waterford"	18
37:1756:41 ...		
Mr. William Hopper & Christopher Cox	pt. "Jamaica"	1

Nathan Harrington	"Beaverdams Addition"	150
	½ "Ingrams Desire" – except 19 a., for your wife Signey	<n/g>
Robert Hawkins	pt. "Macklinborough"	175
	pt. "Tullys Delight"	293
William Hunter	pt. "Chestnutt Meadows" – for h/o Henry Price Williams	100
Thomas Hamer	"Hamers Chance"	178
	pt. "White Hall" – for his wife	18
	pt. "Ratcliffe" pt. "Loyds Freshes"	19
Nathaniel Harrington	"Jadwins Folly"	44
John Higgins & James Sullivane	pt. "Salisbury"	200
William & Thomas Hughlett	pt. "Bakers Plains"	400
37:1756:42 ...		
Matthew Hawkins	pt. "Tullys Delight"	200
Mr. Andrew Hall	pt. "Spread Eagle"	149
	pt. "Spread Eagle"	35
	pt. "Brotherhood"	234
John Holding	"Nicholsons Fancy"	50
	pt. "Woodhouse"	61
	pt. "Woodhouse Addition"	14
William Horne	"Wallnutt Neck Resurveyed" – for his wife	109
	"Barron Ridge" – for his wife	100
Mark Hargadine, Jr.	pt. "Smiths Neglect" – for his wife's daughter Mary Downes	150
Giles & James Hix	pt. "Edmondsons Green Close"	200
MM Robert Hawkins & Kelley (KE)	pt. "Sprigley" – for their wives (N) d/o & coheiresses of Henry Jacobs	300
	pt. "Winchester" – for their wives (N) d/o & coheiresses of Henry Jacobs	125
37:1756:43 ...		
Mrs. Anna Maria Hemsley	"Hardest Fendoff"	150
h/o Mrs. Mary Hemsley	"Towton Fields Addition"	140
	"Hemsleys Discovery"	91
Mrs. Anna Maria & Mary Hemsley	pt. "Towton Fields"	460
Henry Hollyday	pt. "Turners Plains Addition"	120

James Hammond	pt. "Wrenches Adventure"	192
William Hughlett & James Ginn	pt. "Riches Farm" – not patented	74
Thomas Harris	"Addition"	500
	"Steads Go Between"	71
	pt. "Beginning"	429
	pt. "Standford"	174
	pt. "Dilliridge"	251
	pt. "Long Neck"	20½
	pt. "Coursey Upon Wye"	258½
	pt. "Reason"	35
	pt. "Mount Mill"	33
	"Lawrences Delight"	100
	"Johnsons Addition"	100
37:1756:44 ...		
Francis Jackson	"Barbarahs Inlett"	263
Thomas Jackson s/o George	pt. "Winchester"	125
	"Barbarahs Choice"	80
	"Castle Town"	100
Stephen Jerman	pt. "Hogg Hole"	130
h/o Robert Jerman	"Newport"	284
	pt. "Brandford" – from William Diggs	211
John Jerman	pt. "St. Martins"	82
	pt. "Inclosure"	81
Handcock Jones	pt. "Deluge"	80
Henry Jones	pt. "Nobles Range"	58
	pt. "Deluge"	50
37:1756:45 ...		
William Jones	pt. "Deluge"	50
	"Jones's Chance"	100
Mary Jadwin	pt. "Lyford" – for h/o Robert Jadwin	70
Peter Jumpe	pt. "Horse Pasture"	100
Isaac Jumpe	pt. "Horse Pasture"	50
Abraham Jumpe	pt. "Jumps Chance"	100
Vaughn Jumpe	pt. "Pokety Ridge"	45

Solomon Jumpe	pt. "Jumps Chance"	44
	"Jumps Addition"	49
Jeremiah Jadwin	"Cow Range"	100
	"Timms Neglect"	50
	"Jadwins Project"	40

37:1756:46 ...

Edward Jones	"Beaverdam Fork"	100
	"Hopewell"	100
	"Fords Park"	30
	"Fords Folly"	20
	"Jones's Greenwood" – for his son William Kirby Jones	150
	"Jones's Safety"	59
	"Nottingam"	89
Dorothy Isgate	"Fork"	200
John Johnson	"Cloudent"	200
	pt. "Notlars Delight"	80
Thomas Jackson	"Hopewell"	50
	"Nicholsons Chance"	50
William Joyner, Jr.	pt. "Parsons Neck"	60
Jonathan Jolly	"Andeaver"	50
	"Nicholsons Adventure"	50
	"Burton"	50
	"Lester"	50
	"Lester Meadows"	50
Amos Jerman	"Blandford" a/s "Brandford"	37

37:1756:47 ...

Dr. John Jackson	pt. "Providence"	213
	"Smithfield Addition"	327¼
	pt. "Lexton"	184
	pt. "Jamaica"	40
	pt. "Adventure Resurveyed"	27
Thomas Jumpe, Jr.	"Jumps Lott"	34
	pt. "Horse Pasture"	50
Thomas Jones	"Sarahs Portion"	50

Inhabitants of Queen Anns County	pt. "Pierce Land" – whereon Wells's Inspection House is	½
Joseph Jackson s/o Francis	pt. "Jaspers Lott"	200
James Jones	"Jones's Fancy"	100
Archebald Jackson	"Nodd"	113
	"Speedy Contract"	10
	pt. "Rattclife"	300
37:1756:48 ...		
Samuel Jackson	pt. "Oak Ridge" – for h/o Benjamin Boon	175
	pt. "Garden of Roses" – for h/o Benjamin Boon	177¾
Thomas Jumpe s/o Thomas	pt. "Horse Pasture"	50
h/o Richard Kieron	pt. "Confusion"	100
Nathaniel Knotts	pt. "Knotts Addition"	50
	"Knotts Range"	235
	"Knotts Chance"	53
	pt. "Turners Plaines Addition" – for h/o James Bell	120
James Kentin	pt. "Grovly Hoe"	150
	pt. "Upland"	100
37:1756:49 ...		
Solomon Kenton	pt. "Upland"	200
	"Upland Addition"	50
James Kersey	pt. "Scotland"	100
Baldwin Kemp	pt. "Emorys Rich Land"	150
James Knotts	pt. "Knotts Chance"	200
John Knotts	pt. "Knotts Chance"	102
Anne Knotts (widow)	pt. "Emorys Rich Land"	95
	pt. "Relief"	55
William Kent	pt. "Toms Fancey Enlarged"	150
37:1756:50 ...		
Thomas Kersey	pt. "Scotland"	50
Susanah Kirby	"Kirbys Hardship" – for h/o Walter Kirby	199
Benjamin Kirby (cnp)	"Clouds's Chance"	6
	"Bodys Neck"	200
	"Coopers Quarter"	50
	pt. "Sillen" – for h/o John Evans & Andrew Price	200

	pt. "Uper Deal" – for h/o John Evans & Andrew Price	500
James Kelley or Joseph Buckley	pt. "Buckleys Delight" – for his wife	33⅓
Mary Kemp	pt. "Toms Fancy Enlarged"	75
h/o Thomas Kemp	pt. "Willenlew"	106
37:1756:51 ...		
Robert Kent	pt. "Batchelors Plains"	200
William Kirkham	pt. "Stephens Fields" – for h/o Henry Clifts	278
Mr. Robert Loyd	"Hemsleys Park" – for devisees of Phil. Hemsley	800
	"Cloverfields" – for devisees of Phil. Hemsley	1622
	pt. "Trustram Wells" – for devisees of Phil. Hemsley	68
	"Hemsleys Adventure" – for devisees of Phil. Hemsley	200
	"Tilghmans Gift" – for William Hemsley	650
	"Tilghmans Meadows" – for his wife	270
	"Snodland" – for his wife	284
	"Friendship"	175
James London	"Kirkhams Lott"	200
James Lane	pt. "Worleys Outrange"	100
	"Lanes Addition"	75
Elizabeth Longfellow	"Josephs Hope" – for h/o Joseph Longfellow	50
Richard Lambert	pt. "Lowes Arcadia" – for Thomas Phillips s/o David	100
Thomas Lee	pt. "Lees Chance"	166
	pt. "Stratton"	152
	pt. "Hawkins's Pharsalia"	100
37:1756:52 ...		
John Legg	pt. "Linrick" & pt. "Leggs Begining"	186
	pt. "Pentroby" – rightly called "Pentrogay"	14
John Lee	pt. "Camberwell"	100
John Leith	"Horse Penridge"	100
Bexley John Lambden	pt. "Swifts Outlett"	48
	pt. "Northumberland"	52
Mary Lane	"Lanes Folly" – for h/o Walter Lane	161
	pt. "Stevens Fields"	110

Sarah Linsey	"Jadwins Hazard" – for her son Edward	61
John Legg, Jr.	pt. "Limrick" & pt. "Leggs Beginning"	14
	⅓ "Woodland Neck"	16⅔
	⅓ "Oldsons Relief"	33⅓
John Lockerman, Jr.	"Bennetts Tolson Resurveyed"	930
Alexander Lee	"Knave Standoff"	50
Thomas Mooth	pt. "Friendship"	25
	"Wattsons Delight"	50
	"Wattsons Delight Addition"	30
	"Mooths Range"	105
37:1756:53 ...		
William Merson	pt. "Middle Plantation"	66⅔
William Mansfield	pt. "Waltham" – in right of his wife	16⅔
	pt. "Wilkinsons Addition" – in right of his wife	16⅔
Rebecca Meeds	pt. "Brandford" – from William Diggs part of that executed by Richard Bennett, for h/o John Meeds	141
William Meeds	pt. "Brandford"	100
	pt. "St. Martins"	100
John Merideth	"Trustram Ridge"	150
Thomas Meridith	pt. "Plain Dealing"	75
	pt. "Adventure"	100
Anne Meridith	pt. "Shrewsberry" – for h/o William Meridith	150
	"Shrewsberry Addition" – for h/o William Meridith	100
David Mills	1 lot in Kings Town	1
Mr. John Mayne	"New London"	150
	"New London Addition"	114
Thomas Martindale	pt. "Silvesters Forrest"	100
	"Martindales Range"	50
	"Martindales Hope"	316
Mary Merrick	"Merricks Delight" – for h/o Isaac Merrick	50
37:1756:54 ...		
James Millis	"Campersons Choice" – for Samuel & William Cook (minors)	100
William Winchester Mason	"Ephraims Hope"	100
	pt. "Winchesters Folly Resurveyed"	273
William Montague	pt. "Ratcliffe"	140

Queen Anne's County - 1756 – 2nd Set

John Miller	pt. "Oakenthorpe"	229
	pt. "Providence"	150
Thomas Mountsieur	"Hacketts Delight"	150
James Massey	pt. "Friendship"	300
	"Masseys Addition"	23½
Patrick Mooney	⅓ "Nevills Delight"	16⅔
	"Mooney Luck"	75
Mr. Daniel McConnikin	"McConnikin Correar"	150
Mr. Thomas Marsh	"Little Thickett"	200
	"Marshes Forbearance"	150
	"Cabbin Neck"	350
	"Neglect"	200
	2 lots in Kings Town – No. 4, No. 5	2
	pt. "Shepherds Fortune"	266
	1 lot in Kings Town – from Mr. Maxwell	1
	pt. "Poplar Hill"	200
	"Clouds's Choice"	200
	"Lowthers Chance" – from (N) Swift	150
37:1756:55 ...		
James McCoy	pt. "Smiths Delight"	218½
	"Maccoys Pleasure"	129
	pt. "Hamers Addition"	18½
Thomas Meloyd	pt. "Toms Fancy Enlarged"	100
Timothy Mannah	"Mannahs Chance Resurveyed"	50
Joseph Merchant	"Jacks Purchase"	75
	"Musketo Ridge"	50
	"Josephs Own"	30
Thomas McClannahan	pt. "Fox Harbour"	100
	pt. "Collins's Lott"	56¼
	pt. "Brotherhood"	42½
Samuell McCosh	pt. "Upperheathworth"	238
	pt. "Collins's Refusal"	112
	pt. "Heaths Gift"	53
	pt. "Larrington"	119
	pt. "Crumpton"	50

William Matthews – apprentice to William Pindar	pt. "Bridge North"	50
Charles Murphy	pt. "Hawkins's Pharsalia"	200
	"Murphys Chance Resurveyed"	99½
James Miller	"Forrest of Windsor"	250
37:1756:56 ...		
Solomon Mason	pt. "Winchesters Folly Resurveyed"	133
Richard Mason	pt. "Winchesters Folly Resurveyed"	133
Henry Mason	"Masons Hazard"	192
Abraham McCastelow	"Forkalett"	62
Anne Merridith (KI)	pt. "Conners Neck"	60
Abraham Milton	"Crumps Forrest"	150
James Massy, Jr.	pt. "Friendship" – surveyed for (N) Tilghman	50
William Mayner	pt. "Dispute" a/s "Brotherhood" – for his wife	47
	pt. "Notlars Delight" – for his wife	33
John Meeds	pt. "Beginning" – not on Rent Roll	150
John McConnikin	⅓ "Woodland Neck" – for his wife	16⅔
	⅓ "Oldsons Relief" – for his wife	33⅓
	"Georges Codd"	100
Thomas Meeds	pt. "Beginning" – not on Rent Roll	150
John Mason	⅔ "Nevills Delight"	33⅓
37:1756:57 ...		
Samuel Massey	pt. "Poplar Hill"	123
	"Masseys Addition"	40½
William Meridith (Tullys Neck)	"Meridiths Adventure"	100
Peter Maxwell	"Hazard"	175
Nathaniel Moore	pt. "Clouds's Adventure" – for h/o James Ware	112½
	pt. "Brotherhood" – from (N) Roseberrey & wife	67
John Nabb	pt. "Tilghman Addition"	100
	"Jones's Fortune"	100
	pt. "Adventure"	7
	pt. "Toms Fancy Enlarg'd"	150
Solomon Newnam	pt. "Williams Lott"	40
William Newnam (cnp)	"Newnams Chance"	56
	pt. "Johns Meadows"	60

	pt. "Shaver"	107
	"Newnams Addition"	72
	"Addition" – for h/o Joseph Newnam	24
	pt. "Scotton Addition"	10
	pt. "Johns Meadows"	40
	"Shearing"	100
	pt. "Devonishes Chance"	16¾
37:1756:58 ...		
Charles Nabb	pt. "Clouds Adventure"	200
	"Elizabeths Portion"	100
Thomas Newton	pt. "Toms Fancy Enlarged"	100
Mr. Edward Neale	pt. "Hawkins's Farme Resurveyed"	12
	pt. "Green Spring"	550
	"Neales Residence"	899
Mr. Jonathan Nicols	pt. "Hacton" – for his wife	200
	pt. "Redford" – for his wife	150
	"Willsons Addition" – for his wife	70
	pt. "Partnership"	500
Nathaniel Newnam	pt. "Shaver"	93
Rachel Nevill	pt. "Barton" – for h/o John Nevill	40
	"Smiths Addition" – for h/o John Nevill	106
Mr. Charles Nicols	"Jones's Forrest"	500
	pt. "Brandfield" & pt. "Sayers Addition"	50
37:1756:59 ...		
James William Nabb – another account below	pt. "Wrenches Farme" – for his wife	200
	pt. "Moores Hope Addition" – for his wife	172
John Nabb, Jr.	pt. "Batchelors Hope" – for John Brown (minor) s/o John	40
	pt. "Neglect" – for John Brown (minor) s/o John	32⅔
John Nevill s/o John (cnp)	pt. "Wortons & Pindars Outrange"	75
	pt. "Sewalls Fork"	250
	"Nevills Outrange"	46½
	"Nevills Discovery"	3½
	pt. "Tilghmans Discovery"	200
	"Solomons Outlett"	50
	"Nevills Addition"	144

Queen Anne's County - 1756 – 2nd Set

	"Farrington"	250
h/o Dick (Negro)	pt. "Knowles's Range"	244
James William Nabb – another account above	pt. "Hawkins's Farme" tbc William Dockery (f. 24)	8
	pt. "Moores Hope Addition" tbc William Dockery (f. 24)	20
37:1756:60 ...		
John Oldson	pt. "Hawkins's Pharsalia"	150
Thomas OBryan	"Pleasant Spring Resurveyed"	418
	4 lots in Ogle Town – No. 22, No. 38, No. 39, No. 59	4
Robert Offley	pt. "Levells"	80
Samuel Osburn	"Addition"	200
	pt. "Martins Neck Resurveyed"	78
Abraham Oldson	pt. "Hawkins's Pharsalia"	50
	pt. "Hawkins's Farme Resurveyed"	126
William Oxingham	pt. "Olden Lyon"	100
	"Mire Branch"	85
	"Turners Plaines"	128
William Pryor	"Pryors Chance"	271
37:1756:61 ...		
Charles Price	"Lincoln"	200
	pt. "Broomly Lambeth"	247
Thomas Price	pt. "Brandford" – from William Diggs	106
John Phillips	pt. "Vaughans Discovery"	230
William Pratt	pt. "Chaires Addition"	54
	"Bucks Forrest"	187
Henry Pratt, Jr.	"Pleasant Park"	100
	"Pleasant Park Addition"	9½
Thomas Purnall	"Dudleys Chance"	200
Mr. Grundy Pemberton (cnp)	pt. "Dawsons Neck"	142
	pt. "Partnership"	850
	pt. "Hawkins's Pharsalia"	600
	"Pembertons Resurvey"	969
	"Bostons Addition"	150
	"Kingsale"	250
	"Kingsale Addition"	100

Queen Anne's County - 1756 – 2nd Set

	"Change"	200
	pt. "Kelds Inheritance"	52
Mr. Vincent Price	"Andrew & Prudences Satisfaction"	696
	pt. "Lambert" – for h/o Timothy Lane	400
37:1756:62 ...		
John Powell	"Longs Desire"	50
	"Powells Fancy"	94
John Pickerin	pt. "Lowes Arcadia" – for his wife	66⅔
John Pondar	pt. "Smiths Delight"	81½
James Pondar s/o Richard	"Pondars Chance"	38
Margarett Pindar	pt. "Bishopton"	250
	pt. "Ashton"	75
	pt. "Collins's Lott"	116
	pt. "Wortons & Pindars Outrange"	67
Mary Perrey (widow)	"Stafford"	100
Thomas Powell (Choptank)	"Powells Venture"	95½
Martha Primrose	pt. "Shepherds Fortune" – for h/o George Primrose	200
Morgan Pondar	pt. "Spread Eagle" – for his wife	16⅔
37:1756:63 ...		
John Pratt	pt. "Vaughans Discovery" – for his wife (N) d/o Thomas Burk	100
	"Wrights Park"	100
Henry Pollock	pt. "Colne Rectifyed"	284
Mr. Thomas Price s/o Henry	"Goodhap"	126
	"Margaretts Hill"	200
Thomas Price s/o Thomas	pt. "Brandford"	23
	pt. "Conclusion"	64
Robert Pratt	"Pratts Choice"	100
Prudence Primrose	pt. "Kents Lott"	52
George Powell	"Longs Chance"	50
	"Tryangle"	50
William Price (KI)	pt. "Coppidge Range" – for h/o John Carter	198
	"Craney Neck" – for h/o John Carter	168
	pt. "Ridge" – for John Carter (minor)	124⅔
John Price	pt. "Toms Fancy Enlarged"	590
37:1756:64 ...		

Thomas Price (KI)	pt. "Cloverfields"	100
John Primrose	pt. "Whittingtons Lott" & pt. "Hemsleys Britland Resurveyed" – for h/o Jos. Whittington	178½
George Personate	"Smiths Range"	300
Thomas Priest	"Wigg Moore"	61
Thomas Powell (Double Creek)	pt. "Tilghmans Discovery"	1¼
Quakers	"Land of Prophecy" – for a Meeting House	3
Nathaniel Reed	pt. "Toms Fancy Enlarged"	400
	pt. "Wrights Square" – for his wife	100
Richard Ross	pt. "Coldraine"	125
	pt. "Coldraine" – for Andrew Jordan (minor)	183
William Roe	pt. "Dudleys Desire"	100
37:1756:65 ...		
Benjamin Roe	"Clouds's Range"	100
John Roe s/o Thomas	"Downes's Forrest"	300
	"Roes Addition"	70
Patrick Robertson	"Tully Barden"	50
	"Tully Bardin Inclosement"	150
	"Blair Croisk"	200
Alexander Robertson	"Tully Bardins Addition"	62
	"Peith"	66
Peter Rich	"Bridge Town"	11
	3 lots in Bridge Town – No. 4, No. 5, No. 6	3
William Ricketts s/o Edward	pt. "Hinsleys Plains"	59
William Robinson	"Anns Lott"	100
	pt. "Elliotts Addition"	50
	pt. "Ridleys Chance"	96½
	pt. "Parkers Lott" & pt. "Boltons Delight" – for Daniel Bolton (minor)	140
James Reed	pt. "Providence"	100
37:1756:66 ...		
Mr. Benjamin Roberts (cnp)	pt. "Lowes Desire"	178
	pt. "Sayers Range"	200
	pt. "Sheperds Redoubt"	100
	"Dixons Gift" – for h/o James Roberts	100
	"Roberts's Meadows" – for h/o James Roberts	100

	"Watsons Desire"	50
Francis Rochester	"Watry Plains"	150
	pt. "Tullys Lott"	200
	"Collins's Gift"	175
	pt. "Outrange"	80
	pt. "Ripley"	300
John Rochester	"Winchester"	200
	"John & Rachels Choice"	100
Henry Rochester	"Lowders Hazard"	77
	"Philadelphia"	50
John Railey	pt. "Wilsons Begining"	100
	"Raileys Begining"	62
William Ridger	"Hope"	50
	"Small Hopes"	50
	"Ridgers Lott"	100
	"Ridgeways Chance"	50
37:1756:67 ...		
Benjamin Richardson – another account on f. 69	pt. "Cloverfields"	335
h/o John Ruth	pt. "Smiths Neglect"	150
David Register	pt. "Conquest"	138
	"Bradburns Delight" a/s "Bailys Delight"	100
	pt. "Boagley"	60
Christopher Ruth	pt. "Chesnutt Meadows"	100
	pt. "Conclusion"	86
	pt. "Hawkins's Farme Resurveyed" – for h/o Peter Countice	120
	pt. "Baynards Pasture"	37
Thomas Robinson	pt. "Wrights Chance" a/s "Choice"	100
Samuell Roe	pt. "Oakenthorpe"	164
	"Tullys Addition"	300
	"Nedds Begining"	30
	"Roes Lane"	22
	pt. "Sarahs Fancy"	50
William Reed	"Newnothingham Rectified" – for his wife	169

Queen Anne's County - 1756 – 2nd Set

Thomas Richardson Roe	pt. "Oakenthorpe"	226
	pt. "Sarahs Fancy"	30
37:1756:68 ...		
James Roe	"Begining"	85
	pt. "Sarahs Fancy"	540
William Ridgeway, Jr.	"Plain Dealing" – for h/o William Ferrell	100
John Roe s/o Edward	pt. "Narborough"	250
	"Hinesleys Choice"	100
	pt. "Oakenthorpe"	40
	pt. "Sarahs Fancy"	111
Benjamin Ridgeway	"Long Delay"	150
John Roberts (minor)	"Roberts's Desire"	150
Edward Rooke	"For Revival"	1118
Gilbert Reed	pt. "Spread Eagle"	1
Theophilus Randall	"Bacon Neck" a/s "Barrew Neck"	227
	"Jones's" a/s "Janes Lott"	50
James Roberts	pt. "Sandy Hursh"	100
37:1756:69 ...		
William Robinson, Jr.	pt. "Tottingham" – for his wife (N) d/o Samuel Sallisbury	100
John Russam	"Clymores Chance" – for h/o Thomas Clymore	59
Mr. Thomas Ringgold (KI)	"Coxes Neck"	1500
William Robinson (Tuckahoe)	pt. "Todcaster"	500
William Roberts	"Roberts's Chance"	150
Thomas Robinson, Jr.	pt. "Lowes Arcadia" – for his wife	100
Damsel Railey	pt. "Larrington" – for h/o Charles Railey	31
	pt. "Bishops Outlett" – for h/o Charles Railey	73½
Benjamin Richardson	"Pascos Adventure"	150
	"Wading Place"	300
	"Ashburys Addition"	35
	pt. "Cloverfields"	335
Patrick Sexton	"Liberty"	100
37:1756:70 ...		
John Seth (cnp)	pt. "Mount Mill"	79¼
	pt. "Addition"	10
	pt. "Bennetts Outlett"	50

	pt. "Mount Mill" – for his brother Jacob	79¼
	pt. "Addition" – for his brother Jacob	10
	pt. "Bennetts Outlett" – for his brother Jacob	50
John Sullivant	pt. "Sonderfield"	109
	pt. "Dungarnon"	150
	pt. "Fosetts Plains" – for h/o John Hammond	150
	"Sullivants Chance"	66
Andrew Sanders	"Good Luck Range"	50
Thomas Swann	pt. "Jumps Chance"	100
	pt. "Jumps Choice"	2½
	pt. "Sayers Addition"	100
Susannah Steward	pt. "Kearys Discovery"	140
	pt. "Silvesters Forrest"	105
Emanuel Swift	"Swifts Forrest Addition"	50
James Slaughter	"Fern Ridge"	50
	pt. "Partnership" a/s "Ratcliffe"	50
	"Fairn Ridge Addition"	100
	"Golden Rod Ridge"	50
John Swift	"Swifts Forrest"	50
	"Bear Harbour"	50
37:1756:71 ...		
Moses Swift	"Indian Tract"	50
	pt. "Swifts Meadows"	100
James Silvester	pt. "Beargarden"	123
	"Carmarthan"	100
h/o William Starkey	pt. "Oak Ridge"	175
	pt. "Hickory Ridge"	156
	pt. "Codshead Manor"	116
William Shepherd	pt. "Hinesleys Plains"	109
Sollomon Sinnott	pt. "Hawkins's Pharsalia"	150
Robert Smith	pt. "Toms Fancy Enlarged"	100
Joseph Scrivner	pt. "Hackers Meadows"	14
	"Josephs Part of Hackers Meadows Enlarged"	325
Daniel Smith (p)	pt. "Jones's Fancy"	75
Benjamin Smith (cnp)	pt. "Jones's Fancy"	75
	"Marys Chance"	30

Queen Anne's County - 1756 – 2nd Set

	"Teats Desire"	35
37:1756:72 ...		
John Spry	pt. "Friendship" – surveyed for (N) Tilghman	70
Thomas Spry	pt. "Friendship" – surveyed for (N) Tilghman	55
	pt. "Friendship" – another	15
Solomon Seney	pt. "Barton"	110
	"Bradfords Addition"	100
	pt. "Clouds's Adventure"	187½
	pt. "Sewalls Fork" – for his wife (N) w/o John Nevill	250
	pt. "Tilghmans Discovery" – for his wife (N) w/o John Nevill	78¾
	pt. "Poplar Hill" – for his wife (N) w/o John Nevill	150
Thomas Seward	"Outrange"	174
Thomas Sands	"Sands Outlett"	100
	"Dub Hen Ridge"	40
	"Timber Ridge"	70
	pt. "Swifts Outlett"	22
	"Long Swamp"	63
	"Lancaster"	119
	pt. "Northumberland"	48
Mr. Gideon Swift	"Chance"	66
	pt. "Swifts Outlett"	70
	"Constantinople"	100
	pt. "James Choice"	50
	"Crumps Advise" – for his daughters Elizabeth & Mary	100
	"Mulberry Tract"	100
James Sutton	pt. "Sandy Hurst"	100
Absalom Spark	pt. "Sparkes's Own"	25
37:1756:73 ...		
Christopher Spry	"Thief Keep Out"	100
	pt. "Friendship" – surveyed for (N) Tilghman	52
	pt. "Friendship" – another	29
	"Sprys Chance"	21
	"Thief Keep Out Addition"	150
	"Buck Range" – for your son Humphrey	50

Queen Anne's County - 1756 – 2nd Set

Thomas Stanton	"Forrest of Sherwood"	200
	pt. "Security"	40
Mrs. Rebeccah Sudler	"Jones Hole Resurveyed" – for h/o James Sudler	276
	"Stent on Sudler" – for h/o James Sudler	173
Mr. Joseph Sudler	"Sledmore"	800
	pt. "Devonishes Chance"	15
	"Sudlers Purchase"	80
	"Sudlers Fortune"	186
	"Sudlers Island"	64
	pt. "Shepherds Forrest"	200
	pt. "Broad Creek Resurveyed" – for Ann Wells d/o & heiress of John Wells	630
	½ "Cloaks Chance"	50
	"Tilbury"	50
	"Tilburys Addition"	50
Dr. John Smith	"Smiths Neck"	128
	pt. "Spread Eagle"	346
	"Marys Portion"	150
	pt. "Martins Neck" – resurveyed by (N) Orsburn	39
	pt. "Spread Eagle" – for the mill	5
Susannah Stephens	"Derochbourns Neglect"	17½
37:1756:74 ...		
Robert Small	"Ship Point"	100
William Scott	pt. "Sayers Range"	40
	"Scotts Out Range"	304
Nathaniel Smith	"Smiths Desire"	50
	"Smiths Outlett"	100
	"Long Ridge"	124
	"Indian Oldfield"	40
Thomas Scotton	"Scottons Forrest"	50
	"Scottons Desire"	100
Richard Swift	"Williams Pasture"	54
John Stent	pt. "Coldraine"	103
Richard Sparkes – grandson of Richard Collins	1 lot in Kings Town	1
Samuell Swift	"Fosters Folly"	50

William Smith	pt. "Sallisbury Plains"	200
Caleb Sparks	pt. "Sparkes's Own"	25
37:1756:75 ...		
Francis Spry	pt. "Sprys Adventure"	75
William Spry	pt. "Friendship" – surveyed for (N) Spry	149
John Scott	pt. "Stratton"	532½
Solomon Scott	pt. "Stratton"	311
Aaron Saunders	"Purnalls Forrest" – for h/o William Purnall	500
	"Jumps Lane" – for h/o William Purnall	100
Moses Swift	"Swifts Meadows"	100
Lemon Swift	"Soote Hill" – for h/o Fairclough Wright	200
Henry Storey	pt. "Todley"	193
James Silvester, Jr.	"Beargarden Addition"	125
	pt. "Beargarden"	80
Mr. John Seegar	"Johnsons Adventure"	100
	"Newnams Portion"	241½
	"Gwinns Hazard"	100
	pt. "Woodhouse"	39
	pt. "Woodhouse Addition"	11
	"McCleans Addition"	150
37:1756:76 ...		
Nathaniel Saterfield	"Saterfields Venture"	55
Francis Stephens	"Lanark"	86
	"Hunting Tower" – for his son Robertson	100
Joseph Slocum	pt. "Bishops Fields"	50
Charles Seth	pt. "Mount Mill"	158½
	pt. "Addition"	20
	pt. "Bennetts Outlett"	25
Richard Scotton	"Hazle Ridge"	65
Benjamin Silvester	"Bucks Range"	113
	"Silvesters Hazard"	189
Richard Small	"Coles Endeavour"	150
Maurice Sliney	pt. "Petts Gift"	85
	pt. "Timber Ridge"	250
John Smith	"Sandy Hill"	100
Thomas Seward, Jr.	"Hawkins's Range"	90

Millington Sparks	pt. "Sparks's Own"	25
37:1756:77 ...		
George Smith	pt. "Smiths Forrest" – for Thomas Chaires (minor) s/o Joseph	61
	pt. "Confusion" – for Thomas Chaires (minor) s/o Joseph	159
Catherine Scotton	"Scottons Outlett"	50
Mrs. Prissilla Sanders	pt. "Middle Plantation"	33⅓
Absolam Swift	pt. "Content"	50
Robert Scrivner	"Neglect"	190
James Smith	pt. "Hemsleys Britland Rectified"	57
Joseph Spry	pt. "Sprys Adventure"	75
Josias Salloway	½ "Cloaks Chance"	50
David Silvester	pt. "Grubby Neck"	75
Emory Sudler	"Sudlers Chance" – for James Sudler (minor)	87½
	"Little Neck" – for James Sudler (minor)	55
William Silvester	pt. "Grubby Neck"	75
37:1756:78 ...		
John Sweat, Jr.	pt. "Park" – for h/o Benjamin Griffith	220
Daniel Smith (joyner)	"Mary Portion"	100
	"Mantons Addition"	5
Nathaniel Scott, Jr.	pt. "Stratton"	54½
h/o Nathaniel Scott	"Toms Fancy Enlarged"	243
Christopher Spry (TA)	"Doddington"	200
Mr. Richard Tilghman (cnp)	"Tilghmans Hermitage"	1843
	pt. "Bristoll Marsh"	50
	pt. "Forlone Hope"	1050
	pt. "Carpenters Outlett"	9
	pt. "Boagley"	75
	pt. "Park"	500
	"Wyatts Range"	50
	pt. "Confusion"	9
	pt. "Adventure" & pt. "Confusion" – from (N) Alley	110
	pt. "Grays Inn"	75
	"Cheshire"	200
	pt. "Shrewsberry"	150

	"Sintra"	187
	"Tilghmans Recovery Resurveyed"	1050
	"Plains Resurveyed"	112
37:1756:79 ...		
Maj. William Tilghman	"Pauls Fort"	200
	pt. "Bristoll Marsh"	140
	pt. "Tilghmans Discovery"	490
	"Sallisbury"	500
	"Delmore End"	500
	1 lot in Ogle Town	1
	pt. "Poplar Plain"	191
	"Meadows"	28
	pt. "Smiths Mistake"	400
	"Andever"	500
Mr. Edward Tilghman	pt. "Malton"	239
	1 lot in Ogle Town	1
	pt. "Porters Lodge"	200
	"Tilghmans Landing"	68
	pt. "Resurvey of Forlorne Hope Rectified"	2890
	"Tilghmans Resurvey of Long Neck"	539
	pt. "Union"	720
	"Scottons Folly"	50
	pt. "Long Neck"	2½
	pt. "Coursey Upon Wye"	321½
	"Pleasant Banks on Wye"	19
	pt. "Sparkes's Choice"	100
	pt. "Tullys Delight"	200
	"Just Design"	17½
	pt. "Discovery"	216
	pt. "Loyds Meadows" & pt. "Loyds Meadows Addition"	655
	"Beaverdams"	50
	"Hollow Flatt"	50
	⅓ "Reviving Spring"	166⅔
Mr. Nathaniel Tucker (cnp)	pt. "Adventure"	61
	"Jones's Addition"	200

Queen Anne's County - 1756 – 2nd Set

	pt. "Batchelors Plains"	100
37:1756:80 ...		
Mr. James Tilghman	pt. "Adventure"	1030
	"Adventure Addition"	40
	"Tilghman Freshes"	600
	pt. "Jerusalem"	200
	"Coles Bank Enlarged"	703
	"Killkenny"	200
Mr. Mathew Tilghman	"Tilghmans Forrest"	1400
	"Rings End"	100
	"Nottlars Enjoyment"	500
	1 lot in Ogle Town	1
	pt. "Poplar Plains"	191
	pt. "Glocester"	195
	½ "Timber Fork"	250
	½ "Negligence"	22½
	"Tilghmans Chance"	990
	"Ovall"	420
	pt. "Toms Fancy Enlarged"	162
Trustram Thomas 3rd	pt. "Trustram Thomas's Part of Trustram"	127
Baynard Tillotson	pt. "Lords Gift on Resurvey"	270
	pt. "Todley"	170
	"Exchange"	100
	pt. "Lantley" – for his wife Margarett	325
Mr. John Tillotson	"Shepherds Fields on Resurvey"	140
	pt. "Todley"	150
	pt. "Lowes Arcadia"	100
	"Inkersell" – for h/o (N) Chetham	134
	"Timberland" – for h/o (N) Chetham	400
	"Pascalls Chance" – for h/o (N) Chetham	250
	pt. "Park" – for h/o (N) Chetham	354
	"Chethams Landing" – for h/o (N) Chetham	90
37:1756:81 ...		
h/o John Timm	"Society Hill"	50
	"Timms Arcadia"	50
	"Society Hills Addition"	75

Queen Anne's County - 1756 – 2nd Set

Stephen Thomas	pt. "Hawkins's Pharsalia"	80
	pt. "Alcocks Pharsalia"	33⅓
Philemon Thomas	pt. "Hawkins's Pharsalia"	120
	pt. "Lees Chance"	33
	pt. "Alcock's Pharsalia"	66⅔
Trustram Thomas (Long Neck)	"Grubby Neck"	50
	"Trustrams Ridge"	50
	"Trustrams Adventure"	150
Thomas Tanner	"Chance"	50
	"Tanners Advantage"	39
	"Providence"	100
	"Ashford" – for h/o Isaac Hudson	100
Alexander Toalson	pt. "Freshford"	140
	pt. "Partnership"	206½
Amia Toalson	pt. "Philpotts Neck" – for h/o Alexander Toalson	233⅓
Mr. James Tuit	pt. "Youngs Chance"	270
	pt. "Lambeth Fields"	132
37:1756:82 ...		
Richard Tickell	1 lot in Kings Town – No. 22	11
Mary Thomas	"Forrest Plains" – for h/o Christopher Thomas	150
Benjamin Toalson	pt. "Coppidges Range"	211
	pt. "Slaughterton" – for his wife	100
Mr. Samuel Thompson	"Kirbys Recovery"	52
	"Wellmores Range"	1000
Mary Trickey	"Woodberry" – for h/o Thomas Trickey	100
Mr. Dowdall Thompson (cnp)	pt. "Prices Hill"	180
	pt. "Shepherds Discovery"	200
	"Parsons Marsh Addition"	10
	"Good Luck"	100
	pt. "Sparks's Choice"	250
	pt. "Mount Pleasant"	102½
	pt. "Enjoyment"	50
	"Barefield" a/s "Bargholt"	200
	"Parsons Marsh"	34
	pt. "Shepherds Discovery" & pt. "Henfield"	218
	"Courseys Town Resurveyed"	394

	"Whortons Marsh" – as guardian to Arthur Holt	27
	"Highgate Lane" – as guardian to Arthur Holt	100
	"Holt" – as guardian to Arthur Holt	506
	"Holts Castle Hill Resurveyed" – as guardian to Arthur Holt	304½
	pt. "Mount Pleasant" a/s "Mount Pleasure"	52½
	"Parsons Chance"	115
	pt. "Mount Pleasure"	80
	pt. "Enjoyment"	79
Isaac Tharp	pt. "Coleraine"	83
37:1756:83 ...		
John Tittle	1 lot in Kings Town – No. 1	1
Christopher Thomas, Jr.	pt. "Trustram Thomas's Part of Trustram"	100
Joseph Toalson	"Toalsons Desire"	193
	pt. "Philpotts Neck"	116⅔
	½ "Morgans Inclosure" – for h/o Andrew Toalson	218½
Edmond Thomas, Jr.	pt. "Trustram"	450
Joseph Thomas	pt. "Trustram Thomas's Part of Trustram"	200
John Taylor	pt. "Neglect"	51
	pt. "Batchelors Hope"	90
Tilden Thomas	"Addition"	227
Philemon Tanner	⅓ "Woodland Neck"	16⅔
	⅓ "Oldsons Reliefe"	33⅓
Richard Taylor	"Alberts Delight" – for h/o William Mountsieur	200
John Toalson & James	"Partnership"	380
Thomas Teat	"Bee Tree Ridge"	50
37:1756:84 ...		
Henry Thompson	"Baynards Large Range Addition" – for h/o John Baynard	505
	"Vineyard Addition" – for h/o John Baynard	28½
	"Baynards Chance" – for h/o John Baynard	54
	pt. "Pitts's Vineyard" – for h/o John Baynard	166⅔
	"Joans Plackett" – for h/o John Baynard	100
Isaac Turner	"Swann Brook"	770
Visitors of Queen Anns County School	pt. "Forlorne Hope"	100
Vestry of Saint Pauls Parish	pt. "Docters Folly"	½

Richard Vanderford	pt. "Outrange" – in right of his wife Hannah d/o Robert Green	40
John Vanderford	pt. "Wrenches Farme"	200
	"Christophers Hazard"	100
Joshua Vansant	"For Difficulty"	72
37:1756:85 ...		
James Vanderford	pt. "Fox Hill"	28⅓
	pt. "Dispute" a/s "Brotherhood"	15⅔
John Vanderford s/o Rebecca	pt. "Fox Hill"	28⅓
	pt. "Dispute" a/s "Brotherhood"	15⅔
Vestry of Christ Church Parish	pt. "Little Ease" – a glebe	150
h/o or devisees of John Walters	pt. "Smeath"	250
	"Barnstable Hill"	210
	"Westminister"	297
	pt. "Upperheathworth"	143
John Welch	pt. "Partnership"	200
	pt. "Ditteridge"	83
	pt. "Reason"	20
Henry Williams	pt. "Sallisbury Plains"	100
	"Williams Fortune"	150
MM Nathan Samuel Turbutt Wright & Thomas Wright	pt. "Hemsleys Britland Rectified"	50
	pt. "Wrights Reserve"	250
Mr. Thomas Wilkinson	"Barbadoes Hall"	350
37:1756:86 ...		
James Williams	pt. "Courseys Addition"	100
	pt. "Kendall"	100
Elizabeth Wootters	"Richard & Marys Forrest"	80
James Willson	"Willsons Chance"	100
	"Willsons Chance Addition"	200
Jacob Wootters	"New Buckley"	100
	"Cow Range"	38
John Wheatley	pt. "Wheatley" a/s "Daniels Fields"	140
William Wheatley	"Wheatleys Park"	100
Thomas Wheeler	"Killmaiden"	100
	"Killmaiden Addition"	15

Queen Anne's County - 1756 – 2nd Set

William Whitby	"Whitbys Forrest"	50
Mr. Nathaniel Wright	"Brotherhood"	50
	"Wrights Chance"	300
37:1756:87 ...		
Daniel Willcox	pt. "Mount Hope"	250
	"Mount Hope Addition"	100
John Woodall (KE) s/o John	pt. "Crumpton"	10
	pt. "Sandy Hurst"	<n/g>
Matthew Weeks	pt. "Enjoyment" tbc D. Thompson	79
	pt. "Woolverhamton"	120
William Wharton	"Whortons Adventure"	570
	pt. "Sayers Range Addition"	17
Benjamin Whittington	"Whittingtons Lott Resurveyed"	178½
	pt. "Poplar Hill"	34
	pt. "Rattcliffes Part of Lloyds Freshes"	171
Penelope Wright	pt. "Parsons Point"	100
Robert Walters	"Dundee"	368
	"Jamaica"	150
	"Walters Addition to Kirbys Prevention"	33
	pt. "Hope Resurveyed"	50
William White	"Workmans Hazard"	150
	"Sparkes Point"	50
37:1756:88 ...		
George Webb	"Wattsons Lott"	50
	"Webbs Plains"	50
John Willson (KI)	pt. "Eastern Island"	50
	"Willsons Adventure"	54
	"Erricksons Island"	20
Thomas Walker	"Toms Adventure"	56
	"Toms Adventure Addition"	50
Richard Wells, Jr.	pt. "Bath"	145
Mr. Nathan Wright	"White Marsh on Resurvey"	376
	pt. "White Marsh Addition"	250
	pt. "Smiths Reserve"	2½
	"Cork House"	590
	"Jones's Park Resurveyed"	340

John Wright	pt. "Narborough"	250
	"Narborough Addition"	100
	"Littleworth"	50
William Wallace	"Boothbys Fortune"	500
Jacob Walters	"Kerbys Prevention"	50
37:1756:89 ...		
Jonathan Wootters	"Oak Ridge"	24
	"Oak Ridge Addition"	78
h/o Littleton Ward	pt. "Colne Rectified"	286
Nathan Wright s/o Edward	"Tullys Reserve"	300
	"Reserve Addition"	50
	"Marys Portion"	554
	pt. "Content"	400
John Willson, Jr.	"Willsons Adventure" – for his wife	262
h/o Humphrey Wells, Jr.	pt. "Jennys Beginning"	22
	"Baths Meadows"	36
Peter Wrench	"Wrenches Chance"	35
	pt. "Wrenches Farme"	200
Samuell Walters & James	pt. "Partnership"	217½
Samuell Walters	"Walters's Park"	150
James Walters	"Walters's Rambles"	150
37:1756:90 ...		
William Wrench	pt. "Guilford"	26
	pt. "Wrenches Lott"	100
	pt. "Hawkins's Farme Resurveyed"	326
Henry Wrench	pt. "Wrenches Lott"	354
	"Wrenches Reserve"	39
Mr. Thomas Willson	"Sewalls Range"	1120
	"Plain Dealing"	727
	"Jackson Boggs"	46
	pt. "Bennetts Outlett"	495
Josiah Whorton	"Fords Chance"	100
Zerobable Wells	"Teats Folly"	50
	"Buck Island"	100
John Whitby (cnp)	"Batchelors Chance"	69
	"Bite the Biter"	78½

Queen Anne's County – 1756 – 2nd Set

	"Clarks Lott"	112
widow Woodall	pt. "James's Chance" – for h/o Cornelius Comegys	150
	pt. "Crumps Chance" – for h/o Cornelius Comegys	50
	pt. "Hope" – for h/o Cornelius Comegys	228⅔
Mrs. Elizabeth Wells	pt. "Bath"	255
37:1756:91 ...		
Mr. George Wells	"Red Lyon Point"	50
	pt. "Baths Addition"	150
Humphrey Wells s/o Humphrey	"Peirce Land Addition"	50
	"Crumps Fancy"	50
	"Landing"	30
	"Fancys Addition"	150
Benjamin Wells s/o Humphrey	"Low Lands"	45
	"Calebs Lott"	80
John Wells s/o Humphrey	"Peirce Land"	199½
Joseph Whitby	"Buck Range"	100
Henry Ward	"Wards Flower Fields"	50
Mr. William Walls (KE)	pt. "Bath"	100
	pt. "Baths Addition"	150
Richard Warner	pt. "Sayers Range Addition"	66
	pt. "Alberts Desire" a/s "Abbotts Desire"	100
John Watson	pt. "Baileys Delight on Resurvey" – for his wife Esther	100
37:1756:92 ...		
Nathaniel Wright, Jr.	pt. "Sallisbury"	100
	½ "Skinners Expectation"	240
w/o Ambrose Wright	pt. "Wrights Chance"	100
	pt. "Hawkins's Farme Resurveyed"	41
	pt. "Guilford"	12
Mr. Nathan Samuel Turbutt Wright (cnp)	"New Hynson Town"	360
	pt. "Grays Inns"	75
	pt. "Larrington"	100
	2 lots in Kings Town – No. 2, No. 27	2
	pt. "Wrights Square"	140
	pt. "Gould Hawks Enlargement" – as guardian to Elisha Brown	35

	"Claxton" – as guardian to Elisha Brown	100
	1 lot in Ogle Town – as guardian to Elisha Brown	1
	1 lot in Ogle Town	1
Mr. Thomas Wright	"New Reading"	300
	pt. "Grays Inn"	50
	pt. "Neglect"	45
	"Warplesdon"	300
	"Warplesdon Addition" pt. 'Solomons Friendship"	230
	pt. "Lowes Arcadia"	350
Mr. Nathaniel Wright s/o Edward	"Hazard"	100
	½ "Content"	100
	"Content Addition"	200
	"Contents Outlett"	50
37:1756:93 ...		
Mr. Edward Wright s/o Edward	pt. "Partnership"	250
	"Colonells Quarters"	100
Isaac Winchester	½ "Morgans Inclosure" – for h/o Alexander Toalson	218½
	"Purlivant"	180
	"Isaacs Addition"	80
James Walters (KI)	pt. "Conners Addition"	120
Elisabeth White	pt. "Crawford" – for h/o Robert Willson	216
	pt. "Ridge"	62⅓
h/o Ambrose Wright – one of which is a minor & has chosen John Tillotson as his guardian	pt. "Hawkins's Farme Resurveyed"	5
	pt. "Wrights Chance"	408
	pt. "Guilford"	40
Rebecca Williams	"Millford" – for h/o Abraham Williams	123
Mary Webb (widow)	pt. "Lyford" – h/o James Webb	643
Thomas Wilkinson s/o Henry	"Wattsons Chance"	50
Solomon Wright	"Guilford"	300
	"Guilford Addition"	150
	"Hogg Harbour"	100
	pt. "Narborough"	250
37:1756:94 ...		
h/o Nathaniel Wright s/o Nathaniel	pt. "Guilford"	<n/g>

Stephen Weeks	pt. "Woolverhamton"	80
	pt. "Mount Pleasant" & pt. "Lillingstons Enjoyment"	1½
Joshua Walliston	pt. "Condone"	10
	pt. "Crumpton"	10
Solomon Yewell	"Purchase"	86
Stephen Yoe	pt. "Brandford"	100
John Young s/o William	pt. "Stratton"	50
Aaron Yoe	"Courseys Addition"	50
John Young	pt. "Stratton" tbc Nathaniel Scott, Jr. (f. 78)	54½
37:1756:95 ...		
Dr. James Anderson (KE)	pt. "Providence" – in right of his wife	200
	"Ashford" – in right of his wife	200
	pt. "Rambles" – in right of his wife	200
	"Shepherds Fields" a/s "Forrest"	200
James Auld (DO)	1 lot in Kings Town – No. 19	1
Thomas Adcock (TA)	"Wyatts Folly"	50
Stephen Andrews (in Jerseys)	"Mount Gilboa"	50
<erased> (CV)	<erased>	<unr>
Mr. William Anderson (London)	"Darland Resurveyed"	1750
	"Loyds Town"	1000
37:1756:96 ...		
Mr. Rizdon Bozman (TA)	pt. "Killeray"	100
	pt. "Millford"	200
	"Point Landing"	5¼
	"Killerays Addition"	34¾
James Bartlett (TA)	"Partnership"	575
Benjamin Blackiston (KE)	"Benjamins Park"	80
	"Upper Landing"	200
Daniel Bird (Biddeford)	1 lot in Kings Town – No. 8	1
James Benson (TA)	pt. "Spread Eagle" – for his wife	100
	"Collins's Own" – for his wife	92
James Baxter (CE)	"Beaver Neck Resurveyed" – for h/o John Roles	320
h/o William Bunt (VA)	"Kent Fort Manor"	1000
John Blackwell or Thomas Grace	pt. "Alcocks Pharsalia"	100

Queen Anne's County - 1756 – 2nd Set

Anne Brooke (widow) (TA)	pt. "Scarborough"	200
John Barwicke	pt. "Jumps Choice"	97½
37:1756:97 ...		
John Buck, Esq.	pt. "Poplar Hill"	100
	2 lots in Ogle Town	2
Edward Clark (TA)	"Clarks Delight" – for h/o Caleb Clark	76
	"Clarks Struggle" – for h/o Caleb Clark	65
Charles Carroll (Annapolis)	pt. "Thompsons Manor" a/s "Poplar Island"	1000
James Claypole (KE)	pt. "Lambeth"	187½
	"Wells's Chance" – for his wife Elizabeth	100
	pt. "Lambeth" – more	62½
Johannah Carpenter (widow) (Duck Creek)	⅓ "Porters Lodge"	100
37:1756:98 ...		
Elinor Carey	pt. "Silvesters Addition"	112
Amy Carey	pt. "Silvesters Addition"	65
Daniel Cox	pt. "Coleraine" – charged on f. 20	<n/g>
Peter Commerford	"Mount Pleasure" – for h/o (N) Sharp	500
Benjamin Cleave (KE)	"Cleaves's Rambles" – for his son Nathaniel	110
h/o James Dickinson	"Dickinsons Plains"	860
Samuell Dickenson (KEDE)	"Youghall"	175
	"Gorsuches Tryangle"	63
	"Poplar Ridge"	150
	"Poplar Ridge Addition"	200
Mrs. Susannah Douglas (CE)	"Macklins Fancy"	500
John Dixon (TA)	pt. "Jerusalem"	200
37:1756:99 ...		
~~James Dudley (TA)~~	~~pt. "Dudleys <unr>"~~	~~165~~
William Dickenson (TA)	pt. "Scarborough" – for h/o John Dickenson	200
MM Phillip Davis, John Davis, & David Davis	"Partnership"	300
Henry Elbert	pt. "Davis's Range"	200
h/o Abraham Falconar (KE)	"Grove"	150
	"Edenborough"	1074
Col. William Fitzhugh (CV)	"Morgans Neck" – for h/o John Rousby	400
	"Bluff Point" – for h/o John Rousby	496

Thomas Fleming (Annapolis)	pt. "Conners Neck" – for h/o John Granger	100
Mr. Nicholas Gouldsborough (TA)	pt. "Old Town"	740
37:1756:100 ...		
Mr. William Gouldsborough (TA)	"Walnutt Ridge" – for devisees of Mr. George Robins	600
	"Pearle" – for his wife	~~1000~~
Mr. Robert Gouldsborough (TA)	pt. "Controversey"	500
	pt. "Sandishwood" – for his wife	665
	pt. "Jaspers Lott"	570
Jeremiah Gresingham (TA)	pt. "Davis's Range" – for his wife	200
Peter Garon (TA)	pt. "Allocks Pharsalia" – for h/o William Vickers	100
Edward Harding (TA)	pt. "Hemsleys Arcadia"	231
Mr. Samuell Hyde (London)	"Smiths Forrest"	2000
Patrick Hamilton (CE)	pt. "Point Love" – for h/o Jos. Wicks	400
37:1756:101 ...		
h/o Aquilla Johns	pt. "Cold Spring"	430
Alexander Kelley (KE)	pt. "Malton" – in right of his wife (N) one of d/o Maurice McCarty	150
William Lambden (TA)	pt. "Reviving Spring"	333⅓
Mr. Thomas Lane (TA)	pt. "Smiths Ridge"	300
	"Collins's Range" – for his wife	300
John Leeds (TA)	pt. "Scarborough"	200
37:1756:102 ...		
Edward Loyd, Esq. (cnp)	"Ninevah"	600
	"Ninevahs Addition"	200
	pt. "Loyds Freshes"	810
	"Mill Range"	136
	"Chesnutt Neck"	300
	"Hoggs Hole"	50
	"Breek Neck"	100
	"Wilton"	650
	pt. "Addition to Wilton"	600
	"Hemsleys Reserve Rectified on Resurvey"	185
	pt. "Brandford"	186
	pt. "St. Martins"	82
	pt. "Costins Park"	21

Queen Anne's County - 1756 – 2nd Set

	"Scotts Chance"	100
	pt. "Oaken Thorpe"	56
	"Nuttwells Chance Resurveyed"	294
	pt. "Hemsleys Britland Rectified"	223
	"Courseys Range"	600
	pt. "Costins Chance"	32
	"Coopers Hill"	100
	"Woolverton"	250
	pt. "Reward" – for John Coursey	200
	pt. "Macklins Addition" – for John Coursey	18
	pt. "Narborough"	250
~~Stead Lowe~~	~~pt. "Begining"~~	~~100~~
Rev. Mr. Richard Molineaux (popish priest)	"Batchelors Plains"	151¾
	"Johns Forrest"	200
	"Lundy"	200
	"Woodhouse"	200
	"Waterford"	200
37:1756:103 ...		
Nicholas Massey (KE)	"Pacolett"	18
Mr. George Mellegin (CE)	"Edinkelley"	600
Francis Neale (TA)	"Shadwell" – for his son Francis	100
	pt. "Shadwells Addition" – for h/o Robert Jones	100
Edward Neale (TA)	pt. "Shadwells Addition"	100
Jonathan Neale (TA)	"Webbs Chance" – as trustee for John Webb	150
	pt. "Silvesters Addition" – as trustee for John Webb	40
h/o or devisees of Jeremiah Nicols (TA)	pt. "Partnership"	250
Mr. Edward Oldham (TA)	"Exchange"	470
	"Exchange" – another	60
	pt. "Providence"	300
37:1756:104 ...		
Aaron Parrott (TA)	pt. "Cold Spring"	162
John & James Porter (TA)	"Halls Harbour" – in right of their wives (N) d/o Capt. Henry Rippon	500
	pt. "Poplar Hill" – in right of their wives (N) d/o Capt. Henry Rippon	50

Dr. Richard Porter (TA)	½ "Negligence" – for his wife's sister in Newfoundland	22½
	½ "Timber Fork" – for his wife's sister in Newfoundland	250
Thomas Reese (PA)	"Andever Meadows" – for his wife	175
Mr. James Ringgold (TA)	pt. "Courseys Point" or "Smiths Mistake"	623
	pt. "Bishops Outlett"	400
	pt. "Bishops Addition" & pt. "Bishops Outlett" – from (N) Wattson	100
John Robertson (SO)	"Athol"	500
37:1756:105 ...		
h/o George Robotham	"Robothams Park"	500
Elizabeth Robass	pt. "Providence"	150
Tobias Stansbury (BA)	"Robinsons Farme" – for his wife	200
Mr. Jarvas Spencer (KE)	pt. "Connoway" – for h/o Christopher Williams	111
h/o Charles Stevens (TA)	pt. "Willenlew"	212
37:1756:106 ...		
Joseph Turner (TA)	"Turners Lane"	100
Abner Turner (TA)	pt. "Turners Plains Addition"	<unr>
h/o Mr. Lambert Willmore (KE)	1 lot in Kings Town	1
William Webb	pt. "Redford"	150
Park Webb (TA)	pt. "Shadwells Addition" – for h/o Samuel Neale	50
William Willson & wife (TA)	pt. "Beargardon"	150

36:1757:1 ...		Acres
Alce Allyband	"Allybands Hazard Enlarg'd"	114
James Ayler	pt. "Inclosure"	50
Elinor Anthony	pt. "Hoxton"	100
William Austin	pt. "Waterford"	382
	"Rawlins Chance" – for h/o William Elliott	100
John Attkinson	pt. "Rawlins Chance" – for h/o George Elliott	230
	pt. "Mount Hope" – for h/o George Elliott	50
	pt. "Elliotts Addition" – for h/o George Elliott	50
William Aule	pt. "Oaken Thorpe" – for son James	100
Rebekah Ashberry	pt. "Fox Hill"	20⅓
	pt. "Dispute" a/s "Brotherhood"	15⅔
John Attkinson, Jr.	pt. "Toms Fancy Enlarg'd"	332
Stephen Andrews	"Mount Gilboa"	50
John Ayler	"Aylers Fortune"	75
36:1757:2 ...		
Edward Browning	pt. "Hope" – for his wife	33⅓
Phill. Charles Blake	"Blakeford"	555
	"Lloyds Meadows & Lloyds Meadows Addition"	570
	"Bennetts Regulation"	1306
John Burke s/o Thomas	pt. "Dawsons Neck"	172
	"Falconars Lott"	50
Madam Sarah Blake (cnp)	"Rusendale" – for h/o Mr. John Sawyer Blake	250
	"Coursey" – for h/o Mr. John Sawyer Blake	250
	"Hogg Hole" – for h/o Mr. John Sawyer Blake	100
	"Jenkins's Neck" – for h/o Mr. John Sawyer Blake	250
	"Cold Harbour" – for h/o Mr. John Sawyer Blake	100
	"Sawyers Forrest" – for h/o Mr. John Sawyer Blake	2250
	"Gore" – for h/o Mr. John Sawyer Blake	175
	"Jacksons Choice" – for h/o Mr. John Sawyer Blake	100
	"Wading Place" – devised by Esq. Bennett for her son John	1000
	"Burton Upon Walsey" – devised by Esq. Bennett	388
	pt. "Neglect" – devised by Esq. Bennett for her son Charles	440
	"Ulthorp" – devised by Esq. Bennett	100

	"Wrights Chance" – devised by Esq. Bennett	124
	pt. "Bromley Lambeth" – devised by Esq. Bennett for her daughters Henrietta Maria & Mary Blake	1503
William Baning	pt. "Golden Lyon"	100
	"Clarkes Venture"	35
	"Banings Discovery"	48
George Baynard	pt. "Relief"	500
	pt. "Relief & Hawkins's Pharsalia"	185
	"Baynards Pasture"	202
	"Roes Chance"	247
	"Hogg Harbour"	125
	pt. "Codds Head Manor"	100
Margaret Baning	"Bells Venture" – for h/o John	50
	"Purnalls Addition"	300
	"Widdows Choice"	83
Thomas Bostick	"Hynsleys Fancey"	50
	"Bosticks Chance"	50
	"Addition"	100
Charles Bradley	"Aylers Hope"	100
36:1757:3 ...		
Thomas Baggs	pt. "Old Town"	60
	"Chance Hill"	50
	"Hunters Hope"	50
	pt. "Ratcliffe" – from (N) Mountague	42
	"Baggs's Marsh"	51
James Blades	"Good Will"	50
John Baggs	"Hackers Adventure" – for h/o Abner Roe	200
	"Abners Outlett" – for h/o Abner Roe	125
	"Roes Choice" – for h/o Abner Roe	64
Henry Burt	"Burts Fancey"	257
	"Burts Delight"	100
	"Doggwood Ridge"	100
	"Elsbury"	33
Jacob Boon (cnp)	"Boons Park"	240
	"Boons Hazard"	120
	"Boons Struggle"	30

Queen Anne's County - 1757

	"Boons Hazard Addition"	46
	pt. "Sayers Addition" & pt. "Branfield" – for his wife (N) w/o of James Andrews	120
	"Boons Chance"	151
	"Dead Ridge"	85
Isaac Boon	pt. "Haddon"	200
	"Boons Venture"	130
Joseph Boon	pt. "Boons Pleasure"	160
	"Boons Addition"	39
Abraham Boon	pt. "Boons Pleasure"	90
	"Boons Covitt"	75
James Barwick	pt. "Oaken Thorpe"	185
William Bolton	pt. "Spread Eagle" – for his wife	100
	pt. "Carman & Burton" – for his wife	75
	"Littleworth" – for his wife	100
John Bolton	pt. "Tulleys Delight"	100
Thomas Baley s/o Jacob	pt. "Todley"	187
Thomas Baley	pt. "Baleys Delight"	156
36:1757:4 ...		
Ezekiel Betts	pt. "Providence"	200
	"Comby Chance"	50
h/o James Brown	"Ripley Resurveyed"	265
Robert Basnett	pt. "Manahs Chance" – for h/o Timothy Manah	100
Nicholas Broadaway	pt. "Whitall"	82
	pt. "Collington"	100
	pt. "Notlars Desire"	38
	pt. "Carman & Burton"	75
Katherine Buckley (widow)	pt. "Buckleys Delight"	16⅔
Charles Bermingham	"Berminghams Fortune"	100
Francis Bright	"Stoopy Gibson"	200
	"Brights Island"	28
Robert Blunt	pt. "Blunts Marsh" a/s "Great Neck"	220
	"Copartnership"	373
	pt. "Parsons Point"	400
Samuel Blunt	pt. "Blunts Marsh" a/s "Great Neck"	110

Edward Brown	pt. "Pascos Lott" – for h/o John Griffith	50
	pt. "Eastern Island" – for h/o John Griffith	25
	pt. "Addition" – for h/o John Griffith	90
	pt. "Princes" – for h/o John Griffith	48
	pt. "Bonadventure" – for h/o John Griffith	37½
	pt. "Rotterdam" – for h/o John Griffith	25
	pt. "Tulleys Delight"	107
	3 lots in Ogle Town	3
	⅓ "Sudlars Chance" – for his wife	29
Thomas Benton	pt. "Pentrogay"	186
	"Pentrovay"	50
Vincent Benton	pt. "Contention"	50
	"Jaspers Lott"	200
	"Bentons Luck"	79
James Burroughs	"Georges Hazard"	50
36:1757:5 ...		
William Barkhust	"Pensilvania Border"	50
	"Golden Ridge"	80
James Baley	pt. "Baleys Addition"	70
	pt. "Cleaves's Rambles" – for his wife	120
	"Tryangle"	50
Sweatnam Burn	pt. "Royston"	525
	pt. "Royston" tbc Elizabeth Coleman	50
Nathan Baynard	pt. "Relief"	476
h/o James Boon	pt. "Haddon"	160
	pt. "Garden of Roses"	48
	pt. "Garden of Roses" – more	200
	pt. "Haddon" – more	40
William Baxter	"Upper Blunt Point"	324
	pt. "Parsons Neck" – as guardian to Thomas Price	60
	pt. "Pascos Lott" – as guardian to Thomas Price	50
	pt. "Eastern Island" – as guardian to Thomas Price	25
	pt. "Addition" – as guardian to Thomas Price	90
	pt. "Princis" – as guardian to Thomas Price	48
	pt. "Bonadventure" – as guardian to Thomas Price	37½
	pt. "Rotterdam" – as guardian to Thomas Price	25

Queen Anne's County - 1757

George, Thomas, & John Burroughs	"Buck Road"	100
John Brown	"Hambletons Hermitage"	33⅓
	"Sedge Harbour"	167
	"Huntley"	251
	pt. "Hambletons Hermitage" – tbc h/o James Brown	33⅓
William Bancks	pt. "Pitts's Vineard"	166⅔
	"Godferys Folley"	50
	pt. "Pokety Ridge" & pt. "Jumps Chance"	126
	"Hunters Chance"	100
	"Bancks's Addition"	665
	"Aylers Outlett"	97
	"James Park"	50
	"Bancks's Delight"	773½
	"Merricks Delight"	50
	pt. "Pokety Ridge", pt. "Jumps Chance", & pt. "Jumps Addition"	93
	pt. "Jumps Chance" – from Thomas Swan, Jr.	50
Thomas Burroughs	"Scottons Inclosure"	55
36:1757:6 ...		
Charles Brown	"Magreholm"	608
	pt. "Bennetts Choice" – for his wife	1180
	pt. "Neglect" – for his wife	100
	"Halls Discovery"	150
	"Butlers Own Resurveyed"	164
	"Piney Swamp Tract"	50
	"Canaan"	50
	"Alder Branch"	100
	"Wakey Plains"	50
	pt. "Long Marsh Ridge Enlarg'd"	33½
	"Hobbs Venture"	281
	"Burks Expectation"	150
	"Ashley" – escheat	95½
John Bracco (cnp)	"Bracco"	393
	"Bracco's Addition"	98¾
	"Rattle Snake Ridge"	151

Queen Anne's County - 1757

	pt. "Long Marsh Ridge Enlarg'd"		724
John Bostick	"Hazell Point"		75
Samuel Blunt, Jr.	pt. "Fox Harbour" – for his wife		50
	pt. "Bishopton" – for his wife		32
	pt. "Notlars Desire" – for his wife		80
	pt. "Brotherhood" – for his wife		45
William Bennett	"Bennetts Chance"		281
	"Lambden Adventure"		100
Hannah Burroughs	pt. "Adventure"		50
Turbut Betton	pt. "Waltham"		21
	pt. "Wilkinsons Addition"		45
Robert Broadaway	pt. "Henrys Lott"		50
	"Roberts Outlett"		150
	"Society Hill"		50
	pt. "Society Hill Addition"		25
Edward Brown (Chester)	pt. "Brampton"		124
Charles Baker	pt. "Saulsberry Plains" – in right of his wife		33⅓
James Butler	pt. "Fox Hill"		85
	pt. "Notlars Delight"		37
36:1757:7 ...			
James Broadaway	pt. "Salisbury Plains" – for h/o Richard Scotton		50
	pt. "Scottons Addition" – for h/o Richard Scotton		100
	"Nathaniels Addition" – for Nathaniel Scotton		43
Isaac Baggs	"Hazard"		50
	"Sandy Ridge Enlarg'd"		160
John Brown s/o Edward	"Stoke"		100
	"Wellew"		100
	"Stokes Addition Rectified"		60
Thomas Barnes	"Barns's Satisfaction"		23
James Bell	"Turners Plains Addition"		120
Elisha Brown	pt. "Golds Hawk Enlargement"		35
	"Claxton"		100
	1 lot in Ogle Town		1
Thomas Beal, Jr.	"Brothers Discovery"		99
Nathan Baggs	pt. "Ingrams Desire" – in DO, for his wife		<n/g>
	pt. "Bridge Town" – for his wife		17

James Burk	pt. "Cole Rain"	148
	"Locks Point"	50
Joseph Buckley	pt. "Buckleys Delight" – for his wife	33⅓
John Barwick	"Jumps Choice"	97½
John Blackwell	"Alcocks Pharsalia"	100
36:1757:8 ...		
William Campbell	pt. "Detterage"	166
	pt. "Anthorpe"	197
	pt. "Hambletons Hermitage"	250
	pt. "Bishopton"	68
	"Walkers Square"	260
	pt. "Davis's Range"	185
	pt. "Reason"	74
	pt. "Lloyd's Meadows"	66
	pt. "Anthorpe"	203
	"Churnells Neck"	200
	"Adventure"	30
	"Hambletons Hermitage" – more	150
John Carradine	pt. "Forlone Hope"	50
John Clements	pt. "Edmondsons Green Close"	200
	pt. "Smiths Clifts"	100
Christopher Cox	pt. "Smiths Ridge"	300
	pt. "Prophecy"	217
	pt. "Heaths Discovery"	23
	pt. "Adventure"	39
	"Coxes Necessity"	½
	pt. "Partnership"	500
	pt. "Lows Arcadia"	233⅓
	"Plains Dealing Resurveyed" – for his son Christopher	350
	pt. "Walkers Square"	40
	"Jamaca" – with (N) Hopper	1
36:1757:9 ...		
William Coursey (cnp)	"Cheston"	800
	"Coursey Upon Wye"	290
	"Lords Gift"	1050

Queen Anne's County - 1757

	pt. "Smeath"	25
	"Sleford" – for his wife	200
	"Shepherds Hook" – for his wife	200
Solomon Clayton	"Solomons Fancey"	50
	"Barbadoes Hall" – from (N) Wilkinson	350
Charles Clayton	"Mount Molock"	150
Richard Costin	"Newington"	80
	"Newington Addition"	50
	pt. "Carters Forrest"	22
	pt. "Toms Fancy Enlarg'd"	100
James Clayland	pt. "Costins Park" – for h/o James Costin	279
John Cooper, Jr.	pt. "Keareys Discovery"	60
	"Grimes's Folly"	40
Mathew Chilton, Jr.	"Chiltons Chance"	64
Phillemon Croney	pt. "Cold Rain"	75
h/o James Croney	pt. "Cold Rain"	75
John Cahall	pt. "Wheatleys" a/s "Daniels Field" – for h/o Edward Cahall	60
John Cooper	"Taylers Chance"	200
James Countice	pt. "Dublin"	150
h/o William Countice	pt. "Dublin"	150
36:1757:10 ...		
John Colbreath	pt. "Poplar Neck"	200
	pt. "Sollomons Lott Addition"	35
	"Holley Neck Resurveyed"	415
	"Poplar Neck Addition"	70
	"Buck Range"	100
	"Parsons Delight" – for his daughter Mary	80
Elijah Chance	pt. "Bear Point"	100
Batchelor Chance	pt. "Bear Point"	100
John Chance	pt. "Littleworth"	50
Elinor Chance	pt. "Littleworth"	50
	pt. "Littleworth Addition"	50
	pt. "Garden of Roses"	22¼
Henry Council	pt. "Hawkins's Pharsalia"	162

Queen Anne's County - 1757

John Collins	pt. "Tottingham"	200
	pt. "Hackers Meadows" – for his wife	100
William Canon	pt. "Content"	100
Thomas Coleman	pt. "Tilghmans Discovery"	80
John Commyges	pt. "Shepherds Forrest"	173
	pt. "Shepherds Redout"	200
John Clothier	pt. "Clothiers Pharsalia"	150
	pt. "Hinsleys Plains"	4
Robert Certain	"Jones's Delight"	200
	pt. "Leavells" – for Margaret Collins (minor)	170
James Cassey	pt. "Conaway"	289
Nicholas Clouds	pt. "Broad Creek Resurveyed"	200
36:1757:11 ...		
Andrew Cox	½ "Forrest of Winsor"	125
Charles Conner	pt. "Wood Yard Thickett"	205
William Carmichal	pt. "Park"	500
	pt. "Allens Neck"	117
	pt. "Partnership"	36
	"Harmonton" a/s "Harmons Lott"	304
	"Allens Neck Outlett"	18¾
	pt. "Bennetts Choice"	212
	pt. "Stagwell"	526
	"Stagwell Addition"	129
Richard Carter	pt. "Barns's Satisfaction"	50
	"Donns Hazard Corrected"	343¼
Jacob Carter	"Oar Mine"	200
	pt. "Coppidges Range"	30
Henry Carter	"Mattapax Neck"	98
Phillip Coppidge	"Indian Spring"	100
	pt. "Slaughterton"	200
	pt. "Coppidges Range"	13
Henry Casson (cnp)	pt. "Long Range Addition"	124
	"Mistake"	20
	"Jumps Claims"	80
	pt. "Dudleys Desire"	100
	"Cassons Meadows"	490

	"Salvesters Discovery"	241
	"Mistake Addition"	27
	pt. "Jumps Chance"	135
	pt. "Pitts's Vineard"	166⅔
	"Bakers Chance"	127
h/o Henry Culley	pt. "Poplar Hill"	27
	5 lots in Kings Town – No. 1, No. 12, No. 13, No. 24, No. 25	5
Nathaniel Cleave	"Mangy Pockey"	100
	"Troy"	100
	"Pockys Addition"	62
	"Wells Park" – for his wife	110
James Clough	"Cloughs Fancy"	50
	"Cloughs Rambles"	100
36:1757:12 ...		
William Clayton	"Prous's Park"	300
	pt. "Tryangle"	25
	"Winter House"	50
	"Hogg Penn Neck"	55
	pt. "Bishop Fields"	350
	"Claytons Chesterfield"	92
	"Chesterfield"	200
	pt. "Chesterfield" – from (N) Butler	200
	"Tryangle" – from (N) Butler	25
	"Claytons Landing"	20
	"Hogg Hole"	50
Richard Cooke	pt. "Partnership"	20
	pt. "Sandish Woods"	335
Benjamin Coventon	pt. "Toms Fancy Enlarg'd"	100
Edward Cahall	pt. "Hacton" – for his wife	50
	pt. "Hacton" – for his wife	50
Edward Clayton (cnp)	"Chesterfield Addition"	70
	pt. "Neglect"	200
	"Broad Neck"	100
	pt. "Park" – for his wife	146

Queen Anne's County - 1757

	pt. "Courseys Point" & pt. "Brampton Addition" – from (N) Ringgold	9
	pt. "Bishops Addition" & pt. "Bishops Outlett" – from (N) Austin	200
John Covington	pt. "Providence"	100
	pt. "Rawlings Hazard"	179
William Covington	pt. "Kinesleys Plains"	91
James Callaghane	pt. "Hemsleys Arcadia"	70
Sharples Cooper	"Hills Outlett Resurvey'd"	233
Nathaniel Curtis	pt. "Sarah's Fancy"	112
Henry Covington	pt. "Rachells Desire"	471
	pt. "Hinsleys Plains"	140
	pt. "Hinsleys Plains" – from (N) Clothier	60
36:1757:13 ...		
Susannah Cockey (widow)	"Hogg Penn Neck", "Goose Hill", & pt. "Ridge"	95
Henry Council, Jr.	"Swine Range" – for wife	30
	"Widdows Folley" – for wife	70
	pt. "Friendship" – for wife	25
	pt. "Friendship" – more, for wife	50
Thomas Carradine	"Commegys Hazard"	100
	pt. "Lexton"	235
	"Lott"	50
	pt. "Bristol Marsh"	160
	pt. "Toms Fancy Enlarg'd"	150
Benjamin Chaires	pt. "Warplesdon Addition" & pt. "Solomons Friendship"	100
John Council	"Hogg Penn Ridge"	150
John & Gias Bartus Commyges	"Salem"	360
Henry Collester	pt. "Crumpton"	200
	pt. "Sandy Hurst"	216
Daniel Cox	pt. "Cole Rain"	526
James & John Clayland	pt. "Trustram"	300
Anthony Cox	"Coxes Desire"	100
Mary Cockey	"Hogg Penn Neck", "Goose Hill", & pt. "Ridge"	95
Joseph Chaires	"Lantley"	125

Queen Anne's County - 1757

Dennis Carey	pt. "Bennetts Outlett"	75
	pt. "Middle Plantation"	60
	"Bennetts Outlett"	15
36:1757:14 ...		
Joshua Clark	pt. "Lyford"	287
	pt. "Stephen Fields"	412
Edward Cockey	"Hogg Penn Neck", "Goos Hill", & pt. "Ridge"	95
George Cope	"Copes's Range"	250
	"Cohee's Desire" – for h/o James Cohee	100
William Curtis	"Curtis's Lott"	50
Nathaniel Coventon	"Coventons Necessity"	140
	pt. "Rachells Desire"	37
Thomas Clayland	~~pt. "Dungamon"~~	~~116½~~
	"Fossets Plains"	150
Samuel Cocklin	"Wyatts Lott" – for h/o (N) Wyatt	150
Boon Chance	"Stoney Hill"	24
Susannah Clough	"Cloughs Hope" – for h/o Nathaniel Clough	50
	"Boons Hope" – by name of "Broom Hope" for h/o Nathaniel Clough	100
Jere. Colson	pt. "Lambert" – for his wife (N) d/o Timothy Lane	400
Edward Chetham	pt. "Timber Land"	200
	pt. "Pascalls Chance"	125
James Chetham	pt. "Timber Land"	200
	pt. "Pascalls Chance"	125
	pt. "Park"	354
36:1757:15 ...		
John Downes, Jr.	"Wrights Plains"	100
	pt. "Wrights Reserve"	200
	"Wrights Reserve Addition"	50
	pt. "Security"	60
	pt. "Smeath"	106
	pt. "Staggwell"	42
	"Donns Chance"	100
	pt. "Smeath on Resurvey" – for h/o John Burk	412
	pt. "Smeath on Resurvey" – for (N) Barber	50
	pt. "Smeath on Resurvey" – from (N) Hynson	175

Queen Anne's County - 1757

William Dawson	pt. "Trustram"	300
Mrs. Henrietta Maria Dulany	"Lloyd's Insula"	1795
	"Purchas"	1000
	pt. "Brandfield"	228
	"Skinners Expectation"	240
Charles Downes	pt. "Fair Play"	116
	pt. "Macklin Burrough"	199
	"High Gale"	50
	"Wrenches Adventure"	87
Thomas Dockery	pt. "Fishingham"	100
	"Dockerys Meadow"	142
36:1757:16 ...		
John Davis	pt. "Confution"	220
	"Peters Lott"	150
	pt. "Content"	70
Henry Downes, Jr.	pt. "Dullage"	80
Mathew Dockery	pt. "Fishingham"	100
	"Fishingham Addition"	13
	"Mathews Fancy"	8½
	"Dangerfield"	200
	"Davis's Discovery"	52
John Downes	pt. "Nobles Range" & pt. "Hemsleys Arcadia"	192
	pt. "Carters Forrest"	22
Solomon Downes	pt. "Millford"	200
	pt. "Parkers Freshes"	87
	"Porters Folley"	100
Henry Downes	pt. "Carters Forrest"	114
Mrs. Catherine Davis	"Claxton Hill"	150
	"Claxton Hill Addition"	80
John Deford & wife	"Chance"	284
Volentine Downey	"Pigg Quarter Neck"	100
William Dockery	pt. "Suffolk"	10
Sarah Durdin (widow)	pt. "Powells Fancy"	50
Benjamin Denney	"Wotters's Chance"	100
	"Wotters's Chance Addition"	75
	"Outlett"	18

Queen Anne's County - 1757

Hynson Downes	"Shore Ditch"	150
	pt. "Dullage"	50
36:1757:17 ...		
John Downes s/o John	"Downes Chance"	150
Rebeckah Downes (widow)	pt. "Nobles Range" & pt. "Hemsleys Arcadia"	100
Joseph Dodd	"Jamaca's Addition" – for wife	50
	pt. "Jamaca" – for wife	59
Jacob Dodd	pt. "Rye Hall" – for h/o George	184
John Duffey	"Batchelors Adventure" – for wife	150
	"Storeys Park" – for wife	100
James Duhamell	"Hynsons Lott"	199
	"Timber Swamp"	200
Mary Dyre	pt. "Waltham"	16⅔
	pt. "Wilkinsons Addition"	16⅔
Abner Dudley	"Sarah Portion"	300
Thomas Doyle	pt. "Batchelors Hope" – for wife	20
	pt. "Neglect" – for wife	16⅓
	"Marshey Crook" – for Charles Brown (minor)	100
Lewis & Lewis Derochbroom, Jr.	"Friendship Resurveyed"	396
John Derochbroom	"Vaughn's Kindness"	200
Lewis Derochbroom, Jr.	"Josephs Addition" – for his brother Joseph (minor)	60
William Dames	"Danby Resurveyed" – for devisees of Rev. James Cox	275
	"Discovery" – for devisees of Rev. James Cox	100
	pt. "Adventure Resurveyed" – for devisees of Rev. James Cox	124
	"Bridge North" – for devisees of Rev. James Cox	100
36:1757:18 ...		
Daniel Dulaney	pt. "Vaughans Kindness"	200
Robert Dunkin	"Refuse" – for his wife (N) w/o Isaac Hollingsworth	100
Arthor Emory (cnp)	"Welch Ridge"	500
	"Happ Hazard"	116
	"Happ Hazard Addition"	50
	"Mores Hope"	100

	pt. "Mores Hope Addition"	208
John Emory	"Bee Tree"	500
	pt. "Partnership"	165
	pt. "Powells Fancey"	90
	"Batchelors Chance Resurveyed"	253
	"Happ Hazard"	17
	"Emorys Chance"	110
	"Bee Tree Swamp"	76
John Emory, Jr.	"Emorys Resurvey"	537¾
Sarah Emory	pt. "Partnership" – surveyed for (N) Beck	100
36:1757:19 ...		
William Elbert	½ "Reward"	200
	½ "Macklins Addition"	18
	"Lewis's Chance"	50
	pt. "Lambeth"	129½
John Emerson	pt. "Addition"	100
Mary Eagle	"Lambeth Addition" – for h/o William	170
Benjamin Endsworth	pt. "Brandfield & Sawyers Addition" – for h/o John Wilson	200
John Ewbancks	pt. "Ratcliffe"	140
devisees of John Earle	pt. "Upperheathworth"	167
	"Heathworth"	533
John Errickson	"Sarahs Portion"	96
John Elliott	"Forlone Hope"	100
	"Elliotts Choice"	120
	"Donns Hazard Corrected" – for h/o William Price	233¾
Elizabeth Errickson (widow)	pt. "Sarah's Portion"	54
	"Johnsons Lott"	46
Joseph Elliott	"Williams Lott"	10
	"Newnams Hermitage"	50
	pt. "Salisberry Plains"	100
	pt. "Sawyers Range"	60
	pt. "Lowes Desire"	53
	pt. "Slaughterton"	100
	pt. "Lows Desire" – from Thomas Hadaway	35
	pt. "Slaughterton"	100

John Elliott s/o John	"Mathews Enlargement"	155
Charles Errickson	"Stenton Errickson"	200
36:1757:20 ...		
Richard Tilghman Earle	"Earles Begining"	517
Lawrance Everett	"Hunters Forrest"	200
Michael Earle (CE)	"Emorys Fortune Addition"	270
	pt. "Partnership" – surveyed for (N) Emory	175
	"Golden Grove"	20
Thomas Emory	"Emory Paxton"	100
	pt. "Partnership" – surveyed for (N) Beck	150
Gideon Emory	pt. "Fortune"	90
	pt. "St. Pauls"	50
	pt. "Carmans Neck"	50
	pt. "Meconikins Fortune"	236
	pt. "Meconikins Fortune" – more, for his wife	143
	pt. "Wood Ridge" – for his wife	184
James Emory	"Emorys Part of Trustram"	196
Arthor Emory s/o John	pt. "Partnership" – surveyed for (N) Beck	90
	pt. "Partnership" – surveyed for (N) Emory	10
Joseph Elliott s/o George	"Clouds's Hermitage"	200
Sarah Elson (widow)	1 lot in Kings Town – No. 7	1
Thomas Emory s/o John	"Roberts Range"	150
	"Roberts Range Addition"	37
Joseph Everett	"Roes Desire" – for h/o Thomas Roe, Jr. (Choptank)	50
	"Hackers Adventure" – for h/o Thomas Roe, Jr. (Choptank)	50
George Elliott	"Elliotts Luck"	125
36:1757:21 ...		
James Earle	"Cove Point on Resurvey"	200
	"Wood Land Neck"	200
	"Earles Guard"	86
Lawrence Everett, Jr.	pt. "Everetts Content"	100
Henry Elbert	pt. "Davis's Range"	400
Henry Elliott	pt. "Slaughterton"	100
Burton Fra. Falconar & John	"Chesnut Ridge"	200

Queen Anne's County - 1757

Francis Foreman	pt. "Royston"	500
36:1757:22 ...		
Thomas Ford	pt. "Ashton"	142½
Isaac Ford	pt. "Ashton"	82½
James Findley	pt. "Rambles" – stricken off	0
William Fisher	pt. "Large Range"	416⅔
	pt. "Codds Head Manor"	384
Henry Fiddeman	pt. "Hacketts Garden"	600
	pt. "Brandfield"	200
	pt. "Large Range" – from William Thomas	10
	⅓ "Pitts's Vineard"	166⅔
	"Joans Plackett"	100
John Foreacres	pt. "Tulleys Lott"	100
James Findley (wheelright)	pt. "Warplesdon Addition" & pt. "Solomons Friendship"	50
	"Nathan's & Thomas's Begining"	27
James Webb	pt. "Suffolk" – for William Fisher (minor)	290
	"Fishers Plains" – for William Fisher (minor)	164
John Fisher	pt. "Suffolk"	190
	pt. "Brandford" – for William Jerman (minor)	100
	pt. "Suffolk" – more	10
James Fisher	pt. "Fishers Meadows"	167
w/o Thomas Fisher – during life & after to her son Richard	pt. "Fishers Meadows"	167
John Falconar	"Falconars Chance"	12
	"Welch Pool" – as tenant under Daniel Wheatly	150
John Foreman s/o Francis	pt. "Royston"	100
36:1757:23 ...		
John Green	"Greens Adventure Upon Carpenters Square"	212
William Greenwood	"Miss Hitt" – for h/o Selph. Riche	250
Mathew Griffith	pt. "Park"	220
Edward Garratt	"Sandy Hill"	50
Mary Godwin (widow)	pt. "White Mars Addition"	338
Michael Green	"Costin's Hope"	200
William Godwin	pt. "Wrights Chance" a/s "Choice"	100

Richard Gould	pt. "Ripley"	266⅔
	pt. "Spread Eagle"	75
36:1757:24 ...		
John Gafford	pt. "Macklins Begining" & pt. "Smithfield"	150
	"Brotherhood" – for his wife	170½
Charles Gafford	pt. "Macklins Begining" & pt. "Smithfield"	150
Richard Gafford	pt. "Macklins Begining" & pt. "Smithfield"	150
Mathew Graves	"Graves's Begining"	50
Marmaduke Goodhand	pt. "Sillen"	200
	"Broad Oak"	500
	"Poplar Neck"	300
	pt. "Sillin" – more, for Nathaniel Brown	100
	"Wood Yard Thickett" – for his wife	205
	pt. "Point Love"	200
Phillemon Green	"Greens Fortune"	80
	"Greens Fortune Addition"	75
	"Jones's Forrest"	100
Frances Gould (widow)	"Spring Branch"	100
	pt. "Ripley"	133⅓
	pt. "Scivals Fork"	500
James Gould	"Goulds Purchase"	195
William Green	"Bradford"	100
	pt. "Ridleys Chance"	20
Elizabeth Gwin	"Gunners Harbour" – for h/o John Gwin	100
Benjamin Gould	pt. "Camberwell"	100
Anne Gilbert	"Isaac's Chance"	100
Boatswain Tom & Gibbs (Negroes)	pt. "Killmanam Plains"	200
36:1757:25 ...		
James Ginn	pt. "Bakers Plains"	200
Stephen Gudeon	"Outlett" – from Benjamin Denney	50
Thomas Gilpin	pt. "Halls Harbour"	250
Solomon Glanding	"Glandings Begining"	10
Christopher Higgins	pt. "Dunganon"	150
John Hall (cnp)	"Welch Pool" – for his wife	100
	pt. "Dancy"	300

	pt. "Hogg Harbour"	219¾
	"Falconars Hope"	21½
	pt. "Vaughans Discovery" – as guardian for h/o Edward Hall	100
	pt. "Hogg Harbour" – as guardian for h/o Edward Hall	73¼
36:1757:26 ...		
John Hill	"Green Hill"	200
Robert Hardcastle	"Mount Hope"	150
	"Renewell"	154
	"Angle"	50
Ezekiall Hunter	"Boons Ridge"	50
Mary Hunter	"Jumps Lott"	50
	"Hunters Hazard"	50
William Herrington	pt. "Josephs Lott"	100
	pt. "Henrys Lott"	25
h/o David Harrington	"Hope Well"	100
	"Harringtons Desire"	50
	"Buck Bay"	100
	"Beaver Dams"	50
Earnult Hawkins	pt. "Brampton"	126
Richard Harrington	"Solomons Lott"	100
	pt. "Solomons Lott Addition"	15
Richard Hynson	"Anns Portion"	150
Thomas Honey	"Sparks's Outlett"	114
Volentine Thomas Honey	pt. "Adventure"	109
Joseph Harris	pt. "Crumps Chance"	50
	pt. "Upperheathworth"	100
	pt. "Crumps Forrest"	15
James Harris	pt. "Crumps Chance"	50
	pt. "Toms Fancy Enlarg'd" – for his wife	75
Mrs. Sarah Holliday	"Redburn Rectified" – for h/o James Holliday, Esq.	1440
	pt. "Backlin Burrough" – for h/o James Holliday, Esq.	114
36:1757:27 ...		
John Hambleton (cnp)	pt. "Neglect"	50
	"Hambletons Range"	100

	"Mary Ann's Lott"	100
	"Hambletons Addition"	50
	"Hambletons Luck"	100
h/o John Harris	pt. "Contention"	150
James Hackett	"Prices Hill"	200
Thomas Hackett	pt. "Prices Hill"	100
	pt. "Scotland"	50
	pt. "Providence"	330
	pt. "Shepherds Fortune" – for his wife	150
William Hopper	"Chesterfield"	900
	pt. "Providence"	200
	"Bridgewater"	300
	pt. "Gilford"	200
	"Darkin"	210
	pt. "Courseys Point" or "Smiths Mistake"	200
	"Hoppers Industry"	213¼
	pt. "Smiths Mistake"	275
	pt. "Conquest"	256
	pt. "Green Spring"	100
	pt. "Camberwell"	272
	pt. "Stepney"	255½
	"Dockerys Discovery"	73
	pt. "Paxton Lott"	20
John Hollingsworth	"Hambletons Hermitage"	33⅓
John Hadley	"Skinners Pleasure"	50
James Hutchins	"Wrights Fortune"	120
	pt. "Condon"	316
Thomas Hutchins	"Lanes Ridge"	200
Giles Hicks	pt. "Killary"	100
Charles Hines	pt. "Spread Eagle" – for Thomas	33⅓
36:1757:28 ...		
Anthony Herrington	pt. "Warners Discovery" – for his wife (N) d/o William Vickers	195
James Holliday (London)	pt. "Macklin Burrough"	230
	pt. "Waterford"	18

Queen Anne's County - 1757

James Harvey	"Harveys Discovery"	170
	pt. "Gold Hawks Enlargement"	35
h/o Robert Hawkins	pt. "Macklin Burrough"	175
	pt. "Tulleys Delight"	293
Robert Hawkins & William Kendall (KE)	pt. "Sprigley" – in right of their wives (N) d/o & coheiresses of Henry Jacobs	300
	"Winchester" – in right of their wives (N) d/o & coheiresses of Henry Jacobs	125
William Hunter	pt. "Chesnot Meadows" – for h/o Henry Price Williams	100
Thomas Hamer	"Hamers Chance"	178
	pt. "Whiteall" – for his wife	18
	"Ratcliffts Part of Lloyds Freshes"	19
Nathaniel Herrington	"Jadwins Folley"	44
William & Thomas Hughlett	"Bakers Plains"	400
Mathew Hawkins	pt. "Tulleys Delight"	200
Andrew Hall	pt. "Spread Eagle"	149
	pt. "Spread Eagle" – more	35
	pt. "Brotherhood"	234
John Holden	"Nicholsons Fancey"	50
	pt. "Wood House"	61
	pt. "Wood House Addition"	14
	"Waterford" – from Richard Lake	200

36:1757:29   ...

William Horne	"Walnut Neck Resurveyed" – for his wife	109
	"Barren Ridge" – for his wife	100
Mark Hargadine, Jr.	pt. "Smiths Neglect" – for his wife	150
Giles & James Hicks	pt. "Edmondsons Green Close"	200
Mrs. Anna Maria Hemsley	"Hardest Find Off"	150
h/o Mary Hemsley	"Touton Fields Addition"	140
	"Hemsleys Discovery"	91
h/o Anna Maria Hemsley & Mary Hemsley	pt. "Touton Fields"	460
Henry Holliday	pt. "Turners Plains Addition"	120
James Hammond	pt. "Wrenches Adventure"	192
Mr. Thomas Harris (cnp)	"Addition"	500
	"Steads Go Between"	71

	pt. "Begining"	429
	pt. "Standford"	114
	pt. "Ditterage"	251
	pt. "Long Neck Addition"	20½
	pt. "Coursey Upon Wye"	258½
	pt. "Reason"	35
	pt. "Mount Mill"	33
	"Lawrances Delight"	100
	"Johnsons Addition"	100
	"Harris's Hazard"	59½
William Hammond	pt. "Fossetts Plains" tbc Thomas Clayland	0
Nathan Harrington	"Beaver Dams Addition"	150
	½ "Ingrams Desire"	\<n/g\>
36:1757:30 ...		
w/o Francis Jackson	"Barbareys Inlett"	263
Thomas Jackson s/o George	pt. "Winchester"	125
	"Barbareys Choice"	80
	"Castle Town"	100
Stephen Jarman	pt. "Hogg Hole"	130
Robert Jarman	"New Port"	284
Jeremiah Jadwin	"Cow Range"	100
	"Tims Neglect"	50
	"Jadwins Project"	40
Edward Jones	"Beaver Dams Fork"	100
	"Hope Well"	100
	"Jones's Greenwood" – for his son William Kenny Jones	150
	"Jones's Safety"	59
	pt. "Nottingham"	59
Dorothy Isgate	"Fork"	200
John & Hans Johnson	"Cloudent"	200
	"Notlars Delight"	80
Thomas Jackson	"Hope Well"	50
	"Nicholson Chance"	50
William Joyner, Jr.	pt. "Parsons Neck"	60

Jonathan Jolley	"Andeavour"	50
	"Nicholsons Adventure"	50
	"Burton"	50
	"Lester"	50
	"Lesters Meadows"	50
36:1757:31 ...		
Amos Jarman	pt. "Blandford" a/s "Brandford"	37
	pt. "St. Martins"	82
	pt. "Inclosure"	81
	pt. "Brandford" – for John Jarman (minor)	111
John Jackson	"Fords Park" – for his wife	30
	pt. "Nottingham" – for his wife	30
Inhabitants of Queen Anne's County	"Price Land" – whereon Wells Inspecting House stands	½
Dr. John Jackson	pt. "Providence"	213
	"Smithfield Addition"	327¼
	pt. "Lexton"	184
	pt. "Jamaca"	40
	pt. "Adventure Resurveyed"	27
Thomas Jones	"Sarahs Portion"	50
Joseph Jackson s/o Francis	"Bentons Hazard"	87
Mary Jolley	"Hope"	50
James Jones	"Jones's Fancey"	100
Archibald Jackson	"Speedy Contract"	10
	pt. "Ratcliff"	100
	"Controversie"	22
Samuel Jackson	pt. "Oak Ridge" – for h/o Benjamin Boon	175
	pt. "Garden of Roses" – for h/o Benjamin Boon	177¾
Thomas Jumpe s/o Thomas	pt. "Horse Pasture"	50
	"Jumps Lott"	34
Archibald Jackson, Jr.	"Nodd"	113
James Jackson	pt. "Ratcliff"	100
Obednigo Jackson	pt. "Ratcliff" – taken off	100
36:1757:32 ...		
Sarah Jones	pt. "Nobles Range" – for h/o Henry	58
	pt. "Dittlage" – for h/o Henry	50

Queen Anne's County - 1757

Mary Jadwin	pt. "Lyford" – for h/o Robert	70
Peter Jumpe	pt. "Horse Pasture"	100
Isaac Jumpe	pt. "Horse Pasture"	50
Abraham Jumpe	pt. "Jumps Chance"	100
Vaughan Jumpe	pt. "Pokety Ridge"	45
Mary Jones w/o William	"Jones's Chance"	100
h/o Richard Keiron	pt. "Confution"	100
Nathaniel Knotts	"Knotts Addition"	50
	"Knotts Range"	235
	"Knotts Chance"	53
James Kenton	pt. "Grovley Hoe"	150
	pt. "Upland"	100
Solomon Kenton	pt. "Upland"	200
	"Upland Addition"	50
James Kersey	pt. "Scotland"	100
36:1757:33 ...		
Baldwin Kemp	pt. "Emory Rich Land"	150
James Knotts	pt. "Knotts Chance"	200
Anne Jarmon (widow)	pt. "Emorys Rich Land"	95
	pt. "Relief"	55
William Kent	pt. "Toms Fancy Enlarg'd"	150
Thomas Kersey	pt. "Scotland"	50
Benjamin Kerby	"Clouds's Chance"	6
	"Bodys Neck"	200
	pt. "Sillen" – for h/o John Evans & Andrew Price	200
	pt. "Uper Deale" – for h/o John Evans & Andrew Price	500
Mary Kemp	pt. "Toms Fancy Enlarg'd"	75
Robert Kent	pt. "Batchelors Plains"	200
William Kirkham	pt. "Stephens Fields" – for h/o Henry Clift	278
36:1757:34 ...		
Mr. Robert Lloyd (cnp)	"Hemsleys Park" – for devisees of Phill. Hemsley	800
	"Clovar Fields" – for devisees of Phill. Hemsley	1622
	pt. "Trustram Wells" – for devisees of Phill. Hemsley	68
	"Hemsleys Adventure" – for devisees of Phill. Hemsley	200

	"Tilghmans Gift" – for William Hemsley	650
	"Tilghmans Meadows" – for his wife	270
	"Snodland" – for his wife	284
	"Friendship"	175
James London	"Kirkhams Lott"	200
James Lane	pt. "Worleys Out Range"	100
	"Lanes Addition"	75
Elizabeth Longfellow	"Josephs Hope" – for h/o Joseph Longfellow	50
Richard Langford	⅓ "Good Increase" – for his wife (N) d/o Thomas Crupper	66⅔
Richard Lambert	pt. "Low's Arcadia" – for David s/o Thomas Phillips	100
Thomas Lee	pt. "Lees Chance"	166
	pt. "Stratton"	52
	pt. "Hawkins's Pharsalia"	100
John Legg	pt. "Limricks" & pt. "Leggs Begining"	186
	pt. "Pentroby" – rightly called "Pentrogy"	14
John Lee	pt. "Camberwell"	100
John Leith	"Horse Penn Ridge"	100
Bexly John Lambden	pt. "Smiths Outlett"	48
	pt. "Northumberland"	52
Mary Lane	"Lane's Folley" – for h/o Walter Lane	161
	pt. "Stephen Fields" – for h/o Walter Lane	110
36:1757:35 ...		
Edward Linsey	"Jadwins Hazard"	61
John Legg, Jr.	pt. "Limricks" & pt. "Leggs Begining"	14
	⅓ "Woodland Neck"	16⅔
	⅓ "Oldsons Relief"	33⅓
John Lockerman, Jr.	"Bennetts Toalson Resurveyed"	930
Alexander Lee	"Knave Standoff" – for his wife	50
James Lane	"Herringtons Venture"	100
Thomas Mooth	pt. "Friendship"	25
	"Watsons Delight"	50
	"Watsons Delight Addition"	30
	"Mooths Range"	105
William Merson	pt. "Middle Plantation"	66⅔

William Mansfield	pt. "Waltham" – for his wife	16⅔
	pt. "Wilkinsons Addition" – for his wife	16⅔
Rebeccah Meeds	pt. "Brandford" – from William Diggs for h/o John Meeds	141
36:1757:36 ...		
William Meeds	pt. "Brandford"	10
	pt. "St. Martins"	100
John Maridath	"Trustram Ridge"	150
Thomas Maridath	pt. "Plain Dealing"	75
	pt. "Adventure"	100
	pt. "Shrewsbury" & pt. "Shrewsbury Addition"	50
Anne Maridath (widow)	pt. "Shrewsbury" & pt. "Shrewsbury Addition" – for h/o William	200
David Mills	1 lot in Kings Town	1
John Mayne	"New London"	150
	"New London Addition"	114
Anne Martindale (widow)	pt. "Salvesters Forrest" – for h/o Thomas	100
	"Martindales Range" – for h/o Thomas	50
	"Martindales Hope" – for h/o Thomas	316
h/o James Millis	"Campersons Choice" – for Samuel & James Cook (minors)	100
William Winchester Mason	"Ephraims Hope"	100
	pt. "Winchesters Folley"	273
William Mountague	pt. "Ratcliff"	98
John Miller	pt. "Oaken Thorpe"	229
	pt. "Povidence"	150
Timothy Mountseer	"Hacketts Delight"	150
James Massey	pt. "Friendship"	300
	pt. "Masseys Addition"	23½
Patrick Mooney	pt. "Nevells Delight" – for wife	16⅔
	"Mooneys Luck" – for wife	75
Daniel Meconikin	"Meconikins Corcar"	150
36:1757:37 ...		
Thomas Mash (cnp)	"Little Tickett"	200
	"Marshes Forbarance"	150
	"Cabbin Neck"	350
	"Neglect"	200

	2 lots in Kings Town – No. 4, No. 5	2
	pt. "Shepherds Fortune"	266
	1 lot in Kings Town – from (N) Maxwell	1
	pt. "Poplar Hill"	200
	"Clouds's Choice"	200
	"Lowthers Chance"	150
	pt. "Poplar Hill"	100
James Mecoy	pt. "Smiths Delight"	218½
	"Mecoys Pleasure"	129
	pt. "Hamers Addition"	18½
	"Ponders Chance"	38
Thomas Meloyd	pt. "Toms Fancy Enlarg'd"	100
Timothy Mannah	"Mannahs Chance Resurveyed"	50
Jos. Merchant	"Jacks Purchase"	75
	"Musketo Ridge"	50
	"Josephs Own"	30
Thomas Meclannahan	pt. "Fox Harbour"	100
	pt. "Collins's Lott"	56
	pt. "Brotherhood"	42½
Samuel Mecosh	pt. "Upper Heathworth"	238
	pt. "Collins's Refusall"	112
	pt. "Heaths Forrest"	50
	"Heaths Gift"	53
	pt. "Larrington"	119
	"Crumpton"	50
William Mathews	pt. "Bridge North"	50
Charles Murphey	pt. "Hawkins's Pharsalia"	200
	"Murpheys Chance Resurveyed"	99½
James Miller	pt. "Forrest of Windsor"	125
36:1757:38 ...		
Solomon Mason	pt. "Winchesters Folley Resurveyed"	133
Richard Mason	"Winchesters Folley Resurveyed"	133
Henry Mason	"Masons Hazard"	192
Anne Maridath (KI)	pt. "Conners Neck"	60
James Massey, Jr.	pt. "Friendship" – surveyed for (N) Tilghman	50
William Maner	"Notlars Delight" – for his wife	33

John Meeds	pt. "Begining" – on TA Roll	150
John Mason	"Nevells Delight" – for his wife	33⅓
John Meconikin	"Georges Codd"	100
	⅓ "Woodland Neck" – for his wife	16⅔
	⅓ "Oldsons Relief" – for his wife	33⅓
Samuel Massey	pt. "Poplar Hill"	123
	"Masseys Addition"	40½
	"Masseys Right"	23
William Maridath (Tulleys Neck)	"Maridaths Adventure"	100
Nathaniel Moor	pt. "Clouds's Adventure" – for h/o James Ware	112½
	pt. "Brotherhood" – for h/o James Ware	67
James Manor	pt. "Seegars Hazard"	60
Peter Maxwell	pt. "Hazard"	45
36:1757:39 ...		
Thomas Meeds	pt. "Begining" – on TA Roll	150
Charles Mooney	pt. "Southampton" – for wife	75
Elias Meconikin	"Derochbrooms Neglect" – for wife (N) w/o John Steavens	17½
	"Steavens Range" – for h/o John Steavens	315
John Nabb	pt. "Tilghmans Addition"	100
	"Jones's Fortune"	100
	pt. "Adventure"	7
Solomon Newnam	pt. "Williams Lott"	40
William Newnam	"Newnams Chance"	56
	pt. "Johns Meadows"	60
	pt. "Shavour"	107
	"Newnams Addition"	72
	"Addition" – for h/o Jos. Newnam	24
	pt. "Scottons Addition" – for h/o Jos. Newnam	40
	"Shearing" – for h/o Jos. Newnam	100
	pt. "Devonishes Chance" – for h/o Jos. Newnam	16¾
	"Newnams Hazard"	20¼
Charles Nabb	pt. "Clouds's Adventure"	200
	"Elizabeth Portion"	100
Thomas Newton	"Toms Fancy Enlarg'd"	100

Queen Anne's County - 1757

Edward Neale	pt. "Green Spring"	500
	"Neales Residence"	899
36:1757:40 ...		
Jonathan Nicols	pt. "Hacton" – for his wife	200
	pt. "Deford" – for his wife	150
	"Wilsons Addition"– for his wife	70
	pt. "Partnership"	500
James Nevell	pt. "Barton"	40
	"Smiths Addition"	106
	"Southampton"	75
Nathaniel Newnam	pt. "Shavor"	93
Charles Nicols	"Johns Forrest"	500
	pt. "Brandfield & Sayers Addition"	50
h/o Dick (Negro)	pt. "Knowles's Range"	244
John Nevell s/o John	pt. "Whartons & Pendars Out Range"	75
	"Sewals Fork"	250
	"Nevells Discovery"	3½
	pt. "Tilghmans Discovery"	200
	"Solomons Outlett"	50
	"Nevells Addition"	250
	"Farrington"	250
	"Bee Tree Ridge"	50
	"Nevells Out Range"	46½
James Williams Nabb	pt. "Wrenches Farme" – for his wife	200
	"Mores Hope Addition" – for his wife	172
	pt. "Hawkins's Farme" – from William Dockery	8
	pt. "Mores Hope Addition" – from William Dockery	29
Benjamin Newnam	⅓ "Wilsons Begining & Raleys Begining" – in right of his wife	54
John Olson	pt. "Hawkins's Pharsalia"	150
	pt. "Hawkins's Pharsalia" – from your brother Abraham	50
36:1757:41 ...		
Thomas OBryan	4 lots in Ogle Town – No. 22, No. 38, No. 39, No. 59	4
	"Pleasant Spring Resurveyed"	392

Queen Anne's County - 1757

Robert Offley	pt. "Levells"	80
Samuel Osburn	"Addition"	200
	pt. "Martins Neck Resurveyed"	78
Abraham Oldson	pt. "Hawkins's Farme Resurveyed"	126
w/o William Oxenham	pt. "Golden Lyon"	100
	"Mirey Branch"	85
	"Turners Plains"	128
William Pryor	"Pryors Chance"	271
Charles Price	"Lincoln"	200
	pt. "Broomley Lambeth"	83
William Price	pt. "Broomley Lambeth"	164
Henry Punney	pt. "Salisberry" – for his wife (N) d/o John Higgens	50
	pt. "Salisberry" – for his wife's sister	50
Rebekah Purnall (widow)	pt. "Sayers Addition & Brandfield"	100
Thomas Price	pt. "Brandfield" – from William Diggs	106
John Phillips	pt. "Vaughans Discovery"	230
William Pratt	pt. "Chaires's Addition"	54
	"Bucks Forrest"	187
36:1757:42 ...		
Henry Pratt	"Pleasant Park"	100
	"Pleasant Park Addition"	9½
Thomas Purnall	"Dudleys Chance"	200
Grundy Pemberton	pt. "Dawsons Neck"	142
	pt. "Partnership"	850
	pt. "Hawkins's Pharsalia"	600
	"Pembertons Resurvey"	969
	"Bostons Addition"	150
	"King Sale"	250
	"Change"	200
	pt. "Kelds Inheritance"	52
	"King Sale Addition"	100
Vincent Price	"Andrews & Prudences Satisfaction"	696
John Powell	"Longs Desire"	50
	"Powells Fancey"	94
John Pickering	pt. "Lows Arcadia" – for wife	66⅔
John Ponder	pt. "Smiths Delight"	81½

Margrett Pinder	pt. "Crumps Forrest" – for John Shoebrooks (minor)	135
William Pindar	pt. "Bishopton"	250
Edward Pendar	pt. "Ashton"	75
	pt. "Collins's Lott"	116
John Pendar	pt. "Wartons & Pendars Outrange"	67
Mary Perry (widow)	"Stafford"	33⅓
	"Marys Lott"	18
Martha Primrose	pt. "Shepherds Fortune" – for h/o George	200
Thomas Powell (Choptank)	"Powells Venture Addition"	281
36:1757:43 ...		
Morgan Ponder	pt. "Spread Eagle" – for wife	16⅔
John Pratt	"Wrights Park"	100
	"Vaughans Discovery" – for wife	100
	pt. "Suffolk" – from (N) Fisher	100
Henry Pollock	pt. "Coln Rectified"	284
Thomas Price s/o Thomas	pt. "Brandford"	23
	pt. "Conclution"	64
Robert Pratt	"Pratts Choice"	100
Prudence Primrose	pt. "Kent Lott"	52
George Powell	"Tryangle"	50
	"Longs Chance"	280
William Price (KI)	pt. "Coppidges Range" – for h/o John Carter	198
	"Craney Neck" – for h/o John Carter	160
	pt. "Ridge" – for John Carter (minor)	124⅔
	"Barns's Satisfaction" – for h/o John Carter	50
John Price	pt. "Toms Fancy Enlarg'd"	50
Thomas Powell (D.D. Creek)	pt. "Tilghmans Discovery"	1¼
Thomas Price (KI)	pt. "Cloverfield"	100
	pt. "Sillen" – for h/o Edward Brown	100
	pt. "Belcher" – for h/o Edward Brown	100
John Primrose	"Whittingtons Lott & Hemsleys Britland Resurveyed" – for h/o Joseph Whittington	178½
George Personale	"Smiths Range" – tenant under William Thomas	220
	"Smiths Range" – more, for himself	80
Thomas Priest	"Wiggmore"	61

36:1757:44 ...		
Thomas Price s/o Henry	"Good Happ"	126
	"Margretts Hill"	200
George Porter	"New Cunningham"	100
James Pratt	"Christophers Hazard" – from John Vanderford	100
James Phillips	"Phillips Chance"	44
Robert Pratt	"Pratts Hope"	100
William Purnall	⅓ "Purnalls Forrest"	166⅔
John Young Purnall	⅓ "Purnalls Forrest"	166⅔
Quakers	pt. "Land of Phrophecy" – for a Meeting House	3
Nathaniel Read	pt. "Toms Fancy Enlarg'd"	400
	"Wrights Square" – for wife	100
Joseph Roe	"Roes Addition" – 21 year lease from John Roe	70
	"Downes's Forrest" – 21 year lease from John Roe	60
Richard Ross	pt. "Cole Rain"	125
	pt. "Cole Rain" – for Andrew Jordan (minor)	183
36:1757:45 ...		
William Roe	pt. "Dudleys Desire"	100
John Roe	"Woodland"	100
Benjamin Roe	"Clouds Range"	100
John Roe s/o Thomas	pt. "Downes's Forrest"	240
Patrick Robertson	"Tulley Barden"	50
	"Tulley Bardens Inclosement"	150
	"Blear Crook"	200
Alexander Robertson	"Tulley Bardens Addition"	62
	"Peith"	66
Peter Ritch	pt. "Bridge Town"	11
	3 lots in Bridge Town – No. 4, No. 5, No. 6	3
Frances Ricketts (widow)	pt. "Hinesleys Plains"	59
James Read	pt. "Providence"	100
William Robinson	"Anns Lott"	100
	pt. "Elliotts Addition"	50
	pt. "Ridleys Chance"	76½
	pt. "Parkers Lott" & pt. "Boltons Delight" – for Daniel Bolton (minor)	140

Queen Anne's County - 1757

Benjamin Roberts	pt. "Lows Desire"	178
	pt. "Sawyers Range"	200
	pt. "Sheperds Redoubt"	100
	"Roberts Meadows"	50
	"Dixons Gift" – for h/o James Roberts	100
Francis Rochester	"Watery Plains"	150
	pt. "Tulleys Lott"	200
	"Collins's Gift"	175
	pt. "Out Range"	80
	pt. "Ripley"	300
John Rochester	"Winchester"	200
	"John & Rachells Choice"	100
36:1757:46 ...		
Elizabeth Rochester (widow)	"Lowders Hazard"	77
	"Philadelphia"	50
James Raley	pt. "Wilsons Begining" & pt. "Raleys Begining"	108
William Ridger	"Small Hopes"	50
	"Ridgers Lott" [!]	0
	"Ridgaways Chance"	50
	"Ridgaways Range"	93
	"Ridgers Lott Enlarg'd"	408
Benjamin Richardson	pt. "Cloverfields"	335
	"Pascos Adventure"	150
	"Wading Place"	300
	"Ashberrys Addition"	35
	pt. "Cloverfields" – more	335
Thomas Butler	pt. "Smiths Neglect" – for h/o John Rooth	150
David Ragister	pt. "Conquest"	138
	"Bradburns Delight" a/s "Baleys Delight"	100
	pt. "Boagley"	60
Christopher Rooth/Ruth (cnp)	pt. "Chesnut Meadows"	100
	pt. "Conclusion"	86
	pt. "Hawkins's Farme Resurveyed" – for h/o Peter Countice	120
	pt. "Salisberry Plains" – for John Walker (minor)	66⅔
	pt. "Baynards Pasture"	37

Queen Anne's County - 1757

	"Rooths Part of Smiths Branch"	17
	pt. "Rawwlins Hazard"	78
Thomas Robinson	"Wrights Chance" a/s "Choice"	100
Samuel Roe	pt. "Oaken Thorpe"	164
	"Tulleys Addition"	300
	"Nields Begining"	30
	"Roes Lane"	22
	pt. "Sarahs Fancy"	50
William Read	"New Nothingham Rectified" – for wife	169
James Roe	"Begining"	85
	"Sarahs Fancy"	540
William Ridgaway	"Plain Dealing" – for h/o William Farell	100
	"Swifts Meadows"	100
36:1757:47 ...		
John Roe s/o Edward	pt. "Narborough"	250
	"Hinsleys Choice"	100
	pt. "Oaken Thorpe"	40
	pt. "Sarahs Fancey"	111
James Adcock	"Long Delay" – for his wife (N) d/o Benjamin Ridgaway	150
John Roberts (minor) s/o William	"Roberts Desire"	150
Edward Rooke	"Revivall"	1118
Gilbert Read	pt. "Spread Eagle"	1
Theophelus Randolph (KE)	"Baken Neck" a/s "Barren Neck"	227
	"Jones's" a/s "Jones Lott"	50
James Roberts	pt. "Sandy Hurst"	100
	pt. "Rambles" – from James Findley	123
William Robinson	pt. "Tottingham" – for his wife (N) d/o Samuel Salisberry	100
John Russam	"Climers Chance" – for h/o Thomas Climer	59
Thomas Ringgold (KI)	"Coxes Neck"	1000
William Robinson (Tuckahoe)	"Todcaster"	500
William Roberts	"Roberts Chance"	150
Thomas Robinson, Jr.	pt. "Lows Arcadia" – for wife	100

Queen Anne's County - 1757

John Raley	pt. "Bishops Outlett" & pt. "Larrington" – from Thomas Baley s/o Jacob	104½
	⅓ "Good Increase" – for his wife	66⅔
	⅓ "Good Increase" – from (N) Killingsworth	66⅔
William Read s/o James	"Reads Adventure"	50
36:1757:48 ...		
James Rosberry	pt. "Brother Hood" – in right of his wife	107
John Seegar	"Johnsons Adventure"	100
	"Newnams Portion"	241½
	pt. "Wood House Addition"	11
	"McCleans Addition"	150
	"Forkalet"	62
	pt. "Seegars Hazard"	742
James Sullivant	pt. "Saulsberry"	100
Patrick Sexton	"Liberty"	100
John Seth	pt. "Mount Mill"	79¼
	pt. "Addition"	10
	pt. "Bennetts Outlett"	50
John Sullivant	pt. "Ponderfield"	109
	pt. "Dungarnon"	33¾
	"Sullivants Chance"	66
	"Dungarnon"	116¼
Thomas Swan	pt. "Jumps Chance"	100
	pt. "Jumps Choice"	2½
Susanna Stewart	pt. "Kearys Discovery" – for h/o Thomas	140
	pt. "Salvesters Forrest" – for h/o Thomas	105
36:1757:49 ...		
Emanuel Swift	"Swifts Forrest Addition"	50
James Slaughter	"Fern Ridge"	50
	pt. "Partnership" a/s "Ratcliff"	50
	"Fern Ridge Addition"	100
	"Golden Road Ridge"	50
John Swift	"Swifts Forrest"	50
	"Beaver Harbour"	50
	"Swifts Endeavour"	150
Moses Swift	"Indian Tract"	50

James Salvester	"Baregarden"	123
	"Carmathan"	100
William Shepherd	pt. "Hinsleys Plains"	109
Solomon Sennett	pt. "Hawkins's Pharsalia"	150
Robert Smith	pt. "Toms Fancey Enlarg'd"	100
Joseph Scrivner	pt. "Hackers Meadows" – of original	14
	"Joseph Part of Hackers Meadows Enlarg'd"	325
Daniel Smith (planter)	pt. "Jones's Fancey"	75
Benjamin Smith	pt. "Jones's Fancey"	75
	"Marys Chance"	30
	"Tears Desire"	35
John Spry	pt. "Friendship" – surveyed for (N) Spry	70
Thomas Spry	pt. "Friendship" – surveyed for (N) Tilghman	55
	pt. "Friendship" – another	15
Solomon Seaney	pt. "Barton"	110
	"Brandfords Addition"	100
	pt. "Clouds Adventure"	187½
	pt. "Sewals Fork" – for his wife (N) w/o John Nevell	250
	pt. "Tilghmans Discovery" – for his wife (N) w/o John Nevell	78¾
	pt. "Poplar Hill" – for his wife (N) w/o John Nevell	150
36:1757:50 ...		
Thomas Seward	"Outrange"	174
Thomas Sands	"Sands Outlett"	100
	"Dubbin Ridge"	40
	"Timber Ridge"	70
	pt. "Swifts Outlett"	22
	"Long Swamp"	63
	"Landcaster"	119
	pt. "Northumberland"	48
Giddeon Swift (cnp)	"Chance"	66
	pt. "Swifts Outlett"	70
	"Constantinople"	100
	pt. "James's Choice"	50
	"Mulberry Tract"	100

	"Crumps Advice" – for his daughters Elizabeth & Mary	100
Rebekah Sutton (widow)	pt. "Sandy Hurst"	100
Christopher Spry	"Thief Keep Out"	100
	"Friendship" – surveyed for (N) Tilghman	52
	pt. "Friendship" – another	29
	"Sprys Chance"	21
	"Thief Keep Out Addition"	150
	"Buck Range" – for his son Humphrey	50
Thomas Stanton	pt. "Security" tbc Caleb Sparks	0
Rebekah Sudlar	"Jones Hole Resurveyed" – for h/o James Sudlar	276
	"Hint on Sudlar" – for h/o James Sudlar	173
Dr. John Smith	"Smiths Neck"	128
	pt. "Spread Eagle"	346
	pt. "Martins Neck"	39
	pt. "Spread Eagle" – more for "Mill Land"	5
	"Smith Field"	93¾
Anne Sudlar (widow)	"Sledmore"	800
	pt. "Devonishes Chance"	15
	"Sudlars Purchase"	80
	"Sudlars Fortune"	186
	"Sudlars Island"	64
	pt. "Shepherds Forrest"	200
	"Broad Creek" – for Anne Wells d/o & h/o John Wells	630
	½ "Cloaks Chance"	50
	"Tilberry"	50
	"Tilberrys Addition"	50
	"Sudlars Chance"	68
Robert Small	"Ship Point"	100
36:1757:51 ...		
William Scott	pt. "Sawyers Range"	40
	"Scotts Outrange"	304
Nathaniel Smith (cnp)	"Smiths Desire"	50
	"Smiths Outlett"	100
	"Long Ridge"	124

Queen Anne's County - 1757

	"Indian Oldfield"		40
Thomas Scotton	"Scottons Forrest"		50
	"Scottons Desire"		100
Richard Swift	"Williams Pasture"		54
John Stent	pt. "Cole Rain"		103
Richard Sparks – grandson of Richard Collins	1 lot in Kings Town		1
Samuel Swift	"Fosters Folley"		50
William Smith	pt. "Saulsberry Plains"		200
Caleb Sparks	"Forrest of Sherwood"		200
	"Security"		40
Francis Spry	"Sprys Adventure"		75
	pt. "Sprys Adventure" – for your brother Joseph		75
William Spry	pt. "Friendship" – surveyed for (N) Spry		149
John Scott	pt. "Stratton"		532½
Solomon Scott	pt. "Stratton"		311
Aaron Saunders	⅓ "Purnalls Forrest"		166⅔
	"Jumps Lane" – for h/o William Purnall		100
36:1757:52 ...			
Lemond Swift	"Sole Hitt" – for h/o Fairclo Wright		200
James Salvester, Jr.	"Baregarden Addition"		125
	pt. "Baregarden"		80
Nathaniel Satterfield	"Satterfields Venture"		55
Francis Steavens	"Lanark"		86
	"Hunting Tower" – for his son Robertson		100
Joseph Slocham	pt. "Bishops Fields" – for wife		50
Charles Seth	pt. "Mount Mill"		158½
	pt. "Addition"		20
	pt. "Bennetts Outlett"		10
	pt. "Middle Plantation" – from Dennis Carey		40
Benjamin Salvester	"Bucks Range"		113
	"Salvesters Hazard"		189
Richard Scotton	"Hazel Ridge"		65
Richard Small	"Smalls Industry"		177
Maurice Sliney	pt. "Peters Gift"		85
	"Timber Range"		250

John Smith	"Sandy Hill"	100
Thomas Seward, Jr.	"Hawkins's Range"	90
George Smith	pt. "Smiths Forrest" – for Thomas Chaires (minor) s/o Joseph Chaires	61
	pt. "Confution" – for Thomas Chaires (minor) s/o Joseph Chaires	159
Catherine Scotton	"Scottons Outlett"	50
Priscella Saunders	pt. "Middle Plantation"	33⅓
36:1757:53 ...		
Absolem Swift	"Content"	50
Robert Scrivner	"Neglect"	190
James Smith (Wye)	pt. "Hemsleys Britland Rectified"	57
Josias Sallaway	½ "Cloaks Chance"	50
David Salvester	pt. "Grubby Neck"	75
James Sudlar	"Sudlars Chance"	58½
William Salvester	pt. "Grubby Neck"	75
John Sweat, Jr.	pt. "Park" – for h/o Benjamin Griffith	220
Daniel Smith (joyner)	"Mary Portion"	100
	"Mantons Addition"	5
h/o Nathaniel Scott	pt. "Toms Fancey Enlarg'd"	243
Nathaniel Scott, Jr.	pt. "Stratton"	54½
Christopher Spry (TA)	"Doddington"	200
Emory Sudlar	"Little Neck"	55
Ephraim Storey	pt. "Todley"	193
William Saterfield	pt. "Winfield"	102½
36:1757:54 ...		
Col. Richard Tilghman (cnp)	"Tilghmans Hermitage"	1843
	pt. "Bristol Marsh"	50
	pt. "Forlone Hope"	1050
	pt. "Carpenters Outlett"	9
	pt. "Boagley"	75
	pt. "Park"	500
	"Wyatts Range"	50
	pt. "Confution"	9
	pt. "Adventure" & pt. "Confution" – from (N) Alley	110
	pt. "Grays Inn"	75

Queen Anne's County - 1757

	"Cheshire"	200
	pt. "Shrewsberry"	150
	"Sintra"	187
	"Tilghmans Recovery"	1050
	"Plains"	112
Col. Edward Tilghman	pt. "Malton"	239
	1 lot in Ogle Town	1
	pt. "Porters Lodge"	200
	"Tilghmans Landing"	68
	"Resurvey of Forlone Hope Rectified"	2890
	"Tilghmans Resurvey of Long Neck"	539
	pt. "Union"	720
	"Scottons Folley"	50
	pt. "Long Neck Addition"	2½
	pt. "Coursey Upon Wye"	321½
	"Pleasant Banks on Wye"	19
	pt. "Sparks's Choice"	100
	pt. "Tulleys Delight"	200
	"Just Design"	17½
	pt. "Loyds Meadows & Loyds Meadows Addition"	655
	"Beaver Dams"	50
	"Hollow Flatt"	50
	⅓ "Reviving Spring"	166⅔
	pt. "Discovery"	216
	"Tulleys Delight" – more	100
Maj. William Tilghman	"Pauls Forrest"	200
	pt. "Bristol Marsh"	148
	pt. "Tilghmans Discovery"	490
	"Salisberry"	500
	"Delmore End"	350
	1 lot in Ogle Town	1
	"Meadows"	28
	"Smiths Mistake"	355
	"Andeavour"	500
Mr. James Tilghman (cnp)	pt. "Adventure"	1030
	"Addition"	40

Queen Anne's County - 1757

	"Tilghmans Freshes"	600
	pt. "Jerusalem"	200
	"Coles Bank Enlarg'd"	703
	"Killkenny"	200
	pt. "Jerusalem" – from (N) Dixon	200
Nathaniel Tucker	pt. "Adventure"	61
	"Jones's Addition"	200
	"Batchelors Plains"	100
36:1757:55 ...		
Mr. Mathew Tilghman	"Tilghmans Forrest"	1400
	"Rings End"	100
	"Notlars Enjoyment"	500
	1 lot in Ogle Town	1
	pt. "Poplar Plains"	191
	pt. "Glochester"	195
	½ "Timber Fork"	250
	½ "Negligence"	22
	"Tilghmans Chance"	990
	"Ovall"	420
	pt. "Toms Fancey Enlarg'd"	162
	pt. "Poplar Plains"	191
	pt. "Delmore End"	150
Trustram Thomas 3rd	"Trustrams Thomas Part of Trustram"	127
Baynard Tillotson	pt. "Lords Gift on Resurvey"	270
	"Todley"	170
	"Exchange"	100
	"Lantley" – for his wife Margaret	325
John Tillotson	"Shepherds Folds on Resurvey"	140
	pt. "Todley"	150
	pt. "Lows Arcadia"	100
	"Inkersell"	134
	"Chittams Landing"	90
	"Tillotsons Delight"	105½
	pt. "Oaken Thorpe"	226
	pt. "Sarahs Fancey"	20
	"Knotts's Chance" – from James Knotts	302

Queen Anne's County - 1757

h/o John Timms	"Society Hill Addition" – taken off, heir lives in PA	0
Stephen Thomas	pt. "Hawkins's Pharsalia"	80
	pt. "Adcocks Pharsalia"	33⅓
Phillemon Thomas	pt. "Hawkins's Pharsalia"	120
	pt. "Lees Chance"	33
	pt. "Acocks Pharsalia"	66⅓
Trustram Thomas (Long Neck)	"Grubby Neck"	50
	"Trustrams Ridge"	50
	"Trustrams Adventure"	150
Thomas Tanner	"Chance"	50
	"Tanners Adventure"	39
	"Providence"	100
	"Ashford" – for h/o James Hudson	100
36:1757:56 ...		
Alexander Tolson	pt. "Freshford"	148
	pt. "Partnership"	206½
Amia Tolson	pt. "Phillpotts Neck" – for h/o Alexander Tolson	233⅓
James Tute	pt. "Youngs Chance"	270
	pt. "Lambert Fields"	132
Richard Tickell	1 lot in Kings Town	1
Mary Thomas	"Forrest of Plains" – for h/o Christopher	150
Benjamin Tolson	pt. "Coppidges Range"	211
	"Slaughterton" – for wife; tbc Jos. Elliott	0
Samuel Thompson	"Kirbeys Recovery"	52
	"Wilmores Range"	1000
Mary Trickey	"Woodberry" – for h/o Thomas Trickey	100
Isaac Thorpe	"Cole Rain"	83
John Tickell	1 lot in Kings Town – No. 7	1
	1 lot in Kings Town – from (N) Sarell & wife	1
Christopher Thomas	"Trustram Thomas Part of Trustram"	100
w/o Dowdall Thompson (cnp)	pt. "Price Hill"	180
	pt. "Shepherds Discovery"	200
	"Parsons Marsh Addition"	10
	"Good Luck"	100
	"Sparks's Choice"	250
	pt. "Mount Pleasant"	102½

	pt. "Enjoyment"	50
	"Barefield" a/s "Bargolt"	200
	"Parsons Marsh"	34
	pt. "Shepherds Discovery" & pt. "Hinfield"	218
	"Courseys Town Resurveyed"	394
	"Mount Pleasant" a/s "Mount Pleasure"	52½
	"Parsons Chance"	115
	pt. "Mount Pleasure"	80
	pt. "Enjoyment"	79
	"Whartons Marsh" – for Arthur Holt	27
	"High Gate Lane" – for Arthur Holt	100
	"Holt" – for Arthur Holt	506
	"Holts Castle Hill Resurveyed" – for Arthur Holt	304½
36:1757:57 ...		
Joseph Tolson	"Tolsons Desire"	193
	pt. "Phillpotts Neck"	116⅔
	½ "Morgans Inclosure" – for h/o Andrew Tolson	218½
Edmond Thomas	pt. "Trustram"	450
Joseph Thomas	"Trustram Thomas Part of Trustram"	200
John Taylor	pt. "Neglect"	51
	pt. "Batchelors Hope"	90
Tildeon Thomas	"Addition"	227
Phillemon Tanner	⅓ "Woodland Neck"	16⅔
	⅓ "Oldsons Relief"	33⅓
Richard Taylor	"Alberts Delight" – for h/o William Mounsier	200
John & James Tolson	"Partnership"	380
Isaac Turner	"Swann Brook"	770
Henry Thompson	"Baynards Large Range Addition" – for h/o John Baynard	505
	"Vineyard Addition" – for h/o John Baynard	28½
	"Baynards Chance"	54
George Teate	"Jacksons Choice"	100
	"Teats Arcadia"	243
Thomas Taylor	½ "Crumps Forrest" – from (N) Milton & wife	150
Joseph Tarbutton	"Lowcoust Ridge"	100

James Tolson	pt. "Oak Ridge" – for h/o William Starke	175
	pt. "Hickory Ridge" – for h/o William Starke	150
	pt. "Codshead Manor" – for h/o William Starke	116
36:1757:58 ...		
Visitors of Queen Ann's County School	"Forlone Hope"	100
Vestry of St. Pauls Parish	"Docters Folley"	½
Richard Vanderford	pt. "Outrange" – in right of his wife Hannah d/o Robert Green	40
John Vanderford	pt. "Wrenches Farme"	200
	pt. "Wrenches Farme" – more, from Jo. Chaires	200
Joshua Vansant (KE)	"Difficulty"	72
John Vanderford s/o Rebekah	pt. "Fox Hill"	28⅓
	pt. "Dispute" a/s "Brotherhood"	15⅔
Vestry of Christ Church Parish	pt. "Little Ease" – glebe land	150
36:1757:59 ...		
h/o or devisees of John Walters	pt. "Smeath"	250
	"Barnstable Hill Resurveyed"	210
	"Westminster"	297
	pt. "Upper Heathworth"	143
John Welch	pt. "Partnership"	200
	pt. "Dillerage"	83
	pt. "Reason"	20
William Wheeler	"Wheelers Chance"	23½
Henry Williams	"Salisberry Plains"	100
	"Williams Fortune"	150
MM Nathan S. T. Wright & Thomas Wright	pt. "Wrights Reserve"	250
	pt. "Hemsleys Britland Rectified"	50
James Williams	pt. "Courseys Addition"	100
	pt. "Kendall"	100
Hannah Wilson (widow)	"Wilsons Chance"	100
	"Wilsons Chance Addition"	200
Jacob Wotters	"New Buckley"	100
	"Cow Range"	38
John Wheatley	"Wheatleys" a/s "Daniels Fields"	140
William Wheatley	"Wheatleys Park"	100

William Whetby	"Whetby's Forrest"	50
Nathaniel Wright	"Brotherhood"	50
	"Wrights Chance"	300
Thomas Wheeler	"Killmarden"	100
	"Killmarden Addition"	15
Daniel Wilcox	pt. "Mount Hope"	250
	"Mount Hope Addition"	100
Elizabeth Wooters	"Richard & Marys Forrest"	80
36:1757:60 ...		
John Woodall (KE) s/o John	pt. "Crumpton" – taken off; tbc Joshua Walliston	10
Mathew Wicks	"Wolverhampton"	120
William Whorton	"Whartons Adventure"	570
	pt. "Sawyers Range Addition"	17
	"Williams Begining"	6½
Benjamin Whittington	pt. "Whittingtons Lott & Hemsleys Britland Resurveyed"	178½
	pt. "Poplar Hill"	34
	"Ratcliffs Part of Loyds Freshes"	171
Penelope Wright	"Parsons Point"	100
Robert Walters	"Dundee"	368
	"Jamacia"	150
	"Walters Addition to Kerbys Prevention"	33
	pt. "Hope"	50
William White	"Workmans Hazard"	150
	"Sparks's Point"	50
Jonathan Wooters	"Oak Ridge"	20
	"Oak Ridge Addition"	78
John Wilson	"Wilsons Adventure" – for his wife	262
Nathan Wright s/o Edward	"Tulleys Reserve"	300
	"Reserve Addition"	50
	"Marys Portion"	554
	pt. "Content"	400
Peter Wrench	"Wrenches Chance"	35
	"Wrenches Farme"	200
h/o Humphery Wells, Jr.	<n/g>	<n/g>
36:1757:61 ...		

Samuel Walters	"Walters Park"	150
William Wrench	pt. "Guilford"	26
	"Wrenches Lott"	100
	"Hawkins's Farme Resurveyed"	326
Henry Wrench	pt. "Wrenches Lott"	354
	"Wrenches Reserve"	39
Thomas Wilson	"Sewals Range"	1120
	"Plain Dealing"	727
	"Jacksons Boggs"	46
	pt. "Bennetts Outlett"	495
Josias Wharton	"Fords Chance"	100
Zorababell Wells	"Teats Folley"	50
	"Buck Island"	100
John Whetby	"Batchelors Chance"	69
	"Bite the Biter"	78½
	"Clarks Lott"	112
widow Woodall	pt. "James Choice" – for h/o Cornelious Commyges	150
	pt. "Crumps Chance" – for h/o Cornelious Commyges	50
	pt. "Hope" – for h/o Cornelious Commyges	228⅔
Elizabeth Wells	pt. "Bath"	255
James Walters	"Walters Rambles"	150
George Wells	"Red Lyon Point"	50
	pt. "Baths Addition"	150
John Wells s/o Humphery	pt. "Price Land"	199½
Humphery Wells s/o Humphery	"Price Land Addition"	50
	"Crumps Fancey"	50
	"Landing"	30
	"Fanceys Addition"	150
	pt. "Bath"	145
Benjamin Wells s/o Humphery	"Low Lands"	45
	"Calebs Lott"	80
36:1757:62 ...		
Joseph Whetby	"Buck Range"	100
William Walls (KE)	pt. "Bath"	100
	pt. "Baths Addition"	150

Richard Warner	pt. "Sawyers Range Addition"	66
	"Alberts Desire" a/s "Delight"	100
	"Warners Addition"	9¾
John Watson	pt. "Baleys Delight" – for his wife Esther	100
Nathaniel Wright, Jr.	pt. "Salisberry"	100
	½ "Skinners Expectation"	240
w/o Ambrose Wright	pt. "Wrights Chance"	100
	pt. "Hawkins's Farme Resurveyed"	41
	pt. "Guilford"	12
Nathan Samuel Turbut Wright	"New Hynson Town"	360
	pt. "Grays Inn"	75
	pt. "Larrington"	100
	2 lots in Kings Town – No. 2, No. 27	2
	1 lot in Kings Town – more	1
	pt. "Wrights Square"	140
Nathaniel Wright s/o Edward	"Hazard"	100
	½ "Content"	100
	"Content Addition"	200
	"Content Outlett"	50
Isaac Winchester	½ "Morgans Inclosure" – for h/o Alexander Tolson	218½
	"Purlivant" – for h/o Alexander Tolson	180
	"Isaac's Addition"	80
James Walters (KI)	pt. "Conners Neck" – for his wife (N) d/o Phill. Conner	120
Thomas Wright	"New Reading"	300
	pt. "Gray's Inn"	50
	pt. "Neglect"	45
	"Warplesdon"	300
	pt. "Warplesdon Addition" & pt. "Solomons Friendship"	230
	pt. "Lows Arcadia"	350
Edward Wright s/o Edward	pt. "Partnership"	250
	"Colonells Quarters"	100
36:1757:63 ...		
Jonathan Roberts	pt. "Crawford" – in right of his wife Elizabeth White for h/o Robert Wilson	216
	pt. "Bridge" – for his wife	62⅓

Queen Anne's County - 1757

h/o Ambrose Wright – one of which is a minor under the guardianship of John Tillotson	pt. "Hawkins's Farme Resurveyed"	5
	pt. "Wrights Chance"	408
	"Gilford"	40
Rebeccah Williams	"Millford" – for h/o Abraham Williams	123
Mary Webb	pt. "Lyford" – for h/o James Webb	643
Thomas Wilkinson s/o Henry	"Watsons Chance"	50
Solomon Wright	"Guilford"	300
	"Guilford Addition"	150
	"Hogg Harbour"	100
	pt. "Narborough"	250
Steaphen Wicks	"Woolverhampton"	80
	pt. "Mount Pleasure" & pt. "Lillingstons Enjoyment"	1½
Joshua Walliston	pt. "Condon"	10
	pt. "Crumpton"	10
George Webb	"Watsons Lott"	50
	"Webbs Plains"	50
John Wilson (KI)	pt. "Eastern Island"	50
	"Wilsons Adventure"	54
	"Erricksons Island"	20
Thomas Walker	"Toms Adventure"	56
	"Toms Adventure Addition"	50
Nathan Wright	"White Marsh on Resurvey"	376
	"White Marsh Addition"	250
	pt. "Smiths Reserve"	2½
	"Cork House"	590
	"Joans's Park"	340
36:1757:64 ...		
John Wright	"Narborough"	250
	"Narborough Addition"	100
	"Littleworth"	50
w/o William Wallace	"Boothbys Fortune"	500
Jacob Walters	"Kerbys Prevention"	50
Anne Wells	"France Rectified"	62
Alexander Walters	"Kirbys Hardship" – for h/o Walter Kirby	199

Edward Wright	pt. "Batchelors Hope" – for John Brown (minor) s/o John	40
	pt. "Neglect" – for John Brown (minor) s/o John	32⅔
Solomon Yeowell	"Purchas"	86
Steaphen Yoe	"Brandford"	100
John Young s/o William	pt. "Stratton"	50
Aaron Yoe	pt. "Courseys Addition"	50
36:1757:65 ...		
Dr. James Anderson (KE)	pt. "Providence" – in right of his wife	200
	"Ashford" – in right of his wife	200
	pt. "Rambles" – in right of his wife	200
	"Shepherds Fields" a/s "Forrest" – in right of his wife	200
James Aud (DO)	1 lot in Kings Town – No. 19	1
William Anderson (London)	"Darland Resurveyed"	1750
	"Lloyds Town"	1000
John Abbington (CV)	"Abbington" tbc William & Henry Pratt	500
Thomas Adcock (TA)	"Wyats Folley"	50
Rizdon Bozman (TA)	pt. "Hillary"	100
	pt. "Millford"	200
	"Point Landing"	5¼
	"Hillary Addition"	34¾
James Bartlett (TA)	"Partnership"	575
Benjamin Blackeston (KE)	"Benjamins Park"	80
	"Upper Landing"	200
Daniel Bird (Bidford)	1 lot in Kings Town – No. 8	1
James Benson (TA)	pt. "Spread Eagle" – for wife	100
	"Collins's Own" – for wife	92
James Baxter (CE)	"Beaver Neck Resurveyed" – for h/o John Role	320
h/o William Brent (VA)	"Kent Fort Manor"	1000
John Buck, Esq.	"Poplar Hill"	100
	2 lots in Ogle Town	2
36:1757:66 ...		
Samuel Booman (TA)	⅓ "Dickersons Plains" – in right of his wife	286⅔
Edward Clark (TA)	"Clarks Delight" – for h/o Caleb Clark	76
	"Clarks Struggle" – for h/o Caleb Clark	65

Charles Carroll (Annapolis)	"Thompsons Manor" a/s "Poplar Island"	1000
James Claypole (KE)	pt. "Lambeth" – taken off	178½
	pt. "Wells Chance" – for wife	100
	pt. "Lambeth" – more, taken off	62½
Joanna Carpenter (widow, Duck Creek)	⅓ "Porters Lodge"	100
Amia Carey	pt. "Salvesters Addition"	65
Elinor Carey	pt. "Salvesters Addition"	112
Peter Cummerford	"Mount Pleasant" – for h/o (N) Sharp	500
Benjamin Cleaves (KE)	"Cleaves's Rambles" – for his son Nathaniel	110
Samuel Dickenson (KEDE)	"Yough Hall"	175
	"Gersuches Tryangle"	63
	"Poplar Ridge"	150
	"Poplar Ridge Addition"	200
Phillip Davis, John Davis, & David Davis	"Partnership"	300
36:1757:67 ...		
Susanah Duglas (CE)	"Macklins Fancey"	500
William Dickenson (TA)	pt. "Scarborough"	200
George & Empy Dawson	"Padan Aaran"	275
Polard Edmondson (TA)	⅓ "Dickersons Plains" – in right of his wife	286⅔
Col. William Fitzhugh (CV)	"Morgans Neck" – for h/o John Rousbey	400
	"Bluff Point" – for h/o John Rousbey	496
Thomas Fleming (Annapolis)	pt. "Conners Neck" – for h/o John Granger	100
Nicholas Goldsbrough (TA)	pt. "Old Town"	740
William Goldsbrough (TA)	"Walnut Ridge" – for devisees of Mr. George Robins	600
	"Perle" – for devisees of Mr. George Robins	1000
Jeremiah Grassingham (TA)	pt. "Davis's Range"	15
36:1757:68 ...		
Robert Goldsbrough (TA)	pt. "Controversie"	500
	"Jaspers Lott"	570
	pt. "Sandish Woods" – for wife	665
Peter Garoon (TA)	pt. "Alcocks Pharsalia" – for wife (N) w/o William Vickers	100
Edward Harden (TA)	pt. "Hemsleys Arcadia"	231
Samuel Hide (London)	"Smiths Forrest"	2000

Patrick Hamilton	pt. "Point Love" – for his wife (N) d/o Jos. Wicks	400
Alexander Kelly (KE)	pt. "Malton" – for his wife (N) d/o Maurice McCarter	150
36:1757:69 ...		
William Lambden (TA)	pt. "Reviving Spring"	333⅓
Thomas Lane (TA)	pt. "Smiths Ridge" – for wife	300
	"Collins's Range" – for wife	300
John Leeds (TA)	pt. "Scarborough"	200
Edward Lloyd, Esq. (TA)	"Ninevah"	600
	"Ninevahs Addition"	200
	pt. "Lloyd's Freshes"	810
	"Mill Range"	136
	"Chesnot Neck"	300
	"Hoggs Hole"	50
	"Broad Neck"	40
	"Wilton"	650
	"Addition to Wilton"	600
	"Hemsleys Resurvey Rectified on Resurvey"	185
	pt. "Brandford"	186
	pt. "St. Martins"	82
	"Scotts Chance" – taken off	100
	pt. "Oaken Thorpe"	56
	"Nutwells Chance Resurveyed"	294
	pt. "Hemsleys Britland Rectified"	223
	"Courseys Range"	600
	pt. "Costins Chance" – taken off	32
	"Coopers Hill"	100
	"Woolverton"	250
	"Narborough"	250
	½ "Reward" – for John Coursey	200
	"Macklins Addition" – for John Coursey	18
James Loyd Chamberlin (TA)	pt. "Willinle" – from Madam Dulaney	682
36:1757:70 ...		
Nicholas Massey (KE)	"Pascolett"	18
George Meligan (CE)	"Edin Kelly"	600

Francis Neale (TA)	"Shadwell" – for his son Francis	100
	pt. "Shadwells Addition" – for h/o Robert Jones	100
Edward Neale (TA)	pt. "Shadwells Addition"	100
Deborah Nichols (widow, TA)	"Partnership" – for devisees of Jeremiah Nichols	250
Edward Oldham (TA)	"Exchange"	470
	"Exchange" – another	60
	pt. "Providence"	256
36:1757:71 ...		
Aaron Parrot (TA)	pt. "Cold Spring"	162
	"Westford"	247
John & James Porter (TA)	"Halls Harbour" – in right of their wives (N) d/o Capt. Henry Rippen	250
	pt. "Poplar Hill" – in right of their wives (N) d/o Capt. Henry Rippen	50
Daniel Powell (TA)	pt. "Scarborough" – for wife	200
James Ringgold (KE)	"Courseys Point" or "Smiths Mistake"	614
	pt. "Bishops Outlett"	400
	pt. "Bishops Addition" & pt. "Bishops Outlett"	100
	pt. "Smiths Mistake" – from William Tilghman	45
Thomas Rease (PA)	"Andeavour Meadows"	175
36:1757:72 ...		
John Robertson (SO)	"Athel"	500
h/o George Robotham	"Roebothams Park"	500
Elizabeth Robass (TA)	"Providence"	150
Tobias Stansberry (BA)	"Robinsons Farme" – for his wife	200
Jarves Spencer (KE)	pt. "Conaway" – for h/o (N) Williams	111
h/o Charles Steavens (TA)	pt. "Willinew"	212
Esther Turner (widow, TA)	"Turners Lane"	100
Abner Turner	"Abners Park"	130
	"Turners Plains Addition"	58
36:1757:73 ...		
William Webb (TA)	"Redford"	150
h/o Lambert Wilmore (KE)	1 lot in Kings Town	1
Park Webb	"Shadwells Addition" – for h/o Samuel Neale	50
William Wilson & wife (TA)	pt. "Bargarden"	150

John Webb	"Webbs Chance"	150
	"Salvesters Addition"	40
Phillip Walker	⅓ "Dickersons Plains"	286⅔
	Certification	
36:1757:<unnumbered>	**Second Certification**	
36:1757:<unnumbered>	**Recapitulation**	
36:1757:<2 unnumbered>	<blank>	
36:1757:<unnumbered>	…	
	"Slaughterton" tbc: • Phil. Coppidge – 200 a. • Joseph Elliott – 200 a. • Henry Elliott – 100 a.	

Index of Surnames & Tract Names

Abbington	153, 201, 268, 371
Andrew	201, 268
John	94, 153, 371
Abbington Square	71
Abbingtons Square	268
Abbot	
John	63
Abbotts Desire	199, 255, 316
Abbot's Ash	63
Abington	31
Andrew	31, 67
John	31
Abingtons Square	31
Abners Outlet	184, 208, 271, 324
Abners Park	34, 206, 262, 374
Abner's Park	74
Abrahams	
(N)	80
Isaac	80
Abrams	
Isaac	23
Acocks Pharsalia	364
Adams	
Thomas	38, 85
Adcock	
(N)	356
James	356
Thomas	201, 258, 318, 371
Adcocks Pharsalia	364
Addition	3, 4, 7, 10, 25, 27, 31, 33, 37, 39, 41, 47, 67, 69, 74, 79, 80, 82, 84, 86, 88, 105, 116, 124, 138-140, 143, 144, 155, 157, 158, 168, 181, 182, 187, 191, 196, 204, 208, 210, 221, 229, 236, 238, 242, 243, 247, 252, 268, 269, 271, 273, 284, 291, 298, 299, 303, 304, 307, 312, 324, 326, 337, 343, 350, 352, 357, 360, 362, 365
Addition to Freith	59
Addition to Frieth	70, 263
Addition to Fruth	40
Addition to Wilton	204, 261, 320, 373
Addy House	108, 109, 167, 220, 283
Addyhouse	12
Adkinson	
John	119
Adventure	2, 6, 9, 13, 15, 16, 20, 26, 30, 31, 35, 43, 60, 61, 63, 67, 72, 76, 84, 93, 107, 111-113, 125, 126, 131, 135, 159, 160, 172, 178, 181, 192, 193, 212, 213, 226, 233, 236, 248, 249, 263, 264, 266, 275, 276, 295, 297, 308-310, 328, 329, 341, 348, 350, 361-363
Adventure & Confusion	248
Adventure Addition	8, 90, 104, 111, 193, 249, 310
Adventure Point	109
Adventure Resurveyed	107, 160, 176, 221, 231, 283, 292, 336, 345
Ailer	
Henry	78, 79
Ailward	
William	32, 70, 266
Ailward Town	70, 266
Ailwards Town	32
Aires	
George	45, 59
Alberts Delight	21, 132, 135, 196, 252, 312, 365
Alberts Desire	199, 255, 316, 369
Alcock	
Thomas	28
Alcocks Pharsalia	46, 52, 194, 202, 203, 250, 258, 260, 311, 318, 329, 372
Alcock's Pharsalia	311
Alder Branch	15, 114, 158, 211, 327
Aliquare	
Jacob	134
All	
James	154, 207, 270
William	154, 207, 270

Alla		James	121, 156, 209
John	16	William	147
Allaband		Andrew & Prudence Satisfied on	
Thomas	35	Resurvey	57
Allabands Hazard	114	Andrew & Prudences Satisfaction	89, 183, 238, 300
Allcocks Pharsalia	74, 149		
Allen		Andrew & Prudence's Satisfaction	118
John	38	Andrews	
Thomas	38, 78, 266	(N)	325
William	84	James	325
Allens Deceipt	1	John	43, 50, 81, 94, 129, 201
Allens Deceit	136, 137, 258	Stephen	94, 133, 207, 318, 323
Allens Neck	38, 162, 215, 263, 278, 331		
		Stephens	36, 258
Allens Neck Outlett	162, 215, 278, 331	Andrews & Prudences Satisfaction	352
Allen's Deceit	147	Angle	341
Allen's Neck	78, 84, 266	Annes Portion	172
Alley		Anne's Portion	124
(N)	192, 248, 308, 361	Anns Lott	55, 127, 240, 301, 354
John	13, 94, 112, 263	Anns Portion	12, 226, 288, 341
Alleyband		Ann's Chance	60
Thomas	94	Anssiter	
Allins Neck	133	Sarah	28
Allins Neck Outlett	133	Anthony	
Allocks Pharsalia	320	Elinor	154, 323
Allyband		Ellinor	207, 270
Alce	323	Mark	94, 118
Alice	154, 207, 270	Anthorp	7, 17, 144
Thomas	114, 207, 270	Anthorpe	106, 133, 160, 213, 276, 329
Allyband Hazard Enlarged	154	Arcadia	149
Allybands Hazard Enlarg'd	323	Arthurs Chance	7, 266
Allybands Hazard Inlarged	270	Arthur's Chance	76
Allybands Hazard Inlarg'd	207	Ashberry	
Alquare		Rebekah	323
Jacob	94, 152	Ashberrys Addition	355
Andeaver	104, 230, 292	Ashbury	
Andeavour	36, 345, 362	James	47
Andeavour Meadows	374	Joseph	94, 144
Anderson		Rebecca	47, 154, 207, 270
(N)	272	Ashbury Addition	6
James	144, 154, 258, 272, 318, 371	Ashburys Addition	139, 185, 241, 303
		Ashford	4, 25, 41, 69, 137, 144, 154, 194, 250, 258, 311, 318, 364, 371
William	114, 154, 258, 318, 371		
Andever	141, 192, 309	Ashley	327
Andever Meadows	176, 205, 262, 322	Ashton	23, 49, 53, 129, 132, 169, 183, 223, 239, 285, 300, 339, 353
Andevour	248		
Andover	9		
Andrew		Astrick	17, 42, 63
(N)	156	Athel	374

Page 377

Athol	205, 262, 322	
Atkinson		
(N)	164, 280	
John	36, 154, 207, 270	
Attkinson		
John	323	
Aud		
James	258, 371	
Auld		
James	201, 318	
Aule		
James	323	
William	323	
Ausiter		
Sarah	94, 118	
Aussiter		
Sarah	18	
Austin		
(N)	333	
John	94, 128	
Samuel	147, 207, 270	
Samuell	154	
William	15, 85, 94, 124, 154, 207, 270, 323	
Awbry		
John	153	
Richard	153	
Thomas	153	
Ayler		
Henry	18, 264	
James	18, 94, 114, 154, 207, 270, 323	
John	323	
Aylers Fortune	323	
Aylers Hope	44, 155, 208, 271, 324	
Aylers Outlett	158, 211, 274, 327	
Aylor's Hope	119	
Ayres		
George	36, 129, 166, 220, 282	
Backlin Burrough	341	
Backs's Addition	158	
Bacon		
Anthony	94, 149, 264	
Bacon Neck	127, 186, 242, 303	
Baggs		
Isaac	328	
John	45, 80, 94, 120, 155, 208, 213, 271, 275, 324	
Mary	213, 275	
Nathan	202, 212, 275, 328	
Thomas	94, 121, 155, 208, 271, 324	
Baggs's Marsh	324	
Bailey		
(N)	82	
James	94	
Thomas	16	
Baileys Delight	15	
Baileys Delight on Resurvey	199, 316	
Baileys Delight Resurveyed	16	
Baily		
(N)	145, 210, 273	
Jacob	126, 128, 156, 209, 272	
James	82, 95, 145, 157, 210, 273	
Thomas	63, 94, 95, 126, 127, 141, 147, 156, 209, 272	
Bailys Addition	157, 210, 273	
Bailys Delight	29, 185, 255, 302	
Bailys Delight Attached	147	
Bailys Delight on Resurvey	127, 272	
Baily's Delight	63, 209	
Baily's Delight on Resurvey	156	
Baken Neck	356	
Baker		
Charles	31, 159, 212, 275, 328	
John	32, 37, 71, 94, 113	
Bakers Chance	216, 279, 332	
Bakers Plains	37, 173, 225, 228, 287, 290, 340, 343	
Baker's Plains	71	
Baldwin		
John	87	
Baley		
Jacob	325, 357	
James	326	
Thomas	325, 357	
Baleys Addition	326	
Baleys Delight	325, 355, 369	
Ball		
Benjamin	34, 64, 67, 80, 88	
Banckes		
William	158, 274	
Banckes's Delight	274	

Bancks			William	94, 103, 141, 157, 210, 326
Nicholas	28		Barnes	
William	148, 211, 327		Francis	63, 66
Bancks's Addition	211, 274, 327		Thomas	49, 138, 157, 210, 273, 328
Bancks's Delight	158, 211, 327		Barnes Satisfaction	4, 138, 157, 162
Bangor	28, 70		Barnes's Satisfaction	63, 66, 103, 122, 138, 168, 210, 273, 278, 284
Baning				
John	324		Barns	
Margaret	324		Fra.	4
William	324		Thomas	4, 49
Banings Discovery	324		Barns Satisfaction	4, 49
Banks			Barnstable Hill	4, 105, 313
Nicholas	28, 80, 266		Barnstable Hill Resurveyed	105, 196, 252, 366
Banks Addition	28		Barns's Satisfaction	215, 222, 328, 331, 353
Banks Fork	28			
Banks's Addition	80, 266		Barren Neck	11, 127, 242, 356
Banks's Fork	80, 266		Barren Ridge	3, 86, 137, 343
Banning			Barren Ridge Addition	80, 266
John	45, 94, 117, 155, 208, 271		Barrew Neck	303
Margaret	208		Barrick	
Margarett	155, 271		Edward	50
Thomas	19		James	50
William	45, 94, 116, 155, 208, 271		Barron Neck	52
			Barron Ridge	174, 228, 290
Bannings Discovery	155, 208, 271		Barrow Neck	186
Barbadoes Hall	6, 42, 110, 197, 253, 313, 330		Bartlet	
			John	87
Barbados Hall	85		Bartlett	
Barbarah Inlett	109		James	94, 151, 202, 258, 318, 371
Barbarahs Choice	5, 109, 174, 229, 291		John	28, 94, 149
Barbarahs Inlett	174, 229, 291		Rachell	55
Barbareys Choice	344		Thomas	94, 151
Barbareys Inlett	344		Barton	23, 32, 50, 129, 131, 181, 188, 237, 244, 298, 305, 351, 358
Barbars Delight	38			
Barbarys Inlett	54			
Barber			Barwick	
(N)	105, 165, 219, 281, 334		(N)	115
Barber's Delight	68		Ed.	18
Barefield	54, 145, 251, 311, 365		Edward	48
Baregarden	358, 360		James	18, 48, 95, 122, 156, 209, 272, 325
Baregarden Addition	360			
Bargarden	374		John	159, 258, 329
Barghold	251		William	94, 143
Bargholt	311		Barwicke	
Bargolt	365		John	319
Barkhurst				
James	42			
Barkhust				
James	94, 144			

Bashaw		63
	Andrew	63
	Giles	38, 78, 269
Basnett		
	Robert	156, 209, 272, 325
Bastin		
	Henry	32, 64
Batchellor		1
Batchellors Adventure		16
Batchellors Chance		7
Batchellors Hope		20, 36
Batchellors Plains		6, 31
Batchelors Adventure		107, 166, 220, 282, 336
Batchelors Chance		108, 199, 255, 315, 368
Batchelors Chance Resurveyed		108, 167, 221, 283, 337
Batchelors Hope		105, 106, 167, 182, 196, 220, 237, 252, 283, 298, 312, 336, 365, 371
Batchelors Plains		16, 69, 78, 106, 109, 153, 160, 193, 204, 249, 261, 294, 310, 321, 346, 363
Batchelor's Plains		232
Bath		8, 34, 130, 134, 143, 199, 201, 255, 257, 314, 316, 368
	Isabel	147
	John	46
Bath Addition		8, 34, 130
Baths Addition		134, 199, 255, 316, 368
Baths Meadows		198, 254, 315
Bath's Addition		144
Batterfield		42
Batts Neck		63
Baxter		
	James	202, 258, 318, 371
	Roger	4
	Thomas	3
	William	145, 157, 210, 273, 326
Baxtor		
	William	94
Bayley		
	Jacob	49
	Thomas	55, 56
Bayleys Delight on Resurvey		56

Bayly		
	Thomas	15, 29
Baynard		
	(N)	82
	Esther	20, 94
	George	20, 33, 81, 95, 127, 155, 208, 271, 324
	Hannah	155
	John	20, 57, 82, 93, 94, 115, 118, 148, 252, 312, 365
	Nathan	20, 115, 158, 211, 274, 326
	Robert	115, 204
	Susanna	20
	Thomas	20, 115, 204
	William	118, 148
Baynards Chance		57, 155, 252, 312, 365
Baynards Discovery		150, 268
Baynards Large Range Addition		93, 115, 155, 252, 312, 365
Baynards Pasture		155, 185, 241, 271, 302, 324, 355
Baynard's Chance		103
Baynard's Discovery		103
Baynard's Pasture		208
Beal		
	Thomas	328
Bear Garden		20, 50, 84, 120, 150, 187, 190, 206, 243, 246, 262
Bear Garden Addition		190
Bear Garden Point		50
Bear Harbour		119, 187, 243, 304
Bear Point		26, 120, 161, 214, 330
Beargarden		304, 307
Beargarden Addition		246, 307
Beargardon		322
Bearpoint		277
Bears Harbour		25
Beaver Dam		104
Beaver Dams		40, 128, 172, 226, 249, 341, 362
Beaver Dams Addition		344
Beaver Dams Fork		344
Beaver Harbour		357
Beaver Neck		68
Beaver Neck Resurveyed		2, 136, 147,

		202, 258, 318, 371
Beaverdam Addition		36
Beaverdam Fork		44, 130, 230, 292
Beaverdamb		148
Beaverdambs Addition		119
Beaverdams		193, 288, 309
Beaverdams Addition		173, 228, 290
Beaver's Neck		63
Beck		
	(N)	167-169, 221-223, 283, 285, 337, 338
	John	12, 22, 66, 67, 105, 165, 219, 281
Beckeld		
	Rev. Mr.	38
Beckett		
	(N)	70
Bedford		42
Bee Tree		57, 108, 167, 221, 283, 337
Bee Tree Ridge		23, 129, 196, 252, 312, 351
Bee Tree Swamp		167, 221, 283, 337
Beedle		
	Henry	63
Beedles Outlett		63
Begining		186, 204, 303, 321, 344, 350, 356
Beginning		8, 40, 52, 59, 79, 80, 90, 116, 128, 180, 229, 235, 242, 263, 268, 291, 297
Beiglin & Beignlin Addition		14
Belamy		
	Henry	63
Belcher		4, 63, 152, 159, 211, 274, 353
	Thomas	63
Bell		
	Hannah	117
	Jacob	146
	James	45, 57, 68, 117, 176, 231, 293, 328
	John	45
	William	26, 45, 53, 117
Bellin		
	Thomas	21
Bells Adventure		53
Bells Venture		117, 155, 208, 271, 324
Benewell		288
Benfield		195
Benjamans Infancy		112

Benjamin Infancy		52
Benjamin Tasker & Co.		53
Benjamins Infancy		118, 150, 170
Benjamins Park		202, 258, 318, 371
Benjamins Parke		36
Benjamin's Infancy		90, 268
Benjamin's Park		152
Benjamin's Parks		84
Bennett		
	Deborah	63
	Esq.	207, 208, 270, 271, 323, 324
	Esquire	148
	James	51
	R.	13
	Richard	10, 56-58, 63-68, 82, 93, 103, 148, 295
	William	159, 212, 275, 328
Bennetts Addition		63
Bennetts Adventure		7
Bennetts Chance		159, 212, 275, 328
Bennetts Choice		158, 162, 211, 215, 274, 278, 327, 331
Bennetts Choice Resurveyed		11
Bennetts Out Lett Resurveyed		11
Bennetts Out Lott		164
Bennetts Outlett		187, 191, 199, 218, 242, 243, 247, 255, 280, 303, 304, 307, 315, 334, 357, 360, 368
Bennetts Regulation		11, 63, 154, 207, 270, 323
Bennetts Regulation on Resurvey		57
Bennetts Toalson Resurveyed		347
Bennetts Tolson Rest		233
Bennetts Tolson Resurveyed		203, 295
Bennetts Toulson		11, 56
Bennett's Choice		64
Bennett's Outlett		63, 64
Bennett's Regulation		65, 67, 68
Bennett's Toulson		68
Benson		
	James	202, 258, 318, 371
Benton		
	Fra.	3
	Francis	3
	Mark	4, 80
	Thomas	94, 136, 137, 157, 210, 273, 326

Vincent	94, 141, 157, 210, 273, 326	
Vincon	231	
Bentons Hazard	157, 210, 273, 345	
Bentons Luck	326	
Berks	26, 84	
Bermingham		
Charles	157, 210, 272, 325	
John	56, 94, 134	
Berminghams Fortune	56, 157, 210, 272, 325	
Bermingham's Fortune	134	
Bermmington	50	
Berry		
David	43	
James	28	
Margaret	106	
Berrys Point	153	
Berverdams	113	
Betten		
Turbutt	159	
Betton		
(N)	107	
Turbut	328	
Turbutt	212, 275	
Betts		
Ezekiel	325	
Robert	25, 69, 77, 268	
Thomas Peacock	47, 94, 129, 156, 272	
Thomas Peo.	209	
Betts Range	26, 149, 202, 267	
Beverdam Fork	175	
Beverdams	11, 56	
Beverton	41, 92	
Birch		
Christopher	41, 55, 64, 93	
Bird		
Daniel	202, 258, 318, 371	
Biscoe		
John	51, 94, 152	
Bishop		
(N)	93	
Richard	16, 65, 81	
William	16, 61, 63, 65, 69, 80, 81, 84, 88, 91, 93, 94, 112, 128, 159, 212, 275	
Bishop Fields	332	
Bishopfields	163	
Bishopprick	141	
Bishops Addition	11, 16, 22, 45, 126, 147, 154, 205, 207, 262, 270, 322, 333, 374	
Bishops Fields	21, 133, 145, 191, 216, 246, 279, 307, 360	
Bishops Outlet	126	
Bishops Outlett	6, 11, 16, 22, 45, 49, 110, 126, 128, 147, 154, 186, 205, 207, 209, 242, 262, 263, 270, 303, 322, 333, 357, 374	
Bishopsfields	44	
Bishoptan	129	
Bishopton	7, 23, 24, 106, 144, 159, 160, 183, 212, 213, 239, 275, 276, 300, 328, 329, 353	
Bishop's Addition	84	
Bishop's Fields	80, 91	
Bishop's Outlet	80	
Bite the Biter	199, 255, 315, 368	
Bitts		
Robert	69	
Blackeston		
Benjamin	371	
Blackiston		
Benjamin	152, 202, 258, 318	
John	259	
Blackstone		
Benjamin	36	
Blackwell		
John	52, 74, 202, 258, 318, 329	
Blades		
James	53, 94, 119, 155, 208, 271, 324	
Blair Creisk	240	
Blair Croisk	301	
Blair Crook, Athol, & Dunkelld	152	
Blake		
Charles	5, 60-65, 207, 208, 270, 271, 323	
Christopher	5	
Henrietta Maria	208, 271, 324	
John	46, 50, 154, 155, 207, 270, 323	

	John Sawyer	323		325
	John Sayer	5, 207	William	59, 156, 209, 272, 325
	John Sayre	88, 94, 106		
	M.	271	Boltons Delight	59, 124, 184, 240, 301, 354
	Mary	208, 324		
	Phil. Charles	207	Bonadventure	41, 140, 157, 158, 210, 211, 273, 326
	Philemon Charles	94, 106, 154, 270	Bonham	
	Phill. Charles	5, 54, 323	William	68
	Sarah	154, 207, 270, 323	Bonham's Addition	68
Blakeford		5, 54, 63-65, 106, 154, 207, 270, 323	Bonnams Addition	38
			Booman	
Blandford		230, 292, 345	Samuel	371
Blanford		176	Boon	
Blangey			(N)	324
	Lewis	36, 84	Abraham	94, 325
Blangy			Benjamin	95, 293, 345
	(N)	137	Isaac	94, 325
	Jacob	2	Jacob	18, 19, 47, 94, 324
Blear Crook		354	James	28, 94, 326
Bloomsberry		37, 61, 266	John	19
Bloomsbury		71	Joseph	94, 325
Bluff Point		63, 203, 260, 319, 372	Moses	28, 94
Bluff Point Resurveyed		10	William	18
Blunt			Boone	
	Richard	3, 69, 88, 137	(N)	156, 209, 272
	Robert	3, 80, 137, 157, 210, 273, 325	Abraham	148, 156, 209, 272
			Benjamin	148, 156, 231
	Samuel	3, 94, 138, 157, 210, 212, 273, 275, 325, 328	Isaac	121, 156, 209, 272
			Jacob	121, 156, 209, 272
			James	121, 158, 211, 274
	Samuell	159	Joseph	148, 156, 209, 272
Blunts Marsh		3, 69, 88, 137, 138, 157, 210, 273, 325	Moses	148, 156
			William	18
Boadley		248	Boones Addition	156, 209, 272
Boage			Boones Covett	209, 272
	John	63	Boones Covitt	156
Boagley		6, 10, 63, 106, 185, 192, 269, 302, 308, 355, 361	Boones Hazard	156, 209, 272
			Boones Hazard Addition	156, 209, 272
Boagly		241	Boones Hope	80, 120, 161, 164, 218, 269, 280
Bockin		8		
Bocking		63	Boones Park	156, 209, 272
Body of Quakers		30	Boones Pleasure	148, 156, 209, 272
Bodys Neck		1, 137, 177, 232, 293, 346	Boones Ridge	119, 172, 226, 288
Boggs			Boones Struggle	156, 209, 272
	(N)	48	Boones Venture	121, 156
Bolton			Boone's Hazzard	121
	Daniel	59, 95, 124, 184, 240, 301, 354	Boone's Park	121
			Boons Addition	325
	John	95, 124, 156, 209, 272,	Boons Chance	325

Boons Covitt	325	John	159, 212, 275, 327
Boons Hazard	324	Bracco Addition	159, 212, 275
Boons Hazard Addition	325	Bracco's Addition	327
Boons Hope	27, 334	Braco	159
Boons Park	18, 324	Brad Burns Delight	147
Boons Pleasure	19, 325	Bradbeans Delight	15
Boons Ridge	341	Bradbourne's Delight	63
Boons Struggle	324	Bradburns Delight	16, 29, 185, 241, 302, 355
Boons Venture	209, 272, 325	Bradburns Purchase	15
Boothbys Fortune	31, 198, 257, 315, 370	Bradford	22, 127, 148, 171, 225, 287, 340
Boothby's Fortune	146	Elizabeth	136, 147
Bordley		Rev. Mr.	94
Stephen	32, 72, 131	Bradfords Addition	51, 128, 188, 244, 305
Boroughs Ridge	43	Bradley	
Bostick		Charles	44, 94, 119, 155, 208, 271, 324
John	159, 212, 275, 328	Bradnox	
Thomas	47, 59, 155, 208, 271, 324	Thomas	69
Bosticks Chance	47, 155, 208, 271, 324	Bradys Delight	241
Bostock		Bragholl	195
Thomas	94, 119	Bragholt	54
Bostocks Chance	119	Braghott	145
Boston	14, 92	Bramfield	19
Boston Addition	183	Brampton	15, 40, 53, 123, 159, 212, 226, 275, 288, 328, 341
Bostons Addition	14, 117, 238, 299, 352	Brampton Addition	84, 333
Boulton		Bramptons Addition	11
Daniel	17	Bramton	123, 174
John	17	Brandfield	27, 28, 80, 106, 156, 165, 169, 181, 219, 223, 263, 281, 286, 298, 335, 339, 352
William	17	Brandfield & Sawyers Addition	337
Boultons Delight	17	Brandfield & Sayers Addition	39, 168, 221, 237, 284, 351
Bourk		Brandfield & Sayres Addition	121
John	37	Brandford	37, 49, 50, 53, 84, 113, 114, 174, 178, 182, 183, 201, 204, 229, 230, 233, 238, 239, 258, 261, 269, 272, 291, 292, 295, 299, 300, 318, 320, 339, 345, 348, 353, 371, 373
Bourks			
John	37		
Bourn			
Sweatnam	94		
Bowes			
George	40, 74, 81		
Bowles			
James	31, 71		
Bowlingly	11, 104		
Bows			
George	265		
Bowtingly	148		
Bozman			
Rizdon	94, 150, 201, 258, 318, 371	Brandfords Addition	358
Bracco	212, 275, 327	Branfield	60, 325

Branford	53, 176	Broad Creek Resurveyed	1, 136, 162, 189, 215, 245, 278, 306, 331
Brayley			
John	150		
Samuel	150	Broad Neck	5, 108, 163, 217, 224, 279, 332, 373
Break Neck	261		
Breday		Broad Oak	2, 136, 170, 286, 340
Robert	250	Broadaway	
Breek Neck	320	Isaac	150
Breek Nock	204	James	212, 328
Bremington	227	Nicholas	30, 156, 209, 272, 325
Brent			
William	70, 202, 258, 371	Robert	28, 85, 86, 328
Brentford	53	William	150
Bridge	369	Broadnox	
Bridge North	67, 106, 160, 180, 221, 235, 283, 297, 336, 349	Thomas	63, 66
		Broadrib	
		John	81
Bridge North Resurveyed	26	Broadway	
Bridge Town	52, 80, 121, 147, 184, 202, 212, 240, 275, 301, 328, 354	Isaac	94, 263
		James	275
		Nicholas	23, 50, 94, 133
Bridge Walter	111	Robert	267
Bridge Water	171, 225, 287	Samuel	29, 75, 263
Bridges		William	94, 263
Richard	64, 91	Broady	
Bridgewater	342	Robert	159, 212, 275
Bridgnorth	28	Brocknock	11
Bridgwater	14	Brodaway	
Bridling's Addition	92	Robert	28
Bright		Bromley Lambeth	324
Fra.	3, 53	Brooke	
Fran.	210	Anne	202, 258, 319
Francis	1, 66, 67, 94, 136, 157, 273, 325	Broom Hope	164, 334
		Broomhope	218, 280
Brights Island	137, 157, 210, 273, 325	Broomley	63, 271
Brigland & Briglands Addition	14	Broomley Lambeth	63, 65, 155, 182, 208, 238, 352
Briglin	76		
Briglin & Briglins Addition	263	Broomly Lambeth	65, 112, 299
Brigling	92	Brother Hood	122, 357
Briglins Addition	76	Brotherhead	200
Brimmington	84	Brotherhood	35, 44, 48, 130, 133, 142, 144, 154, 159, 180, 196, 197, 207, 212, 225, 228, 235, 236, 252, 253, 270, 275, 287, 290, 296, 297, 313, 314, 323, 328, 340, 343, 349, 350, 366, 367
Briscoe			
John	269		
Bristol Marsh	72, 104, 106, 218, 248, 333, 361, 362		
Bristoll Marsh	8, 13, 43, 187, 192, 308, 309		
Britton			
William	54		
Broad Creek	4, 38, 63, 69, 359	Brotherhood Resurveyed	53

Page 385

Brothers Annexion		38		Katharine		210
Brothers Discovery		328		Katherine		157, 272, 325
Brother's Annextion		72		Richard		94, 133
Browley Lambeth Resurveyed		11		Robert		56
Brown				Buckleys Delight		56, 157, 177, 210, 232, 272, 294, 325, 329
	Charles	147, 158, 167, 211, 220, 274, 283, 327, 336		Buckley's Delight		133
	Edward	1, 15, 94, 95, 127, 140, 157, 159, 210-213, 273-275, 326, 328, 353		Bucks Expectation		274
				Bucks Forrest		182, 238, 299, 352
				Bucks Range		191, 247, 307, 360
				Bullin		
	Elisha	200, 256, 316, 317, 328			Thomas	61, 142
				Bullock		
	James	23, 130, 156, 209, 272, 325, 327			Fra.	46
					Fran.	259
	John	1, 20, 36, 94, 105, 152, 159, 167, 182, 212, 213, 220, 237, 274, 275, 283, 298, 327, 328, 371		Bunt		
					William	318
				Burk		
					(N)	300
					James	329
	Let.	94			John	58, 94, 112, 116, 155, 164, 208, 218, 271, 280, 334
	Letitia	138				
	Mathew	1, 138				
	Nathaniel	159, 171, 224, 275, 287, 340			Sarah	94
					Thomas	94, 112, 155, 208, 271, 300
	Thomas	26, 80				
	William	74		Burke		
Browne					John	51, 85, 323
	Edward	173			Precilla	12
Browning					Thomas	18, 45, 323
	Edward	207, 270, 323		Burkhust		
Browns Lott		60			William	273
Bruff				Burks Expectation		158, 211, 327
	Richard	38, 75, 268		Burlers Marsh		78
Bruffe				Burn		
	Richard	38			Darias	213
Buck					Daris	275
	John	94, 134, 157, 259, 319, 371			Martha	267
					Sweat.	211
Buck Bay		172, 226, 288, 341			Sweatnam	146, 158, 273, 326
Buck Island		199, 255, 315, 368		Burner		
Buck Range		62, 148, 149, 189, 197, 199, 214, 245, 255, 277, 305, 316, 330, 359, 368			William	9
				Buroughs		
					Thomas	212
Buck Road		35, 135, 158, 211, 274, 327		Burroughs		
Buckley					George	94, 141, 157, 158, 210, 211, 273, 274, 327
	Jo.	232				
	Joseph	294, 329			Hannah	159, 212, 275, 328

	James	326
	John	158, 211, 274, 327
	Thomas	158, 159, 211, 274, 275, 327
	William	35, 94, 135
Burroughs Ridge		149, 264
Burt		
	Henry	57, 94, 121, 156, 209, 272, 324
Burton		141, 175, 230, 292, 345
	Edm.	266
	Edmund	63
	Edward	39, 78
	Judith	95, 123
	William	30, 46, 56, 123
Burton Upon Wallsey		63
Burton Upon Walsey		155, 207, 270
Burton Upon Walsey Resurveyed		11
Burtons Lott		39, 266
Burton's Lott		78
Burts Delight		121, 156, 209, 272, 324
Burts Fancey		324
Burts Fancy		57, 121, 156, 209, 272
Bussells		
	John	134
	Margaret	94
	Margarett	134
Bussey		
	Samuel	60
Butler		
	(N)	332
	James	159, 212, 275, 328
	John	38
	Thomas	29, 35, 38, 78, 95, 125, 159, 212, 266, 274, 355
Butlers Marsh		38, 266
Butlers Neck		38, 266
Butlers Own		125, 211
Butlers Own Resurveyed		158, 274, 327
Butlers Owne		35
Butler's Neck		78
Butterfield		107
Cabbin Branch		37, 69, 266
Cabbin Neck		2, 140, 179, 234, 296, 348
Cabin Branch		78
Caedar Branch		39
Cahal		
	Edward	161
	John	161
	Mary	117
Cahall		
	Edm.	117
	Edmund	46, 95
	Edward	165, 214, 217, 277, 279, 330, 332
	John	214, 277, 330
Calebs Lott		34, 130, 199, 316, 368
Caleb's Lott		255
Callaghan		
	Fard	45
Callaghane		
	Ferdinando	89
	James	165, 217, 279, 333
Callington		124, 133
Callister		
	Henry	164, 280
Calvin		
	William	81, 128, 264
Camberwel		131
Camberwell		23, 47, 80, 84, 131, 134, 171, 177, 225, 226, 233, 288, 294, 340, 342, 347
Campbell		
	William	7, 20, 24, 29, 94, 106, 160, 213, 276, 329
Campe		
	Thomas	47
Camper		
	John	95, 150
Campersons Choice		51, 120, 179, 234, 295, 348
Canaan		35, 123, 158, 211, 274, 327
Cannon		
	William	95, 161, 215, 277
Cannoway		135
Canon		
	William	331
Caradine		
	John	6, 106
Carey		
	Amia	259, 372
	Amy	202, 319
	Dennis	164, 218, 280, 334, 360
	Elinor	202, 319, 372

Ellionor		259
William		50, 75, 150
Caridine		
Ann		106
Carman		
James		128
John		51, 95, 128
Thomas		86, 95, 128, 268
William		51, 96, 128, 142
Carman & Burton		30, 123, 133, 156, 157, 209, 272, 325
Carmans & Burton		23
Carmans Neck		12, 104, 107, 148, 222, 285, 338
Carmarthan		243, 304
Carmarthen		120
Carmarthin		187
Carmathan		19, 358
Carmichal		
William		331
Carmichall		
William		24, 38, 95, 133, 162, 215, 278
Carmons Neck		169
Carpenter		
Joanna		372
Johannah		202, 259, 319
John		45
Simon		64
Carpenter Outlett		192
Carpenters Meadow		9
Carpenters Meadows		64
Carpenters Outlett		10, 26, 248, 263, 308, 361
Carpenters Square		12
Carpenter's Outlett		76
Carpenter's Square		63
Carr		
John		29, 74, 265
Carradine		
Anne		160
John		9, 16, 85, 94, 213, 276, 329
Thomas		164, 217, 280, 333
Carriday		
John		42
Carridine		
John		266
Carroll		
Charles		37, 53, 109, 152, 202, 259, 319, 372
Daniel		37
Daniell		53
Mary		51, 109
Carslake		
Edward		54
Carter		
(N)		26
Elizabeth		164
Henry		142, 162, 216, 278, 331
Jacob		96, 142, 162, 215, 278, 331
John		33, 37, 48, 63, 96, 139, 184, 239, 300, 353
Margaret		147
Richard		4, 26, 49, 74, 75, 96, 138, 162, 215, 263, 278, 331
Vallentine		4
Volentine		140
Carters Addition		4, 138, 149, 162, 168, 215, 222, 267, 278, 284
Carters Chance		61
Carters Forrest		115, 161, 166, 214, 219, 263, 277, 282, 330, 335
Carter's Addition		90
Carter's Forrest		74
Cary		
Edm.		268
William		96
Casbury		209
Cash		
Edward		23
Cassey		
James		16, 23, 31, 96, 135, 165, 215, 278, 331
Joseph		31
Casson		
Henry		141, 162, 216, 278, 331
Cassons Meadows		162, 216, 278, 331
Castle Miles		21, 31, 64
Castle Town		32, 139, 291, 344
Castle Towne		173, 229
Cedar Branch		64
Certain		
(N)		131

Page 388

	Robert	44, 135, 162, 215, 278, 331	Ed.	14
Certaine			Edward	14
	Robert	44	Cheshire	26, 107, 192, 248, 308, 362
Chaires			Richard	28, 70, 267
	Benjamin	164, 218, 280, 333	Cheshires Delight	28, 70, 267
	James	95	Chesnot Meadows	343
	Jo.	366	Chesnot Neck	373
	John	16, 85, 164, 217, 247, 252, 280	Chesnut Meadows	355
			Chesnut Ridge	338
	Joseph	96, 164, 191, 218, 280, 308, 333, 361	Chesnutt Meadow	173
			Chesnutt Meadows	185, 228, 241, 302
	Thomas	95, 191, 247, 308, 361	Chesnutt Neck	131, 204, 260, 320
			Chesnutt Ridge	169, 285
Chaires Addition		16, 114, 299	Chester Field	125
Chaires's Addition		182, 217, 238, 352	Chester Fields	108
Chairs			Chesterfield	6, 14, 29, 52, 86, 87, 111, 114, 159, 163, 171, 212, 216, 225, 274, 279, 287, 332, 342
	James	16, 116		
	John	107		
	Joseph	142		
	Thomas	16, 53, 62, 89, 107	Chesterfield Addition	40, 163, 217, 279, 332
Chais				
	John	60	Chesterfields Addition	108
Chamberlin			Chesterton	31, 266
	James Loyd	373	Chestnut Meadows	113
Chance	3, 4, 13, 23, 31, 46, 52, 59, 72, 74, 80, 84, 132, 137, 138, 153, 162, 166, 168, 189, 194, 205, 215, 222, 242, 244, 250, 259, 263, 266, 269, 278, 282, 284, 305, 311, 335, 358, 364		Chestnut Ridge	116
			Chestnutt Meadows	6, 40, 113, 290
			Chestnutt Neck	152
			Chestnutt Ridge	53
			Cheston	12, 108, 160, 214, 276, 329
			Daniel	96, 151
			Chestorton	78
			Chesutt Ridge	223
			Chetham	
	Batchelor	214, 277, 330	(N)	111, 310
	Boon	334	Ed.	5
	Elijah	214, 277, 330	Edward	30, 76, 264, 334
	Elinor	277, 330	James	250, 334
	Ellinor	215	Chethams Landing	30, 111, 194, 250, 310
	John	214, 277, 330		
	Richard	26, 27, 57, 80, 120, 161, 269	Chettham	
			(N)	250
Chance Hill		120, 271, 324	Chew	
Chance Hills		48	Henrietta Maria	28
Chance Hitt		155, 208	Samuel	20, 28
Change		14, 117, 183, 238, 300, 352	Chichester	34, 72, 267
Charleville		69, 74	Chilton	
Chatham			Mathew	44, 277, 330
	(N)	194	Matthew	95, 115, 161, 214
Chattam			Chiltons Chance	330
			Chittams Landing	363

Page 389

Choice	125, 127, 170, 172, 185, 224, 241, 286, 302, 339, 356		Claylands Purchase	28, 266
			Clayland's Purchase	76
			Claypole	
Christophers Hazard	196, 252, 313, 354		Elizabeth	319
			James	95, 152, 259, 319, 372
Churnalls Neck	72, 131		Claypoole	
Churnells Neck	32, 160, 213, 276, 329		Elizabeth	202
Clapham			James	202
Josias	55		Clayton	
Clark			(N)	72, 123
(N)	27, 49		Charles	165, 219, 281, 330
Caleb	95, 150, 259, 268, 319, 371		Edward	95, 108, 163, 217, 279, 332
Edward	58, 74, 202, 259, 319, 371		Solomon	7, 15, 16, 28, 29, 33, 40, 53, 57, 108, 214, 276, 330
Joshua	164, 218, 281, 334		William	7, 29, 61, 80, 96, 145, 163, 216, 279, 332
Clarke				
Benjamin	27			
Caleb	47			
Jos.	45		Claytons Chesterfield	216, 332
Joshua	45, 57, 115		Claytons Chesterfields	163, 279
Clarkes Venture	324		Claytons Landing	163, 216, 279, 332
Clarke's Struggle	74		Cleans Addition	246
Clarks Adventure	47, 150, 268		Cleave	
Clarks Delight	47, 202, 259, 319, 371		(N)	210
Clarks Lott	47, 202, 255, 316, 368		Benjamin	96, 202, 259, 319
Clarks Struggle	202, 259, 319, 371		Hannah	96
Clarks Strugle	58		Kath	142
Clarks Venture	57, 155, 208, 271		Katherine	96
Clarkson Hill	124, 166, 220, 282		N.	210
Clarkson Hill Addition	124, 166, 220		Nat.	96
Clarksons Hill Addition	282		Nathaniel	17, 59, 96, 142, 163, 202, 216, 259, 279, 319, 332
Clarksons Hills	22			
Clarksons Hills Addition	22			
Claton			Cleaves	
Charles	108		(N)	273
Solomon	108		Benjamin	372
Claxton	40, 105, 200, 256, 317, 328		Nathaniel	17, 56, 273, 372
Claxton Hill	335		Cleaves Ramble	145
Claxton Hill Addition	335		Cleaves Rambles	56, 202, 259
Clay Neck	64		Cleaves's Addition	210
Clay Pitt Neck	41		Cleaves's Ramble	157
Clayland			Cleaves's Rambles	273, 319, 326, 372
James	161, 164, 214, 218, 276, 280, 330, 333		Clemens	
			John	54
John	12, 28, 76, 106, 164, 218, 266, 280, 333		Clement	
			John	109
Thomas	218, 334, 344		Clements	
William	28, 74, 267		John	45, 95, 329
Claylands Part of Trustram	164		Clemments	

	John	160, 213, 276			136, 137, 144, 159, 162, 215, 265, 278, 331
Clemonds					
	John	54			
Clerks Delight		150		Richard	24, 53, 144, 159
Clerks Lott		150		Ruth	136
Clerks Venture		116	Clouds Adventure		6, 31, 47, 181, 188, 200, 298, 358
Cleve					
	(N)	145	Clouds Choice		35
	Benjamin	145	Clouds Hermitage		24, 59
	Nathaniel	145	Clouds Range		19, 24, 59, 184, 354
Clevefields		177	Clouds's Adventure		129, 134, 144, 236, 244, 297, 305, 350
Cleves's Rambles		145			
Clift			Clouds's Chance		137, 177, 232, 293, 346
	Elizabeth	164			
	George	47	Clouds's Choice		137, 179, 235, 296, 349
	Henry	47, 95, 116, 164, 232, 346			
			Clouds's Hermitage		126, 169, 223, 285, 338
Clifts					
	Henry	294	Clouds's Range		123, 240, 301
Climer			Clough		
	Charles	75		James	96, 136, 163, 216, 279, 332
	Fran.	216			
	Francis	117, 279		Mary	164, 218, 280
	John	60		Nathaniel	147, 164, 218, 280, 334
	Thomas	356			
Climers Chance		356		Susannah	334
Cloak			Cloughs Fancy		163, 216, 279, 332
	Maurice	96, 135, 141	Cloughs Hope		147, 164, 218, 280, 334
Cloake			Cloughs Rambles		163, 216, 279, 332
	Morris	36	Cloughton		
Cloaks Chance		189, 191, 245, 247, 306, 308, 359, 361		James	63
			Clough's Fancy		136
Cloather			Clovar Fields		346
	Lewis	47	Clover Kelds		113
Clockerton		24, 130, 134, 237	Cloverfeilds		20
Closcester		249	Cloverfield		67, 353
Clothier			Cloverfields		64, 65, 67, 68, 80, 88, 138, 139, 144, 184, 185, 195, 232, 239, 241, 294, 301-303, 355
	(N)	333			
	John	96, 144, 161, 215, 278, 331			
	Lewis	95, 133	Cloverfields Resurveyed		34
Clothiers Pharsalia		144, 161, 215, 278, 331	Clymer		
				C.	46
Clouden		47		Charles	46
Cloudent		134, 175, 230, 292, 344		Francis	165
Clouds			Clymore		
	Benjamin	1, 2, 25, 35		Thomas	186, 242, 303
	Elizabeth	137	Clymores Chance		186, 242, 303
	Mrs.	96	Coaley		
	Nicholas	24, 59, 78, 86, 96,		Daniel	152

Page 391

	Mary	152	Coldrain		115, 116, 118, 146
Cobrieth			Coldraine		150, 161, 184, 190, 206, 240,
	John	56			246, 277, 301, 306
Coburn			Cole		
	William	80		John	96, 142
Cockar				Mary	13, 15, 53, 59
	(N)	1		Ri	53
Cockayne				William	48, 89
	(N)	26	Cole Rain		329, 333, 354, 360, 364
	Samuel	89	Cole Raine		251
	Thomas	90, 96, 149, 202, 267	Coleman		
	Thomas	26		Elizabeth	163, 217, 279, 326
Cockey				John	129
	Charles	163, 217, 280		Thomas	45, 131, 161, 215,
	Edward	37, 48, 96, 139, 164,			277, 331
		196, 218, 281, 334	Colement		
	John	1, 69		Thomas	95
	Mary	164, 218, 280, 333	Colerain		74, 76, 165, 264
	Susannah	333	Coleraine		49, 51, 52, 147, 164, 218,
Cocklin					280, 312, 319
	Samuel	147, 218, 334	Coles Bank		61, 89, 151
Cocks Neck		3	Coles Bank Addition		151
Codds Head Manor		324, 339	Coles Bank Enlarged		193, 310
Coddshead Mannor		18, 28, 47	Coles Bank Enlarg'd		363
Cods Head Manner		145	Coles Endeaver		142
Cods Head Mannor		120	Coles Endeavour		48, 191, 247, 307
Cods Head Manor		208, 243	Cole's Bank Addition		90
Codshead Mannor		70, 121, 285	Collester		
Codshead Manor		169, 187, 195, 223,		Henry	333
		234, 262, 271, 304,	Collier		
		366		Alice	45, 95, 126
Codshead Manour		87		Allice	22
Coffin				Mathew	22
	Richard	95	Collings		
Cohee				Thomas	64
	James	146, 164, 218, 281,	Collington		17, 22, 30, 64, 85, 156, 272,
		334			325
	Martha	164	Collins		
Cohees Desire		164, 218, 281		John	21, 31, 58, 64, 81, 95,
Cohee's Desire		146, 334			103, 122, 126, 161,
Colbreath					215, 277, 331
	John	90, 92, 95, 119, 330		John Offley	269
	Mary	330		Margaret	162, 215, 278, 331
Cold Harbour		5, 106, 154, 207, 270,		Richard	22, 144, 190, 246,
		323			306, 360
Cold Rain		330		Sarah	30, 81
Cold Raine		175, 214		Thomas	64, 67, 84, 85, 278
Cold Spring		37, 71, 74, 150, 203, 205,	Collins Chance		263
		260, 262, 320, 321,	Collins Lott		23, 45
		374	Collins Owne		45

Collins Range	7	Cornelious	368
Collins Refusall	29	Gias Bartus	333
Collins's Gift	185, 241, 302, 355	John	331, 333
Collins's Lott	14, 17, 76, 129, 142, 180, 183, 235, 239, 264, 296, 300, 349, 353	Conaway	78, 331, 374
		Conclusion	33, 113, 183, 185, 239, 241, 300, 302, 355

Collins's Own   131, 202, 258, 318, 371
Collins's Range   260, 320, 373
Collins's Refusal   70, 87, 180, 296
Collins's Refusall   144, 235, 264, 349
Collins's Ridge   151, 203
Collister
    Henry   218
Collonells Quarter   35
Collonells Quarters   200
Coln   70
Coln Rectified   353
Colne   27
Colne Rectified   183, 239, 254, 315
Colne Rectifyed   300
Colonells Quarters   256, 317, 369
Colonels Quarter   123
Colpe Rectified   198
Colson
    (N)   334
    Jere.   334
Colt
    Robert   8
Comberwell   21
Comby Chance   325
Come by Chance   156, 209, 272
Comegies
    Nathaniel   47
Comegys
    Cornelius   85, 96, 134, 199, 255, 316
    Gias Bartus   164
    John   95, 131, 164
    Nath.   21
Commagys Hazard   164
Commegys
    Gias Bartus   218, 280
    John   161, 215, 218, 277, 280
Commegys Hazard   280, 333
Commegy's Hazard   217
Commerford
    Peter   319
Commins Freehold   4, 109
Commins's Freehold   105
Commyges

Conclution   353
Condon   2, 88, 151, 227, 342, 370
Condone   139, 173, 201, 257, 289, 318
Coney Hall   105
Confusion   13, 16, 17, 42, 64, 72, 111-113, 165, 176, 191, 192, 219, 231, 248, 263, 282, 293, 308
Confution   335, 346, 361
Connally
    Dennis   74
Connally's Park   74, 267
Connaway   23, 31, 215, 264
Connelly
    Dennis   28
Conner
    (N)   256, 369
    Charles   138, 162, 215, 278, 331
    Nathaniel   105
    Phil.   256
    Phill.   369
Connerly
    Dennis   267
Conners Addition   317
Conners Neck   151, 171, 200, 235, 256, 297, 320, 349, 369, 372
Connolly
    Dennis   28
Connollys Park   28
Connor
    Charles   1, 96
    Nathaniel   1, 94
    Philip   64, 67, 69, 88
    Phill.   1, 139
Connors Neck   1, 40, 64, 180
Connor's Neck   69, 88, 139, 148
Connoway   23, 136, 165, 205, 262, 278, 322
Conny Hall   3
Conquest   15, 40, 85, 108, 123, 147, 171, 185, 225, 241, 288, 302, 342, 355

Constantinople	23, 132, 189, 244, 305, 358		138, 157, 162, 168, 210, 215, 222, 273, 278, 284, 325
Content	10, 35, 58, 63, 64, 68, 113, 119, 123, 128, 161, 165, 191, 198, 200, 215, 219, 247, 254, 256, 277, 282, 308, 315, 317, 331, 335, 361, 367, 369	Cope	
		George	164, 218, 281, 334
		Copes Range	281
		Copes's Range	334
		Copidges Range	139
		Coppedge Range	33
		Coppidge	
Content Addition	35, 123, 200, 256, 317, 369	Elizabeth	2, 63
		Elizabeth	68
Content Outlett	200, 256, 369	Jane	63
Content Resurveyed	39	John	2, 84
Contention	22, 42, 80, 84, 109, 131, 141, 157, 173, 210, 227, 266, 273, 289, 326, 342	Martha	2, 63, 68
		Phil.	375
		Philip	96, 140
		Phill.	2, 46
Contents Outlett	123, 317	Phillip	162, 216, 278, 331
Contest	23, 130	Coppidge Range	41, 184, 300
Controversey	28, 37, 56, 150, 155, 203, 260, 275, 320	Coppidges Range	139, 142, 162, 195, 215, 216, 239, 251, 278, 311, 331, 353, 364
Controversie	264, 345, 372		
Controversy	80		
Controversye	120, 213		
Cook		Coppidge's Range	84, 144
Her.	133	Coppin	
Hercules	46, 164, 216, 217, 279, 280	Edward	92
		Cork	69, 74
James	51, 95, 120, 234, 348	Cork House	22, 198, 257, 314, 370
Richard	147, 163, 216, 279	Corke Horse	124
Samuel	179, 234, 295, 348	Cornelius	
William	179, 295	Daniel	52, 96, 151, 267
Cooke		Cossens	
Richard	332	Edward	40
Cooper		Cossens Lott	40
(N)	41	Cossens Neck	40
John	46, 57, 95, 115, 118, 161, 214, 277, 330	Costin	
		Henry	13, 65, 76, 85, 265, 266
Richard	87		
Robert	163, 217, 279	James	112, 161, 214, 276, 330
Sharples	333		
Sharpless	163, 217, 280	Richard	13, 36, 115, 161, 214, 277, 330
Thomas	4, 82, 266		
William	18, 95, 116	Costins Chance	115, 204, 261, 321, 373
Coopers Freehold	25, 152, 264		
Coopers Hill	137, 204, 261, 321, 373	Costins Hope	170, 224, 286
Coopers Hills	1	Costins Park	13, 112, 161, 204, 261, 276, 320, 330
Coopers Quarter	3, 136, 177, 232, 293		
Cooper's Freehold	63	Costin's Chance	89
Copartnership	4, 27, 60, 62, 80, 137,	Costin's Hope	339

Page 394

Costin's Park		214			270, 287, 322, 333, 342, 374
Coston		61			
Coston's Hope		14, 127	Courseys Range		10, 109, 204, 261, 321, 373
Costtens Park		13			
Cottington		209	Courseys Town		145
Council			Courseys Town Resurveyed		195, 251, 311, 365
	Henry	161, 164, 277, 280, 330, 333			
			Courseys Towne		25
	John	164, 333	Coursey's Choice		64
Councill			Coursey's Neck		63
	Henry	42, 95, 215, 217	Coursey's Point		63, 225
	John	218, 280	Coursey's Town Resurveyed		145
Counell			Cousins		
	Henry	124		Edward	72, 152
Countice				Elizabeth	152
	James	95, 161, 214, 277, 330	Cousins Lott		72
	Peter	185, 302, 355	Cove Point		64
	William	95, 165, 214, 277, 330	Cove Point on Resurvey		192, 223, 285, 338
Countis			Cove Point Resurveyed		34
	James	15	Coventon		
	Peter	15, 241		Benjamin	332
	William	15		Nathaniel	334
Countiss			Coventons Necessity		334
	James	119	Covepoint on Resurvey		104
	Peter	95	Covington		23
	Rebecca	112		Benjamin	163, 217
	William	119		Henry	16, 44, 95, 163, 217, 280, 333
Coursey		5, 103, 106, 154, 207, 270, 323			
				James	124
	Col.	39		John	124, 163, 217, 333
	Henry	63-66		Nathaniel	218
	John	6, 10, 39, 64, 76, 95, 109, 160, 214, 261, 268, 276, 321, 373		William	163, 217, 333
			Covingtons Necessity		163, 218
			Covinton		
	Otho	10, 63		Benjamin	279
	William	10, 12, 72, 95, 108, 160, 214, 276, 329		John	279
				Nathaniel	281
Coursey on Wye		30		William	279
Coursey Upon Wye		7, 12, 107, 108, 110, 145, 160, 174, 193, 214, 223, 229, 249, 276, 291, 309, 329, 344, 362	Covintons Necessity		281
			Cow Bank Enlarg'd		249
			Cow Range		120, 175, 197, 230, 253, 292, 313, 344, 366
			Cows Range		36
Courseys Addition		18, 42, 112, 113, 197, 201, 253, 258, 313, 318, 366, 371	Cox		
				Andrew	331
				Anthony	26, 80, 164, 218, 264, 280, 333
Courseys Part		110			
Courseys Point		16, 111, 128, 147, 154, 171, 205, 207, 262,		Christopher	12, 43, 95, 112, 160, 173, 213, 228,

		276, 289, 329
Daniel		164, 218, 280, 319, 333
James		43, 49, 53, 93, 95, 107, 160, 221, 283, 336
Cox Neck		138
Coxes Desire		333
Coxes Necessity		213, 329
Coxes Neck		186, 303, 356
Coxes Range		218
Coxs Desire		218
Cox's Desire		164, 280
Cox's Necessity		160, 276
Cox's Neck		3, 242
Craney Neck		63, 139, 184, 239, 300, 353
Crany Neck Resurveyed		33
Crawford		63, 72, 152, 164, 256, 264, 317, 369
Crawford Resurveyed		25
Crew		
	Edward	24, 96, 151, 266
Crocker		
	Josua	1
Crompton		87
Croney		
	James	214, 277, 330
	John	51, 95, 118, 161
	Mary	51, 95, 115
	Phil.	214
	Phill.	277
	Phillemon	330
	William	165
Crony		
	(N)	52
	John	51
	Mary	51, 52
Cross		
	William	60
Crouch		
	Josiah	58
Crump		
	Robert	30
Crumps Advice		55, 130, 189, 359
Crumps Advise		305
Crumps Chance		22, 125, 172, 199, 227, 255, 288, 289, 316, 341, 368
Crumps Choice		134
Crumps Fancey		368

Crumps Fancy		30, 130, 199, 316
Crumps Forrest		29, 39, 43, 46, 124, 125, 180, 187, 213, 227, 235, 288, 297, 341, 353, 365
Crumps Forrests		39
Crumpton		15, 26, 30, 129, 143, 151, 164, 180, 197, 201, 218, 235, 253, 257, 280, 296, 314, 318, 333, 349, 367, 370
Crump's Advice		244
Crump's Fancy		255
Crums Forrest		275
Cruper		
	Ann	95
Crupper		
	(N)	347
	Thomas	12, 57, 68, 127, 172, 227, 289, 347
Culbreath		
	John	214
	Mary	214
Culbreth		
	John	161, 277
	Mary	161, 277
Culley		
	Henry	96, 142, 152, 162, 216, 279, 332
Cummerford		
	(N)	34
	George	34
	Peter	202, 259, 372
Cummins Freehold		40
Cummins's Freehold		140
Curtice		
	Nathaniel	163, 217, 280
	Rebecca	118
	Thomas	95, 118
Curtices Lott		164, 218, 281
Curtice's Lott		118
Curtis		
	Nathaniel	333
	Thomas	57, 60
	William	164, 218, 281, 334
Curtis's Lott		57, 334
Daily		
	John	82, 225
Dalton		

	James	39
Dambewell		287
Dames		
	William	221, 283, 336
Danby		60
Danby Resurveyed		221, 336
Dancey		37, 171, 288
Dancy		28, 78, 112, 340
Daney		264
Dangerfield		21, 61, 69, 80, 166, 219, 335
Daniels Fancy		52, 151, 267
Daniels Field		46, 277, 330
Daniels Fields		27, 117, 161, 197, 214, 253, 313, 366
Dareland Resurveyed		53
Darkin		111, 171, 225, 287, 342
Darland		8, 27, 64, 86
Darland Resurveyed		114, 154, 258, 318, 371
Darvill		
	William	27, 78, 267
Davenport		84
	Humphry	84
Daventport		16, 39, 42
David Prospect		48
Davids Prospect		117, 264
Davis		
	Catharine	220, 282
	Catherine	166, 335
	David	167, 259, 319, 372
	John	16, 38, 74, 95, 108, 113, 114, 165, 167, 219, 259, 267, 282, 319, 335, 372
	Ka.	22
	Katharine	22
	Katherine	17, 95
	Kathrine	124
	Philip	72
	Phill.	32
	Phillip	167, 259, 319, 372
	Thomas	17, 39, 42, 58, 63, 64, 68, 95, 113, 167, 220, 283
Davis Pharsalia		38
Davis Range		38
Davis's Discovery		335
Davis's Pharsalia		74, 267
Davis's Range		70, 106, 149, 151, 160, 203, 213, 259, 260, 276, 319, 320, 329, 338, 372
Dawson		
	Empy	372
	George	372
	James	29, 74, 75, 267
	John	29
	Ralph	105
	William	7, 95, 105, 165, 219, 281, 335
Dawsons Neck		14, 18, 26, 45, 117, 155, 183, 208, 238, 264, 271, 299, 323, 352
Dawson's Neck		78
Day		
	Edward	38, 87, 267
Dayly		
	John	2
Dead Ridge		325
Deer		
	Stephen	23, 95
Deford		351
	(N)	110
	John	45, 95, 128, 166, 282, 335
Dehiniosa		
	(N)	80
Dehorty		
	William	51
Delight		255, 369
Delmore End		9, 104, 192, 248, 250, 309, 362, 363
Deluge		13, 116, 174, 175, 229, 230, 291
Dempster		
	John	24, 52, 95, 133
Denbigh		64
Denbigh Addition		64
Denby		49
Denby Resurveyed		53, 107, 160
Denbys Addition		49
Denley Resurveyed		283
Denney		
	Benjamin	335, 340
	John Earle	109
Denny		
	Ann	10
	Benjamin	141, 166, 220, 282
	Christopher	10

John Earle	10	William	202
Dennys Range	164, 218, 281	Dickinsons Plains	150, 202, 319
Denton Holm	87	Dickinson's Plains	74
Derochbourns Neglect	190, 245, 306	Difficulty	196, 252, 366
Derochbroom		Diggs	
John	336	(N)	113, 229
Joseph	336	Edward	37
Lewis	336	William	84, 174, 178, 233, 238, 269, 291, 295, 299, 348, 352
Derochbrooms Neglect	350		
Derochbrume		Dillerage	366
Jos.	139	Dilliridge	291
Lewis	139	Discovery	31, 43, 104, 107, 148, 160, 193, 221, 249, 283, 309, 336, 362
Derochbrune			
Jo.	95, 103		
John	167, 220, 283	Dispute	44, 130, 133, 154, 180, 196, 207, 235, 252, 270, 297, 313, 323, 366
Jos.	283		
Joseph	92, 167, 220		
Lewis	92, 95, 103, 167, 220, 283	Distance	
		Ralph	2, 82, 267
DeRochburne		Ditterage	64, 344
Jos.	42	Ditteridge	7, 91, 106, 108, 160, 174, 196, 213, 229, 253, 276, 313
Joseph	1		
Lewis	1		
Derouchbrume			
Joseph	139	Dittlage	345
Detterage	329	Dixon	
Devenish Chance	26, 28, 34	(N)	363
Devenish's Chance	23	Isaac	9, 96, 149, 150
Devonish		John	149, 150, 203, 259, 319
Robert	95, 152	Dixons Gift	48, 54, 59, 185, 301, 355
Devonishes Chance	141, 181, 189, 236, 245, 264, 269, 298, 306, 350, 359	Dixon's Gift	84, 240
		Dixsons Gift	132
		Dobbs	
Devonishes's Chance	132	John	4, 80, 267
Devonishe's Chance	80	Dobbs Adventure	4, 80
Devonishs's Chance	74	Dobb's Adventure	267
Devonish's Chance	143	Dobson	
Dickenson		Nathan	202
James	28	William	52, 74, 267
John	259, 319	Dobsons Westmoreland	52, 202, 267
Samuel	50, 61, 75, 259, 372	Dobson's Westmoreland	74
Samuell	319	Dockery	
William	28, 259, 319, 372	Mat.	80
Dickensons Plains	28, 259	Mathew	95, 335
Dickersons Plains	371, 372, 375	Matthew	166, 219, 282
Dickinson		Thomas	95, 112, 165, 219, 282, 335
James	74, 150, 202, 259, 319		
Samuel	19, 74, 75, 89, 96, 153	William	95, 104, 142, 166, 220, 282, 299, 335, 351
Samuell	202		

Dockerys Discovery	226, 288, 342	
Dockerys Meadow	219, 282, 335	
Dockeys Discovery	172	
Dockrey		
Matthew	114	
Dockwra		
Mathew	49	
Docraw		
Mathew	49	
Docters Folley	366	
Docters Folly	312	
Doctors Folley	64	
Doctors Folly	39, 55, 110, 196, 252	
Doctor's Folly	93	
Docwra		
Mathew	50	
Docwray		
Mathew	60	
Dodd		
George	336	
Jacob	166, 220, 282, 336	
Jo.	220	
Joseph	166, 282, 336	
Peter	69	
Doddington	28, 69, 74, 308, 361	
Dodington	206	
Dodlington	247	
Doggwood Ridge	121, 209, 324	
Dogwood Ridge	36, 156, 272	
Doile		
John	53, 59	
Donns Chance	334	
Donns Hazard Corrected	331, 337	
Double Kill	13, 31, 72, 80, 263, 264	
Douglas		
Susannah	319	
Douglass		
Archibald	51	
Susanna	51, 203, 259	
Dover	61	
Downes		
Charles	44, 107, 165, 219, 281, 335	
Hawkins	95, 115, 166, 219, 282	
Henry	61, 95, 115, 166, 219, 282, 335	
Hynson	166, 220, 282, 336	
James	166, 220, 282	
John	60, 95, 105, 115, 165, 166, 218-220, 281, 282, 334-336	
Mary	290	
Nathaniel	95, 114	
Rebeckah	336	
Solomon	335	
Downes Chance	336	
Downes Forrest	184	
Downes's Chance	115, 165, 166, 219, 220, 281, 282	
Downes's Forrest	123, 240, 301, 354	
Downey		
Alexander	1	
T. Valentine	95	
Valentine	1, 166, 282	
Volentine	138, 335	
Downs		
Hawkins	19, 53, 89	
James	51	
John	5, 48	
Mary	228	
Downs Chance	5	
Downs Forrest	34	
Downy		
Alexander	1, 69	
Val.	69	
Vallentine	1	
Dowsons Neck	112	
Doyle		
John	83	
Thomas	167, 220, 283, 336	
Driskell		
William	19, 52, 56, 89, 95, 115, 269	
Drumfield	11, 54, 74	
Dub Hen Ridge	188, 244, 305	
Dubb Hen Ridge	132	
Dubbin Ridge	358	
Dublin	15, 119, 161, 165, 214, 277, 330	
Dudleigh		
(N)	46	
Richard	28	
Dudleighs Chance	27	
Dudleighs Demeans	28	
Dudleighs Desire	19	
Dudley		
Abner	49, 75, 166, 220, 283, 336	
James	319	

Marsh	49, 75	
Richard	74	
Dudleys Chance	117, 183, 238, 299, 352	
Dudleys Choice	61, 117	
Dudleys Desire	118, 141, 162, 184, 240, 278, 301, 331, 354	
Dudley's Demesne	74	
Dudley's Desire	216	
Duffey		
John	166, 220, 282, 336	
Duglas		
Susanah	372	
Duhamell		
James	336	
Duhamil		
Dr.	95	
Peter	128, 283	
Duhamill		
(N)	220	
Rachel	166	
Rachell	220, 283	
Dulaney		
Daniel	336	
Madam	373	
Dulany		
Daniel	95, 221, 283	
Daniell	167	
Darby	41	
Henrietta Maria	165, 219, 335	
Mrs.	281	
William	39, 41, 105, 335, 336	
Dullage		
Dullany		
Daniel	105	
Dundee	2, 137, 197, 254, 314, 367	
Duney	226	
Dungamon	187, 243, 334	
Dunganon	340	
Dungarnen	10	
Dungarnon	218, 225, 287, 304, 357	
Dungarnow	109	
Dungarron	171	
Dunkin		
(N)	336	
Robert	336	
Dunn		
Pasco	69	
Dunnington	80, 267	

Dunns Hazard	4, 162, 168, 215, 278, 284	
Dunn's Hazard	138	
Duns Hazard	138	
Duns Lott	184	
Durdin		
Sarah	335	
Durding		
William	95, 144, 166, 220, 282	
Dwiggin		
John	46	
Dyre		
Mary	167, 220, 283, 336	
Eadsworth		
Benjamin	168	
Eagle		
Mary	168, 221, 284, 337	
Michael	77	
William	44, 96, 116, 168, 221, 284, 337	
Earle		
Elizabeth	29, 43	
James	8, 10, 34, 43, 60, 64, 90, 96, 104, 127, 192, 223, 285, 338	
John	43, 96, 127, 144, 168, 222, 284, 337	
Joseph	47, 107	
Michael	10, 39, 76, 146, 168, 222, 263, 284, 338	
Richard Tilghman	168, 222, 284, 338	
Earles Begining	338	
Earles Beginning	168, 222, 284	
Earles Guard	338	
Eastern Island	4, 137, 139, 140, 157, 158, 198, 210, 257, 273, 314, 326, 370	
Easterne Island	2	
Easterne Part of Easterne Island	41	
Edenborough	203, 319	
Edenburgh	35	
Edgerton		
Charles	268	
Edin Kelly	373	
Edinborough	72, 259	
Edinkelley	204, 321	
Edinkelly	261	

Edmondson			Joseph		96, 168, 169, 284, 285, 337, 338, 375
	Polard	372		Rebeccah	168
Edmondsons Green Close		109, 118, 160, 213, 290, 329, 343		Sufia	140
				Tabitha	169
Edmonsons Freshes		61		William	3, 15, 49, 64, 80, 81, 126, 138, 168, 169, 207, 222, 269, 270, 284, 323
Edmonsons Green Close		174, 276			
Edmundson					
	James	38			
Edmundsons Green Close		11, 54, 228	Elliotts Addition		15, 126, 127, 154, 184, 207, 240, 270, 301, 323, 354
Edmundson's Green Close		89			
Edwards					
	George	36, 96, 118, 169, 223, 285	Elliotts Choice		3, 81, 138, 168, 222, 284, 337
	William	14, 45, 53	Elliotts Luck		169, 223, 285, 338
Edwards Chance		36, 118	Ellis		
Edwards's Chance		169, 223, 285		Benjamin	36, 84
Egerton			Ellors		
	Charles	71		(N)	144, 169
	John	71		Henry	144, 169
Elbert			Ellstone		
	Frances	96, 149		Roger	96, 142
	Henry	203, 259, 319, 338	Elsbury		324
	widow	74		Thomas	36
	William	6, 14, 20, 27, 38, 76, 108, 167, 221, 268, 284, 337	Elson		
				Sarah	338
Elina			Elston		
	Andrew	66		Roger	169, 285
Elisbury		156, 272		Sarah	169, 223, 285
Elizabeth Portion		181, 350	Emerson		
Elizabeths Portion		236, 298		John	37, 60, 61, 116, 168, 221, 284, 337
Elk Point		84		Phil.	103
Ellers				Philip	96, 149
	Henry	96		Phill.	7
Elliot			Emory		
	Joseph	139		(N)	52, 84, 168, 169, 222, 223, 284, 285, 338
Elliott		30, 64			
	(N)	23, 52		Arther	107, 114
	Benjamin	40, 46, 96		Arthor	336, 338
	Edward	59		Arthur	7, 42, 43, 96, 103, 167, 169, 221, 223, 283, 285
	George	15, 24, 59, 96, 126, 169, 207, 223, 270, 285, 323, 338			
				Gideon	222, 285, 338
	Henry	338, 375		Gidion	169
	Jo.	223		James	169, 223, 285, 338
	John	15, 46, 96, 138, 140, 163, 168, 217, 222, 280, 284, 337, 338		John	7, 12, 34, 42, 55, 57, 91, 96, 103, 107, 108, 167, 169, 221, 223, 283, 285, 337, 338
	Jos.	34, 46, 222, 364			

Page 401

Sarah	167, 221, 283, 337	
Thomas	168, 169, 222, 223, 285, 338	
William	12, 34, 96, 104, 109, 148	

Emory Chance 283
Emory Paxton 84, 168, 222, 236, 285, 338
Emory Rich Land 346
Emorys Addition 42
Emorys Chance 57, 108, 221, 337
Emorys Fortune 47
Emorys Fortune Addition 47, 134, 146, 168, 222, 284, 338
Emorys Neglect 42, 107
Emorys Part of Trustram 223, 338
Emorys Paxton 41
Emorys Resurvey 167, 221, 283, 337
Emorys Rich Land 52, 55, 124, 176, 231, 293, 346
Emory's Addition 107
Emory's Chance 91, 167
Emory's Fortune 84, 221
Emory's Rich Land 91, 125, 232
Endeavour 175
Endsworth
    Benjamin 96, 121, 221, 284, 337
Enewell 172
Enjoyment 13, 21, 49, 72, 145, 195, 197, 251, 263, 311, 312, 314, 365
Enjoyment & Mount Pleasant 84
Ephraims Hope 148, 179, 234, 236, 295, 348
Epsom 27, 74
Erickson
    John 65
    Mathew 3
Errecksons Island 2
Errickson
    Charles 3, 139, 168, 222, 284, 338
    Elizabeth 168, 222, 284, 337
    John 3, 55, 96, 139, 168, 222, 284, 337
    Mathew 3
Erricksons Island 139, 198, 257, 314, 370
Errickson's Island 137

Esgate
    Caleb 23, 52, 59, 96
    Dorothy 52
Eubanks
    William 85
Evans
    James 3, 67, 96, 137
    John 2, 42, 47, 96, 127, 138, 177, 232, 293, 294, 346
    Jonathan 223
Everard
    Lawrence 81
Everett
    Jo. 223
    Joseph 285, 338
    Law. 222, 223
    Lawrance 284, 338
    Lawrence 35, 96, 141, 338
Everetts Content 223, 284, 338
Everitt
    Joseph 169
    Lawrence 168
Everitts Content 168
Evett
    Nathaniel 64, 67
Ewbancks
    John 337
Ewbanks
    widow 284
    William 96, 122, 168, 221, 284
Exchange 17, 56, 57, 126, 151, 194, 205, 250, 262, 310, 321, 363, 374
Expectation 31, 78, 265
Fair Play 6, 20, 44, 84, 219, 253, 335
Fairfield 261
Fairn Ridge Addition 187, 243, 304
Fairplay 107, 141, 165, 281
Falconar
    Abraham 72, 203, 259, 319
    B. F. 96
    Benjamin 96
    Burton F. 223
    Burton Fra. 338
    Burton Francis 169
    Gilbert 35
    John 96, 169, 197, 223, 224,

		338, 339
Falconars Chance		224, 339
Falconars Hope		224, 226, 341
Falconars Lott		155, 208, 271, 323
Falconer		
	Benjamin	121
	Burton Francis	116, 285
	John	116, 285, 286
Falconers Chance		286
Falconers Hope		286
Falconer's Lott		121
Fanceys Addition		368
Fancys Addition		199, 255, 316
Farell		
	William	356
Farrington		24, 84, 128, 182, 237, 299, 351
Faulkner		
	Benjamin	34
	John	53
Faulkners Lott		34
Faulkonar		
	Burton Fr.	53
	Burton Fra	53
Feddeman		
	Elizabeth	27, 60
	Henry	97, 169
	Phill.	27, 60
Fedeman Purchase		60
Fedemon Hill		60
Feney		
	John	66
Fentry		90, 117
Fern Ridge		119, 187, 243, 304, 357
Fern Ridge Addition		357
Ferne Ridge		48
Ferrell		
	William	186, 242, 303
Ferress		
	Charles	264
Ferrill		
	William	12
Ferris		
	Charles	28, 78
Fiddeman		
	Henry	146, 223, 285, 339
Field		
	Samuel	97
Fieldin		
	John	45
Fields		
	Samuel	150
Findley		
	Andrew	50
	James	339, 356
Finley		
	Andrew	96, 134, 169
	James	170, 223, 224, 285, 286
	Robert	47, 80, 82
Finney		
	Rachell	37
	William	37
Firth		
	William	96, 131, 268
Fishburne		
	Ralph	30
	William	30
Fisher		
	(N)	353
	Flower	97, 145
	Go.	18
	James	170, 224, 286, 339
	John	18, 170, 224, 286, 339
	Joseph	55, 87
	Ladia	286
	Lidia	224
	Richard	48, 76, 170, 224, 265, 286, 339
	Thomas	18, 28, 76, 116, 118, 170, 224, 265, 286, 339
	William	169, 223, 224, 285, 286, 339
Fishers Chance		55, 120, 226, 234
Fishers Meadows		170, 224, 286, 339
Fishers Plains		170, 224, 286, 339
Fishingham		49, 50, 112, 114, 165, 166, 219, 282, 335
Fishingham Addition		114, 166, 282, 335
Fishinghams Addition		219
Fitzhugh		
	William	203, 260, 319, 372
Fleming		
	Thomas	320, 372
Flemming		
	Thomas	260
Fling		
	Michael	43, 78, 267

Floyd			Forrest Lodge Resurveyed		7
	(N)	151	Forrest of Plains		364
	Robert	46	Forrest of Sherwood	24, 135, 189, 245, 306, 360	
Follingham		126			
Fool Play		84, 253	Forrest of Windsor	180, 235, 297, 349	
Foome			Forrest of Winsor		331
	Peter	127	Forrest Plains	144, 195, 251, 311	
For Difficulty		313	Forrests Plains		12
For Revival		303	Fortune	21, 84, 107, 169, 222, 264, 285, 338	
Forbes					
	Alexander	4	Fosetts Plains		304
Ford			Fossets Plains		334
	Isaac	119, 169, 223, 285, 339	Fossetts Plains	109, 187, 243, 344	
	Jacob	53	Fosters Folley		81, 360
	Thomas	23, 223, 285, 339	Fosters Folly	36, 56, 146, 192, 246, 306	
	William	49, 96, 132, 169			
	Winnefred	132, 169	Foster's Folly		69
Fords Chance		199, 255, 315, 368	Fotterell		
Fords Folley		175		Edward	51
Fords Folleys		119	Foul Play		33
Fords Folly		23, 230, 292	Fouracres		
Fords Park		23, 119, 230, 292, 345		John	97, 146, 169, 223, 286
Fords Parks		175	Fowler		
Foreacres				John	22
	John	339		Robert	96, 128
Forelorne Hope		109	Fox Harbour	24, 45, 81, 133, 142, 144, 159, 180, 212, 235, 275, 296, 328, 349	
Foreman					
	Fr.	49			
	Fra.	15, 49	Fox Hill	44, 61, 69, 125, 130, 154, 159, 196, 212, 252, 270, 275, 313, 323, 328, 366	
	Fran.	50, 223, 224			
	Francis	96, 129, 169, 285, 339			
	John	224, 339	France		36, 84
Fork		23, 52, 59, 60, 67, 133, 175, 230, 292, 344	France Rectified		370
			Franckford		21
Forkalet		357	Frankford		72, 267
Forkalett		180, 235, 297	Fray		
Forlone Hope		192, 196, 308, 329, 337, 361, 366		William	51
			Freeman		
Forlorne Hope		3, 8, 9, 42, 64, 67, 84, 85, 103, 106, 110, 138, 160, 168, 213, 222, 248, 252, 276, 284, 312		John	29
			Freemans Forest		61
			Freeman's Rest		147
			Fresford		43
			Fresh Run		32, 90, 152, 267
Forrest		40, 144, 145, 154, 163, 216, 258, 318, 371	Freshford	38, 43, 78, 81, 128, 149, 194, 250, 264, 311, 364	
	Patrick	64	Freshford Addition		81, 215
Forrest Lodge		7, 42, 63, 64, 103, 104, 107, 148	Freshfords Addition		30
			Friendship	1, 9, 36, 44, 81, 92, 107, 119, 130-132, 134,	
Forrest Lodge on Resurvey		57			

		164, 177-180, 188-190, 217, 232-235, 244-246, 280, 294-297, 305, 307, 333, 347-349, 358-360
Friendship Resurveyed		139, 167, 220, 283, 336
Frisby		
	Elizabeth	87
	P.	72
	Pere	264
	Peregrine	152
Froen		
	Peter	43
Froom		
	Peter	96, 269
Froon		
	Peter	29
Gadd		
	Thomas	27, 82, 268
Gafford		
	Charles	97, 134, 170, 224, 225, 286, 287, 340
	John	225, 287, 340
	Richard	170, 224, 286, 340
Gale		
	George	27, 53, 66, 87, 97, 152, 266
	John	53, 66, 87, 152, 266
Gall		
	Jan	10
	Thomas	10
Garden of Roses		19, 121, 148, 156, 158, 161, 209, 211, 215, 231, 274, 277, 293, 326, 330, 345
Garon		
	Peter	203, 320
Garoon		
	(N)	372
	Peter	372
Garratt		
	Edward	339
Garrett		
	Edward	97, 122, 170, 224, 286
Garron		
	(N)	260
	Peter	260

Gasha		
	Giles	68
Gawell		
	Seth	18
George		
	Jos.	52
	Joshua	87
George Whitehead & Co.		40, 59, 70, 263
Georges Codd		4, 138, 180, 236, 297, 350
Georges Hazard		141, 157, 210, 273, 326
Gersuches Tryangle		372
Gibb		
	John	97, 135
Gibbs		
	Bess	171, 287
	Boatswain Thomas	287
	Boatswain Tom	171, 225
	Hannah	171, 287
	John	22, 25
Gibson		
	John	66
Gilaspy		
	Terrence	10
Gilbert		
	Anne	171, 225, 287, 340
	John	82, 225
Gilford		342, 370
Gillespy		
	Terr.	44
Gills		
	Henry	27
Gilpin		
	Robert	153
	Thomas	340
Ginn		
	James	225, 287, 291, 340
Glanding		
	Solomon	340
Glandings Begining		340
Glinn		
	Nicholas	97, 124
Glocester		28, 72, 74, 81, 128, 193, 267, 310
Glochester		363
Gloscoster		249
Gloster		13, 43
Glover		

	(N)	32	George	19
	Daniel	26, 32, 86, 268	William	19, 81
Goddard			Good Encrease	57
	Thomas	86	Good Hap	239
Goddin			Good Happ	354
	Thomas	17	Good Hope	32
Godferys Folley		327	Good Increase	12, 68, 122, 127, 172, 227, 289, 347, 357
Godferys Folly		146		
Godfreys Folly		51, 52, 158, 274	Good Luck	25, 60, 145, 195, 251, 311, 364
Godfrey's Folly		211		
Godhand			Good Luck Range	39, 114, 191, 243, 304
	Marmaduke	136		
Godman			Good Will	208, 324
	Thomas	3	Goodhand	
Godwin				Christopher	2
	Edward	55, 61, 89, 97, 170, 224, 286		Mar.	275
				Marmaduke	2, 97, 170, 224, 286, 340
	Edwin	5, 42			
	Mary	339	Goodhap	30, 183, 300
	Thomas	97, 127	Goodhope	118
	William	97, 125, 170, 224, 286, 339	Goodman	
				Richard	142
Godwyn			Goodmans Purchase	142
	Edward	17	Goodridge Choice	153
	Thomas	17	Goodwill	53, 119, 155, 271
	William	17	Goodwin	
Gold				Ed.	45
	William	19, 53		Edward	122
Gold Hawks Enlargement		140, 343	Goos Hill	334
Golden Grove		81, 88, 134, 168, 222, 264, 285, 338	Goose Hill	164, 196, 217, 218, 280, 281, 333
Golden Groves		47	Goose Neck	139
Golden Lion		271	Goose Quarter	8, 64
Golden Lyon		45, 116, 117, 155, 205, 208, 238, 324, 352	Gore	5, 88, 106, 154, 207, 270, 323
			Gorsuch Triangle	50
Golden Ridge		157, 210, 273, 326	Gorsuches Tryangle	259, 319
Golden Road Ridge		357	Gorsuch's Triangle	74
Golden Rod Ridge		55, 120, 187, 243, 304	Gould	
				Benjamin	131, 171, 225, 287, 340
Goldhawks Enlargement		105, 109			
Golds Hawk Enlargement		328		Fran.	225
Goldsborough				Frances	51, 97, 170, 287, 340
	Nicholas	45, 97, 149, 260		Francis	38, 131
	Robert	81, 97, 150, 260		James	8, 21, 66, 147, 171, 225, 287, 340
	William	260			
Goldsbrough				Richard	97, 131, 170, 224, 286, 340
	Nicholas	372			
	Robert	372	Gould Hawk	
	William	372		George	88
Golt			Gould Hawks Enlargement	173, 200,

		228, 256, 316
Gould Hawk's Enlargement		88
Gouldhawks Enlargement		40
Goulds Purchase		21, 38, 131, 147, 171, 225, 287, 340
Gouldsborough		
	Nicholas	203, 320
	Robert	28, 37, 203, 320
	William	203, 320
Gould's Purchase		66
Grace		
	Thomas	52, 74, 202, 258, 318
Grafton		
	Richard	14, 97, 153
Grafton Mannor		60
Grainger		
	John	40
Granger		
	Christopher	2, 3, 76, 97, 139, 266
	John	40, 97, 148, 151, 171, 260, 320, 372
Grantham		14, 27, 38, 74
Grassingham		
	Jeremiah	372
Graves		
	Mat.	97
	Mathew	340
	Matthew	143, 171, 225, 287
Graves's Begining		340
Graves's Beginning		143, 171, 225, 287
Grays Inn		26, 33, 45, 107, 110, 192, 200, 256, 308, 317, 361, 369
Grays Inns		316
Gray's Inn		248, 369
Great Neck		69, 137, 138, 157, 210, 273, 325
Green		
	Ann	15
	Elizabeth	152
	Hannah	146, 313, 366
	Henry	14, 15
	John	12, 63, 64, 112, 170, 224, 286, 339
	Mary	152
	Michael	97, 114, 127, 170, 224, 286, 339
	Philemon	146, 171, 225, 287
	Phillemon	340

	Rebecca	152
	Robert	32, 134, 141, 146, 152, 252, 313, 366
	William	127, 148, 171, 225, 287, 340
Green Hill		90, 117, 171, 226, 288, 341
Green Spring		12, 104, 148, 171, 181, 225, 237, 288, 298, 342, 351
Greene		
	Philemon	97
	Robert	32
Greenfield		
	Archebald	127
	Archibald	97
Greenhood		
	William	114
Greens Adventure		13
Greens Adventure Upon Carpenter Square		12, 13
Greens Adventure Upon Carpenters Square		224, 339
Greens Adventure Upon Carpenters Square Resurveyed		112, 170, 286
Greens Fortune		146, 171, 225, 287, 340
Greens Fortune Addition		146, 171, 225, 287, 340
Greenwood		
	Bartholomew	60
	John	43
	Jonathan	19, 97
	William	5, 97, 108, 170, 224, 286, 339
Green's Adventure		64
Green's Adventure Upon Carpenter's Square		63, 64
Gregory		
	(N)	52
	John	52
	William	97, 112, 170, 268
Gresham		
	John	38, 72, 203, 260
Gresingham		
	Jeremiah	203, 320
Gressingham		
	Jer.	151
	Jeremiah	97
Grevely Hoe		176
Grey		

	John	68		John	1
Griffen			Gunners Harbour		26, 108, 171, 225, 287, 340
	Mathew	62			
Griffens Adventure		62	Gutteridge		
Griffin				John	113
	Benjamin	97	Gwider		
	Matthew	89		Thomas	71
Griffin's Adventure		89	Gwider's Range		71
Griffith			Gwin		
	Benjamin	41, 114, 170, 247, 308, 361		Elizabeth	340
	John	140, 157, 210, 273, 326		John	171, 225, 340
			Gwinn		
	Mathew	4, 41, 339		Elizabeth	171, 225, 287
	Matthew	97, 114, 170, 224, 268, 286		John	26, 97, 108, 287
				Robert	97, 144
	Samuel	4	Gwinns Hazard		144, 190, 246, 307
Griffiths Adventure		138, 268	Gwyders Lott		31
Griffiths Purchase		142	Gwyders Range		31
Grimes			Gwyn		
	Jeremiah	97, 140		John	26
Grimes's Folly		115, 161, 277, 330	Gwyther		
Grime's Folly		214		Thomas	267
Grisingham			Gwythers Lott		267
	Jere	260	Gwythers Range		267
Groom					
	Samuel	27, 66	Hacker		
Grose Hill		164		John	76, 81
Grouches Tryangle		202	Hackers Adventure		44, 122, 184, 208, 223, 271, 285, 324, 338
Grove		203, 259, 319			
Grovely Hoe		18, 118, 231			
Grovley Hoe		346	Hackers Forrest		127
Grovly Hoe		293	Hackers Meadow		277
Grubby Neck		48, 62, 120, 132, 191, 194, 247, 250, 308, 311, 361, 364	Hackers Meadows		7, 128, 161, 188, 215, 304, 331, 358
			Hackers Meadows's		243
Grundy			Hacker's Forrest		81
	(N)	76	Hacker's Meadows		76
	Robert	14, 263	Hacket		
Gudeon				Michael	64
	Stephen	340	Hackett		
Guider's Lott		71		James	342
Guildford Addition		45		John	21, 97, 128, 172, 227, 289
Guilford		17, 35, 44, 81, 124, 171, 199-201, 225, 254, 256, 257, 264, 287, 315-317, 368-370		Mary	172, 227, 289
				Michael	30, 72, 84
				Nicholas	91
Guilford Addition		124, 201, 257, 317, 370		Thomas	21, 97, 128, 172, 227, 289, 342
				William	23, 81, 85, 88
Guilfords		111	Hackett Garden		19
Guin					

Hacketts Chance	30	Halls Fortune	121
Hacketts Delight	32, 128, 129, 179, 234, 296, 348	Halls Harbour	51, 53, 151, 205, 262, 321, 340, 374

Hacketts Garden 27, 50, 74, 118, 146, 169, 223, 264, 285, 286, 339
Hacketts Lott 23
Hackett's Chance 84
Hackett's Delight 81
Hackett's Lott 85
Hackney Marsh 64
Hackton 91, 118, 150, 165, 181, 207, 217, 237
Hacton 19, 42, 154, 270, 279, 298, 332, 351
Hadaway
    Thomas 337
Haddaway
    George 46
    Thomas 47, 74, 265
Hadden 18, 28, 121, 158, 274
Haddin 156
    William 61
Hadding 18, 28
Haddon 209, 211, 272, 325, 326
Hadley
    (N) 179
    John 9, 92, 134, 173, 227, 289, 342
Haldey
    John 97
Hale
    Thomas 65
Hale's Neck 65
Hall
    Andrew 173, 228, 290, 343
    Edward 112, 171, 225, 287, 341
    Elinor 112
    Ellinor 171, 225, 287
    John 112, 171, 224, 226, 288, 340
    Lawrence 90, 96, 112, 269
    William 269
Hallaway
    John 152
Hallings
    Thomas 67
Hallow Hatt 113
Halls Discovery 158, 211, 274, 327

Hambleton
    James 97, 127
    John 172, 227, 289, 341
    John Hawkins 97, 130
Hambletons Addition 172, 227, 289, 342
Hambletons Hermetage 173
Hambletons Hermitage 106, 129, 130, 132, 156, 159, 160, 209, 212, 213, 227, 272, 274, 276, 289, 327, 329, 342
Hambletons Luck 227, 289, 342
Hambletons Range 172, 227, 289, 341
Hamer
    John 69, 76, 97, 131, 135, 269
    Thomas 173, 228, 290, 343
    William 97, 122
Hamers Addition 129, 235, 296, 349
Hamers Chance 228, 290, 343
Hamers Choice 173
Hamers Lott 269
Hamer's Addition 90
Hamer's Choice 76
Hamer's Lott 69, 76, 135
Hamesleys Discovery 20
Hamilton
    (N) 260, 373
    Hance 52
    John 30, 33
    John Hawkins 24
    Patrick 203, 260, 320, 373
    William 16
Hamiltons Hermitage 7, 20, 21
Hamiltons Range 30, 127
Hammer
    John 59
Hammers Addition 50
Hammers Lott 59
Hammilton
    John 127
Hammond
    James 173, 229, 291, 343
    John 12, 109, 187, 243, 304
    Katharine 14
    Katherine 97

	Mordicai	26
	Thomas	26, 29, 97, 107
	William	344
Hamond		
	Thomas	45
Hamour		
	John	15
Hamours Choice		15
Hamours Lott		15
Hampton		60
Hamton		115, 120
Hannonton		162, 278
Hap Hazard		42, 43, 167, 221
Hap Hazard Addition		221
Haphazard		114, 167, 283
Haphazard Addition		114, 167, 283
Happ Hazard		336, 337
Happ Hazard Addition		336
Hardcastle		
	Robert	44, 96, 115, 172, 226, 288, 341
Harden		
	Edward	372
Hardest Fend Off		20, 229
Hardest Fendoff		174, 290
Hardest Find Off		343
Hardestfindoff		113
Harding		
	Edward	97, 149, 203, 260, 320
	Robert	26
Hargadine		
	Mark	228, 290, 343
Harmans Lott		24
Harmions Lott		215
Harmons Lott		331
Harmonton		32, 64, 215, 331
Harmon's Lott		64
Harrington		
	(N)	82, 146, 173, 227, 289
	Anthony	146, 173, 227, 289
	David	23, 51, 96, 119, 172, 226, 341
	George	97, 146, 173, 227, 289
	John	29, 82, 267
	Nathan	173, 228, 290, 344
	Nathaniel	173, 228, 290
	Richard	51, 97, 120, 172, 226, 288, 341
	Sedney	228
	Signey	290
	William	52, 97, 120, 172, 226, 288
Harringtons Desire		119, 172, 226, 288, 341
Harringtons Venture		146, 173, 227, 289
Harris		
	Edward	7
	Isaac	40, 97
	James	44, 227, 289, 341
	John	22, 24, 97, 173, 227, 289, 342
	Jos.	227
	Joseph	22, 97, 125, 288, 341
	Mary	105
	Rebecca	289
	Susanna	44, 97
	Thomas	91, 98, 108, 229, 263, 291, 343
	William	22, 97
	Workman	40
Harrison		
	William	89
Harriss		
	James	125, 172
	John	131
	Joseph	172
	Rebecca	172
	Thomas	174
Harrisson		
	William	266
Harris's Hazard		344
Harris's Range		61
Hart		
	John	97, 143
Hartshorne		
	John	97, 135
Harvey		
	James	46, 173, 228, 343
Harveys Discovery		173, 228, 343
Harvy		
	James	140
Hawkins		
	(N)	52, 147, 174, 228, 290, 343
	Arnal	60
	Col.	7, 12
	Earnult	341

Elizabeth	81, 93, 97, 104	Hazell Point	328
Ern.	147	Hazle Ridge	191, 247, 307
Ernault	11, 37, 57, 81, 97, 123, 174, 226, 288	Head	
		Thomas	17
John	11, 15, 61, 81, 84, 93, 97, 122, 147, 157, 210, 265, 273	Hearys Discovery	115
		Heath	
		James	15, 29, 203, 264, 265
Major	21	James Paul	29, 30, 87, 88
Mathew	343	Heaths Discovery	29, 113, 153, 160, 213, 276, 329
Matthew	173, 228, 290		
Mrs.	81, 82, 103	Heaths Forrest	29, 46, 126, 235, 265, 349
Robert	173, 174, 228, 290, 343		
		Heaths Gift	126, 180, 235, 296, 349
Hawkins Farm Resurveyed	148, 182, 237, 241	Heaths Parcell	30
		Heathworth	43, 88, 127, 168, 222, 284, 337
Hawkins Farme	12		
Hawkins Farme Resurveyed	104, 143	Heath's Forrest	87
Hawkins Pharsalia	5, 11, 42, 117, 122-125, 127, 128, 143, 155, 161	Heath's Gift	90
		Heath's Parcells	87
		Hemsley	42, 107
Hawkins Range	11, 128	(N)	81, 82, 177
Hawkins's Farm	81, 220, 282	Anna Maria	174, 229, 290, 343
Hawkins's Farm Resurveyed	112, 185, 199, 200, 254, 256, 257		
		Elizabeth	82
		Mary	174, 229, 290, 343
Hawkins's Farme	93, 166, 299, 351	Phil.	232, 294
Hawkins's Farme Resurveyed	112, 142, 181, 201, 238, 298, 299, 302, 315-317, 352, 355, 368-370	Philemon	65, 113
		Phill.	177, 346
		William	20, 64, 65, 68, 74, 81, 82, 86, 114, 177, 232, 294, 347
Hawkins's Pharsalia	81, 109, 177, 180, 182, 183, 187, 194, 208, 215, 233, 235, 237, 238, 243, 250, 271, 277, 294, 297, 299, 304, 311, 330, 347, 349, 351, 352, 358, 364		
		Hemsley Arcadia	166
		Hemsley Britland Rectified	33
		Hemsleys Adventure	20, 113, 177, 232, 294, 346
		Hemsleys Arcadia	60, 74, 115, 165, 166, 203, 260, 279, 282, 320, 333, 335, 336, 372
Hawkins's Range	191, 247, 307, 361		
Hays		Hemsleys Arcadia Moore	115
John	24, 97, 133	Hemsleys Britland	25, 33, 135, 145, 197, 254
Haysel Point	275		
Haysell Point	212	Hemsleys Britland Rectified	56, 110, 191, 197, 204, 247, 253, 261, 308, 313, 321, 361, 366, 373
Haysil Point	159		
Hazard	35, 47, 48, 84, 107, 120, 123, 155, 180, 200, 213, 256, 267, 275, 297, 317, 328, 350, 369		
		Hemsleys Britland Resurveyed	301
		Hemsleys Brittland	24
William	48	Hemsleys Brittland Rectified	109
Hazel Ridge	360	Hemsleys Discovery	113, 174, 290, 343

Hemsleys Dispute		247	John	173, 290
Hemsleys Park	20, 113, 177, 294, 346		Higgs	
Hemsleys Plains		163	Aron	151
Hemsleys Reserve Rectified		11	High Gale	15, 219, 335
Hemsleys Reserve Rectified on Resurvey			High Gate Lane	17, 64, 365
		204, 261, 320	Highgate	107, 165, 281
Hemsleys Resurvey Rectified on			Highgate Lane	103, 122, 195, 251, 312
	Resurvey	373	Hill	
Hemsley's Britland		65	James	48
Hemsley's Britland Rectified		65	John	90, 96, 117, 171, 226,
Hemsley's Discovery		229		288, 341
Hemsley's Park		232	Robert	31
Hemsley's Reserve		65	William	84
Hemsley's Reserve Rectified		65	Hillary	371
Hemsly			Hillary Addition	371
	William	67	Hilleray	143
Hemslys Arcadia		219	Hills Addition	27, 267
Hemsly's Arcadia		217	Hills Cabbin	1, 41
Hemsly's Choice		64	Hills Out Lett	18
Hemsly's Plains		217	Hills Outlett	116
Heneslys Plains		51	Hills Outlett Resurveyed	163, 217, 280
Henfield	25, 42, 85, 144, 145, 195, 251,		Hills Outlett Resurvey'd	333
		311	Hill's Addition	78
Henry			Hill's Cabbin	92
	Thomas	25	Hill's Lott	84
Henrys Lott	159, 172, 212, 226, 275,		Hindman	
		288, 328, 341	Jacob	98, 151
Hensleys Plains		184	Hinds	
Hermonton		133	Mary	21
Herrington			Thomas	21
	(N)	342	Hindsleys Plains	122-124
	Anthony	342	Hindsly	
	David	287, 288	Thomas	91
	Nathaniel	343	Hines	
	William	341	Ann	97, 143
Herringtons Venture		347	Benjamin	122, 127
Hiccory Ridge		121	Charles	97, 143, 227, 289,
Hickory Ridge	89, 187, 243, 304, 366			342
Hicks			James	97
	Giles	81, 174, 342, 343	Thomas	143, 227, 289, 342
	James	13, 174, 343	Hinesley	
	John	13	Thomas	268
Hide			Hinesleys Addition	268
	Samuel	372	Hinesleys Choice	186, 303
Higgens			Hinesleys Fancy	119
	(N)	352	Hinesleys Plain	128
	John	96, 111, 171, 225, 228,	Hinesleys Plains	161, 176, 187, 215,
		287, 352		280, 304, 354
Higgins			Hinesly	
	Christopher	340	Nathaniel	97, 125

Peter	97, 125	Hoggpen Ridge	280
Thomas	68, 76	Hoggs Harbour	112
Hinesly Fancy	208	Hoggs Hole	5, 10, 12, 154, 204, 207, 260, 270, 320, 373
Hineslys Addition	76		
Hineslys Choice	125, 242	Holden	
Hineslys Plains	106, 125, 240, 243	John	343
Hinesly's Plains	91, 217	Holding	
Hinesly's Reserve	68	John	173, 228, 290
Hinfield	269, 365	William	97, 144
Hinsleys Choice	356	Hole Haven	60
Hinsleys Fancy	155, 271	Holley Neck Resurveyed	330
Hinsleys Plains	278, 279, 301, 331, 333, 358	Holliday	
		Henry	343
Hint on Sudlar	359	James	341, 342
His Lordships Mannor	39	Sarah	341
His Lordships Manour	86	Hollingsworth	
Hitt or Miss	16, 31, 43, 93, 120, 234	(N)	336
Hitt or Miss Resurveyed	146	Isaac	336
Hix		John	17, 56, 81, 97, 132, 227, 289, 342
Giles	81, 143, 174, 227, 228, 289, 290		
		Sarah	133, 227, 289
James	96, 118, 228, 290	Thomas	7, 63, 64, 103
Roger	42	William	59, 80, 268
Hobbs		Hollingworth	
James	49, 97, 119	Thomas	57
Jo.	36	William	8
Hobbs Venture	49, 158, 211, 274, 327	Hollinsworth	
Hobbs's Venture	119	John	17, 21, 172, 173
Hocken		Sarah	173
John	2	William	8
Hodden	148	Hollow Flatt	193, 249, 309, 362
Hog Harbour	17	Holloway	
Hog Pen Neck, Goose Hill, Mattapax Neck, & Ridge	48	John	267
		Holly Neck	56, 92
Hogg Harbour	57, 90, 124, 151, 155, 171, 201, 208, 225, 226, 257, 269, 271, 287, 288, 317, 324, 341, 370	Holly Neck Resurveyed	92, 119, 161, 214, 277
		Hollyday	
		George	36, 69
		Henry	229, 290
		James	50, 66, 126, 147, 172, 173, 227, 228, 289
Hogg Hole	40, 49, 106, 113, 145, 163, 174, 216, 229, 279, 291, 323, 332, 344		
		Samuel	38
		Sarah	172, 227, 289
Hogg Pen Neck	25, 40, 64-66, 93, 163, 164, 196, 216-218, 279, 280	Holme Hill	153
		Holt	92, 122, 195, 251, 312, 365
		Arther	122
Hogg Pen Neck & Goose Hill	64	Arthur	17, 30, 62, 64, 92, 93, 97, 195, 251, 312, 365
Hogg Pen Ridge	164, 218		
Hogg Penn Neck	145, 332-334		
Hogg Penn Ridge	333		
Hoggpen Neck	139, 280, 281	Edward	32

Holts Castle Hill		62, 64, 93
Holts Castle Hill Resurveyed		122, 195, 251, 312, 365
Holt's Castle Hill Resurveyed		93
Hommond		
	Katherine	149
Honey		
	Thomas	97, 124, 172, 226, 288, 341
	Val. Tho.	226
	Valentine	288
	Valentine Thomas	172
	Volentine	125
	Volentine Thomas	341
Hoopers Ensel		61
Hoopers Ensul		147
Hope		26, 32, 61, 86, 127, 136, 185, 207, 241, 254, 255, 268, 270, 302, 316, 323, 345, 367, 368
Hope Resurveyed		158, 314
Hope Well		341, 344
Hopewell		23, 51, 52, 65, 119, 135, 172, 175, 226, 230, 288, 292
	Richard	37, 71, 266
Hopkins		
	Dennis	28
	Thomas	30
Hopper		
	(N)	329
	William	8, 14, 34, 82, 96, 111, 112, 128, 171, 173, 225, 228, 287, 289, 342
Hoppers Industry		171, 225, 288, 342
Horn		
	William	174
Horne		
	William	228, 290, 343
Horney		
	Jeffry	54, 59
	Thomas	44
Horse Pasture		44, 64, 118, 175, 230, 231, 291-293, 345, 346
Horse Pen Ridge		233
Horse Penn Ridge		347
Horse Penridge		294
Horseley		
	James	44
Horsependridge		177
Horsley		
	James	97, 133
Hoxton		323
Hudson		
	Isaac	41, 137, 194, 250, 311
	James	364
Huet		
	Robert	63
Hughes		
	John	31
Hughlett		
	Thomas	71, 173, 228, 290, 343
	William	71, 173, 228, 290, 291, 343
Hunns Hazard		222
Hunter		
	Ezekiall	341
	Ezekiel	226, 288
	James	35, 52
	Joseph	96, 119, 172
	Mary	226, 288, 341
	Samuel	35, 81, 137
	William	173, 228, 290, 343
Hunters Chance		52, 119, 158, 211, 274, 327
Hunters Forrest		35, 168, 222, 284, 338
Hunters Hazard		119, 172, 226, 288, 341
Hunters Hope		52, 119, 155, 208, 271, 324
Hunter's Forest		141
Hunter's Forrest		81
Hunting Field		60
Hunting Tower		191, 246, 307, 360
Hunting Town		119
Huntley		159, 274, 327
Huntly		212
Hurlock		
	James	29, 75, 268
Husbands		
	Richard	84
Hussey		
	(N)	271
	Michael	42
Hussy		
	(N)	127, 208
	Michael	51

Hutchings
    James   76, 227
    Thomas   227
Hutchins
    James   2, 32, 57, 68, 85, 97, 139, 173, 289, 342
    Thomas   173, 289, 342
Hyde
    Samuel   38, 70, 153, 260
    Samuell   203, 320
Hyndman
    Jacob   26
Hyndsleys Plains   33
Hyndson
    Richard   12
Hynes
    Charles   173
    Thomas   173
Hynesby
    Thomas   39
Hynesleys Fancy   47
Hynesly
    Charles   51
    Nathaniel   51
    Peter   39
Hynesly Plains   51
Hyneslys Plains   51
Hynsley Choice   39
Hynsley Plain   43
Hynsleys Fancey   324
Hynsleys Plains   42
Hynsleys Reserve   39
Hynson
    (N)   105, 165, 219, 281, 334
    John   84, 86
    Nathaniel   66
    Richard   6, 84, 97, 124, 172, 226, 288, 341
    Thomas   65, 67, 68
Hynson New Haven   84
Hynson Town   65
Hynson Town Addition   10
Hynson Towne   33
Hynsons Hill   11
Hynsons Lott   166, 220, 283, 336
Hynsons Towne   8
Hynson's Hill   68
Hyson Town Addition   111

Ilive

    Isaac   64
Imbert
    Andrew   5, 65, 66
Impey
    (N)   29
Inch
    John Davis   80
Incklingborough   15
Inclosure   18, 61, 79, 114, 154, 174, 207, 229, 264, 270, 291, 323, 345
Indian Oldfield   190, 246, 306, 360
Indian Spring   2, 140, 162, 216, 278, 331
Indian Tract   55, 122, 187, 243, 304, 357
Ingrains Desire   147
Ingrams Desire   212, 275, 290, 328, 344
Ingram's Desire   228
Inhabitants of Queen Anne's County   176, 345
Inhabitants of Queen Anns County   293
Inhabitants of Queen Ann's County   231
Injoyment   133
Inkersal   111
Inkersel   65
Inkersell   5, 14, 194, 250, 310, 363
Irish Discovery   37, 71, 266
Isaac Addition   2, 200
Isaac Chance   2, 45
Isaacs Addition   256, 317
Isaacs Chance   225, 287
Isaac's Addition   139, 369
Isaac's Chance   34, 81, 146, 171, 340
Isgate
    Caleb   133
    Dorothy   175, 230, 292, 344
Ivey
    (N)   263
    Anthony   13
    Robert Smith   13
Ivy
    Anthony   64
    Robert   73
    Robert Smith   72
Jackerman
    John   198
Jackman
    Ann   146

Jacks Purchase	57, 141, 179, 235, 296, 349	Jadwins Folley		173, 343
Jackson		Jadwins Folly		228, 290
Archebald	120, 176, 293	Jadwins Hazard	55, 121, 178, 233, 295, 347
Archibald	48, 51, 98, 231, 345	Jadwins Project	175, 230, 292, 344
D.	72	Jadwin's Project	120
Fra.	231	Jaimaca Addition	111
Francis	5, 81, 109, 174, 176, 229, 291, 293, 344, 345	Jamaca	329, 336, 345
		Jamaca's Addition	336
		Jamacia	367
George	1, 5, 98, 109, 174, 229, 291, 344	Jamaica	6, 10, 107, 129, 166, 173, 176, 197, 220, 228, 231, 254, 282, 289, 292, 314
James	231, 345		
Jo.	231	Jamaica Addition	41, 166, 220, 282
John	18, 54, 84, 91, 93, 98, 146, 175, 231, 292, 345	James Camp	32
		James Choice	23, 189, 199, 305, 368
		James Lott	52, 242
Joseph	54, 176, 293, 345	James Park	327
Mary	98	James's Camp	76, 227
Obednego	231	James's Chance	316
Obednigo	345	James's Choice	132, 134, 255, 358
Richard	65	James's Lott	10, 65
Samuel	231, 293, 345	James's Park	158, 211, 274
Thomas	5, 31, 52, 81, 98, 110, 135, 174, 175, 191, 213, 229, 230, 275, 291, 292, 344	Janes Lott	127, 186, 303
		Jarman	
		Amos	345
		John	50, 345
William	62, 82	Robert	45, 49, 344
Jackson Boggs	315	Stephen	174, 344
Jacksons Boggs	5, 108, 199, 255, 368	William	12, 49
Jacksons Choice	5, 155, 191, 213, 270, 275, 323, 365	Jarmon	
		Anne	346
Jackson's Choice	65, 207	Jaspars Lott	5, 11
Jacob		Jaspers Lott	203, 231, 260, 293, 320, 326, 372
(N)	228		
Henry	228	Jasper's Lott	81, 176
Jacobs		Jasson Choice	106
(N)	83, 174, 290, 343	Jemmett	
Henry	26, 83, 98, 104, 174, 290, 343	Samuel	116
		Jenifer	
Jacsons Choice	110	Daniel	66, 78, 93
Jadwin		Jenkins Neck	5, 106
Jer	36	Jenkins's Neck	154, 207, 270, 323
Jere.	230	Jennett	
Jeremiah	36, 56, 60, 98, 120, 175, 292, 344	Samuel	19
		Jennys Begining	198
Mary	175, 230, 291, 346	Jennys Beginning	54, 59, 78, 254, 315
Robert	45, 49, 98, 116, 175, 230, 291, 346	Jerman	
		Amos	176, 230, 292

John	98, 114, 174, 229, 291	
Joseph	98, 114, 174	
Robert	113, 174, 229, 291	
Stephen	229, 291	
William	113, 339	
Jerusalem	9, 149, 150, 193, 203, 249, 310, 319, 363	
Jerusaley	259	
Joanes Park	22	
Joane's Hole	65	
Joans Placket	155	
Joans Plackett	252, 312, 339	
Joans Plackett Addition	27	
Joans's Park	370	
John & Rachaels Choice	133	
John & Rachell Choyce	43	
John & Rachells Choice	58, 241, 355	
John & Rachels Choice	185, 302	
John Forrest	31	
Johnes		
John	65	
Johns		
Aquilla	203, 260, 320	
Richard	37, 71	
Johns Forrest	204, 261, 321, 351	
Johns Fortune	142	
Johns Hole etc. Resurveyed	2	
Johns Hole Resurveyed	245	
Johns Meadows	34, 135, 143, 181, 236, 297, 298, 350	
Johnson		
Absolem	41	
Albert	41, 47, 98, 132, 266	
Fr.	47	
Gabriel	34, 72, 267	
Hans	344	
Henry	16, 21, 52, 55, 85	
John	23, 47, 64, 98, 134, 175, 230, 292, 344	
Peter	92	
Johnson Addition	229	
Johnson Lott	55, 222	
Johnsons Addition	55, 132, 174, 291, 344	
Johnsons Adventure	24, 131, 152, 190, 246, 307, 357	
Johnsons Lott	168, 284, 337	
Johnson's Adventure	85	
Johnson's Lott	65, 139	
John's Forrest	78, 153	

John's Hole	63, 65	
John's Meadows	236	
Joiner		
William	93, 98, 137, 140	
Jolley		
Anne	176	
Jonathan	141, 345	
Mary	345	
Jolly		
Jonathan	98, 175, 230, 292	
Jommett		
Samuel	19	
Jones		
Ed.	46	
Edward	2, 44, 46, 82, 98, 130, 175, 230, 266, 292, 344	
Handcock	116, 174, 229, 291	
Henry	44, 98, 116, 175, 229, 291, 345	
James	176, 231, 293, 345	
John	10, 13, 85, 267	
Jos.	89	
Mary	346	
Nehemiah	260	
Ner.	10	
Neriah	27, 46, 111	
Nerish	98	
Richard	10, 27, 39, 63, 64, 70, 86, 268	
Robert	67, 149, 205, 261, 321, 374	
Sarah	345	
Thomas	176, 231, 292, 345	
Wat.	6	
William	45, 98, 116, 175, 230, 291, 346	
William K.	230	
William Kenny	344	
William Kerby	175	
William Kirby	292	
Jones Addition	6, 10, 111	
Jones Delight	44	
Jones Fancy	51	
Jones Forrest	42, 46, 111	
Jones Fortune	6, 106	
Jones Hall	10, 111	
Jones Hole Resurveyed	139, 189, 306, 359	
Jones Lott	356	

Jones Park	16, 124	Edward	98, 146
Jones Plackett	10, 20, 111, 115	Thomas	44, 64, 98, 118
Jones Plackett Addition	10, 111	William	18, 64, 88, 98, 118
Jones Plott	4, 138	Jump Chance	175
Jones Tryangle	10	Jumpe	
Jones's	186, 242, 303, 356	Abraham	230, 291, 346
Jones's Addition	109, 193, 249, 309, 363	Isaac	230, 291, 346
		Peter	230, 291, 346
Jones's Armour	65	Solomon	175, 230, 292
Jones's Chance	175, 230, 291, 346	Thomas	175, 176, 231, 292, 293, 345
Jones's Delight	135, 162, 215, 278, 331		
Jones's Fancey	176, 345, 358	Vaughan	346
Jones's Fancy	129, 188, 231, 244, 293, 304	Vaughn	291
		Volentine	230
Jones's Forrest	150, 181, 225, 237, 287, 298, 340	Jumps Addition	18, 118, 175, 230, 292, 327
Jones's Fortune	181, 236, 297, 350	Jumps Chance	18, 44, 116, 118, 158, 162, 175, 187, 211, 216, 230, 243, 274, 278, 291, 292, 304, 327, 332, 346, 357
Jones's Greenwood	175, 230, 292, 344		
Jones's Park	124, 257		
Jones's Park Reserved	198		
Jones's Park Resurveyed	314	Jumps Choice	18, 50, 116, 119, 143, 159, 187, 243, 304, 319, 329, 357
Jones's Plott	138, 162, 168, 215, 222, 278, 284		
Jones's Safety	175, 292, 344	Jumps Claims	162, 216, 278, 331
Jones's Safty	230	Jumps Lane	18, 116, 190, 246, 307, 360
Jones's Tryangle	85, 267		
Jordan		Jumps Lott	18, 119, 172, 176, 226, 231, 288, 292, 341, 345
Andrew	51, 240, 301, 354		
James	51, 98, 116, 175	Jump's Addition	88
Joseph Part of Hackers Meadows Enlarg'd	358	Jump's Chance	118
		Jump's Choice	258
Josephs Addition	167, 220, 283, 336	Jump's Claims	141
Josephs Hope	61, 122, 232, 294, 347	Jurusalem	111
Josephs Hopes	177	Just Design	193, 249, 309, 362
Josephs Lott	52, 120, 172, 226, 265, 288, 341	Keareys Discovery	330
		Keary	
Josephs Own	180, 235, 296, 349	William	57
Josephs Part of Hackers Meadows Enlarged	188, 304	Kearys Discovery	57, 116, 161, 187, 214, 243, 277, 304, 357
Josephs Part of Hackers Meadows Inlarg'd	243		
Joseph's Addition	139	Keary's Discovery	149
Joseph's Lott	87	Keen	
Joy		Thomas	93
Charles	153	Keiran	
Ignatius	153	Richard	16
Joyner		Keiron	
William	1, 175, 230, 292, 344	Richard	346
		Kelds Inheritance	183, 238, 300, 352
Jump			

Kelley		
	(N)	290, 320
	Alexander	320
	James	177, 294
Kelly		
	(N)	174, 203, 260, 373
	Alexander	203, 260, 373
	Edmond	99
	Edmund	146
	James	232
Kemp		
	Baldwin	52, 98, 124, 176, 231, 293, 346
	Balwin	55
	Mary	177, 232, 294, 346
	Thomas	177, 232, 294
Kendal		60
Kendall	40, 42, 51, 61, 74, 81, 113, 115, 141, 197, 253, 265, 313, 366	
	(N)	228, 343
	William	343
Kent		
	Robert	6, 77, 98, 106, 232, 265, 294, 346
	William	6, 98, 128, 176, 232, 293, 346
Kent Fort Mannor		51
Kent Fort Manor		38, 202, 258, 318, 371
Kent Fort Manour		70
Kent Lott		183, 239, 353
Kentin		
	James	176, 231, 293
	Solomon	176, 231
Kenting		
	William	19, 61
Kenton		
	James	18, 98, 118, 346
	Solomon	98, 118, 293, 346
Kents Lott		300
Kerby		
	Benjamin	1, 177, 346
	James	1
	Walter	1, 176
	William	1
Kerbys Addition		1
Kerbys Hardship		176, 232
Kerbys Prevention		1, 315, 370
Kersey		
	James	98, 123, 176, 231, 293, 346
	Thomas	99, 142, 176, 232, 293, 346
Kersley		
	James	91
Keys		
	John	98, 129
	Richard	17, 98, 111
Kieran		
	Richard	176
Kieron		
	Richard	111, 231, 293
Kilkenney		249
Kilkenny		24, 173
Kill Maiden		36, 120
Kill Maiden Addition		120
Killary		342
Killeray		81, 150, 174, 201, 227, 258, 289, 318
Killerays Addition		150, 202, 258, 318
Killeroy		19
Killingsworth		
	(N)	357
Killkenny		19, 131, 310, 363
Killmaiden		197, 253, 313
Killmaiden Addition		197, 253, 313
Killmainam Plains		78
Killmainam Plains Addition		76
Killmanam Plains		135, 171, 225, 287, 340
Killmanam Plains Addition		267
Killmanams Plains		22, 32
Killmanams Plains Addition		21
Killmarden		367
Killmarden Addition		367
Kindness		87, 268
Kinesleys Plains		333
King		
	Andrew	6
	Thomas	36, 56, 69, 81, 83
King Hammer		64, 107
King Hammer on Resurvey		57
King Sale		352
King Sale Addition		14, 352
King Town		179
Kings Sale		117
Kings Sale Addition		117
Kings Town		117, 140, 142, 143, 147, 151, 162, 169, 178,

		179, 190, 194, 195, 200-202, 206, 216, 223, 234, 246, 251, 256, 258, 262, 279, 285, 295, 296, 306, 311, 312, 316, 318, 322, 332, 338, 348, 349, 360, 364, 369, 371, 374		346
			Knotts Chance	176, 231, 293, 346
			Knotts Range	176, 231, 293, 346
			Knotts's Chance	176, 363
			Knowles	
			James	37
			John	25, 42, 98, 115
			Lawrence	31
			Knowles Range	148, 237
Kingsale		183, 238, 299	Knowles's Range	135, 166, 237, 299, 351
Kingsale Addition		183, 238, 299		
Kinnimont			Knowls Range	31
	John	89, 98, 141		
Kirbeys Recovery		364	Labour in Vain	10, 111
Kirby			Laine	
	(N)	137	Walter	116
	Benjamin	232, 293	Lake	
	Susanah	293	Richard	343
	Susanna	232	Lambden	
	Walter	69, 98, 232, 293, 370	Bexley John	178, 294
	Warter	136	Bexly John	233, 347
Kirbys Addition		136, 232	George	48, 132
Kirbys Hardship		293, 370	John	99, 132
Kirbys Prevention		137, 201, 258	William	150, 203, 260, 320, 373
Kirbys Recovery		195, 251, 311		
Kirby's Prevention		147	Lambden Adventure	48, 328
Kirkham			Lambdens Adventure	132, 159, 212, 275
	James	19		
	William	19, 232, 294, 346	Lambert	19, 118, 183, 238, 265, 300, 334
Kirkhams Lott		44, 115, 177, 232, 294, 347		
			Richard	123, 177, 233, 294, 347
Knatchbull				
	Norton	13, 26	Lambert Fields	364
Knave Stand Off		23, 81, 233	Lambeth	13, 19, 37, 44, 45, 65, 76, 85, 89, 141, 152, 167, 202, 221, 259, 265, 284, 319, 337, 372
Knave Standoff		178, 295, 347		
Kniver Heath		29, 74, 267		
Knott				
	Edward	151	Lambeth Addition	44, 168, 221, 284, 337
	Frances	151		
	John	40	Lambeth Fields	13, 26, 74, 142, 194, 250, 263, 311
Knotts				
	Ann	232	Lambeths Addition	116
	Anne	293	Lampson	
	James	52, 55, 98, 125, 176, 231, 293, 346, 363	William	74
			Lampton	32, 74, 151, 206, 263
	John	231, 293	Lanark	191, 246, 307, 360
	Nath.	231	Lancaster	54, 59, 81, 188, 244, 305
	Nathaniel	52, 117, 176, 293, 346	John	54, 59, 81
			Land	
Knotts Addition		52, 117, 176, 231, 293,	John	71

Land of Benjamin	153, 263
Land of Phrophecy	354
Land of Prophecy	30, 43, 78, 184, 269, 301
Land of Prophesy	127, 240
Landcaster	358
Landing	34, 130, 199, 255, 316, 368
Landy	153

Lane
- (N) 334
- Charles 31, 71
- Gallan 44
- James 99, 118, 177, 232, 294, 347
- John 19, 65, 68, 69, 76, 81, 265
- Mary 19, 178, 233, 294, 347
- Thomas 89, 90, 98, 151, 203, 260, 320, 373
- Timothy 19, 37, 44, 99, 118, 238, 300, 334
- Walter 55, 65, 178, 233, 294, 347
- William 19

Lanes Addition	232, 294, 347
Lanes Chance	142
Lanes Folly	19, 116, 178, 233, 294
Lanes Folly Addition	19, 265
Lanes Folly on Resurvey	55
Lanes Forrest	19, 29, 265
Lanes Ridge	32, 139, 174, 227, 289, 342
Lane's Folley	347
Lane's Folly	65
Lane's Folly Addition	76
Lane's Forrest	65, 68, 74

Lang
- John 17, 49, 64, 103, 265

Langford
- (N) 347
- Richard 347

Lanington	180
Lantley	107, 142, 164, 194, 250, 280, 310, 333, 363
Lantly	218
Large Range	18, 50, 76, 93, 115, 118, 169, 223, 265, 285, 286, 339
Large Range Addition	48, 50, 76, 141, 162, 216, 265, 278
Larington	126
Larrington	15, 30, 110, 141, 186, 200, 235, 242, 256, 296, 303, 316, 349, 357, 369
Lawes Addition	177
Lawrances Delight	344

Lawrence
- John 17, 60
- Richard 52

Lawrence Delight	52
Lawrences Delight	174, 229, 291
Lawrence's Delight	132

Layton
- (N) 43

Leatherberry
- John 26

Leavells	331

Lee
- Alexander 55, 178, 233, 295, 347
- Elizabeth 81, 83
- John 23, 134, 177, 233, 294, 347
- Thomas 48, 99, 128, 177, 233, 294, 347
- William 23

Leeds
- John 203, 260, 320, 373

Lees Chance	194, 233, 250, 294, 311, 347, 364
Lee's Chance	177

Legg
- John 28, 41, 98, 99, 136, 137, 177, 178, 233, 294, 295, 347
- William 41

Leggs Begining	294, 347
Leggs Beginning	136, 177, 178, 295
Leicester Fields	45

Leith
- John 177, 233, 294, 347

Lemare
- Charles 99

Lemarr
- Charles 36

Lemarre
- Charles 121

Lentley	16
Leonard	

John		19
Rebecca		99, 118
Lester		141, 175, 230, 292, 345
Lester Meadows		175, 230, 292
Lesters Meadows		345
Levell		64
Levells		21, 58, 122, 162, 182, 215, 238, 278, 299, 352
Levills		134
Lewells		31
Lewis		
	(N)	52
	Ch.	61
	George	269
	John	27
	Thomas	6, 27, 99, 106
Lewis Addition		92
Lewis Chance		27
Lewis's Chance		106, 167, 221, 284, 337
Lexon		26, 43, 85
Lexton		106, 127, 147, 151, 176, 187, 217, 231, 265, 280, 292, 333, 345
Liberty		12, 53, 69, 106, 186, 242, 303, 357
Liecester Fields		114
Lihon		
	Thomas	151
Lillingston		
	John	26, 67, 76, 84, 263
	Mary	67
Lillingstons Addition		26, 152, 267
Lillingstons Castle		26, 152, 267
Lillingstons Enjoyment		257, 318, 370
Limbrick		41
Limrich		28
Limrick		44, 136, 149, 177, 178, 264, 295
Limrick & Leggs Beginning		233
Limricks		347
Lincoln		112, 182, 238, 299, 352
Lincolne		13
Linrick		294
Linsey		
	Edward	178, 233, 295, 347
	Patrick	55, 99
	Sarah	178, 295
	Sarh	233
Little Ease		1, 41, 137, 139, 152, 196, 252, 267, 313, 366
Little Neck		4, 138, 191, 247, 308, 361
Little Thickett		2, 57, 68, 85, 140, 179, 227, 234, 296
Little Tickett		348
Little Worth		120, 123, 198
Little Worth Addition		120
Littleworth		27, 39, 40, 46, 56, 66, 125, 146, 156, 161, 209, 214, 215, 257, 272, 277, 315, 325, 330, 370
Littleworth Addition		57, 161, 215, 277, 330
Litton		
	Thomas	98
Lloyd		
	Alice	65
	Anne	266
	Edward	150, 177, 214, 260, 373
	Phil.	266
	Philemon	64-66, 68, 76
	Rebecca	64
	Robert	81, 82, 177, 232, 346
Lloyds Freshes		84, 260
Lloyds Insula		219
Lloyds Meadows & Lloyds Meadows Addition		249, 323
Lloyds Town		84, 258, 371
Lloyd's Freshes		68, 373
Lloyd's Insula		66, 335
Lloyd's Meadows		65, 329
Lock Point		58
Lockerman		
	John	203, 295, 347
Locks Point		116, 164, 218, 280, 329
London		
	James	44, 99, 115, 177, 232, 294, 347
Long		
	John	34, 70, 266
Long Delay		186, 242, 303, 356
Long Marsh Ridge		48, 153
Long Marsh Ridge Enlarged		158, 159, 274, 275
Long Marsh Ridge Enlarg'd		211, 212, 327, 328
Long Neck		30, 108, 110, 145, 174, 193, 291, 309

Long Neck Addition	229, 249, 344, 362	Lower Fords		152, 206
Long Neglect	65	Lowerfords		50
Long Point	61, 90, 117	Lowerford's		269
Long Range	18, 76, 119, 169, 265	Lowes Arcadia		17, 39, 45, 110, 123, 124, 128, 160, 177, 183, 186, 194, 200, 213, 233, 239, 250, 256, 265, 276, 294, 300, 303, 310, 317
Long Range Addition	331			
Long Ridge	190, 245, 306, 359			
Long Run	45, 122			
Long Swamp	188, 244, 305, 358			
Longfellow		Lowes Bennington		19
Elizabeth	232, 294, 347	Lowes Birmington		265
Jo.	232	Lowes Desire		34, 46, 47, 132, 134, 168, 185, 222, 240, 244, 265, 284, 301, 337
Joseph	61, 99, 122, 177, 294, 347			
Longs Chance	34, 184, 239, 300, 353	Lowe's Arcadia		76
Longs Desire	24, 120, 183, 238, 300, 352	Lowe's Bennington		76
		Lowe's Desire		74, 78
Long's Chance	70	Lows Arcadia		39, 329, 352, 356, 363, 369
Lookerman				
John	233	Lows Desire		132, 337, 355
Lord		Lowther		
John	146	Charles		23, 59, 99, 134, 264
Lords Gift	10, 22, 31, 108, 160, 214, 276, 329	Lowthers Chance		179, 235, 296, 349
		Low's Arcadia		347
Lords Gift on Resurvey	122, 194, 250, 310, 363	Loyd		
		Alice		5, 99
Lords Gift Resurveyed	56	Ann		99
Lord's Gift	65	Anne		114, 177
Lott	40, 43, 106, 187, 217, 280, 333	Ed.		27
Louder's Hazard	133	Edward		27, 98, 114, 204, 320
Louther		John		15, 40, 178
Charles	23	Phill.		20
Lovely	39, 85	Rebecca		27, 53
Deliverance	39, 85	Robert		99, 113, 294
Low		Loyd Costin		74
(N)	60	Loyd Town		85
Low Land	34	Loyds Costin		20
Low Lands	199, 255, 316, 368	Loyds Freshes		27, 150, 197, 204, 290, 320
Lowcoust Ridge	365			
Lowd		Loyds Insula		20, 105, 165, 281
Charles	50	Loyds Meadows		5, 20, 113, 160, 213, 276, 309
Lowder				
Charles	57, 59	Loyds Meadows & Loyds Meadows		
Lowders Hazard	185, 241, 302, 355	Addition		106, 109, 154, 193, 207, 270, 362
Lowe				
Nicholas	28			
Stead	204, 263, 265, 321	Loyds Meadows Addition		5, 309
Vincent	31, 66, 78, 79, 82	Loyds Town		10, 114, 154, 318
Lowe Lands	130	Loyds Towne		9, 27
Lower Arcadia	22, 242	Lundy		31, 78, 204, 261, 321

Page 423

	John	31, 78, 79
Lyford		25, 45, 49, 115-117, 164, 175, 201, 218, 230, 257, 281, 291, 317, 334, 346, 370
Lynsey		
	Partrick	121
Macarthy		
	Morrice	44
Macclannahan		
	Thomas	142
Macclinborough		147
Macconakin		
	John	50
Maccoys Pleasure		296
Maccoy's Pleasure		179
Macdaniell		
	Edward	41
Mackleys Addition		276
Macklin		11, 104, 148
Macklin Borough		126, 173
Macklin Burrough		335, 342, 343
Macklinborough		76, 127, 165, 172, 173, 219, 227, 228, 265, 281, 289, 290
Macklinbourough		107, 122
Macklingboroug		15
Macklins Addition		108, 109, 167, 261, 284, 321, 337, 373
Macklins Begining		340
Macklins Beginning		6, 134, 170, 286, 287
Macklins Fancey		372
Macklins Fancy		6, 319
Macklyn		
	(N)	76
	Richard	86
	Robert	6
Macklynborough		228
Macklyne		
	Robert	69
Macklyns Addition		6, 214, 221
Macklyns Beginning		224, 225
Macklyns Fancy		259
Macklyn's Beginning		85
Macklyn's Fancy		76, 203
Macklys Addition		160
Maclean		
	Da.	52

Maclinborough Division		85
Maclinburgh		85
Maconakin		
	Elizabeth	4
Magreholm		327
Maidens Choice		2, 137
Malborough		48
Malden		15, 85, 268
Malloony		
	Teague	32
Mallory		
	Teague	78
Malton		44, 110, 151, 192, 203, 248, 260, 309, 320, 362, 373
Manah		
	Susanna	98
	Susannah	129
	Timothy	31, 129, 325
Manahs Chance		325
Manahs Chance Resurveyed		129
Maner		
	William	349
Manfield		
	William	233
Mangey Pockey		17
Mangy		59
Mangy Pockey		59, 332
Mangy Pocky		142, 216
Mangy Pokey		163, 279
Mannah		
	Timothy	156, 179, 209, 235, 272, 296, 349
Mannahs Chance		156, 209, 272
Mannahs Chance Resurveyed		179, 235, 296, 349
Manor		
	James	350
Mansfield		
	William	98, 109, 178, 295, 348
Manton		24, 130, 134, 236
Manton Addition		61
Mantons Addition		134, 188, 247, 308, 361
Marborough Addition		39
Margaretts Hill		183, 239, 300
Margaretts Hills		27
Margarett's Hill		76
Margretts Hill		354

Maridath		
	Anne	348, 349
	John	348
	Thomas	348
	William	348, 350
Maridaths Adventure		350
Marks		
	H.	46
	John	84
Marlborough		17
Marphys Chance		122
Marsh		
	Thomas	2, 41, 98, 140, 179, 234, 296
Marshall		
	(N)	53
	Ann	33
	Charles	53, 59, 78
	Thomas	26, 68
Marshall Outlett		53
Marshalls Outlett		59
Marshall's Outlett		78
Marshes Forbarance		348
Marshes Forbearance		2, 140, 179, 234, 296
Marshey Crook		336
Marshs Portion		140
Marshy Brook		105
Marshy Creek		34
Marshy Crook		7, 167, 220, 283
Martaindale		
	Thomas	118
Martains Neck Resurveyed		145
Martin		
	(N)	80
	Henry	31, 80, 266
	Robert	65
Martindale		
	Anne	348
	Thomas	98, 178, 234, 295, 348
Martindales Hope		179, 234, 295, 348
Martindales Range		234, 295, 348
Martindale's Range		178
Martins Neck		38, 138, 189, 245, 306, 359
Martins Neck Resurveyed		3, 182, 238, 299, 352
Martin's Neck		65
Mary Ann Lott		30
Mary Anns Lott		227, 289
Mary Ann's Lott		127, 172, 342
Mary Branch		57
Mary Portion		308, 361
Marys Chance		36, 135, 244, 304, 358
Marys Lott		353
Marys Portion		3, 188, 189, 198, 245, 247, 254, 306, 315, 367
Mary's Chance		146, 188
Mash		
	Thomas	348
Mason		
	Henry	235, 297, 349
	John	236, 297, 350
	Leonard	41
	Mathew	6
	Matthew	80, 263
	Rebecca	148
	Richard	28, 98, 148, 235, 297, 349
	Solomon	235, 297, 349
	William	236
	William Winchester	234, 295, 348
Masons Hazard		235, 297, 349
Massey		
	James	9, 44, 98, 179, 180, 296, 348, 349
	Nicholas	24, 85, 321, 373
	Peter	131, 152
	Samuel	152, 180, 297, 350
	William	48, 98
Masseys Addition		179, 296, 297, 348, 350
Masseys Hazard		24, 152
Masseys Right		350
Massy		
	James	44, 131, 234, 235, 297
	Nicholas	84, 204, 261, 267
	Peter	236
	Samuel	142, 236
	William	130
Massys Addition		234, 236
Massys Hazard		131, 236, 267
Massy's Hazard		85
Mathews		
	Elizabeth	28
	Timothy	45
	William	349

Mathews Enlargement	3, 338			320
Mathews Fancy	335	McCastelow		
Mathewshaw		Abraham		235, 297
George	6	McClallyn		
Jeffry	6	Abigail		98
Mattapax	65	McClallyon		
Mattapax Neck	33, 37, 142, 162, 216, 331	Abigail		116
		McClannahan		
Mattapox Neck	278	Thomas		98, 180, 235, 296
Mattershaw		McCleans Addition		190, 307, 357
George	98, 107	McConnakin		
Matthews		John		180
Timothy	81	McConnickins Fortune		222
William	81, 180, 235, 297	McConnikin		
Matthews Enlargement	140, 163, 280	Daniel		179, 234, 296
Matthews Fancy	166, 282	Elizabeth		98, 138
Matthew's Enlargement	217	John		98, 135, 236, 297
Matthew's Fancy	219	McConnikin Correar		296
Maxby	11, 65	McConnikins Correar		179, 234
Maxfield	28, 78, 264	McConnikins Fortune		135, 169, 179, 234, 285
Maxwell				
(N)	179, 234, 349	McCosh		
Alexander	65	Samuel		70, 99, 144, 180, 235
Mr.	296	Samuell		296
Peter	180, 297, 350	McCoy		
Maynard		James		99, 144, 179, 235, 296
Thomas	267	McCoys Pleasure		235
Mayne		McCustalow		
John	98, 118, 178, 234, 295, 348	Abraham		180
		McDaniel		
Mayner		Edmund		84, 85
William	235, 297	Edward		236
Maynor		McKittrick		
William	180	Andrew		125
Mayson		Dr.		98
Henry	180	McLean		
John	180	Da.		11
Richard	180	Mead		
Solomon	180	William		50
William Winchester	179	Meadow		192
Maysons Hazard	180	Meadows		248, 309, 362
Mayton		Meads		
Leonard	138	John		49, 50
McCarter		Thomas		52
(N)	373	Meagreholm		274
Maurice	373	Meaguholm		158, 211
McCarty		Meanah		
(N)	144, 169, 203, 260, 320	Timothy		59
Major	151	Meanahs Chance		59
Maurice	144, 169, 203, 260,	Meanor		

	James	236		Anne	295
Meclannahan				John	295
	Thomas	349		Thomas	295
Meconikin			Meridith		
	(N)	350		Anne	178, 235
	Daniel	348		John	126, 139, 178, 233
	Elias	350		Thomas	233
	John	350		William	126, 236, 295, 297
Meconikins Corcar		348	Meridiths Adventure		297
Meconikins Fortune		338	Meridith's Adventure		236
Mecosh			Merrick		
	Samuel	349		Isaac	52, 98, 119, 179, 295
Mecoy				Mary	179, 295
	James	349	Merricks Delight		52, 119, 179, 211, 295, 327
Mecoys Pleasure		349			
Medcalf			Merridith		
	William	65		Ann	234
Medcalfe				Anne	180, 297
	William	64		John	35
Meeds				Lewis	1
	John	98, 113, 178, 180, 233, 235, 295, 297, 348, 350		William	22, 234
			Merridith Adventure		35
			Merrydith		
	Rebecca	178, 233, 295		John	15, 35
	Rebeccah	348		William	22
	Thomas	90, 98, 116, 180, 235, 297, 350	Merson		
				William	12, 98, 108, 178, 233, 295, 347
	William	45, 98, 114, 178, 233, 295, 348			
			Mersons Freehold		40, 105, 109, 140
Meligan			Merydith		
	George	373		Thomas	178
Mellegin			Middle Plantation		108, 109, 178, 191, 218, 233, 247, 281, 295, 308, 334, 347, 360, 361
	George	321			
Meloyd					
	Thomas	235, 296, 349			
Meloy'd			Midle Plantation		12
	Thomas	179	Miles		
Merchant				Thomas	65
	Jo.	235	Milford		19, 53, 124
	Jos.	349	Mill Land		78, 267, 359
	Joseph	98, 141, 179, 296	Mill Range		16, 81, 128, 149, 204, 260, 320, 373
Meredeth					
	Thomas	114	Milland		43
Meredith			Millegin		
	John	81, 90, 98		George	204
	Thomas	98	Miller		
	William	81, 181		James	180, 235, 297, 349
Merediths Adventure		81		John	32, 37, 42, 128, 179, 234, 296, 348
Meredith's Adventure		181			
Merideth				Michael	25, 63, 72, 152

Page 427

Milles		
Jeremiah		31
Millford		19, 56, 81, 115, 150, 166, 201, 257, 258, 282, 317, 318, 335, 370, 371
Millford Addition		35, 114, 154
Millican		
George		261
Millington		
Oliver		25, 27, 74
William		204
Millis		
James		31, 48, 98, 120, 179, 234, 295, 348
Jos.		55
Millrange		88
Mills		
David		48, 99, 117, 178, 234, 264, 295, 348
Milton		
(N)		365
Abraham		180, 235, 297
Minn		
Golt		81
Mire Branch		117, 205, 238, 299
Mirely Branch		68
Mirey Branch		352
Mischief		85, 243
Mischiefe		19
Miss Hitt		56, 114, 170, 224, 286, 339
Mistake		16, 65, 141, 162, 216, 278, 331
Mistake Addition		332
Mistakes Addition		162, 216, 278
Mitchell		
John		84
Richard		27, 70
Mitchells Adventure		125, 226
Mitchels Adventure		288
Mitchels Adventure & Adventure		226
Mittford		219
Mocklinborough Division		15
Moffit		
John		98
Molineaux		
Richard		153, 261, 321
Mollineaux		
Richard		204
Molton		9
Monroe		
John		28
Monrowe		
Dun		28
Montague		
William		122, 295
Montaque		
(N)		208
Montecue		
William		62
Montecues Luck		62
Mooney		
Charles		236, 350
Patrick		179, 234, 296, 348
Mooney Luck		296
Mooneys Luck		234, 348
Moor		
Charles		17, 98
Nathaniel		350
Moore		
Charles		113
John		57
Nathaniel		236, 297
Richard		17
Moore Hope		57
Moores Hope		114, 167, 221, 283
Moores Hope Addition		114, 142, 166, 167, 182, 220, 221, 237, 282, 283, 298, 299
Mooth		
Thomas		36, 57, 98, 107, 178, 233, 295, 347
Mooths Range		178, 233, 295, 347
Mores Hope		336
Mores Hope Addition		337, 351
Morgains Inclosure		256
Morgan		
Evan		67
Henry		63, 65, 93
Herbert		25, 140
Martin		85, 269
Mary		140
Morgans Enlargement		25
Morgans Hope		269
Morgans Inclosure		139, 140, 195, 200, 251, 312, 317, 365, 369
Morgans Neck		10, 11, 58, 203, 260, 319, 372
Morgan's Enlargement		93

Morgan's Hope	85			348
Morgan's Inclosure	93	Mountagues Luck		234
Morgan's Neck	65, 103	Mountague's Luck		85
Morrice		Mountecue		
Anne	35	William		36
William	35	Mounthope		143, 154, 270
Morris		Mountseer		
Ann	35, 78	Thomas		32
Robert	65	Timothy		348
Samuel	35	Mountsier		
Morriss		(N)		32
Anne	268	Thomas		81
Morris's Chance	35, 78, 268	Mountsieur		
Moscropp		Thomas		128, 179, 234, 296
Thomas	45	William		196, 312
Moun		Mulberry Tract		189, 244, 305, 358
William	252	Mullican		
Mounsier		Daniel		40
William	365	Mullicans Delight		40
Mounsieur		Mullikin		
Thomas	98	Daniel		262
William	98, 135	Mullikins Delight		262
Mount Gilboa	50, 129, 201, 207, 258, 318, 323	Murphey		
		Charles		235, 349
Mount Hope	15, 23, 60, 61, 89, 118, 123, 126, 146, 172, 197, 207, 226, 253, 288, 314, 323, 341, 367	William		41
		Murpheys Chance Resurveyed		349
		Murphy		
		Charles		180, 297
		James		32
Mount Hope Addition	23, 314, 367	Thomas		42
Mount Hopes Addition	123, 197, 253	William		41, 55
Mount Malick	72	Murphys Chance		55
Mount Mill	7, 41, 65, 105, 187, 191, 229, 242, 243, 247, 291, 303, 304, 307, 344, 357, 360	Murphys Chance Resurveyed		180, 235, 297
		Muskata Range		28
		Musketa Ridge		19
Mount Mills	174	Musketo Range		85, 267
Mount Molock	330	Musketo Ridge		141, 179, 235, 296, 349
Mount Moluck	32, 108, 165, 219, 281			
Mount Pleasant	21, 31, 49, 81, 145, 195, 251, 263, 264, 311, 312, 364, 365, 372	Nabb		
		Charles		99, 134, 181, 236, 298, 350
		James William		182, 298, 299
Mount Pleasant & Enjoyment	264	James Williams		237, 351
Mount Pleasure	133, 195, 201, 202, 251, 257, 259, 312, 318, 319, 365, 370	John		6, 99, 106, 181, 182, 236, 237, 297, 298, 350
Mountague		Narborough		82, 123, 124, 145, 186, 198, 201, 204, 242, 257, 261, 303, 315,
(N)	324			
William	85, 98, 179, 234,			

		317, 321, 356, 370, 373
Narborough Addition		145, 198, 257, 315, 370
Naseby		38, 74, 267
Nathan & Thomas's Beginning		170, 224, 286
Nathaniels Addition		191, 212, 275, 328
Nathan's & Thomas's Begining		339
Neal		
	Edward	99, 151
	Francis	99, 149
	Jeremiah	205
	Samuel	150, 206
Neale		
	Charles	13
	Edward	148, 181, 205, 237, 261, 298, 321, 351, 374
	Fra.	46
	Fran.	29, 261
	Francis	29, 205, 321, 374
	Jere.	269
	Jeremiah	52, 74
	Jonathan	46, 205, 261, 321
	Samuel	262, 322, 374
Neales Residence		237, 298, 351
Neales's Residence		181
Neck		72
Nedds Begginning		123
Nedds Begining		186, 302
Nedds Beginning		241
Neds Beginning		33
Needles		
	John	142
Neglect		6, 10, 11, 30, 33, 34, 36, 40, 63, 66, 77, 86, 105, 106, 108, 110, 126, 127, 140, 155, 158, 163, 167, 179, 182, 191, 196, 200, 208, 211, 217, 220, 227, 234, 237, 247, 252, 256, 265, 271, 274, 279, 283, 289, 296, 298, 308, 312, 317, 323, 327, 332, 336, 341, 348, 361, 365, 369, 371
Neglect Resurveyed		57

Negligence		47, 74, 193, 205, 249, 262, 310, 322, 363
Negro		
	Dick	166, 237, 299
Negroes		
	Boatswain Tom	340
	Dick	351
	Gibbs	340
Nemo		
	John	265
Nevell		
	(N)	244
	James	351
	John	24, 237, 244, 351, 358
	Rachell	237
Nevells Addition		237, 351
Nevells Delight		234, 348, 350
Nevells Discovery		351
Nevells Out Range		351
Nevells Outrange		237
Nevil		
	Walter	129
Nevill		
	(N)	188, 305
	David	129
	Elizabeth	99, 129
	John	24, 51, 99, 128, 181, 182, 188, 298, 305
	Marian	143
	Mat.	10
	Rachel	298
	Walter	23, 32, 50, 129, 181
	William	55, 99, 143
Nevills Addition		129, 182, 298
Nevills Delight		143, 180, 236, 296, 297
Nevills Discovery		128, 182, 298
Nevills Outrange		128, 182, 298
Nevils Delight		179
New Buckley		39, 117, 197, 253, 313, 366
New Cunningham		44, 115, 161, 214, 277, 354
New Hall		17, 64, 71, 103, 265
New Hynson Town		6, 20, 33, 65, 67, 110, 200, 256, 316, 369
New Hynson Town Resurveyed		56
New London		39, 53, 118, 178, 234, 295, 348
New London Addition		178, 234, 295,

		348
New Nothingham		105
New Nothingham Rectified		242, 356
New Nottingham		39
New Port		344
New Reading		6, 66, 67, 110, 200, 256, 317, 369
New Reading on Resurvey		56, 109
Newhall		49
Newington		13, 52, 61, 89, 115, 161, 214, 226, 269, 277, 330
Newington Addition		36, 115, 161, 214, 277, 330
Newman		
	Da.	34
	Daniel	21, 33, 59
	John	121
Newnam		
	Benjamin	351
	Daniel	33, 34, 99, 132, 266
	David	23
	Jo.	80
	John	99
	Jos.	236, 350
	Joseph	99, 133, 143, 181, 298
	Nathaniel	181, 237, 298, 351
	Solomon	181, 236, 297, 350
	William	99, 135, 181, 236, 297, 350
Newname		
	William	90
Newnams Addition		181, 236, 298, 350
Newnams Chance		135, 181, 297, 350
Newnams Hazard		350
Newnams Hermitage		33, 132, 168, 222, 284, 337
Newnams Portion		190, 246, 307, 357
Newnam's Chance		90, 236
Newnothingham Rectified		186, 302
Newport		174, 229, 291
Newton		
	Thomas	181, 237, 298, 350
Nichols		
	Deborah	374
	Jeremiah	374
Nicholson		
	John	52
	Thomas	55, 135

Nicholson Chance		344
Nicholsons Addition		52
Nicholsons Adventure		175, 230, 292, 345
Nicholsons Chance		55, 175, 230, 292
Nicholsons Fancey		343
Nicholsons Fancy		173, 228, 290
Nicholson's Adventure		141
Nickolson		
	Thomas	99, 136
Nickolson's Chance		136
Nickolson's Fancy		136
Nicols		
	Charles	181, 237, 298, 351
	Deborah	261
	Jere	261
	Jeremiah	205, 321
	Jonathan	150, 181, 237, 298, 351
Nields Begining		356
Nimrods Pleasure		163, 217, 279
Ninevah		72, 149, 204, 320, 373
Ninevahs Addition		204, 320, 373
Ninevah's Addition		149
Nineveh		260
Ninevehs Addition		260
Nineveth		1, 26
Nineveth Addition		26
No Name		66, 69, 85
Noble		
	Robert	76
Noble Range		76
Nobles Range		5, 13, 115, 116, 166, 175, 219, 229, 282, 291, 335, 336, 345
Nobles Range & Hemsleys Arcadia		220
Nodd		51, 120, 176, 231, 293, 345
Nollars Enjoyment		111
Norman		
	Thomas	33
Norrest Addition		124
Norrests Addition		16, 17
Norrestts Addition		124
Norris		
	Robert	22
	Thomas	85
Norris Derry		85
North East Thickett		67
Northumberland		47, 59, 132, 178, 188, 233, 244, 294, 305,

	347, 358	Oakridge	156
Norward		Oar Mine	33, 142, 162, 215, 278, 331
John	268	Obryan	
Norwood	26, 85, 268	Patrick	16
John	26, 85	Thomas	16, 182, 238, 299, 351
Notingam	175		
Notlars Delight	21, 24, 125, 134, 144, 159, 175, 180, 212, 230, 235, 275, 292, 297, 328, 344, 349	OBryon	
		Thomas	99, 125
		Ocklyn	
		Margaret	92
Notlars Desire	24, 133, 157, 159, 209, 212, 265, 272, 275, 325, 328	Offley	
		John	21, 82
		Robert	99, 134, 182, 238, 299, 352
Notlars Enjoyment	193, 249, 363	Offleys Fortune	21
Notlar's Desire	78	Offly	
Notlers Delight	133	Dorrothy	31
Notleys Delight	44	Ogle Town	104, 105, 110, 111, 127, 134, 144, 147, 157, 182, 192, 193, 200, 210, 238, 248, 249, 256, 259, 273, 299, 309, 310, 317, 319, 326, 328, 351, 362, 363, 371
Nottingam	292		
Nottingham	230, 344, 345		
Nottlars Enjoyment	310		
Nottleys Desire	50		
Nottleys Enjoyment	9		
Nuthall			
Elias	66		
Nuthall's Chance	66	Old Indian Cabbin	37, 85
Nuthead		Old Town	86, 121, 149, 155, 203, 208, 260, 271, 320, 324, 372
William	78, 267		
Nutheads Choice	267		
Nutheads Coyce	32	Old Towne	45
Nuthead's Choice	78	Olden Lyon	299
Nutthead		Older	
William	32	John	86
Nuttwells Chance Resurveyed	11, 321	Older Branch	274
Nutwells Chance Resurveyed	204, 261, 373	Oldham	
		Edward	99, 151, 205, 262, 321, 374
		Oldson	
Oak Ridge	47, 121, 147, 148, 187, 198, 231, 243, 254, 304, 315, 345, 366, 367	Abraham	99, 143, 182, 238, 299, 352
		Henry	99, 143, 182
Oak Ridge Addition	198, 254, 315, 367	John	5, 78, 99, 122, 143, 182, 237, 268, 299
Oake Ridge	18		
Oaken Thorpe	123, 125, 179, 241, 242, 261, 321, 323, 325, 348, 356, 363, 373	Oldsons Pasture	5, 78, 268
		Oldsons Relief	136, 178, 180, 196, 233, 236, 252, 295, 297, 347, 350, 365
Oakenthorp	39, 186		
Oakenthorpe	42, 51, 66, 86, 122, 128, 154, 156, 186, 204, 207, 209, 234, 270, 272, 296, 302, 303	Oldsons Reliefe	41, 312
		Olson	
		Abraham	351
Oakenthorpe Resurveyed	11		

	John	351
On Long Creek		33
Oneal		
	Charles	99, 112
Original of Friendship		103
Original Stagwell		103
Orsburn		
	(N)	189, 306
Osborne		
	Samuel	99, 145
	William	3, 65, 88, 138
Osburn		
	Samuel	238, 299, 352
	Samuell	182
Out Lett		35
Out Range		21, 61, 62, 132, 355
Outlett		166, 220, 282, 335, 340
Outrange		32, 69, 85, 131, 134, 141, 146, 152, 185, 188, 196, 221, 241, 244, 252, 260, 265, 302, 305, 313, 358, 366
Outson		
	Andrew	5
	Henry	5
	Thomas	5
Oval		43
Ovall		43, 90, 127, 193, 310, 363
Owen		
	Thomas	115
Oxenham		
	William	238, 352
Oxingham		
	William	205, 299
Pack		45
Pacolett		130, 204, 261, 321
Padan Aaran		372
Padan Aaron		75
Padan Aran		267
Padan Haran		29
Paine		
	Isaac	53
Painter		
	Nicholas	87, 268
Painters Point		32
Pamphilion		
	Thomas	100, 150, 269
Pamphillion		
	Thomas	46

Pamplilion		
	Edward	205
Panther Point		82, 269
Park		30, 76, 84, 85, 87, 111, 114, 133, 153, 162, 163, 170, 192, 194, 215, 217, 224, 247, 248, 250, 265, 266, 278, 279, 286, 308, 310, 331, 332, 334, 339, 361
Parke		26, 41
Parker		
	Henry	63, 66
	William	33, 53
Parker Freshes		170
Parkers Freshes		61, 115, 166, 219, 224, 243, 282, 286, 335
Parkers Lott		38, 124, 184, 240, 301, 354
Parkers Range		60, 120
Parker's Freshes		89
Parker's Lott		66
Parrot		
	Aaron	374
Parrott		
	Aaron	37, 74, 205, 262, 321
	Aron	150
Parson		
	John	72
Parsons		
	(N)	25
	John	21, 59, 76, 100, 135, 146, 267
	Samuel	36
	Solomon	25
	Thomas	36, 99, 106
	William	36
Parsons Chance		59, 135, 195, 251, 312, 365
Parsons Delight		214, 277, 330
Parsons Lott		4
Parsons Marsh		25, 195, 251, 311, 365
Parsons Marsh Addition		25, 145, 195, 251, 311, 364
Parsons Neck		4, 41, 93, 128, 139, 140, 157, 175, 210, 212, 230, 266, 273, 275, 292, 326, 344
Parsons Point		3, 41, 136, 137, 157, 197, 210, 254, 273, 314,

	325, 367	Pear Plantation	78, 269
Parson's Marsh	90, 145	Pearce	
Parson's Neck	69, 82, 93, 159	Daniel	52
Partnership	7, 8, 12, 14, 17-19, 24, 27,	Pearl	55
	31, 34, 53, 57, 59, 60,	Pearle	149, 203, 260, 320
	62, 66, 67, 75, 85, 87,	Pears Plantation	38
	90, 104, 107-109, 111,	Pearson	
	117, 119, 121, 123,	Ralph	141
	125, 133, 134, 143,	Pearsons Delight	161
	147, 148, 151, 153,	Peirce Land	199, 316
	160, 162, 163, 167-	Peirce Land Addition	199, 316
	169, 181, 183, 187,	Peith	184, 240, 301, 354
	194-196, 198, 200,	Pemberton	
	202, 205, 213, 215,	(N)	52
	216, 221-223, 237,	Benjamin	60, 62, 117
	238, 243, 250, 252-	Elizabeth	14, 100, 117
	254, 256, 258, 259,	Grundy	14, 17, 61, 90, 92,
	261, 265, 276, 278,		100, 117, 183, 238,
	279, 283-285, 298,		299, 352
	299, 304, 311-313,	John	14, 92
	315, 317-319, 321,	Pembertons Resurvey	117, 183, 238,
	329, 331, 332, 337,		299, 352
	338, 351, 352, 357,	Pemberton's Resurvey	92
	364-366, 369, 371,	Pendar	
	372, 374	Edward	353
Pascalls Chance	14, 194, 250, 310, 334	John	353
Pascall's Chance	111	Pennsylvania Border	103
Pascoes Adventure	241	Pensilvania Border	326
Pascoes Lott	139, 273	Pensylvania Border	141, 157, 210, 273
Pascoe's Lott	82, 140	Pentreby	136
Pascolett	373	Pentroby	177, 233, 294, 347
Pascos Adventure	41, 185, 303, 355	Pentrogay	3, 137, 157, 177, 210, 273,
Pascos Lott	157, 210, 265, 273, 326		294, 326
Pascos's Lott	4	Pentrogy	233, 347
Pasco's Adventure	139	Pentrovay	137, 157, 210, 326
Pasco's Lott	69	Pentrovey	273
Patsy Plains	148	Perle	372
Pauls Forrest	362	Perrey	
Pauls Fort	8, 104, 192, 248, 309	Mary	300
Pauls Park	7	Perry	
Paxton		Daniel	33, 59
Daniel	100	John	33, 100, 135
Daniel Bridges	143	Mary	183, 239, 353
Hugh	41, 69	Personale	
Paxton Lott	342	George	353
Paxtons Lott	14, 226, 288	Personate	
Paxton's Lott	69, 82	George	239, 301
Payne		Peters Gift	360
Isaac	39	Peters Lott	22, 55, 114, 165, 219, 335
Peale Place	12, 108, 109, 163, 217, 279	Peter's Lott	282

Pett		
	Thomas	66, 269
Petts		
	Thomas	38
Petts Gift		41, 307
Petts Neck		38, 78, 269
Pett's Gift		66
Pharsalia		12, 34, 51
Philadelphia		34, 134, 185, 241, 302, 355
Philips		
	Christopher	107
	David	123
	Hannah	126
	John	91, 113
	Thomas	69, 123
Phillips		
	Christopher	6, 99
	David	22, 100, 177, 233, 294, 347
	George	6
	Hanah	45
	James	354
	John	182, 238, 299, 352
	Richard	26, 45
	Thomas	37, 41, 78, 177, 233, 266, 294, 347
Phillips Chance		354
Phillips Neck		251
Phillpott		
	Robert	66
Phillpotts Neck		47, 140, 194, 364, 365
Phillpott's Neck		66
Philpott		
	Robert	66
Philpotts Neck		195, 250, 311, 312
Philpott's Neck		66
Pickerin		
	John	183, 300
Pickering		
	Fra.	43
	John	17, 40, 239, 352
Pickeron		
	John	81, 100, 128
Pierce Land		130, 176, 293
Pierce Land Addition		130
Pig Quarter Neck		166, 282
Pigg Quarter Neck		1, 69, 138, 335
Pindar		
	William	81, 92, 180, 297, 353
Pinder		
	Margaret	100, 129, 239
	Margrett	353
	Mary	55
	William	14, 23, 24, 49, 55
Piney Neck		2, 137
Piney Swamp Tract		158, 211, 274, 327
Pitt		
	Thomas	78
Pitts		
	John	49, 76, 264
Pitts Gift		4, 138, 191, 247
Pitts Vineyard		20, 115, 148, 155, 204, 252
Pitts's Vineard		327, 332, 339
Pitts's Vineyard		118, 158, 211, 216, 274, 278, 312
Plain Dealing		5, 43, 47, 65, 66, 82, 108, 112, 126, 133, 178, 186, 199, 232, 233, 242, 255, 295, 303, 315, 348, 356, 368
Plain Dealing Resurveyd		213
Plain Dealing Resurveyed		160, 276
Plains		22, 29, 86, 107, 192, 248, 267, 362
Plains Dealing Resurveyed		329
Plains Resurveyed		309
Plean Dealing		35
Pleasant		195
Pleasant Bank on Wye		249
Pleasant Banks on Wye		193, 309, 362
Pleasant Park		43, 114, 182, 238, 299, 352
Pleasant Park Addition		182, 238, 299, 352
Pleasant Spring		16, 51, 125, 152
Pleasant Spring Resurveyed		182, 238, 299, 351
Pleasant Springs		269
Pocayes Addition		279
Poccoyes Addition		216
Pochickory Ridge		260
Pock. Hiccory Ridge		203
Pockedy Ridge		18
Pocketty Ridge		175
Pockety Ridge		158
Pockhiccory Ridge		38
Pockhickory Ridge		72

Pockys Addition		332
Pocolett		48
Pocoyes Addition		163
Point Landing		150, 201, 258, 318, 371
Point Love		2, 85, 136, 147, 170, 203, 224, 260, 287, 320, 340, 373
Pokely Ridge		230
Pokety Ridge		118, 274, 291, 327, 346
Pollock		
	Henry	183, 239, 300, 353
Pondar		
	James	183, 300
	John	183, 300
	Margarett	183, 300
	Morgan	183, 300
	Richard	183, 300
Pondars Chance		183, 300
Ponder		
	James	31, 100, 129, 239
	John	82, 239, 265, 352
	Morgan	46, 82, 100, 143, 239, 353
	Richard	43, 90, 100, 129, 239
Ponderfield		21, 82, 109, 187, 243, 265, 357
Ponders Chance		239, 349
Pooley		
	(N)	34
	Mathias	3
Poplar Hill		46, 52, 82, 133, 134, 142, 151, 152, 157, 162, 179, 180, 188, 197, 205, 216, 234, 236, 244, 254, 259, 262, 279, 296, 297, 305, 314, 319, 321, 332, 349, 350, 358, 367, 371, 374
Poplar Hills		50
Poplar Island		152, 202, 259, 319, 372
Poplar Neck		2, 90, 119, 136, 152, 161, 170, 214, 224, 269, 277, 287, 330, 340
Poplar Neck Addition		214, 277, 330
Poplar Plain		85, 111, 192, 248, 250, 309
Poplar Plains		47, 104, 193, 249, 261, 310, 363
Poplar Ridge		50, 51, 75, 87, 202, 259, 319, 372
Poplar Ridge Addition		50, 75, 202, 259, 319, 372
Porter		
	(N)	151, 262, 321, 374
	Dr.	262
	George	354
	James	151, 205, 262, 321, 374
	John	262, 321, 374
	R.	72
	Richard	74, 75, 100, 144, 205, 322
	Thomas	100, 118
	William	93
Porters Folley		335
Porters Folly		166, 219, 282
Porters Lodge		45, 192, 202, 248, 259, 309, 319, 362, 372
Porter's Lodge		110
Povidence		348
Powel		
	Thomas	136, 184
Powell		
	Daniel	74, 374
	George	24, 85, 184, 239, 265, 300, 353
	James	24
	John	56, 100, 120, 183, 238, 300, 352
	Mary	48
	Thomas	24, 48, 100, 131, 183, 239, 300, 301, 353
Powells Fancey		337, 352
Powells Fancy		24, 41, 108, 121, 143, 144, 166, 167, 183, 220, 221, 238, 282, 283, 300, 335
Powells Venture		136, 183, 239, 300
Powells Venture Addition		353
Power		
	(N)	147
	John	76, 85, 147
	Richard	15
Powers		
	John	265
Pox Hill		207
Pratt		
	(N)	300
	Henry	99, 114, 182, 238, 299,

		352, 371
	James	354
	John	147, 183, 239, 300, 353
	Robert	171, 183, 225, 239, 287, 300, 353, 354
	William	38, 99, 114, 182, 238, 299, 352, 371
Pratts Choice		183, 239, 300, 353
Pratts Hope		171, 225, 287, 354
Prevention		60
Price		
	Andrew	57, 60, 61, 68, 69, 89, 93, 100, 118, 139, 177, 232, 293, 294, 346
	Ann	4, 41
	Charles	13, 99, 112, 182, 238, 299, 352
	Henry	27, 30, 60, 62, 76, 80, 100, 118, 183, 239, 300, 354
	John	30, 32, 91, 92, 184, 239, 300, 353
	Oneal	100, 144, 240
	Prudence	57
	T.	210, 211
	Thomas	49, 53, 80, 99, 113, 138, 157, 158, 182-184, 238, 239, 273, 299-301, 326, 352-354
	Vincent	118, 183, 238, 300, 352
	William	4, 49, 66, 80, 138, 168, 184, 222, 239, 284, 300, 337, 352, 353
Price Hill		364
Price Land		231, 255, 345, 368
Price Land Addition		255, 368
Prices Hill		21, 25, 30, 128, 145, 172, 195, 227, 289, 311, 342
Prices Hills		25
Prices Land		34
Pricess Hill		172
Price's Hill		91, 92, 251
Price's Hills		66
Priest		
	Thomas	239, 301, 353
Primrose		
	(N)	160, 276
	George	20, 100, 142, 183, 239, 300, 353
	John	20, 131, 239, 301, 353
	Martha	183, 239, 300, 353
	Prudence	183, 239, 300, 353
	Rachel	100, 131
	Violet	100
	Violett	134
	William	20, 100, 129
Primus		41, 140, 157, 158, 210, 211, 273
Princes		326
Princis		326
Prior		
	Edmund	7
	William	99, 109
Priors Mannor		38
Prophecy		85, 153, 160, 213, 276, 329
Prophesy		112
Prouse Park		7
Prouss's Park		279
Prous's Park		145, 163, 332
Providence		3, 14, 16, 25, 27, 30, 32, 33, 37, 38, 42, 44, 47, 66, 69, 87, 91, 110-112, 124, 128, 129, 137, 142, 144, 146, 149, 151, 154, 156, 163, 171, 172, 175, 179, 184, 194, 205, 209, 217, 225, 227, 231, 234, 240, 250, 258, 262, 267, 272, 279, 287, 289, 292, 296, 301, 311, 318, 321, 322, 325, 333, 342, 345, 354, 364, 371, 374
Pryor		
	Edm.	266
	Edmund	76
	Katherine	69
	William	42, 182, 238, 299, 352
Pryors Chance		182, 238, 299, 352
Pryor's Chance		109
Pryor's Manour		85
Puney		

	Thomas	16		James	355
Punney				John	357
	(N)	352		Raleys Begining	355
	Henry	352		Ralphs Frolick	2, 267
	Thomas	16		Ralphs Frollick	225
Purchas		335, 371		Ralph's Frolick	82
Purchase		20, 26, 29, 68, 105, 112, 165, 201, 219, 258, 281, 318		Ramble	50, 134
				Rambles	25, 144, 154, 169, 223, 258, 285, 318, 339, 356, 371
Purlivant		2, 88, 139, 200, 256, 317, 369		Ramseys Folly	38, 268
Purnal				Ramseys Forest	61
	Juliana	116		Ramsey's Folley	75
	Mc.	116	Randal		
	Thomas	61, 75, 117		Samuel	78
Purnall			Randall		
	John Young	354		Samuel	38
	Juliana	99		Theophilus	186, 242, 303
	Rebekah	352	Randolph		
	Richard	27		Theophelus	356
	Thomas	27, 99, 183, 238, 299, 352	Randon		32, 77, 268
			Range		41, 85, 115, 213
	William	190, 307, 354, 360	Ratcelife		53
Purnalls Addition		26, 117, 155, 208, 271, 324	Ratcliff		345, 348, 357
				Jane	146
Purnalls Chance		29, 267		William	45
Purnalls Forrest		18, 190, 246, 307, 354, 360	Ratcliffe		27, 85, 87, 119, 120, 122, 152, 168, 176, 179, 187, 208, 231, 243, 284, 290, 295, 304, 324, 337
Purnall's Chance		82			
Purnals Forrest		116			
Purnell				James	150
	Margaret	45		John	27
	William	18, 246		William	22, 68, 131
Purnells Addition		45	Ratcliffe Resurveyed		56
			Ratcliffes Part of Loyds Freshes		151
Quakers		30, 184, 240, 301, 354	Ratcliffs Part of Lloyds Freshes		146
			Ratcliffs Part of Loyds Freshes		131, 173, 367
Rachells Desire		333, 334			
Rachels Desire		163, 217, 218, 280, 281	Ratclifts Part of Lloyds Freshes		343
Ragan			Ratcliff's Part of Lloyd's Freshes		68
	Richard	166	Rattclife		293
Ragister			Rattcliffe		197, 221, 231, 234, 266
	David	355	Rattcliffes Part of Lloyds Freshes		314
Railey			Rattcliffs Part of Lloyds Freshes		254
	Charles	186, 242, 303	Rattcliffs Part of Lloyd's Freshes		228
	Damsel	242, 303	Rattle Snake Ridge		32, 113, 159, 212, 275, 327
	John	99, 146, 185, 241, 302			
Raileys Begining		185, 302	Rawlings		
Raily's Beginning		241		Joseph	265
Raley					

Rawlings Chance		126, 154, 169, 207, 270	Redford		37, 149, 150, 181, 206, 237, 262, 298, 322, 374
Rawlings Hazard		333	Reed		
Rawlins				Elizabeth	6, 56
	James	52		Gilbert	186, 242, 303
	Joseph	87		James	99, 142, 184, 240, 301
Rawlins Chance		15, 49, 323		Mat.	67
Rawwlins Hazard		356		Mathew	6, 56
Rayley				Matthew	63
	John	55		Nat.	67
Raymond				Nathaniel	6, 56, 100, 109, 110, 184, 240, 301
	Jonathan	52, 70		Noll.	56
	Presley	263		William	186, 242, 302
Raymond Folly		52	Reese		
Raymonds Travells		52		Thomas	262, 322
Raymond's Travells		263	Refuge		8, 173
Raymond's Travels		70	Refuse		8, 133, 227, 289, 336
Read			Register		
	George	66		David	123, 147, 185, 241, 302
	Gilbert	356	Releaf		176
	James	354, 357	Relief		115, 125, 127, 155, 208, 211, 232, 271, 293, 324, 326, 346
	Mat.	66			
	Mathew	6			
	Matthew	66			
	Nat.	66	Relief & Hawkins's Pharsalia		324
	Nathaniel	354	Reliefe		20, 33, 42, 158, 274
	William	356, 357	Renewell		341
Readbourn Rectified		126, 172	Rereguard		85
Readbourne		66, 84	Reserve Addition		56, 123, 198, 254, 315, 367
Readbourne Rectified		66			
Readburn Rectified		227, 289	Ressum		
Reading		6, 33, 66		John	100
Reads Adventure		357	Resurvey of Forlone Hope Rectified		193, 362
Rear Guard		16			
Reare Guard Addition		16	Resurvey of Forlorne Hope Rectified		248, 309
Reareguard		59			
Rearguard		77	Resurvey of Smiths Mistake		16
Rease			Revival		186
	Thomas	374	Revivall		242, 356
Reason		13, 72, 160, 174, 196, 213, 229, 253, 264, 276, 291, 313, 329, 344, 366	Reviving Spring		32, 150, 193, 203, 249, 260, 309, 320, 362, 373
Recovery		8, 135, 254			
Red Lion Point		199	Reward		6, 108, 109, 160, 167, 221, 261, 276, 284, 321, 337, 373
Red Lyon Point		130, 255, 316, 368			
Redburn Rectified		341			
Redburne		50	Reynolds		
Redburne Rectified		50		John	31, 78, 266
Reddar			Rich		
	(N)	4		Peter	52, 80, 99, 184, 240,

		301
Robert		52
Stephen		16, 56, 82, 114, 170
Rich Range		115, 117
Richard & Marys Forrest		62, 116, 197, 253, 313, 367
Richard & Mary's Forrest		60, 90
Richards		
Richard		37
Richardson		
Anthony		44, 50, 74, 149, 264
Benjamin		99, 139, 185, 241, 302, 303, 355
Daniel		34, 41
Nathaniel		34, 80
Thomas		44
Richardson Adventure		44
Richardsons Adventure		149, 264
Riche		
Selph.		339
Stephen		286
Riches Farm		291
Ricketts		
Edward		51, 99, 128, 184, 240, 301
Frances		354
John		17, 22, 99, 127, 148
William		148, 184, 240, 301
Ridgaway		
(N)		356
Benjamin		356
William		356
Ridgaways Chance		355
Ridgaways Range		355
Ridge		37, 66, 139, 140, 164, 184, 196, 217, 218, 239, 256, 280, 281, 293, 300, 317, 333, 334, 353
Ridger		
William		61, 99, 136, 185, 241, 302, 355
Ridgers		
William		48
Ridgers Lott		48, 136, 185, 241, 302, 355
Ridgers Lott Enlarg'd		355
Ridgeway		
Benjamin		186, 242, 303
William		186, 242, 303
Ridgeways Chance		241, 302
Ridgways Chance		136, 185
Ridley		
James		31
Walter		32
Ridleys Chance		31, 184, 240, 301, 340, 354
Ridley's Chance		87, 240
Ring Hammer		253
Ringgold		
(N)		333
James		205, 262, 322, 374
Thomas		186, 242, 303, 356
Ringold		
James		3, 138
William		25, 27
Rings End		9, 111, 142, 193, 310, 363
Ring's End		249
Ripley		21, 23, 129-131, 170, 185, 224, 225, 241, 286, 287, 302, 340, 355
John Johnson		129
Ripley Resurveyed		156, 209, 272, 325
Rippen		
(N)		374
Henry		374
Rippon		
(N)		82, 151, 262, 321
Henry		51, 53, 151, 262, 321
Ritch		
Peter		121, 354
Stephen		51, 224
Ritches Chance		121
Ritches Folly		121
Robass		
Elizabeth		262, 322, 374
Robass Mill & Land		259
Robatham		
George		32
Robathams Park		262
Robberts		
William		143
Roberts		
Benjamin		185, 240, 301, 355
James		21, 46, 99, 132, 185, 186, 240, 242, 301, 303, 355, 356
John		186, 242, 303, 356
Jonathan		369
William		52, 100, 186, 242, 303, 356

Roberts Chance		242, 356
Roberts Desire		186, 242, 356
Roberts Meadow		132
Roberts Meadows		185, 355
Roberts Meadow's		240
Roberts Outlett		159, 212, 275, 328
Roberts Range		169, 223, 285, 338
Roberts Range Addition		169, 223, 338
Robertson		
	Alexander	184, 240, 301, 354
	John	205, 262, 322, 374
	Patrick	99, 119, 184, 240, 301, 354
Roberts's Chance		186, 303
Roberts's Desire		303
Roberts's Meadows		301
Roberts's Range		143
Roberts's Range Addition		143, 285
Robins		
	G.	260
	George	42, 149, 203, 320, 372
	Henrietta Maria	100, 149
	John	46
	Thomas	42
Robinson		
	(N)	242, 303, 356
	John	37, 66, 69, 79
	Patrick	48
	Thomas	185, 186, 241, 242, 302, 303, 356
	William	127, 184, 186, 240, 242, 301, 303, 354, 356
Robinsons Adventure		37, 69
Robinsons Farm		262
Robinsons Farme		14, 149, 205, 322, 374
Robinson's Adventure		79
Robison		
	William	55
Robotham		
	George	32, 205, 262, 322, 374
Robotham Park		32
Robothams Park		205, 322
Robrass		
	Elizabeth	205
Rochester		
	Elizabeth	355

Fra.		58
Fran.		43, 241
Francis		99, 133, 185, 302, 355
Henry		185, 241, 302
John		185, 241, 302, 355
Roe		
	Abner	184, 208, 271, 324
	Anthony	99, 118
	Benjamin	184, 240, 301, 354
	Edward	17, 33, 56, 61, 79, 99, 123, 186, 242, 303, 356
	James	186, 242, 303, 356
	John	19, 34, 62, 66, 100, 118, 152, 184, 186, 240, 242, 301, 303, 354, 356
	Joseph	354
	Samuel	241, 356
	Samuell	186, 302
	Thomas	19, 22, 24, 44, 59, 99, 122, 123, 143, 169, 176, 184, 223, 240, 285, 301, 338, 354
	Thomas Richardson	186, 242, 303
	William	19, 100, 118, 184, 240, 301, 354
Roebothams Park		374
Roes Addition		34, 62, 123, 184, 240, 301, 354
Roes Chance		155, 208, 271, 324
Roes Choice		184, 208, 271, 324
Roes Desire		143, 169, 223, 285, 338
Roes Lane		56, 123, 186, 241, 302, 356
Roe's Addition		66
Roe's Chance		79
Rogers		
	David	80, 266
	John	125
Role		
	John	371
Roles		
	John	258, 318
Rooke		
	Edward	186, 242, 303, 356
Rooth		
	Christopher	355
	John	355

Rooths Part of Smiths Branch		356	Richard	79, 266
Rosberry			Royton	79
	James	357	Rufsindale	5
Roseberrey			Ruse	
	(N)	297	Thomas	205
Roseberry			Rusendale	323
	(N)	236	Russam	
	James	225, 287	John	186, 303, 356
Ross			Russell	
	James	28, 70, 262	John	67
	John	38, 52, 57, 68, 71, 152	Russendale	106, 154, 207, 270
	Richard	52, 100, 116, 184, 240, 301, 354	Russum	
			John	46, 242
Rosseth		8, 66	Ruth	
Rotterdam		41, 140, 157, 158, 210, 211, 273, 326	(N)	180
			Christopher	185, 241, 302, 355
Rousbey				
	John	372	John	30, 99, 141, 186, 241, 302
Rousby		70, 268		
	Christopher	30, 70, 268	Thomas	29, 46, 90, 99, 126
	John	37, 64-66, 203, 260, 319	Ryan	
			Darby	30
Rousbye		30	Rye Hall	129, 151, 166, 220, 266, 282, 336
Rouse				
	Sarah	4	Ryhall	24, 45
	Thomas	4	Ryley	
Rous's Park		216	Charles	22
Routh				
	Thomas	45	Sadler	
Rowbotham			Giles	86
	George	67, 78	James	157
Rowbotham's Park		78	Joseph	1
Rowland			Sadlers Chance	157
	Thomas	48, 66, 100, 150	Sadlers Rest	86
Rowlands Hazard		27, 48, 163, 217, 279	Saint Martains	114
Rowland's Hazard		66, 150	Saint Martins	45, 84, 204, 229, 233
Rowlens			Saint Paul	8
	John	136	Saint Pauls	7, 69, 107
Rowles			Salem	164, 218, 280, 333
	John	2, 47, 147	Salisberry	352, 362, 369
Rowls			(N)	356
	John	47	Samuel	356
Roylen			Salisberry Plains	337, 355, 366
	John	24	Salisbury	9, 13, 42, 54, 104, 112, 290
Royston		15, 43, 49, 50, 129, 146, 152, 158, 163, 169, 211, 217, 223, 224, 266, 273, 279, 285, 326, 339	James	23, 100, 126
			John	23, 66
			Salisbury Meadows	38, 72
			Salisbury Plain	17
			Salisbury Plains	23, 35, 44, 111, 112, 135, 143, 159, 275,
	(N)	52		

	284, 328		305, 314, 333, 356, 359
Sallaway			
Josias	361	Sandy Ridge Enlarg'd	328
Sallen	1	Santee	
Sallisbury	192, 200, 228, 248, 255, 309, 316	Christopher	81
		Sarah Portion	336
(N)	242, 303	Sarahs Fancey	356, 363
Samuel	242, 303	Sarahs Fancy	163, 186, 217, 242, 280, 302, 303, 356
Sallisbury Meadow	260		
Sallisbury Meadows	203	Sarahs Portion	3, 49, 139, 166, 168, 176, 220, 222, 283, 284, 292, 337, 345
Sallisbury Plains	168, 189, 190, 196, 212, 222, 246, 253, 307, 313		
		Sarah's Fancy	333
Salloway		Sarah's Portion	75, 168, 231, 337
Josias	191, 247, 308	Sarell	
Salsbury	11, 173	(N)	364
Salter		Saspers Lott	210
(N)	84	Saterfield	
John	84	Nathaniel	190, 246, 307
Salvester		William	100, 248, 361
Benjamin	360	Saterfields Venture	190, 246, 307
David	361	Satterfield	
James	358, 360	Nathaniel	360
William	361	William	43, 125
Salvesters Addition	372, 375	Satterfields Venture	360
Salvesters Discovery	332	Saulsberry	357
Salvesters Forrest	348, 357	Saulsberry Plains	328, 360
Salvesters Hazard	360	Saunders	
Sanders		Aaron	190, 307, 360
Andrew	243, 304	Andrew	100, 114, 191
Aron	246	James	100, 109
Priscilla	191, 247	Priscella	361
Prissilla	308	Saw Pitt Neck	41
Sandish Wood	133, 260	Sawpitt	67
Sandish Woods	46, 217, 332, 372	Sawpitt Neck	67
Sandishwood	150, 203, 320	Sawyers Forrest	323
Sandishwoods	164, 280	Sawyers Range	337, 355, 359
Sands		Sawyers Range Addition	367, 369
Thomas	46, 81, 101, 132, 188, 244, 305, 358	Sayer	
		Frances	63
Sands Outlett	132, 188, 244, 305, 358	Peter	67, 80, 92
Sandwich	27, 69, 86, 268	Sayers Addition	27, 156, 181, 198, 272, 298, 304, 325
Sandy Bite	60		
Sandy Hill	48, 122, 170, 191, 224, 247, 286, 307, 339, 361	Sayers Addition & Brandfield	209, 243, 352
		Sayers Forrest	5, 60, 62, 154, 207, 270
Sandy Hinst	164	Sayers Range	5, 41, 168, 185, 190, 222, 240, 245, 284, 301, 306
Sandy Hursh	303		
Sandy Hurst	4, 34, 46, 70, 82, 129, 130, 133, 186, 188, 218, 242, 244, 266, 280,		
		Sayers Range Addition	7, 41, 47, 197,

		199, 253, 255, 265, 266, 314, 316
Sayer's Forrest		85, 86
Sayer's Range Addition		82, 92
Sayres Forrest		106
Sayres Range		118
Sayres Range Addition		132
Sayre's Addition		117, 146
Sayre's Forrest		67
Sayre's Range		141
Sayward		
	Thomas	21
Scandell		
	William	40
Scandret		
	William	100
Scandrett		
	William	43, 100, 106, 127, 147, 187
Scarborough		89, 202, 203, 230, 258-260, 266, 319, 320, 372-374
Scarbrough		120
Scivals Fork		340
Scotland		123, 142, 172, 176, 231, 232, 293, 342, 346
Scott		
	Dr.	153
	Edward	47
	James	65, 69
	John	54, 59, 190, 246, 307, 360
	Nathaniel	7, 59, 82, 100, 101, 122, 143, 192, 247, 265, 308, 318, 361
	Solomon	190, 246, 307, 360
	William	5, 101, 141, 190, 245, 306, 359
Scott Inclosure		7
Scotten		
	John	57
	Richard	35
Scottens Addition		275
Scottens Folly		57
Scottens Inclosure		275
Scottings Addition		34
Scottland		142, 227, 289
Scotton		
	Catherine	191, 247, 308, 361
	James	101, 143
	John	81, 101, 135
	Mary	189
	Nathaniel	191, 212, 328
	Richard	101, 135, 189, 191, 212, 247, 275, 307, 328, 360
	Thomas	101, 143, 190, 246, 306, 360
Scotton Addition		298
Scottons Addition		132, 136, 181, 189, 212, 236, 266, 328, 350
Scottons Desire		190, 246, 306, 360
Scottons Folley		362
Scottons Folly		135, 193, 249, 309
Scottons Forrest		143, 190, 246, 306, 360
Scottons Inclosure		135, 159, 212, 327
Scottons Outlett		135, 191, 247, 308, 361
Scotton's Addition		143
Scotts Chance		19, 54, 59, 204, 261, 321, 373
Scotts Inclosure		143, 265
Scotts Out Range		306
Scotts Outrange		245, 359
Screvener		
	(N)	17
Scrivener		
	Richard	17, 100
Scrivenor		
	(N)	57
	Robert	57
Scriviner		
	Robert	63
Scrivner		
	Joseph	188, 243, 304, 358
	Richard	128
	Robert	191, 247, 308, 361
Seaney		
	(N)	358
	Solomon	358
Sebergham		51, 71, 153, 268
Security		130, 165, 189, 218, 245, 281, 306, 334, 359, 360
Sedge Harbour		159, 212, 274, 327
Sedgwick		
	James	64, 84
Seegar		
	Capt.	85

	John	190, 307, 357	Shadwell's Addition		75, 149
Seegars Hazard		246, 350, 357	Sharp		
Segarr				(N)	259, 319, 372
	John	246		William	202
Seney			Shaver		135, 181, 236, 237, 298
	(N)	188, 244, 305	Shavor		351
	Denis	31	Shavour		350
	Solomon	23, 50, 100, 131, 188, 244, 305	Shearing		59, 143, 181, 236, 298, 350
Sennett			Shefeild		
	Solomon	358		Samuel	46
Serjeant			Sheife Keep Out		34
	Mary	14	Sheild		
Seth				Edmund	41
	Charles	7, 41, 60, 105, 164, 191, 247, 280, 281, 307, 360	Shenton	Thomas	245
			Shepards Fields		154
			Shepards Fold		17
	Jacob	60, 85, 187, 243, 269, 304	Sheperds Forrest		125, 131
			Sheperds Redoubt		131, 301, 355
	John	187, 242, 303, 357	Shephard		
Sewall				(N)	22
	Nicholas	93		William	22
Sewalls Fork		128, 132, 182, 188, 225, 237, 244, 287, 298, 305	Shephard Discovery		25
			Shephards Discovery		25
			Shephards Forrest		29
Sewalls Manour		87	Shephards Fortune		19, 20, 22
Sewalls Range		255, 315	Shephards Redoubt		21
Sewall's Manour		71	Shepherd		
Sewall's Range		93		Francis	67
Sewals Fork		351, 358		William	61, 67, 100, 101, 187, 243, 269, 304, 358
Sewals Range		199, 368			
Seward			Shepherd Fortune		239
	Thomas	101, 131, 188, 191, 244, 247, 305, 307, 358, 361	Shepherds Discovery		85, 144, 145, 195, 251, 269, 311, 364, 365
Sewell			Shepherds Field		67
	Nicholas	37	Shepherds Fields		144, 258, 318, 371
Sewells Fork		170	Shepherds Fields on Resurvey		194, 310
Sewells Fort		51	Shepherds Fold		61
Sewells Mannor		37, 53	Shepherds Folds		135
Sewell's Range		93	Shepherds Folds on Resurvey		111, 122, 363
Sexton					
	Patrick	12, 53, 106, 186, 242, 303, 357	Shepherds Forrest		108, 161, 189, 215, 245, 277, 306, 331, 359
Shadwell		29, 149, 205, 261, 321, 374			
Shadwell Addition		205	Shepherds Fortune		128, 133, 142, 172, 179, 183, 227, 289, 296, 300, 342, 349, 353
Shadwells Addition		46, 117, 150, 151, 165, 205, 206, 216, 261, 262, 279, 321, 322, 374			

Shepherds Hook	108, 161, 276, 330
Shepherds Redoubt	132, 161, 185, 215, 277
Shepherds Redout	331
Shepherd's Folds on Resurvey	250
Shepherd's Forrest	269
Shepherd's Fortune	234
Shepherd's Hook	214
Shepherd's Redoubt	240

Sheppard
- William   30, 86, 122, 135

Sheppard Discovery & Henfield	7
Sheppard Folds	30
Sheppard Forrests	30
Sheppards Discovery	42
Sheppards Fold	54
Sheppards Forrest	30, 47
Sheppards Fortune	45
Sheppards Hook	40
Shepperd's Forrest	86
Sherin	33

Sherlock
- Ann   100

Shermer
- Benjamin   70

Shervin	34
Shield	72
Ship Point	1, 140, 190, 245, 306, 359

Shirlock
- Nicholas   51

Shoebrook
- (N)   82
- Thomas   22, 29, 39, 46, 59, 82, 100, 124

Shoebrooks
- John   353

Shoobrook
- Thomas   187

Shore Ditch	115, 166, 220, 282, 336
Shoreditch	5

Short
- Henry   32, 101, 132, 265

Shover	10
Shrewsberry	22, 126, 128, 192, 248, 295, 308, 362
Shrewsberry Addition	22, 126, 234, 295
Shrewsbury	178, 234, 348
Shrewsbury Addition	178, 348

Shurlock
- Nicholas   51

Shurman
- Benjamin   40

Sibery
- Jonathan   86

Sidly
- William   264

Sigbye
- William   31

Sigley
- (N)   32
- William   80, 81

Silbery
- Jonathan   65

Sillen	103, 137, 138, 159, 170, 171, 177, 224, 232, 274, 275, 286, 287, 293, 340, 346, 353
Sillen Chance	287
Sillin	2, 66, 136, 152, 211, 340

Silvester
- Benjamin   19, 191, 247, 307
- David   191, 247, 308
- James   19, 50, 62, 82, 84, 85, 89, 187, 190, 243, 246, 304, 307
- Thomas   50
- William   191, 247, 308

Silvesters Addition	37, 50, 202, 205, 259, 261, 319, 321
Silvesters Discovery	162, 216, 278
Silvesters Forrest	50, 187, 234, 243, 246, 295, 304
Silvesters Hazard	191, 247, 307
Silvester's Addition	75
Silvester's Forrest	82

Singleton
- John   39, 64, 67, 86

Sinnett
- Solomon   187

Sinnold
- Barnaby   39

Sinnott
- Sollomon   304
- Solomon   243

Sinott
- John   123

Sintia	248
Sintra	23, 66, 192, 309, 362
Sintra Resurveyed	126

Sipple		
	John	191
	Weightman	263
	Wrightman	153
Skeggs Springs		151
Skinner		
	(N)	52
	Andrew	28, 67, 91
Skinners Expectation		28, 106, 165, 200, 219, 255, 281, 316, 335, 369
Skinners Pleasure		52, 134, 173, 289, 342
Skinners Swineyard		151
Skinner's Pleasure		92, 227
Slaugherton		217
Slaughter		
	James	48, 100, 187, 243, 304, 357
	John	119
Slaughterton		46, 139, 140, 162, 163, 168, 216, 222, 251, 278, 280, 284, 311, 331, 337, 338, 364, 375
Sledmore		37, 141, 189, 245, 306, 359
Sleeford		40, 108, 160, 214, 276
Sleford		330
Slinah		
	Morrice	2
Sliney		
	James	138
	Maurice	191, 247, 307, 360
	Sarah	101, 138
Slocham		
	Joseph	360
Slocum		
	Joseph	191, 246, 307
Slomans Friendship		224
Slyney		
	James	2
Small		
	Richard	191, 247, 307, 360
	Robert	1, 101, 140, 190, 245, 306, 359
Small Hope		61
Small Hopes		136, 185, 241, 302, 355
Smalls Industry		360
Smeath		7, 12, 13, 22, 66, 91, 105, 149, 160, 165, 196, 214, 219, 252, 276, 281, 313, 330, 334, 366
Smeath on Resurvey		165, 219, 281, 334
Smeathen Resurvey		105
Smith		
	Benjaman	129
	Benjamin	51, 188, 244, 304, 358
	Casparus	51
	Da.	51
	Daniel	61, 100, 101, 134, 188, 244, 247, 304, 308, 358, 361
	Danniel	129
	Elizabeth	191
	George	17, 56, 57, 100, 126, 191, 247, 308, 361
	James	32, 79, 82, 90, 101, 152, 191, 247, 267, 308, 361
	Jane	56
	John	49, 53, 56, 64, 101, 138, 189, 191, 245, 247, 306, 307, 359, 361
	Jonathan	110
	Katharine	38
	Katherine	69
	Mathew	10
	Nathaniel	47, 87, 245, 269, 306, 359
	Renatus	15, 85, 268
	Richard	38, 51, 82, 101, 141, 190, 269
	Robert	59, 63, 64, 66, 67, 69, 77, 81, 84, 86, 88, 91, 188, 243, 263, 304, 358
	Thomas	38, 100, 110
	Walter	37
	William	10, 63, 101, 143, 190, 246, 307, 360
Smith Field		359
Smith Lott		10
Smith Ridge		12
Smithfield		7, 13, 15, 72, 85, 134, 146, 170, 207, 224, 231, 286, 340
Smithfield Addition		146, 175, 231, 292, 345

Smiths Addition	11, 32, 42, 129, 181, 237, 266, 298, 351	Smith's Range	72
Smiths Begining	10	Smith's Reserve	72
Smiths Beginning	131, 268	Smith's Ridge	151
Smiths Chance	11	Snod Land	9
Smiths Clifts	117, 119, 213, 329	Snodland	114, 177, 232, 294, 347
Smiths Delight	43, 50, 129, 144, 179, 183, 235, 239, 296, 300, 349, 352	Snowden Charles	14
		Society Hill	35, 120, 194, 212, 250, 310, 328
Smiths Desire	141, 190, 245, 306, 359	Society Hill Addition	328, 364
Smiths Farme	22	Society Hills Addition	194, 212, 250, 310
Smiths Forrest	5, 17, 38, 112, 113, 153, 191, 247, 260, 263, 308, 320, 361, 372	Sodden Thomas	49
Smiths Forrest Addition	13, 263	Soden Thomas	116
Smiths Forrests	203	Soder Thomas	100
Smiths Inlett	11	Sokely Ridge & Jumps Chance	211
Smiths Lott	6, 104, 107, 192, 223, 285	Sole Hitt	360
Smiths Mistake	65, 88, 110-112, 128, 147, 154, 171, 192, 205, 207, 225, 248, 262, 270, 287, 288, 309, 322, 342, 362, 374	Sollomons Lott Addition	330
		Solomon Friendship	44
		Solomons Fancey	330
		Solomons Fancy	40, 161, 214, 276
		Solomons Friendship	110, 164, 170, 200, 256, 280, 286, 317, 333, 339, 369
Smiths Mistake Resurveyed	16	Solomons Lott	51, 120, 172, 226, 288, 341
Smiths Neck	189, 306, 359		
Smiths Neglect	33, 51, 114, 141, 186, 228, 241, 290, 302, 343, 355	Solomons Lott Addition	119, 120, 161, 172, 214, 226, 277, 288, 341
Smiths Outlett	141, 190, 245, 306, 347, 359	Solomons Outlet	129
		Solomons Outlett	182, 237, 298, 351
Smiths Polygon	11	Solomon's Fancy	108
Smiths Range	13, 44, 144, 151, 169, 206, 239, 301, 353	Sonderfield	304
		Soot Hill	55
Smiths Range Addition	13, 53, 122	Soote Hill	122, 190, 307
Smiths Reserve	13, 16, 125, 198, 257, 263, 314, 370	Southampton	32, 88, 129, 236, 237, 350, 351
Smiths Ridge	29, 45, 109, 112, 160, 203, 213, 260, 276, 320, 329, 373	Southamton	129
		Southerins Addition	1
		Southerne Valentine	92
Smithson Thomas	32	Southern's Addition	92
Smith's Addition	66, 85	Spakes's Outlett	172
Smith's Chance	67	Spark Absalom	305
Smith's Forrest	70, 72		
Smith's Forrest Addition	72	Sparkers Choice	249
Smith's Inlett	67	Sparkes	
Smith's Mistake	63, 84		
Smith's Neck	245		
Smith's Polygon	67		

Absalom	188	
Absolom	125, 147	
Caleb	100, 126, 147, 188, 246	
George	125	
John	100	
Millington	100, 126, 147, 188, 247	
Richard	101, 144, 190, 306	
Sparkes Choice	125, 126, 145, 147, 251	
Sparkes Own	125, 126, 188, 244, 246	
Sparkes Point	198, 314	
Sparkes's Choice	125, 195, 309	
Sparkes's Own	125, 305, 307	
Sparkes's Point	137	
Sparks		
Absolam	244	
Caleb	307, 359, 360	
George	172	
John	15, 43, 82, 266	
Millington	308	
Richard	246, 360	
Samuell	288	
William	15	
Sparks Choice	25, 44, 193	
Sparks Choyce	43	
Sparks Outlett	44, 226	
Sparks Own	247	
Sparks Owne	43	
Sparks Point	3	
Sparks's Choice	266, 311, 362, 364	
Sparks's Outlett	124, 288, 341	
Sparks's Own	172, 226, 288, 308	
Sparks's Point	254, 367	
Spark's Choice	82	
Speedy Contract	55, 120, 176, 231, 293, 345	
Spencer		
Jarvas	205, 322	
Jarves	374	
Jarvis	262	
Spicey Grove	153	
Spicie Grove	40, 70, 263	
Spread Eagle	21, 22, 30, 45, 46, 66, 122, 123, 127, 131, 143, 156, 170, 173, 183, 186, 189, 190, 202, 209, 224, 227, 228, 239, 242, 245, 258, 269, 272, 286, 289, 290, 300, 303, 306, 318, 325, 340, 342, 343, 353, 356, 359, 371	
Sprigg		
Thomas	66	
Sprigley	66, 77, 104, 174, 222, 228, 269, 290, 343	
Sprigly	10	
Spriglye	9, 26	
Spring Branch	8, 131, 170, 225, 287, 340	
Spry		
(N)	130, 190, 246, 307, 358, 360	
Christopher	74, 101, 130, 189, 245, 247, 305, 308, 359, 361	
Fran.	246	
Francis	100, 130, 190, 307, 360	
Humphrey	189, 245, 305, 359	
Jo.	130, 247	
John	130, 188, 244, 305, 358	
Jonathan	9	
Joseph	191, 308, 360	
Thomas	130, 188, 206, 244, 269, 305, 358	
William	130, 190, 246, 307, 360	
Sprye		
(N)	244	
Christopher	28, 34	
Fran.	36	
Francis	36	
Spryley	46, 150, 205	
Sprys Adventure	36, 130, 190, 191, 247, 307, 308, 360	
Sprys Chance	130, 189, 245, 305, 359	
Spry's Adventure	130, 246	
St. Jones's Forrest	171	
St. Martins	37, 49, 50, 86, 114, 174, 178, 229, 261, 291, 295, 320, 345, 348, 373	
St. Pauls	12, 103, 104, 148, 169, 222, 285, 338	
St. Tee		

Christopher		264
Stafford		33, 135, 183, 239, 300, 353
Staggwell		334
Stagwell		7, 10, 66, 149, 162, 165, 215, 219, 278, 281, 331
	Thomas	66
Stagwell Addition		162, 215, 278, 331
Stagwells Addition		11
Standford		41, 105, 174, 229, 291, 344
Stansberry		
	Tobias	374
Stansbury		
	Tobias	205, 262, 322
Stant		
	John	101
Stanton		
	Thomas	24, 101, 135, 189, 306, 359
Starke		
	William	366
Starkey		
	Edward	27, 80
	John	32, 77, 101, 141, 268
	William	47, 89, 100, 121, 187, 243, 304
Starkeys Folly		141
Start		
	(N)	16
Stavely		
	William	51
Steads Go Between		204, 229, 291, 343
Steavens		
	(N)	350
	Charles	374
	Francis	360
	John	350
	Robertson	360
Steavens Range		350
Stenewell		226
Stent		
	John	146, 190, 246, 306, 360
Stent on Sudler		189, 306
Stenton Erickson		3
Stenton Errickson		338
Stephen Fields		334, 347
Stephens		
	Fran.	246
	Francis	191, 307
	John	139, 140, 190
	Robertson	191, 246, 307
	Susannah	190, 306
Stephens Adventure		139
Stephens Fields		115, 116, 164, 178, 232, 281, 294, 346
Stephens's Adventure		190
Stephens's Range		245
Stephen's Fields		218
Stephney		171
Stepney		27, 47, 79, 82, 226, 268, 288, 342
Sterling		
	James	122
Stevens		
	Charles	32, 37, 75, 83, 205, 262, 322
	Elizabeth	32, 37, 101, 149
	John	1, 72, 101, 245
	Simon	32
	Susanna	245
Stevens Adventure		1
Stevens Fields		47, 75, 294
Stevensfield		11, 26
Stevenson		
	Richard	7
Stevens's Fields		233, 263
Steward		214
	Susanna	243
	Susannah	304
	Thomas	243
Stewart		
	Susanna	187, 357
	Thomas	357
Stint Land		64
Stint on Errickson		139
Stint on Sudlar		139
Stint on Sudler		64, 67, 245
Stinton Errickson		168, 222, 284
Stoke		39, 84, 124, 187, 213, 275, 328
Stoke Addition		39
Stokes Addition Rectified		188, 213, 276, 328
Stoney Hill		334
Stoop		
	Henry	66
Stoopley Gibson		3, 66, 157, 210, 273
Stooply Bright		53
Stooply Gibson		1, 136
Stoopy Gibson		325
Storey		
	Ephraim	361

	Henry	190, 246, 307	
Storeys Park		53, 107, 166, 220, 282, 336	
Storey's Park		89	
Storys Park		60, 62	
Stradon		104	
Stradtton		104	
Straton		190	
Stratton		12, 82, 148, 177, 201, 233, 246, 247, 258, 294, 307, 308, 318, 347, 360, 361, 371	
Stroke		59	
Stroke Addition		124	
Stuard			
	Thomas	57	
Stuart			
	Thomas	100, 116	
Sudborough			
	(N)	82	
	William	37, 82, 268	
Sudborough Hill		82	
Sudborough Hills		268	
Sudboroughill		37	
Sudlar			
	Anne	359	
	Emory	361	
	James	359, 361	
	Joseph	141	
	Rebekah	359	
Sudlars Chance		326, 359, 361	
Sudlars Fortune		141, 359	
Sudlars Island		359	
Sudlars Purchase		359	
Sudlar's Island		141	
Sudlar's Purchase		141	
Sudler			
	Emory	191, 247, 308	
	James	2, 4, 41, 63-65, 67, 138, 139, 189, 245, 247, 306, 308	
	Jos.	245	
	Joseph	41, 92, 101, 189, 306	
	Rebecca	139, 245	
	Rebeccah	189, 306	
Sudlers Chance		247, 308	
Sudlers Fortune		189, 245, 306	
Sudlers Island		189, 245, 306	
Sudlers Purchase		189, 245, 306	
Sudler's Fortune		92	
Sudler's Purchase			92
Suffolk		18, 116, 170, 224, 286, 335, 339, 353	
Sullivane			
	James	228, 290	
Sullivant			
	James	357	
	John	100, 109, 187, 243, 304, 357	
Sullivants Chance		243, 304, 357	
Sullyvant			
	James	173	
Sumpter			
	Robert	148	
Sutton			
	James	4, 133, 188, 244, 305	
	John	4, 82, 265	
	Rebekah	359	
Swan			
	Thomas	18, 327, 357	
Swan Brook		149	
Swanbrook		28	
Swann			
	Thomas	18, 116, 187, 243, 304	
Swann Brook		196, 252, 312, 365	
Sweat			
	John	247, 308, 361	
Sweatnam			
	William	14, 47, 80, 82	
Sweetnam			
	William	60	
Swift			
	(N)	179, 296	
	Absalom	191	
	Absolam	247, 308	
	Absolem	361	
	Elizabeth	189, 244, 305, 359	
	Emanuel	100, 121, 243, 304, 357	
	Emanuell	187	
	Giddeon	358	
	Gideon	189, 244, 305	
	John	23, 34, 35, 47, 59, 100, 101, 121, 132, 187, 243, 304, 357	
	Lemon	190, 246, 307	
	Lemond	360	
	Mary	189, 244, 305, 359	
	Moses	187, 243, 246, 304,

Page 451

		307, 357
Ralph		35, 100, 119, 122, 191
Richard		100, 121, 190, 246, 306, 360
Samuel		101, 146, 192, 246, 360
Samuell		306
William		35, 55, 86, 101, 134, 191, 266
Swifts Endeavour		357
Swifts Forrest		35, 121, 187, 243, 304, 357
Swifts Forrest Addition		35, 121, 187, 243, 304, 357
Swifts Meadows		35, 121, 134, 191, 243, 246, 304, 307, 356
Swifts Out Lett		34
Swifts Outlett		132, 178, 188, 189, 233, 244, 294, 305, 358
Swine Range		48, 132, 164, 217, 280, 333
Syberry		
Jonathan		39
Sylvester		
James		100, 120
Sylvesters Addition		150
Sylvesters Forrest		118, 178
Sylvester's Addition		149, 150
Sylvester's Forrest		149
Tally Gardin		48
Tanner		
Phil.		252
Philemon		196, 312
Phillemon		365
Thomas		3, 4, 41, 102, 137, 194, 250, 311, 364
Tanners Advantage		3, 137, 194, 250, 311
Tanners Adventure		364
Tappahanah		40
Tappahannah		70, 153, 263
Tappanah		40
Tarboton		
William		46
Tarbutton		
Joseph		365
William		195
Tarr Kill		1
Tasker		

Benjamin		37, 51, 53, 71
Tatnell		79
Tautnell		32
Taylers Chance		330
Taylerton		47, 87, 269
Taylor		
(N)		46
John		3, 196, 252, 312, 365
Richard		196, 252, 312, 365
Rubin		102
Ruebin		128
Samuel		22, 76, 265
Thomas		365
Taylors Chance		118, 161, 214, 277
Teagues Hazard		236
Tears Desire		358
Teass Desire		244
Teat		
Thomas		146, 312
Teate		
George		365
Thomas		252
Teats Arcadia		365
Teats Desire		146, 188, 305
Teats Folley		368
Teats Folly		199, 255, 315
Teet		
Thomas		196
Tell Tales Loss		13, 264
Tell Tale's Loss		86
Tenton Fields		150
Tewton Fields		20
Tharp		
Isaac		251, 312
John		206
Thief Keep Out		69, 130, 189, 245, 305, 359
Thief Keep Out Addition		189, 245, 305, 359
Thomas		
(N)		35, 43
Benjamin		125
Charles		251
Christopher		102, 144, 195, 251, 311, 312, 364
Edm.		251
Edmond		196, 312, 365
Edmund		12, 144
Gabriel		78
Jo.		252

	John	19, 80, 263	Tilberry		359
	Joseph	196, 312, 365	Tilberrys Addition		359
	Mary	195, 251, 311, 364	Tilbury		36, 189, 245, 306
	Philemon	194, 250, 311	Tilburys Addition		189, 245, 306
	Philimon	125	Tilghman		
	Phillemon	364		(N)	130, 131, 179, 180, 188, 189, 235, 244, 245, 297, 305, 349, 358, 359
	Stephen	125, 194, 250, 311, 364			
	Teus.	48			
	Thomas	12, 102, 127		Anna Maria	104
	Tilden	144, 196, 252, 312		Col.	31, 39, 55, 57, 84
	Tildeon	365		Edward	68, 69, 71, 73, 75, 77, 79, 83, 86-91, 93, 102, 110, 192, 248, 309, 362
	Trustram	12, 36, 88, 101, 102, 107, 110, 132, 194, 250, 310, 311, 363, 364			
	W.	169, 223, 286		James	90, 101, 111, 193, 249, 310, 362
	William	38, 74, 101, 151, 206, 239, 263, 339, 353		Mathew	111, 310, 363
				Matthew	102, 248, 249
				Mattthew	193
Thompson				Richard	8, 9, 55, 57, 61, 63-68, 76, 86, 88, 101, 104, 192, 248, 308, 361
	A.	25			
	Aug.	9, 21			
	Augustine	25, 31, 34, 38, 54, 268		William	8, 68, 101, 104, 192, 248, 309, 362, 374
	D.	314	Tilghman Addition		297
	Dowdal	100, 145	Tilghman Freshes		310
	Dowdall	90, 195, 251, 311, 364	Tilghmans Addition		6, 8, 67, 106, 181, 236, 350
	Dowdell	91	Tilghmans Chance		193, 249, 310, 363
	Elizabeth	100, 144, 195	Tilghmans Discovery		8, 24, 36, 45, 104, 129, 131, 161, 182, 188, 192, 215, 237, 239, 244, 248, 277, 298, 301, 305, 309, 331, 351, 353, 358, 362
	Henry	252, 312, 365			
	Samuel	144, 195, 251, 311, 364			
Thompsons Mannor		37			
Thompsons Manor		25, 152, 259, 319, 372			
Thompsons Manour		75			
Thorn			Tilghmans Forrest		8, 111, 193, 249, 310, 363
	William	101			
Thorpe			Tilghmans Freshes		8, 111, 193, 249, 363
	Isaac	147, 364			
	William	150	Tilghmans Gift		61, 177, 232, 294, 347
Tickel			Tilghmans Hermitage		8, 9, 39, 55, 192, 248, 308, 361
	Richard	102			
Tickell			Tilghmans Landing		193, 248, 309, 362
	John	364	Tilghmans Lott		8, 268
	Richard	194, 251, 311, 364	Tilghmans Meadows		9, 114, 177, 294, 347
Tickett					
	Richard	142	Tilghmans Meadow's		232

Page 453

Tilghmans Pasture	8	
Tilghmans Range	8	
Tilghmans Recovery	192, 248, 362	
Tilghmans Recovery Resurveyed	309	
Tilghmans Resurvey of Long Neck	193, 248, 309, 362	
Tilghman's Discovery	133, 184	
Tilghman's Gift	114	
Tilghman's Hermitage	64-66, 68, 88	
Tilghman's Landings	110	
Tilghman's Lott	86	
Tilghman's Pasture	68	
Tilghman's Range	68	
Tilghman's Resurvey of Long Neck	110	
Till		
William	45, 101, 153	
Tillbury	135	
Tillburys Addition	135	
Tillinpher		
William	26	
Tillotson		
Baynard	194, 310, 363	
John	17, 22, 65, 101, 194, 201, 310, 317, 363, 370	
Margaret	363	
Margarett	194, 310	
Martha	102, 122	
Tillotsons Delight	363	
Tillottson		
Baynard	250	
Charles	36	
Christopher	17, 54	
J.	257	
John	31, 39, 56, 111, 250	
Margaret	250	
Tillottson's Chance	122	
Timber Fork	47, 75, 193, 205, 249, 262, 310, 322, 363	
Timber Land	250, 334	
Timber Neck	3, 138, 245	
Timber Range	360	
Timber Ridge	2, 34, 132, 138, 188, 191, 244, 247, 305, 307, 358	
Timber Swamp	56, 128, 166, 220, 283, 336	
Timberland	14, 69, 111, 194, 310	
Timm		
John	35, 55, 102, 120, 194, 250, 310	
Timms		
John	364	
Timms Arcadia	35, 194, 250, 310	
Timms Neglect	56, 175, 292	
Timm's Arcadia	120	
Timm's Neglect	120	
Tims Neglect	344	
Tittle		
John	147, 195, 251, 312	
Toadley	46	
Toalson		
Alexander	102, 140, 194, 200, 250, 256, 311, 317	
Amia	194, 311	
Andrew	102, 195, 251, 312	
Anna	102, 140, 250	
Benjamin	100, 144, 195, 251, 311	
James	195, 252, 312	
John	195, 252, 312	
Joseph	195, 251, 312	
Mary	140	
Toalsons Desire	195, 251, 312	
Todcaster	60, 61, 85, 89, 142, 186, 242, 303, 356	
Todley	17, 125, 156, 190, 194, 209, 246, 250, 272, 307, 310, 325, 361, 363	
Tolson		
Alexander	364, 369	
Amia	364	
Andrew	365	
Benjamin	364	
James	365, 366	
John	365	
Joseph	365	
Tolsons Desire	365	
Tomelin		
Ann	45	
Tomlin		
Ann	45	
Tompsons Manor	202	
Toms Adventure	48, 136, 143, 198, 257, 314, 370	
Toms Adventure Addition	143, 198, 257, 314, 370	
Toms Fancey Enlarged	293	
Toms Fancey Enlarg'd	358, 361, 363	

Toms Fancy		33
Toms Fancy Enlarged		122, 127, 128, 143, 146, 154, 161, 163, 176, 179, 181, 184, 188, 193, 270, 277, 279, 289, 294, 296, 298, 300, 301, 304, 308, 310
Toms Fancy Enlarg'd		172, 177, 192, 207, 214, 217, 227, 232, 235-237, 239, 240, 243, 247, 249, 297, 323, 330, 332, 333, 341, 346, 349, 350, 353, 354
Toms Fancy Resurveyed		56
Tom's Fancy		67
Tom's Fancy Enlarged		67, 109, 110, 119, 126, 141
Tom's Fancy Enlarg'd		178
Tom's Neglect		230
Tool		
	Timothy	60, 61, 81, 265
Toole		
	Timothy	40
Toole Hill		246
Tooley		122, 142
Tooll		
	Timothy	141
Tote		
	George	250
Tottenham		22, 29, 87, 203, 265
Tottingham		125, 161, 186, 215, 242, 277, 303, 331, 356
Toulson		68
	Alexander	33, 47, 66, 93, 139
	Andrew	25, 41, 93, 139
	Mary	93
	Rebecca	93
	Susanna	33, 41
	Thomas	68
Tounton Fields		263
Touton Fields		75, 343
Touton Fields Addition		343
Townton Fields		29, 113
Towntons Fields Addition		113
Towton Fields		174, 229, 290
Towton Fields Addition		20, 174, 229, 290
Treshford		16

Triangle		62, 67, 72
Triangle Addition		72
Trickey		
	Mary	195, 251, 311, 364
	Thomas	100, 146, 195, 251, 311, 364
Troy		144, 163, 216, 279, 332
Truelock		
	William	206
Trulock		
	William	101, 152, 269
Trusham		218, 219
Trustam		105
Trustram		7, 12, 88, 106, 107, 144, 165, 169, 196, 223, 251, 280, 281, 285, 312, 333, 335, 365
Trustram Bridge		126
Trustram Ridge		35, 90, 178, 233, 295, 348
Trustram Thomas Part of Trustram		194, 195, 364, 365
Trustram Thomas's Part of Trustram		196, 250-252, 310, 312
Trustram Wells		20, 67, 113, 177, 232, 294, 346
Trustrams Adventure		194, 250, 311, 364
Trustrams Ridge		132, 194, 250, 311, 364
Trustrams Thomas Part of Trustram		363
Tryall		
	John	7
	Joseph	7
Tryangle		13, 29, 56, 82, 120, 125, 145, 157, 159, 163, 184, 210, 212, 216, 239, 269, 274, 279, 300, 326, 332, 353
Tryangle Addition		13, 263, 269
Tucker		
	John	6
	Jos.	1
	Nathaniel	6, 101, 109, 193, 249, 309, 363
Tuit		
	James	142, 194, 250, 311
Tulley Barden		354

Tulley Bardens Addition		354
Tulley Bardens Inclosement		354
Tulleys Addition		123, 356
Tulleys Delight		104, 122, 124, 325, 326, 343, 362
Tulleys Lott		146, 339, 355
Tulleys Reserve		367
Tulley's Lott		133
Tullington		27, 79, 268
Tully		
	Stephen	27, 65, 69, 79, 86, 268
	Steven	66
Tully Barden		119, 184, 240, 301
Tully Bardens Addition		119, 184
Tully Bardens Inclosement		184
Tully Barden's Addition		240
Tully Barden's Inclosement		240
Tully Bardin Inclosement		301
Tully Bardins Addition		301
Tully Lott		241
Tullys Addition		33, 34, 61, 186, 241, 302
Tullys Delight		17, 123, 127, 157, 173, 228, 272, 273, 290, 309
Tullys Lott		30, 169, 185, 223, 286, 302
Tullys Reserve		35, 123, 198, 254, 315
Tully's Delight		84, 148, 156, 193, 209, 210, 249
Turbut		
	Foster	25
	Mary Ann	46
Turbutt		
	Foster	75
	Richard	56
	Samuel	80, 264
	William	30
Turlo		
	Maj.	76
	William	84
Turloe		
	William	7
Turner		
	Abner	206, 262, 322, 374
	Archibald	55
	Easter	55
	Edward	34, 55, 65, 74, 75
	Ester	29
	Esther	65, 69, 75, 374

	Isaac	196, 252, 312, 365
	Jo.	262
	Joseph	55, 206, 322
	Rebecca	29, 55
	Richard	44
	T.	46
	Thomas	46, 75
Turner Plains		55
Turners Lane		29, 55, 75, 206, 262, 322, 374
Turners Plain Addition		55
Turners Plaines		299
Turners Plaines Addition		293
Turners Plains		29, 65, 205, 238, 352
Turners Plains Addition		117, 151, 176, 185, 206, 229, 231, 262, 290, 322, 328, 343, 374
Turner's Lane		65, 69
Turner's Plains		75
Turner's Plains Addition		75
Tute		
	James	364
Tutlefields		50
Tuttle Fields		75, 153, 259
Tuttlefields		19
Tyburn Neck		3
Ubank		
	William	62
Ulthorp		323
Ulthorpe		37, 155, 208, 271
Union		8, 63, 66, 104, 193, 248, 309, 362
Union on Resurvey		57
Uper Deal		294
Uper Deale		346
Upland		19, 118, 176, 231, 293, 346
Upland Addition		118, 176, 231, 293, 346
Uplands Addition		56
Upper Blunt Point		3, 138, 145, 210, 326
Upper Blunt Point Resurveyed		158, 273
Upper Deal		137, 138, 177, 232
Upper Deale		2
Upper Heath		29, 39
Upper Heath Worth		29, 87, 144
Upper Heathworth		43, 227, 235, 349,

	366
Upper Landing	202, 258, 318, 371
Upper Range	60, 61
Upperheathworth	124, 127, 168, 180, 188, 196, 222, 253, 265, 284, 288, 296, 313, 337, 341
Vandeford	
Hannah	146
Richard	146
William	53, 130
Vanderford	8, 47, 111
Charles	12, 21, 264
George	44, 53
Hannah	252, 313, 366
James	196, 252, 313
John	196, 252, 313, 354, 366
Michael Paul	69
Rebecca	196, 313
Rebekah	366
Richard	196, 252, 313, 366
Robert	252
Thomas	24, 44
William	44, 101
Vanderfords Agreement	21, 264
Vanderfort	67
Charles	86
Michael Paul	67
Vanderforts Agreement	86
Vansant	
Joshua	252, 313, 366
Vaughan	
Thomas	91
Vaughans Discovery	18, 45, 112, 113, 171, 182, 183, 225, 238, 239, 287, 299, 300, 341, 352, 353
Vaughans Dives	26
Vaughans Kindness	41, 42, 105, 167, 220, 221, 283, 336
Vaughan's Discovery	91, 147
Vaughan's Kindness	139
Vaughn's Kindness	336
Vestry of Christ Church Parish	41, 252, 313, 366
Vestry of Christs Church Parish	196
Vestry of Saint Pauls Parish	196, 312
Vestry of St. Pauls Parish	111, 252, 366
Vestry of St. Paul's Parish	101
Vickars	
William	46
Vickers	
(N)	146, 173, 227, 260, 289, 342, 372
William	2, 101, 146, 149, 173, 203, 227, 260, 289, 320, 342, 372
Vincent	
Joshua	196
Vincents Lot	60
Vincents Lott	61, 116
Viney	
Godfrey	52
Vineyard	14, 67
Vineyard Addition	57, 82, 155, 252, 312, 365
Visitors of Queen Ann County School	101
Visitors of Queen Annes County School	109
Visitors of Queen Anns County School	196, 312
Visitors of Queen Anns Free School	42
Visitors of Queen Ann's County School	252, 366
Waddy	
Thomas	92
Wadeing Place	10, 12, 41
Wading Place	139, 155, 185, 207, 241, 270, 303, 323, 355
Wakey Plains	327
Walcutt	
John	68
Walcutt's Addition	68
Walker	
Daniel	23
Flower	30
James	101
John	29, 101, 112, 212, 275, 355
Phillip	375
Thomas	102, 136, 143, 198, 257, 314, 370
Walkers Square	29, 106, 160, 213, 276, 329
Wall	249
Wallace	

	J.	72
	John	269
	William	198, 257, 315, 370
Walleston		
	Joshua	201
Wallis		
	William	102, 146
Walliston		
	Joshua	257, 318, 367, 370
Wallnutt Neck Resurveyed		3, 290
Wallnutt Ridge		42
Walls		
	Peter	26
	William	255, 316, 368
Wallters		
	Robert	197
Walnut Neck Resurveyed		343
Walnut Ridge		372
Walnutt Neck		67
Walnutt Neck Resurveyed		137, 174, 228
Walnutt Ridge		67, 85, 149, 203, 260, 320
Walter		
	John	252
Walters		
	(N)	256, 369
	Alexander	2, 370
	Jacob	137, 147, 201, 258, 315, 370
	James	198, 200, 201, 254, 256, 315, 317, 368, 369
	John	3, 4, 13, 101, 105, 196, 313, 366
	Robert	1, 2, 102, 137, 254, 314, 367
	Samuel	198, 254, 368
	Samuell	198, 315
Walters Addition		2
Walters Addition to Kerbys Prevention		367
Walters Addition to Kirbys Prevention		254, 314
Walters Park		368
Walters Rambles		368
Walters's Addition		137
Walters's Park		198, 254, 315
Walters's Rambles		201, 254, 315
Waltham		9, 10, 68, 109, 159, 167, 212, 220, 233, 275, 283, 295, 328, 336, 348
Waltters Addition to Kirbys Prevention		197
Waplesdon Addition		280
Ward		
	Col.	26
	Henry	46, 199, 255, 316
	Littleton	198, 254, 315
	Margaret	102, 149
	Mathew	26
	Mathew Tilghman	26
	Matthew	67
Wards Flower Fields		255, 316
Wards Flowers Fields		199
Wards Hermitage		26
Ward's Hermitage		67
Ware		
	James	200, 236, 297, 350
Warner		
	Richard	199, 255, 316, 369
Warners Addition		369
Warners Discovery		2, 146, 227, 342
Warners Discovery Resurveyed		173, 289
Warners Fairest Discovery		46
Warplesdon		110, 200, 256, 317, 369
Warplesdon Addition		33, 110, 164, 170, 200, 224, 256, 286, 317, 333, 339, 369
Warplesdon Addition & Solomons Friendship		218
Warplesdone		17
Warterford		126
Wartons & Pendars Outrange		353
Waterford		15, 31, 79, 124, 153, 154, 173, 204, 207, 228, 261, 270, 289, 321, 323, 342, 343
Watery Plains		241, 355
Watry Plains		35, 133, 158, 185, 211, 274, 302
Watson		
	(N)	205
	Esther	199, 316, 369
	John	199, 316, 369
Watsons Chance		370
Watsons Delight		347
Watsons Delight Addition		178, 347
Watsons Desire		185, 240, 302

Watsons Lott		370
Watson's Delight		178
Wattham		178
Wattson		
	(N)	322
	Benoni	36
	Benony	132
	Elizabeth	48
	Esther	255
	Fra.	48, 57
	Francis	87
	John	255
	Margaret	126
	William	48, 102, 153
Wattson Chance		48
Wattsons Chance		144, 201, 257, 317
Wattsons Delight		57, 107, 233, 295
Wattsons Delight Addition		107, 233, 295
Wattsons Desire		57, 143
Wattsons Lott		48, 128, 144, 198, 257, 314
Wattson's Desire		87
Waxford		53
Weatheral		
	Thomas	79
Weatherall		79
Webb		
	Edgarr	25
	George	198, 257, 314, 370
	James	25, 101, 117, 201, 257, 317, 339, 370
	John	19, 37, 50, 102, 149, 205, 261, 321, 375
	Mary	201, 257, 317, 370
	Park	46, 102, 150, 206, 262, 322, 374
	Richard	19
	Timothy	102, 144
	William	206, 262, 322, 374
Webbs Chance		19, 149, 205, 261, 321, 375
Webbs Plains		198, 257, 314, 370
Week		86
Weeks		
	Matthew	197, 314
	Stephen	201, 257, 318
Welch		
	John	7, 57, 64, 90, 107, 196, 253, 313, 366

Welch Pool		224, 286, 339, 340
Welch Poole		112, 171, 197, 226, 288
Welch Ridge		114, 167, 221, 283, 336
Welch Ridge Addition		86, 266
Wellenlew		232
Welles Park		130
Wellew		328
Wellies		124
Wellmores Range		311
Wellow		188, 213, 275
Wells		
	Ann	306
	Anne	189, 245, 359, 370
	Ben.	255
	Benjamin	199, 316, 368
	Elizabeth	199, 255, 316, 368
	George	199, 255, 316, 368
	Hum.	254, 255
	Humphery	367, 368
	Humphrey	8, 34, 198, 199, 315, 316
	Humphry	55, 78, 102, 130
	John	1, 63, 67, 83, 189, 199, 245, 255, 306, 316, 359, 368
	Richard	8, 21, 86, 102, 134, 143, 201, 257, 266, 314
	Ruth	102, 136
	William	199
	Zerobabel	144
	Zerobable	315
	Zorababell	368
	Zorob.	255
	Zorobabel	102
	Zorobable	199
Wells Chance		259, 372
Wells Inspecting House		345
Wells Inspection House		231
Wells Park		332
Wells's Chance		202, 319
Wells's Inspection House		293
Wells's Park		55, 163, 216, 279
Welsh Poole		45
Welsh Ridge		42
Welsh Ridge Addition		8
West		
	Francis	27
	Simon	27, 79, 268
Westberry		25, 268

Westbury	25, 69, 77		Wheelers Chance	366
Westford	374		Whetby	
Westminister	313		John	368
Westminster	38, 57, 71, 105, 152, 196, 252, 366		Joseph	368
			William	367
Westminster Escheated	68		Whetby's Forrest	367
Wetherell	38		Whitall	228, 325
Thomas	38		Whitby	
Wexford	59, 83, 167, 220		Jo.	255
Weyatt			John	199, 255, 315
Jane	59		Joseph	199, 316
Whale			William	62, 101, 148, 197, 253, 314
Daniel	30			
Wharton			Whitbys Forrest	148, 197, 253, 314
(N)	55		White	
Josias	255, 368		Elisabeth	317
Robert	17, 55, 83, 92, 103, 130, 197		Elizabeth	256, 369
			Row	27
William	253, 314		Rowland	83
Wharton & Pinders Out Range	128		William	3, 137, 198, 254, 314, 367
Wharton & Pinders Outrange	55, 129			
Wharton Addition	55		White Hall	131, 133, 156, 173, 272, 290
Whartons & Pendars Out Range	351			
Whartons Addition	233		White Mars Addition	339
Whartons Adventure	130, 197, 253, 367		White Marsh	22, 124, 198
			White Marsh Addition	22, 124, 170, 198, 224, 257, 286, 314, 370
Whartons Marsh	17, 122, 251, 365			
Wharton's & Pindar's Outrange	92			
Wharton's & Pinders Outrange	239		White Marsh on Resurvey	257, 314, 370
Wharton's Addition	83, 92			
Wharton's Adventure	92		Whiteall	343
Wheadle			Whitehead	
John	46		George	40, 59, 70, 263
Whealor			Whittabl	209
William	120		Whittall	30
Wheatley	313		John	30
Daniel	197		Whittby	
John	197, 313, 366		William	48
William	197, 313, 366		Whittbys Forrest	48
Wheatleys	161, 197, 330, 366		Whitthall	50
Wheatleys Park	197, 313, 366		Whittington	
Wheatly	214		Ben	135
Daniel	27, 101, 112, 224, 339		Benjamin	102, 197, 254, 314, 367
John	27, 101, 117, 118, 253		John	24, 77, 239
William	253		Jos.	102, 301
Wheatlys	117, 253, 277		Joseph	135, 353
Wheatlys Park	118, 253		Thomas	16, 43, 102, 149, 264
Wheeler			Whittingtons Lott	24, 135, 197, 254, 301
Thomas	197, 253, 313, 367			
William	36, 101, 366			

Whittingtons Lott & Hemsleys Britland		Wild		
Resurveyed	239, 353, 367	Daniel		22
		John		89
Whittingtons Lott Resurveyed	254, 314	Peter		22, 55
Whittingtons Luck	24, 32, 254	Wilkinson		
Whittington's Luck	77	(N)	81, 110, 112, 131, 330	
Whorton		Charles		15
Josiah	199, 315	Christopher	43, 102, 134	
William	367	Edward		32
Whortons & Pindars Outrange	182, 183	Henry	90, 102, 201, 257, 317, 370	
Whortons & Pinders Outrange	237			
Whortons Addition	178	John		68
Whortons Adventure	314	Thomas	15, 39, 41, 42, 55, 93, 101, 110, 197, 201, 253, 257, 313, 317, 370	
Whortons Marsh	195, 312			
Wickersby	39			
Wickersly	86			
Wickes		William	21, 43, 81, 101, 128	
Jo.	136	Wilkinsons Addition	9, 10, 109, 159, 167, 212, 220, 233, 275, 283, 295, 328, 336, 348	
Joseph	85			
Matthew	133			
Wicks				
(N)	260			
Benjamin	2	Wilkinson's Addition	68, 178	
Jo.	202, 260	Willaby		
John	49, 133	Ed.		27
Jos.	47, 320, 373	Willcocks		
Joseph	2, 147	Henry		23
Mathew	367	Willcox		
Matthew	253	Daniel	123, 146, 197, 253, 314	
Steaphen	370			
Stephen	133	James	143, 146	
Widdows Choice	324	Willenlew	20, 37, 47, 75, 83, 165, 205, 219, 262, 281, 294, 322	
Widdows Folley	333			
Widdows Folly	48			
Widdows Lott	47	Willew		82
Widdows Lott Resurveyed	25	William, John, & Joseph's Lott		121
Widows Choice	155, 208, 271	Williams		
Widows Folly	132, 164, 280	(N)		374
Widows Lott	136, 147, 258	Abraham	5, 56, 101, 124, 201, 257, 317, 370	
Widow's Folly	217			
Widow's Lott	63	Ann		6
Wigg Moore	239, 301	Christopher	23, 50, 102, 136, 205, 262, 322	
Wiggins				
John	39	Edward	62, 102, 135	
Wiggmore	353	Henry	6, 196, 253, 313, 366	
Wilcocks		Henry Price	113, 173, 290, 343	
Henry	23			
Wilcox		James	17, 42, 44, 70, 113, 136, 197, 253, 269, 313, 366	
Daniel	101, 367			
James	102	John	54, 112	

Mathew	15, 44, 111	
Price	228	
Rebecca	201, 257, 317	
Rebeccah	370	
Tabitha	101, 112	
Thomas	39, 64	
Williams Adventure	2, 62, 257	
Williams Begining	367	
Williams Fancy	269	
Williams Fortune	253, 313, 366	
Williams Hazard	35, 266	
Williams Lott	33, 132, 168, 181, 222, 236, 284, 297, 337, 350	
Williams Pasture	35, 121, 190, 246, 306, 360	
Williamson		
John	82, 102	
Williams's Adventure	135, 143	
Williams's Fancy	70, 136	
Williams's Fortune	196	
William's Hazard	86	
Willin	16	
Willinew	374	
Willinle	373	
Willinlee	105	
Willinlew	177	
Willkinson		
Henry	144	
Willmore		
Lambert	206, 322	
Willmores Range	9, 25, 38, 251	
Willoby		
Edward	101	
Willoughby		
Edward	117	
Willson		
(N)	169, 286	
James	52, 102, 117, 197, 253, 313	
John	2, 39, 121, 137, 139, 168, 198, 221, 254, 257, 284, 314, 315	
Joseph	90, 102, 152, 269	
Mary	39, 45	
Phineas	142	
Phinehas	198	
Rachel	20	
Robert	164, 256, 317	
Thomas	199, 255, 315	
William	2, 12, 20, 50, 102, 206, 262, 322	
Willsons Addition	150, 181, 237, 298	
Willsons Adventure	137, 198, 254, 314, 315	
Willsons Begining	185	
Willsons Beginning	24, 146, 241, 265	
Willsons Chance	52, 117, 142, 197, 253, 313	
Willsons Chance Addition	197, 253, 313	
Willson's Adventure	257	
Willson's Beginning	86	
Wilmer		
Lambert	151	
Simon	72	
Wilmore		
Lambert	102, 262, 374	
Wilmores Range	144, 195, 364	
Wilson		
Hannah	366	
John	102, 337, 367, 370	
Joseph	87	
Robert	369	
Thomas	368	
William	101, 107, 150, 374	
Wilsons Addition	42, 351	
Wilsons Adventure	367, 370	
Wilsons Begining	302, 355	
Wilsons Begining & Raleys Begining	351	
Wilsons Chance	366	
Wilsons Chance Addition	366	
Wilton	10, 204, 261, 320, 373	
Winchester	1, 5, 43, 77, 83, 104, 109, 133, 174, 185, 228, 229, 241, 268, 290, 291, 302, 343, 344, 355	
Isa	2	
Isaac	200, 256, 317, 369	
Jacob	2, 88, 102, 139	
John	67, 77, 83, 268	
Winchester Folly	28, 46	
Winchesters Folley	348	
Winchesters Folley Resurveyed	349	
Winchesters Folly	148	
Winchesters Folly Resurveyed	148, 179, 180, 234, 235, 295, 297	

Windfield	11	Wooleys Outrange	44
Windsor Forrest	11	Woollahand	
Winfield	12, 13, 42, 43, 73, 104, 112, 125, 127, 144, 148, 223, 240, 248, 361	Maurice	80, 267
		Woollverhamton	197, 201
		Woolverhampton	31, 253, 257, 370
Winkfield Park	13	Woolverhamton	145, 314, 318
Winn		Woolverton	116, 204, 261, 321, 373
Ephraim	46, 101, 125	Wooters	
Winter House	145, 163, 216, 279, 332	Elizabeth	367
Winterfields	263	Jacob	39
Winterhouse	40	John	39
Winton	26, 67, 153	Jonathan	367
Winton Addition	26	Phill.	36
Wintons Addition	26, 153	Richard	60, 62
Winton's Addition	153	Wooters Choice	36
Wise		Wootters	
Christopher	38, 74, 267	Elizabeth	197, 253, 313
Wolverhampton	367	Jacob	101, 117, 197, 253, 313
Wood House	228, 246, 261, 343		
Wood House Addition	228, 246, 343, 357	John	101, 119
		Jonathan	147, 198, 254, 315
Wood Land	240	Phillip	153
Wood Land Neck	10, 223, 233, 236, 252, 338	Richard	90, 101, 116, 118
		Wootters's Choice	141, 166, 220, 282
Wood Ridge	36, 135, 234, 338	Wootters's Choice Addition	166, 220, 282
Wood Ridge Addition	36, 135		
Wood Yard Thickett	1, 331, 340	Wooverton	19
Woodall		Work Mans Hazard	137
John	26, 46, 101, 127, 197, 253, 265, 314, 367	Workman	
		Anthony	80, 266
Martha	101, 129	Workmans Hazard	3, 198, 254, 314, 367
widow	199, 255, 316, 368		
Woodberry	146, 195, 251, 311, 364	Worley	
Woodhall		John	18
John	85	Worleys Out Range	347
Woodhouse	31, 79, 135, 136, 153, 173, 190, 204, 290, 307, 321	Worleys Outrange	49, 118, 232, 294
		Worley's Outrange	177
		Worly's Outrange	116
Woodhouse Addition	135, 136, 174, 190, 290, 307	Worthington	
		William	102, 152
Woodland	19, 118, 186, 354	Wortons & Pindars Outrange	298, 300
Woodland Neck	41, 104, 136, 178, 180, 192, 196, 285, 295, 297, 312, 347, 350, 365	Wotters	
		Jacob	366
		Wotters's Chance	335
		Wotters's Chance Addition	335
Woodridge	169, 179, 222, 285	Wrench	
Woodridge Addition	69	Henry	199, 255, 315, 368
Woodward Thickett	162	Peter	198, 254, 315, 367
Woodyard Thickett	1, 67, 138, 171, 215, 224, 278, 287	William	14, 67, 76, 92, 101, 112, 199, 254, 263,

Wrenches Adventure	315, 368 165, 173, 219, 229, 281, 291, 335, 343	Nathan	124, 145, 148, 198, 257, 314, 315, 367, 370
Wrenches Chance	198, 254, 315, 367	Nathan S. T.	366
Wrenches Discovery	14	Nathan Samuel Turbut	369
Wrenches Farm	217, 237, 252	Nathan Samuel Turbutt	313, 316
Wrenches Farme	14, 67, 116, 164, 182, 196, 198, 254, 280, 298, 313, 315, 351, 366, 367	Nathaniel	17, 35, 40, 48, 59, 82, 101, 122, 128, 197, 200, 253-256, 314, 316, 317, 367, 369
Wrenches Farme Resurveyed	14, 112	Neriah	36
Wrenches Lott	14, 112, 199, 254, 255, 315, 368	Penelope	3, 41, 102, 136, 197, 254, 314, 367
Wrenches Reserve	199, 255, 315, 368	Robert Nor.	22, 53, 101
Wrenche's Discovery	92	Robert Norrest	124
Wrenche's Farme	67	Samuel	3, 61, 69, 137
Wrenhams Plains	15	Sarah	24, 48, 53, 201
Wrexam Plains	114, 263	Solomon	17, 81, 82, 201, 257, 317, 370
Wrexamplaine	177	Solomon Coursey	201
Wrexham Plains	73, 266	T. H.	6, 9, 22, 26, 39, 53, 56, 57, 102, 112, 128
Wrexhams Plains	5, 13, 14	T. Hynson	6, 17, 20
Wright		Thomas	61, 197, 200, 253, 256, 313, 317, 366, 369
(N)	44, 180	Thomas H.	105, 145
Alice	101, 123	Thomas Hynson	33, 56, 57, 65, 67, 92, 101, 110
Ambrose	101, 112, 200, 201, 256, 257, 316, 317, 369, 370	Wrights Chance	37, 39, 40, 48, 59, 122, 125, 127, 155, 170, 172, 185, 197, 200, 201, 208, 224, 241, 253, 256, 257, 271, 286, 302, 314, 316, 317, 324, 339, 356, 367, 369, 370
Charles	22		
Edward	17, 35, 53, 56, 133, 180, 198, 200, 254, 256, 315, 317, 367, 369, 371		
Fair.	246		
Fairclo	360		
Fairclough	56, 101, 122, 190, 307		
Henry	5, 45		
Hynson	102, 141, 264		
John	17, 39, 41, 67, 79, 86, 102, 145, 198, 257, 268, 315, 370	Wrights Choice	17, 30, 79, 268
		Wrights Choice	122
Mary	3, 17, 35, 45, 48	Wrights Fortune	2, 139, 173, 227, 289, 342
N.	17, 72	Wrights Neglect	172
N. S. T.	253	Wrights Park	53, 110, 183, 239, 300, 353
N. Samuel T.	256		
N. Samuel Turb.	197	Wrights Plains	48, 105, 165, 218, 281, 334
N. Samuel Turbutt	200		
Na.	48	Wrights Point	86
Nat.	81	Wrights Reserve	105, 110, 165, 197,

		218, 253, 281, 313, 334, 366
Wrights Reserve Addition		105, 165, 218, 281, 334
Wrights Square		184, 200, 240, 256, 301, 316, 354, 369
Wrightson		
	Mary	32
Wright's Chance		69
Wrixham		38
Wyats Folley		371
Wyatt		
	(N)	36, 218, 334
	James	24, 32, 64, 130
	Jane	54, 59, 78
	Jo.	151
	Thomas	23, 102, 134, 146
	William	36, 77, 147
Wyatts Folly		144, 201, 258, 318
Wyatts Lott		36, 147, 218, 334
Wyatts Range		134, 146, 192, 248, 308, 361
Wyatt's Folley		90
Wyatt's Lott		77
Yarmouth		6, 69, 86, 268
Yarnton		29, 75
Yarpton		268
Yarton		29
Yeo		
	Stephen	49, 53
Yeowell		
	Solomon	371
Yewell		
	(N)	19
	Solomon	26, 29, 102, 112, 201, 258, 318
	Thomas	29, 64, 65
Yoe		
	Aaron	112, 201, 258, 318, 371
	Steaphen	371
	Stephen	102, 113, 201, 258, 318
Yough Hall		259, 372
Youghal		153, 202
Youghall		319
Young		
	John	102, 104, 125, 148, 201, 258, 318, 371
	William	7, 59, 63, 65, 68, 83, 88, 102, 104, 125, 148, 201, 258, 318, 371
Young Hall		19
Youngs Adventure		27
Youngs Chance		13, 27, 142, 194, 250, 268, 311, 364
Young's Adventure		83, 88
Young's Chance		68, 70
Young's Fortune		68

www.ingramcontent.com/pod-product-compliance
Lightning Source LLC
Chambersburg PA
CBHW071222290426
44108CB00013B/1264